Making Alternative Histories

Publication of the Advanced Seminar Series
is made possible by generous support from
The Brown Foundation, Inc., of Houston, Texas.

School of American Research
Advanced Seminar Series
Douglas W. Schwartz, General Editor

Making Alternative Histories
Contributors

Bassey W. Andah
Department of Archaeology and
Anthropology
University of Ibadan, Nigeria

Michael L. Blakey
Department of Sociology and
Anthropology
Howard University

Partha Chatterjee
Centre for Studies in Social
Sciences
Calcutta, India

Russell G. Handsman
Department of Sociology and
Anthropology
University of Rhode Island

Augustin F. C. Holl
Laboratoire d'Ethnologie
Université de Paris X

Thomas C. Patterson
Department of Anthropology
Temple University

Trudie Lamb Richmond
Institute of American Indian Studies
Washington, Connecticut

Peter R. Schmidt
Department of Anthropology and
Center for African Studies
University of Florida, Gainesville

Jalil Sued Badillo
Faculty of Social Sciences
University of Puerto Rico

Iraida Vargas Arenas
Universidad Central de Venezuela
Caracas

Alison Wylie
Department of Philosophy
University of Western Ontario

Making Alternative
HISTORIES

The Practice of Archaeology and History
in Non-Western Settings

Edited by Peter R. Schmidt
and Thomas C. Patterson

SCHOOL OF AMERICAN RESEARCH PRESS ı SANTA FE ı NEW MEXICO

School of American Research Press
Post Office Box 2188
Santa Fe, New Mexico 87504-2188

Director of Publications: Joan K. O'Donnell
Editor: Jane Kepp
Designer: Deborah Flynn Post
Indexer: Andrew L. Christenson
Maps: Carol Cooperrider
Typographer: Tseng Information Systems, Inc.

Distributed by the University of Washington Press

Library of Congress Cataloging-in-Publication Data:
Making alternative histories : the practice of archaeology and history in non-
    Western settings / edited by Peter R. Schmidt and Thomas C.
    Patterson.
            p.   cm. -- (School of American Research advanced seminar
    series)
        Includes bibliographical references (p.) and index.
        ISBN 0-933452-92-6 (cloth). -- ISBN 0-933452-93-4 (paper)
        1. Archaeology and history--Developing countries. 2. Developing
    countries--Historiography. 3. Developing countries--History.
    I. Schmidt, Peter R. (Peter Ridgway), 1942-   . II. Patterson,
    Thomas Carl. III. Series.
    CC77.H5M34 1996
    930.1--dc20   95-47242
                                                              CIP

Cover art: "The Battle of Rorke's Drift, about 1879, between
Zulus and British." Linocut by John N. Muafangejo, 1981.
© 1995 John Muafangejo Trust.

 Contents

CONTENTS

Illustrations

Preface

T his book and the seminar on which it is based began to take form in the early 1980s during many late-night conversations in Dar es Salaam, Tanzania, with a friend and fellow archaeologist, Jonathan Karoma of the University of Dar es Salaam. Like many African archaeologists, Karoma found that the processualists of the 1960s and 1970s in North American archaeology offered little that fit with African needs and attempts to construct histories free from colonial paradigms. The North Americans' emphasis on scientific archaeology of one specific denomination seemed to deny history and at the same time to remain oblivious to creative attempts in Africa and elsewhere in the Third World to develop a historically informed scientific archaeology that spoke to local concerns and sensibilities. Together we wondered if the historical concerns of archaeology in the Third World could positively affect Western theorists. Was the intellectual contribution of Third World thinkers and their compatriots from the West destined to remain on the periphery? Or was there a way to enter into a dialogue, to create a forum that would allow both sides to learn and grow?

As it happened, during this period I had occasion to participate in a School of American Research (SAR) advanced seminar in 1981 on shipwreck archaeology, led by Richard Gould. During a reception given by Douglas Schwartz, SAR's president, for the seminar participants, he and I discussed the current state of archaeology in Africa. He took particular interest in how African and Africanist archaeologists were struggling to overturn established colonial interpretations. He encouraged me to consider a seminar on this topic. I was soon caught up, however, in building from scratch a new archaeology program at the University of Dar es Salaam, and the idea of a seminar languished.

In 1990 I again had the good fortune to be invited to participate in an SAR seminar, this time on historical ecology, led by Carole Crumley. That seminar brought me together again with Thomas Patterson, who has had a long and distinguished career in Latin American archaeology. Tom and I immediately fell to renewing a long-standing conversation about how archaeology and other historical research can be used to recuperate the histories of peoples that have been erased, marginalized, or misrepresented—usually for reasons pertaining to maintenance of state or elite interests. I shared with Tom the long-dormant idea of a seminar focused on making alternative histories, with the added concern that this was an issue which included but was much wider than the continent of Africa. He responded immediately and positively, suggesting a number of Latin Americans who might participate, as well an Indian. In common we agreed on three other North Americans who would bring a well-informed concern with the histories of the peoples among whom they did their research.

Before we departed Santa Fe, a rough outline of the seminar and its participants had taken shape. We approached Jane Kepp, then director of publications, and Doug Schwartz about possible SAR interest in such a seminar and met with an encouraging response.

Shortly thereafter, SAR accepted our proposal for an advanced seminar. The topic went beyond the usual theoretical scope of advanced seminars and was unusually diverse in terms of world areas represented. It was also clear that the SAR leadership was committed to a considerable financial investment to ensure diverse participants, including five people of color, among whom were one African American, two Africans, one Indian, and one Native American. There were also three women and two Latin Americans. The ethnic and racial heterogeneity of the seminar participants is also seen in their academic backgrounds and careers: six archaeologists, one historian, one educator/outreach specialist, one social-political theorist, one philosopher of science, and one physical anthropologist.

During seminar discussions in April 1992, Jane Kepp played a key role in asking hard questions demanding that the seminar participants constantly employ the self-reflective discipline that many of us were asking of contemporary archaeology. We were grateful for her critical scrutiny during the seminar and for her later careful editing of the manuscript. We also appreciated the gracious hospitality of Doug Schwartz and all of the SAR staff, who made us feel so welcomed on the Santa Fe campus.

We owe much to Doug's willingness to sponsor *Making Alternative Histories.* We are also grateful to Joan O'Donnell, Jane's successor as director of publications. She has been forever patient, encouraging, and generous in her assistance. Finally, to the two outside reviewers of the volume, we are indebted for their careful and exhaustive comments on individual chapters. Their assistance has, I hope, helped us craft a product that will realize the promise of the seminar experience. Our thanks also goes to the Center for African Studies at the University of Florida for help in organizational logistics and for helping to sponsor the trip of Bassey Andah from Nigeria. Deepest thanks go to Jim Ellison, who read all the papers and had many thoughtful comments and penetrating insights. His assistance was central to our timely completion of the project.

I would like to dedicate this book to the memory of Victor O. Schmidt, gentleman, lawyer, lover of history, arbiter of fair play, and supergenerational soul mate.

Peter R. Schmidt
Timber Cove, California
January 1995

Making Alternative Histories

Introduction

From Constructing to Making Alternative Histories

PETER R. SCHMIDT AND THOMAS C. PATTERSON

A fter interacting with peoples from the Third World for more than a century, many archaeologists from the West, especially the United States, have yet to hear and understand the voices and concerns of colleagues in those countries. Yet in some ways the Third World is also within the West—particularly for Native Americans whose nations have treaties with the United States and for African Americans whose ancestors were enslaved and brought to the United States against their will. This plurality extends to archaeologists like us, who, while working in mainstream U.S. institutions, have listened to and adopted modes of thought of Third World colleagues only to find that advocacy for alternative views on the use of archaeology and history sometimes leads to censure by colleagues on methodological grounds. Methodological censure, of course, is one of the ways in which a dominant paradigm reproduces itself, but its effect is also to forge an even stronger bond between anthropologists and other social scientists from the First World and the Third who are mutually concerned with alternative ways of constructing the past.

Genesis of the Seminar

Because one of the tenets of North American archaeology is that archaeology is anthropology, and archaeologists should therefore be trained in a four-field approach, it is paradoxical that many North American archaeologists remain unreceptive to and uninfluenced by anthropological perspectives and practices. This contradiction manifests itself in a number of ways. It subdues and mutes the distinctive contributions of Third World archaeologists and historians to contemporary archaeology in the Western world; it militates against the sensibilities and understandings of local societies and their histories; and it precludes wider dissemination of theoretical and methodological innovations that arise out of the perceptions of local investigators. These observations suggest that, in North America at least, archaeologists have been working within a paradigm that incorporates perspectives and behaviors contradictory to those on which the discipline of anthropology is based. This is disturbing.

The absence of a common language and mutually respected methodologies among First and Third World archaeologists compels us to confront and overcome these disabilities and to revitalize anthropology within archaeology. This was one of the reasons we convened an advanced seminar at the School of American Research (SAR) in Santa Fe, New Mexico, in April 1992, inviting historians and archaeologists from India, Cameroon, Venezuela, Puerto Rico, Nigeria, Schaghticoke (a Mahican nation in Connecticut), the United States, and Canada. This mix of scholars provided regional diversity and at the same time assured interaction among individuals with different theoretical perspectives and educational experiences. The five days of seminar discussions affirmed that this sort of dialogue is an essential first step in bringing to the attention of Western scholars perspectives that challenge dominant colonial and postcolonial paradigms embedded in First World archaeology and history. The seminar setting provided an opportunity for open debate about how we respond to the erasure of local histories by colonialism, by neocolonial influences, and by the practice of anthropology as we know it today in North America and much of the Western world.

As discussion unfolded during the seminar, it became clear that there were natural tensions within the group. Some of us were members of the Western academy (Schmidt, Patterson, Handsman, Blakey, and Wylie), whereas others had made their careers entirely in Third World institutions (Andah as an archaeologist in Nigeria, Sued Badillo as a historian in Puerto Rico, and Vargas Arenas as an archaeologist in Venezuela). Others, such as Trudie Lamb Richmond (a Native American working for a U.S. research institution), Augustin Holl (a Cameroonian archaeologist working within the French academy), and Partha Chatterjee (an Indian social theorist who regularly visits U.S. universities), had more pluralistic backgrounds that shared Third World and First World experiences. These distinctions and differences, with the initial tensions that accompanied them, soon blurred as the seminar participants came to realize that philosophical affinities underlay the group and that the "Western group" also had significant Third World credentials: Wylie as a reasoned advocate of feminist perspectives in archaeology, Blakey as an African American within mainstream anthropology, Schmidt as a long-time practitioner of alternative archaeologies in the Third World itself, and Patterson as a close colleague to many Third World theorists.

One of the first tasks facing the seminar was to assemble an agenda for intellectual action. What were the reasons we had come together, and what did we want to gain from the seminar to share with others? One reason that quickly emerged was the importance of enhancing the texture of the historical analyses and narratives we write about other cultures by incorporating the richness and diversity of local histories, which we ignore or obliterate when we disregard the interests of Third World colleagues, their assumptions, and the circumstances in which they work. We all agreed that it was essential to discover concerns and views that we usually are incapable of imagining, given the assumptions under which we work. This insight was as pertinent for the Third World participants—who often work in isolation and are unaware of allies else-where—as it was for the other participants.

The issues raised by these concerns caused us to question whether there is a way to recover the principles of anthropology in American archaeology and to expose the contradictions within the dominant para-digm in archaeology today. To do so means reconceptualizing archae-ology with concerned colleagues from North America and abroad. Like the social archaeologists of Latin America, we came to see archaeology as more than a set of practices and techniques. It is a historical social science that relates the study of past societies to the present and incorpo-rates the historical value of oral accounts, folklore and folklife, and writ-ten documents that reflect the voices of groups whose views of history are commonly ignored or erased. A dialogue between archaeologists and historians of the First and Third Worlds is a necessary first step to reveal the power relations that govern the flow of ideas, to bring into awareness alternate voices and their distinctive messages, and to construct programs of action that challenge an incomplete and dominant First World para-digm. The SAR seminar provided an ideal setting in which these issues could be explored.

Among the initial questions around which seminar participants were asked to focus their discussions were (1) Is there sufficient common ground between First and Third World archaeologists and historians to make a dialogue possible? (2) What role do First World historians and

archaeologists have in examining the legitimacy of dominant historical paradigms? and (3) What are the consequences of Third World approaches to history and archaeology? Let us briefly consider the most
important issues that arose out of our examination of these questions.

Peripheral, Marginal, and Erased History

The opening discussion of the seminar established an important
common thread that all the participants had directly experienced or observed: the erasure of local histories—one of the most cancerous products of international capitalism in both its colonial and its metropolitan
manifestations. This theme was quickly elaborated in a number of directions, all of which provided essential insights into how colonial and
neocolonial powers manipulate the production of histories, encouraging
certain forms of history while discouraging and even silencing others.
The state exercises power over the production of local histories in various ways: censorship, the appointment of official state historians, the
allocation of resources for research and training that serve to amplify
knowledge only about the period with which the state is identified, the
sponsorship of archaeological methods that ensure the erasure of local
histories from the landscape, and sanctions against and outright suppression of those who attempt to challenge official histories.

The participants recognized within the first day of discussions that
some First and Third World archaeologists and historians embraced common concerns for examining and deconstructing dominant historical
paradigms. In many instances, First World archaeologists conduct research under the same dominant paradigms as their colleagues in the
Third World. Critical examination of these paradigms has the potential
to demystify the social relations and practices of archaeology and history
as well as to create ideological space for the practice of archaeology in
constructing alternative histories. Such examinations have three components: (1) an inquiry into what kinds of empirical information are used
and suppressed within the dominant historiography, (2) an analysis of the
concepts used in interpretation, and (3) a close look at the power relations between those who produce information and those who interpret
it and package it for broader consumption.

The first component, examination of what constitutes acceptable information, encourages discovery of information contradictory to orthodoxy that is ignored or suppressed. Differential selection of data provides
an index of what is valued or presumed to support particular interpretations. An example that arose during discussion was the evidentiary basis

for claims that African technology was inferior to that of the West and that this inferiority helps explain the rapid conquest of the continent (Curtin 1964). Historical research reveals that there is no evidence to support views of technological inferiority, and moreover, archaeological investigations have revealed empirical data suggesting the contrary—for example, an innovative, technologically complicated African iron industry that developed in the early first millennium A.D. (Schmidt and Childs 1985).

The second level of inquiry examines analytical concepts and frameworks that organize interpretations in the colonial library—the historiography that grew up as part of the colonial domination of non-Western peoples (Mudimbe 1988). Such inquiries reveal the hidden premises and structures of thought that, in the case of African technology, derive from Enlightenment beliefs such as the progressive development of technology and the existence of hierarchies of social types and races, and from the projection of these beliefs onto both the historical and contemporary landscapes. The example of how iron industry has been treated illustrates this transformation: recent historical African technology was equated with ancient European technology and used to explain the "primitive" ancient technology (Schmidt 1995; Schmidt and Childs 1985). Because Enlightenment and nineteenth-century thought viewed non-Western cultures as representative of earlier stages of human development, temporalizing the idea of a hierarchy (capped by contemporary conditions in the West) ipso facto homogenizes and assigns all non-European technology, through all of historical time, to earlier, primitive stages.

The third form of inquiry requires us to ask how particular historical interpretations mystify, sustain, and reproduce existing power relations. For example, the incorporation of the notion that Africa was techno-. logically inferior to the West is now so widely accepted by orthodox historiography that historians, anthropologists, and archaeologists did not seriously questioned the claim until the 1970s. The assertion is still widely accepted today, even by schoolchildren, and forms the basis of a consciousness which accepts that Africans are incapable of technological innovation and sustainable development. This view provides fertile ground for those who require cheap labor. The existence of debilitated, dependent populations lacking faith in their abilities to experiment and to invent technological solutions for their own development problems also provides a rich medium in which the World Bank and others in the international donor community can carry out their technologically based development schemes without question or opposition.

The seminar participants found that when using these forms of critical analyses, historians and archaeologists would challenge existing orthodoxies. In the African case, empirical evidence has, in fact, been marshaled. Reinterpretations of concepts have been proposed that challenge the received African historiography, but some of these important new perspectives have been either ignored or rejected. Those who manage and control the production and dissemination of knowledge about Africa or other Third World regions do not accept ideas that overturn the unquestioned givens of the established discourse and order. These are the experiences of Westerners working in the Third World. They mirror the experiences of Third World colleagues and illustrate the intersection of interests that archaeologists and historians in the First and Third Worlds have in examining and challenging dominant historical paradigms.

Similar processes occur in the West. Historians and archaeologists concerned with roles of women in history and society can recount similar experiences in which important, widely accepted interpretive positions remain unsupported by empirical evidence and in which evidence has not been assembled in ways that make its origins clear or allow alternatives to be tested. Moreover, theory-laden concepts — such as man the hunter — are not examined to reveal underlying, unstated assumptions and implications. Most importantly, historians and archaeologists rarely reflect critically about or inquire into how such data and concepts refract, sustain, and reproduce existing structures of power. The vital issue here is that uncritical approaches are an integral part of what we teach and export to the Third World. It is precisely at this juncture that critical views become significant in the dialogue between First and Third World scholars.

Neocolonialism

One of the most notable critical contributions of the Third World scholars to the seminar—one that sharpened everyone's awareness of the influences encompassing the practice of archaeology and history — was the issue of neocolonialism. Iraida Vargas Arenas of Venezuela and Bassey Andah of Nigeria argued eloquently that neocolonialism in their countries was a major force in the production of historical knowledge, a perspective that inevitably led to collateral discussions examining the effects of colonialism as well as neocolonialism on the production of knowledge, particularly but not exclusively in the Third World. Whereas colonialism is the expression of power relations between dominant metropolitan countries in the West and the politically, economically, and culturally subordinated peoples on their margins, neocolonialism is based on economic and cultural subordination in the era after colonized peoples gained political independence. Because economic domination carries with it a variety of cultural implications, and because it is in the cultural sphere that most struggles for identity and production of knowledge take place, it is necessary to understand both how economic relations interpenetrate everyday life in the neocolonial world and how everyday life itself is more than a mere reflection of its economic dimensions and must encompass a sense of cultural well-being.

One of the seminar's most poignant examples of neocolonialism at work was that of the changing content of the secondary-school history curriculum in Venezuela. History is no longer taught as a separate subject in secondary schools; it has been subsumed within the vague category of "civics," a subject instructing students how to be good citizens. This shift illustrates the influence of Western philanthropic foundations in reformulating curricula in Third World states (Berman 1983). As history disappears from the Venezuelan school curriculum, so do accounts of resistance to colonialism and economic exploitation, which, by diminishing local self-awareness of the historical consequences of such activities, opens new avenues for foreign economic exploitation. In such circumstances, where history is produced by the state and its officially sanctioned historians, it is often virtually impossible for alternative views to be heard, let alone accepted into the approved curricula. One of the few remaining avenues by which alternative views can reach a popular audience is that of museum exhibits depicting history from different angles of view.

As the seminar began to explore the role of neocolonialism in the making of history, it became apparent that effects similar to those in Venezuela could also be seen in Nigeria (Andah, this volume). Western investment in Nigerian oil production is similar in scope and importance to oil investment in Venezuela. In Nigeria, vast tracts of land are opened to oil exploitation without any attempt to assess the archaeological resources and history of the regions impacted. Inquiry into the history of these large tracts of land "without history" is actively resisted by both the oil companies and the state because the production of such historical knowledge is seen as a dangerous impediment to unlimited access to potential resources and the production of wealth. Archaeological investigations of these landscapes, if allowed and encouraged, could provide a vastly enriched understanding of Nigerian history in the oil-producing region. The state, however, is not prepared to empower archaeology in Nigeria so that its capacity to produce such knowledge might be realized.

Such vivid examples of the effects of neocolonialism on local capacity to make histories disabused the seminar participants of all assumptions that neocolonialism is anything less than a major force in the erasure of history in the non-Western world today.

The State and Archaeology

State sponsorship of research into the very ancient past may also figure prominently in the ways history is represented. As the seminar explored issues of state involvement in either the construction of history or its erasure, we turned to contemporary Kenya, where there has been significant state investment in discovering the ancient history of humankind. For decades Kenya has been faced with the intersection of ethnicity and class structures that threaten national unity. In this volatile context, Kenya has used paleoanthropology as a means of masking deep-seated class and ethnic divisions (Schmidt, this volume). Several decades of official sponsorship of paleoanthropological research through the National Museum of Kenya, with the close collaboration of the National Science Foundation, the National Geographic Society, and the Foundation for Research into the Origins of Man, have produced a host of spectacular finds and a neutral historical symbol of national unity.

The attraction of "early man" in Kenya is that it homogenizes ancient cultures and peoples and makes them appear to be a unity. It identifies them, and by extension all Kenyans, as marking the first step out of nature. The great antiquity of "early men" separates them both from the primitive and from the ethnic/class divisions and struggles in contemporary Kenyan society. The state's identification with paleoanthropology has resulted in the de-emphasizing of local archaeologies, which are all too easily identified with regional ethnic groups. So long as Kenya remains torn by class and ethnic conflict, we would expect the Kenyan state to continue its strong support of paleoanthropology and its underwriting of a national myth of common origin.

State involvement with archaeology and its official sponsorship arose for very different reasons in Mexico between the 1930s and the 1960s, when the Mexican state provided vast sums to support the excavation of royal tombs and the restoration of monumental architecture to serve as tourist attractions. The goal of these investments in archaeology was to obtain foreign exchange and to diversify the Mexican economy. As the seminar considered these examples of both state resistance to archaeology and state sponsorship of archaeology, it became apparent that each incorporated an element of neocolonialism or the influence of foreign interests. In the instance of Mexico it was development in the service of the foreign tourist. Mexican development of archaeology focused research exclusively on ancient states, involved most trained archaeologists in the study of ancient state systems, and diverted resources away from inquiries into kin-organized communities that resisted the incursions and exactions of their state-based neighbors (Patterson, this volume). This meant that large areas of Mexico remained unexamined and that the histories of their ancient inhabitants could not be woven into the fabric of the modern nation-state. The peripheralized regions saw none of the benefits, such as roads and jobs resulting from tourism, that state sponsorship of archaeology led to elsewhere in Mexico. The state attempted to integrate the inhabitants of these peripheries into everyday life through rural education and public health projects based on extensive ethnographic research. This experience has inhibited archaeologists in Mexico from examining the histories of disenfranchised regions and from constructing accounts that might enrich and add variety to local histories or challenge or contradict the views of the state.

If the production of historical knowledge through archaeology and other forms of historical research is limited by neocolonial forces or skewed by special state interests, opportunities to conduct such research in the Third World are also severely limited by access to resources. The impoverished conditions under which Third World scholars work are shaped by the relationships of their countries to the First World and to international lending agencies such as the World Bank and the International Monetary Fund. Conditions imposed by the heavy debts incurred in the 1970s and 1980s and the continued calls for debt restructuring and devaluation, with concomitant massive curtailment of social and educational services, accelerate impoverishment in many countries (Gladwin 1991). The consequences are far-reaching, especially when few resources are available (Alatas 1977; Okpoko 1991). Colleagues who labor under these circumstances find it difficult to write, to contextualize their research, and to disseminate their work because of their isolation from national and international communities of scholars. The setting of our seminar — on the beautiful and affluent campus of the School of American Research — presented an ironic contrast to the conditions under which Third World scholars in the group labor. That contrast created another set of tensions that brought to the fore the very real differences between those who operate at the center and those who exist on the periphery.

The Science and History Dichotomy

Those who fall back on local resources and write about regional history and archaeology often find it difficult, if not impossible, to gain an audience or acceptance in the West because their inquiries do not comply with the canons of established scientific discourse. They are silenced by the very scientists they are trying to reach, because they are not doing "real science" (Rahman 1983).

In this context, science is distinguished by two attributes: the tools and devices of scientific research and the idioms and tropes of scientific language. Everyone knows that science is expensive. Orthodox science requires costly equipment to conduct investigations, collect data, and carry out analyses. It also requires an elaborate infrastructure composed of support personnel, technicians, and principal investigators. The last must have the theoretical sophistication required to integrate disparate data and present well-reasoned arguments in prestigious international journals in order to meet the basic criteria of standard science. These conditions create at least three responses. One is seen in what one First World archaeologist has described as a "scientific swat team" (Joel Grossman, personal communication 1984), which swoops into the Third World to collect data—rarely interacting with local colleagues—before retiring to a high-tech lab where information is analyzed and reports are prepared (but not necessarily disseminated).

Third World archaeologists who have been trained in the West and conditioned to the latest scientific devices find that upon returning home they invariably lack access to the scientific apparatus that such conditioning demands. The result is often professional paralysis, expressed as an inability to conceptualize projects using local labor and tools, eventually leading to a profound alienation from all forms of inquiry. This disablement opens the door for First World archaeologists to control the tempo and modes of research. More insidiously, the seminar participants found, imbalances in scientific resources lead to power relationships that resemble neocolonial relationships, with the Third World scholar financially indentured to research programs controlled and dominated by First World scholars.

An example of the marginalization of history by science is manifest in the policy of the Anthropology Division of the United States National Science Foundation. This policy perpetuates the dominant paradigm, which draws a false dichotomy between history and science: historical approaches within contemporary archaeology are viewed as unscientific and are referred to the National Endowment for the Humanities for possible funding. The implications of such a policy are profound, for, in perhaps one of the most extreme expressions of historical marginalization, it denies the historical configurations of a landscape. This is a process that Russell Handsman and Trudie Lamb Richmond brought to light in their seminar discussion of New England (see chapter 5). There, whole communities were rendered invisible for several hundred years until alternative histories challenged the dominant historiography — which had been reinforced, ironically, by the methodologies of scientific archaeology.

The capacity of "real science" to stifle creativity in the Third World has other expressions as well. For instance, scholars who conduct archaeological research with the few local tools available often lack access to the latest scientific journals, such as *World Archaeology, American Antiquity, Antiquity,* and *Journal of Archaeological Science.* Such journals either are not included in most official exchanges of scientific journals or are beyond the financial capacity of Third World university and museum library budgets. Most African university libraries, for example, have not subscribed to archaeological journals (as well as many other scientific journals) since the mid-1970s because of budgetary restrictions. The consequence is that archaeologists and others concerned with ancient history are unable to situate their work in current scientific idioms and tropes. When the language of their work does not replicate the standards set by international journals and "peer" review, their efforts are neither validated nor legitimated. This rejection by Western scholars leads to increasing marginalization and alienation and may reinforce power relations that already prevail in research endeavors.

Another response is seen among small groups of Third World scholars who refuse to be discouraged when they encounter Western rejection and who respond by publishing their views in locally distributed journals and books. The Nigerian archaeologist Bassey Andah, who participated in the seminar, epitomizes this type of intrepid, independent, and iconoclastic Third World intellectual. For two decades Andah sustained almost single-handedly the *West African Journal of Archaeology,* which often advocated alternative methodologies and histories but is read outside of Africa by perhaps only several dozen archaeologists with African interests. Westerners with little interest in Africa or in the methodologies employed by West African archaeologists ignore or are uninterested in reading these publications, which are often printed on newsprint and otherwise do not meet the standards of presentation found in the prestigious international journals. The major consequence for archaeologists in the West is that they shut themselves off from significant alternative perspectives and different ways of investigating and interpreting the past.

History as Political Engagement

A common link among all the seminar papers and a theme that repeatedly came to the fore during seminar discussions is that history is a political undertaking. A parallel case is made by historians and sociologists of science who claim that science is a cultural and political activity, just as history is. This is a highly contested view, though the observation is commonplace in scientific and philosophical circles. As a philosopher of science and an archaeologist, Alison Wylie helped clarify our debate over this issue by arguing that awareness of the political qualities of contemporary scientific archaeology provides us the means to move between the "unsustainable objectivism" of "real science" and the relativism and skepticism of the more extreme postmodern critiques of science. Wylie's observations helped to open the door for an unprejudiced discussion among the seminar participants of the potential of history to challenge dominant paradigms in science as well as conventional historiographies based on the colonial library, and the potential of those challenges to bring about change.

One of the dilemmas in bringing about change is the disadvantage of using the "master's tools to dismantle the master's house" (Lorde 1984:110). That is, we risk reproducing the oppressive structures we are attempting to reject if we use those structures' own terms of reference (Wylie, this volume). This dilemma was vividly illustrated during the seminar by a discussion of the rejection of archaeology by historians in Tanzania, who initially saw archaeology as a tool for nationalist perspectives based on a cultural evolutionary paradigm ("the master's tools") (Schmidt, this volume). The political confrontation that developed in the Tanzanian academy over ways to make history in a postcolonial setting shifted the debate from revisionism using the categories and unconscious givens of the colonial library to a dynamic archaeological critique of paradigms of historical interpretation and the conditions under which they arose. Wylie added significantly to this discussion by showing that recent feminist contributions to the philosophy of science offer a way out of the dilemma by recognizing the contingency and standpoint specificity of master narratives and their analytical categories: knowledge claims must be assessed from a variety of standpoints that unmask the conditions under which knowledge is produced.

A change occurred during the seminar as dialogue about the political qualities of history developed. Our initial language, which used terms like "constructing history," gradually shifted away from this more analytical concept—in which one assumes full and reflexively informed responsibility for a historical product—to "making history," a phrase that more accurately captures the political processes, also reflexively informed, inherent in giving voice to histories that have been silenced or erased. The title of this introduction captures this shift, in which participants accepted the necessity for constant scrutiny of the presuppositions and foundations of knowledge claims while inexorably moving to the idea that acting on information which contradicts and overturns orthodox historical knowledge involves political engagement.

Accepting Other Histories

If the false separation between science and history silences the contribution of Third World archaeologists within science, so too does the dichotomy between prehistory and history. Both archaeologists and historians of the First World widely accept the validity of prehistory as a concept that applies to preliterate or nonliterate societies, whose pasts can be known to us only through study of archaeological remains. This idea carries with it the additional implication that nonliterate societies lack histories, a view that represents their pasts as mythic because they are expressed through folk histories and oral traditions (Schmidt 1983a, 1983b).

Many historians working in Africa and Latin America have overcome this limitation to develop richly informed local histories based on the critical study of written records, oral accounts, and ethnographic observations (e.g., Feierman 1974, 1990; Hunt 1977; Miller 1980; Packard 1981; Vansina 1985). Their contributions, however, have had little effect on archaeological thinking in Europe and North America, where the dichotomy between science and history remains firmly entrenched. This means that research in the Third World which successfully incorporates oral history into interpretation for periods preceding written accounts is seen as mixing two very distinct domains of knowledge. The mixing of "prehistoric" archaeology with "mythic" oral information further reinforces the idea that such innovative research is not only unscientific (it confuses categories) but also ahistoric. The most unfortunate consequence of these ideas is that some of the most important historical research from the Third World is not read elsewhere.

Most historical archaeologists err in ways similar to those of their prehistorian colleagues by subscribing to categories that exclude the contributions we present in this volume. So long as historical archaeology is seen predominantly as the history of European settlement and colonization, as well as the history of capitalism and its industrial expressions, then it will continue to dismiss and ignore perspectives arising out of indigenous milieus in the Third World (see, for example, Leone and Potter 1988 for a recent expression of this perspective). The chapters in this book challenge the provincialism of historical archaeology, with its framing of problems in strictly Eurocentric categories that reproduce the false distinctions between scientific, mythic, and historical domains of knowledge. The failure of historical archaeology to accommodate the histories of the non-Western world continues to amplify an already deeply Eurocentric bias and a propensity to substitute documentary redundancy for revitalization of pasts forgotten or erased.

The papers presented to the seminar by Handsman and Lamb Richmond, Andah, Schmidt, and Holl showed a more textured awareness and appreciation of the interplay between archaeological remains, written accounts, and oral traditions than is usually allowed by prehistoric archaeology, historical archaeology, or history, which constitute them as distinct domains of knowledge separated by insurmountable barriers. One explanation for the more integrative perspective in these four papers is that the practice of archaeology and history in Third World settings occurs under conditions of poverty, displaced historical identity, and political and economic oppression. Thus, scholars have compelling reasons to recuperate histories that express the experiences and cultural understandings of people whose identities have been denied—by the state, by ruling elites, and by foreign scientists. The certainty and legitimacy of categories like "authentic history" (Andah, this volume) flow directly out of the experiences of authors who, like Andah, have interrogated and examined the intersection of myth, history, and archaeology in their search for histories that fit the needs and circumstances of their communities.

It is essential, however, that we not misunderstand Andah's call for an authentic or "genuine" African history. His is not a chauvinistic claim that only Africans can make history about Africa. It is a signal that African archaeologists are weary of the uneven power relations controlling representations of the African past and that African representations need not meet "objective" standards imposed by the state or foreign scientists who steadfastly refuse to acknowledge their role in reproducing the structures of power. But it also has a strongly applied dimension. A "genuine" history creates a past that forms the basis of an identity empowering Africans to negotiate justice and to develop their communities in ways that overcome the ethnocide, displacement, and genocide caused by the slave trade, as well as the erasures of historical identity perpetrated by state collusion with international capitalism (e.g., the Nigerian state's allowing international oil companies to alter vast tracts of land).

The themes and issues taken up by the seminar participants address the need to set aside the scientific categories and tropes that characterize contemporary archaeology and begin to learn from the problems confronting archaeologists who are trying to recuperate erased historical memory as well as meet pressing community needs under conditions of neocolonialism in the Third World. We now turn to the chapters in this book—which began as papers presented during the seminar—focusing on the themes and issues we have just highlighted.

Key Issues in the Chapters that Follow

By examining the institutions and practices of "official" state historians, Jalil Sued Badillo, a Puerto Rican historian long engaged in the *independentista* movement, powerfully illustrates the need to decolonize the Caribbean historical mind. His analysis in chapter 2 shows how official Caribbean history, with its exclusive focus on particular domains such as trade and production figures, prevents new knowledge from entering the mainstream and how its practices perpetuate incomplete historical understandings of the region. He points out that official histories suppress the extent of the slave trade in Amerindians; this silence was compounded by the fact that colonial censuses typically classified people according to quasi-racial categories that ignored culture. He also points out that in the nineteenth century the state forcibly suppressed advocates of indigenous history. He argues that these influences on the historiography of the Greater Antilles have led to skewed histories that marginalize the local actors and create a false historical reality. A similar process of erasure by classification occurs today in South Africa.

Sued Badillo also unwraps the mystifications surrounding the history of Puerto Rico and the eastern Caribbean. He sees the recuperation of historical memory as a project crucial to overcoming official policies of historical disinformation that have extended over many generations. His analysis shows how chroniclers writing in the sixteenth century erased the centrality of the eastern Caribbean during the early stages of colonial expansion in the New World. These erasures were accepted and further elaborated upon by subsequent official historians, who stressed the idea of economic marginality and fabricated a myth of dependence on the metropolis. Sued Badillo also shows how these state agents suppressed local histories that had the potential to correct the erasures and could have provided points of identity for working-class Puerto Ricans.

Sued Badillo's creative use of the colonial library reveals that there is submerged evidence for the early economic centrality of the eastern

Caribbean. For example, archival evidence for the sixteenth century suggests a vital gold-mining economy and other activities such as hide trading. Smuggling emerged as an economically and culturally important activity that identified rural indigenous communities and differentiated them from the urban colonial ruling class. Conventional historiographies of the region, based on a highly selective use of official records, miss fundamentally important features of economic and cultural activity. Sued Badillo's insights pose a significant challenge to conventional historiography and its assertions about the economic marginality of the region. Though archaeology has the capacity, for example, to recover economic history erased by the early chroniclers, the failure of archaeology to correct orthodox accounts makes Sued Badillo's research all the more trenchant a critique.

The practice of archaeology and history in Venezuela, like that in Puerto Rico, has been shaped by official historians who act as agents of the state and its ruling class. In chapter 3, Iraida Vargas Arenas, using a Marxist-informed analysis that also typifies many of her mostly male Latin American counterparts, argues that for official historians, history is based exclusively on written documents. This perspective segregates official history from all of pre-Hispanic history—which is reserved for archaeologists, who deal with a dead past. Official validation of a dead past also legitimizes the diversion of ancient cultural goods into the commercial marketplace. While such practices mask the underlying processes of capitalist and neocolonial development, alternative currents of thought followed by archaeologists and historians in Venezuela and several other Latin American countries are attempting to recuperate the pasts of Indian, black, and mestizo cultures as an integral part of a project of democratic incorporation (Fonseca 1989; Sanoja 1990; Sanoja and Vargas Arenas 1989; Vargas Arenas and Sanoja 1993a).

Vargas Arenas also identifies how history in Latin America is conceptualized and structured in terms of a lineal succession of periods, each of which expresses particular power relations and forms of domination. The names of the periods—pre-Hispanic, colonial, and republican—further express the centrality of the relationship with the colonial metropolis. Each period is a self-contained and self-explained block of time and events that has neither antecedents nor consequences. The segmentation of the past into a series of unrelated periods creates the illusion that early history is disconnected from and thus unrelated to more recent history, an illusion amplified by archaeology's overwhelming attention to the pre-Columbian era and its almost complete inattention to periods following the arrival of Europeans.

The processes of segmentation and discontinuity illuminated by Vargas Arenas operate with different tempos and rhythms in countries like Venezuela where communities with diverse social structures have been enveloped by the state and variously continue to resist its exactions. Simplifying assumptions and practices, such as the notion of the historical continuity of the civilizing process started by the Spanish Crown, have deprived many local cultures of information about their own history and relations with the state. Vargas Arenas shows how the practices of archaeologists, ethnohistorians, and anthropologists who continue to search for the "objective past" of these communities reproduce the practices of official history, which buttress class and state structures that differentially distribute wealth, access to justice, and the hope for a better future.

Vargas Arenas argues that archaeology has the potential to create a historical consciousness that challenges the simplifications and distortions of official history. To do so, she suggests that it must reject the analytical categories and unilineal sequences of official history and the functionalist approaches of ecological anthropology and become a historical science exposing the contradictions existing within local communities and between them, the state, and their environment.

In chapter 4, Thomas Patterson adds to our understanding of Latin American experiences with archaeology when he examines how archaeology and history have been constructed in Mexico and Peru—states characterized by different power structures and processes of class formation. He argues that archaeology has largely been constituted by the state in Mexico, where significant investments in the archaeology of ancient civilizations were made for the purpose of enhancing tourism, whereas in Peru it has been constructed by agents of the agrarian capitalist and mining-finance-merchant factions of the ruling class and, at times, by intellectuals whose voices resonated with those of urban and rural workers and peasants.

An important result of the difference is that archaeological discourse has historically exhibited more diversity and multivocality in Peru than in Mexico. This means that the politically dominant ruling-class faction in Peru has consistently had to confront alternative understandings of the Peruvian reality. These challenges have ranged from principled silences to the construction of alternative explanations that link pre- and post-Columbian history with everyday life in contemporary rural communities. The various viewpoints provide different explanations of present-day power relations and alternative scenarios of what might be possible in the future if different courses of action are pursued. Explanations that build on liberal and neoliberal models of society (and sustain

World Bank or International Monetary Fund agendas) marginalize urban and rural workers. Other views that take cognizance of the dialectics of everyday life, shaped by both class formation and civil war, clarify rather than obscure power relations and bring into focus the differences and implications of alternative courses of action in the near future.

If official erasure of Puerto Rican history is a clear political and economic statement by the colonial state, then the silencing of Mahican history in New England is a much more complex process that involves local representations followed by state sanctions. Russell Handsman, an archaeologist, and Trudie Lamb Richmond, a Mahican who directs educational programs for the Institute of American Indian Studies, discuss in chapter 5 the inexorable truncation of Mahican history over the last four centuries, showing how the Mahican people have resisted ethnocide—the erasure of cultural differences. The Mahican story of survival is one of ethnogenesis during which the Mahicans have appropriated symbols of identity from the West as well as rediscovered deep-time traditions, those folk histories that have fallen from common usage but have been maintained by a very small number of people.

Mahican history is a case study of ethnocide, exposing the various ways in which the state eliminates cultural diversity. One such device Handsman and Lamb Richmond find that parallels the racial reclassification described by Sued Badillo for Puerto Rico is the use of census categories that ignore the ambiguities of individual identities and smother them under homogeneous categories to produce individuals with uniform, unambiguous, and clearly defined characteristics. Through judicial processes, the state subsequently reaffirms the validity of these categories and the data that deny the presence of different groups on the landscape. In this instance, archaeologists have underwritten state policies by employing survey methods scientifically inadequate to delimit Mahican settlements, thus ensuring that ancient Mahican communities will not be observed in the contemporary landscape. Handsman and Lamb Richmond offer an archaeological methodology that puts these communities back into the landscape, creating points of identity obscured by the practices of archaeologists and historians.

The structuring concepts and categories of the colonial library also have profound effects on the way contemporary historians in Africa view the ancient past. Peter Schmidt, who has engaged in the long-term development of methodologies incorporating African histories, examines in chapter 6 the development of recent Tanzanian historiography to illustrate how and why nationalist histories served the state by glorifying resistance movements, often at the expense of well-developed regional histories. Schmidt's analysis also isolates a strong resistance to archaeological research that discovers histories which differ from and contradict those found in the colonial library; this resistance is partly a struggle over the production of knowledge in which some local historians accept the validity of the Western dichotomy between prehistory and history.

Schmidt argues that archaeology has the often unrealized potential to create new knowledge and interpretations free of the values of the colonial library, as well as to create knowledge that contradicts African historiography arising from the colonial library. For example, European preoccupation with state systems and their histories has led to sponsorship of research along the East African coast that focuses on the emergence of foreign-influenced civilizations (Chittick 1968, 1974, 1975, 1984; Kirkman 1963). Employing this historical emphasis, scholars have characterized the East African hinterland as an economic backwater and have remained noticeably silent about peoples who resided in vast areas in the interior and who were not subject to coastal state authorities. Schmidt illustrates how archaeology can be employed to give voice to the ancient societies ignored by colonial and postcolonial historians.

The project set out in Schmidt's paper illustrates how the archaeology of preliterate periods can be used to critique historical interpretations based on written documents. This interplay of archaeological data with written accounts sets up contradictions to preestablished categories and shows how the boundaries of historical archaeology as it is conventionally practiced can be expanded. Schmidt is also concerned with unequal power relations between First and Third World archaeologists, a condition that is partly ameliorated by the development of local methodologies and capabilities as a first step in challenging the dominant concepts and practices in archaeology emanating from the First World.

As we noted earlier, one of the most important commonalities to emerge from the seminar discussions and from the chapters in this volume is the belief that making alternative histories is an important form of political action. We accept that history provides us ways of knowing the present. When we engage any dominant historiography and its gaps, silences, and dead spaces, we open up new understandings of social relations and of the vested interests of the social groups who want to see that historiography perpetuated. When we develop and consider alternative understandings of history, new vistas of what might be possible in the future unfold. Bassey Andah addresses the issue of the maintenance of historical "dead zones" by vested interests when he argues in chapter 7 that in Nigeria, urban development is taking place as if the landscape lacks a history. He sees that archaeological inquiry into the history of landscapes not only adds a human texture but also confronts advocates of uncontrolled development with the need to incorporate symbolic and substantive historical meanings into their planning designs. This is a process that involves a struggle to be heard, a struggle to develop a popular base of understanding, and a struggle to get alternative histories accepted into curricula and planning.

Andah addresses the dilemma of making alternative histories within the constraints of a neocolonial state (Nigeria) that serves international capitalist interests. He queries how archaeology and history can serve the needs of communities pushed into increasing poverty and those displaced from their traditional landscapes by rampant urbanization and uncontrolled growth. The erasure of cultural diversity, although not an expression of official history, is potentially more insidious than official history; it permanently removes generations of history from the landscape and creates a national historical rootlessness under official state sponsorship.

Andah also argues that archaeology as it has been practiced in Africa fragments the history of African peoples and societies into false temporal and cultural units that ignore the frames of meaning African peoples used to express themselves culturally. He identifies this fragmentation of African societies, both past and present, as a neocolonial device to gain economic control by separating people from their rich traditions of economic and technological achievement. These separations are exacerbated, Andah believes, by the emic-etic distinction in anthropology, which distances the investigator from local people and their historical ideas.

He argues that archaeology must become both a historical and an educational discipline that produces knowledge allowing people to challenge the stereotypes derived from the colonial library (and its widely accepted chronological and typological categories) and to understand contemporary social relations and power structures and their implications. Doing so would help communities pursue programs enabling their members to meet authentically human needs. This project requires that archaeology and its role in making history must be liberated from the assumption that only scientific knowledge reveals the past; this liberation necessarily means a rediscovery and revaluation of histories that ordinary Africans can understand, histories that provide a sense of historical self and creativity rather than of attributes and wants created by international capital or the state.

Augustin Holl, in chapter 8, illustrates an ongoing struggle over the legitimacy of an alternative history in his discussion of the acceptance of the thought of Cheikh Anta Diop, a Senegalese historian who popularized a view of African antiquity that challenged the most fundamental assumptions and conclusions of Western historiography about Africa. Anta Diop's importance is that he provided an alternative way of thinking about the origins of state systems, science, and technology in Africa.

Holl provides an African view of Anta Diop's historical thought by drawing on his personal knowledge of the francophone educational tradition and the profound impact of Anta Diop's historical thinking in francophone Africa. He explains that Anta Diop's historical constructs were important to African intellectuals because they liberated francophone Africans from the categories of colonial history. They came to accept Anta Diop's views about African history in the 1950s and 1960s, immediately before and after the struggles for independence. Holl relates how Anta Diop's historical constructs, which asserted the primacy of Egyptian cultural origins, simultaneously homogenized African history and erased the particularities of various regional developments. Anta Diop's arguments also underwrote and provided legitimacy for a program of pan-African unity, a program that soon proved incompatible with the official agendas of the newly independent states. Holl shows that Anta Diop failed to recognize the implications and limitations of using the terms and concepts of European historiography, especially in accepting European concepts of diffusionism and race. He finds that by engaging in arguments that drew on scientific and linguistic analyses, Anta Diop opened himself to substantive and damaging critiques from those disciplines which sustained the dominant paradigm.

If Anta Diop's explanation homogenizes the histories of African regions by deriving them from one corner of the continent, then, as Michael Blakey points out in chapter 9, the same danger exists when his model is uncritically imported and used in North America. An African American physical anthropologist, Blakey speaks with personal knowledge from the crucible of Afrocentric ideas. He shows how Anta Diop's views were appropriated and introduced into a new context by cultural nationalist (Afrocentric) writers in the United States during the 1980s and 1990s to underpin the construction of African American identity in a context where the history of African Americans is still actively suppressed. Blakey sees this appropriation simultaneously as an important corrective to Eurocentrism and as a failure because of its uncritical acceptance of the categories and modes of analysis found in the colonial library.

Blakey critically examines aspects of the ideology of Afrocentrism: the notion of a singular African epistemology and culture derived historically from Egypt; a belief in the cultural purity and extricability of this primordial "African" epistemology and ethos from the multicultural influences of the African diaspora; and the delineation of naturally

21

occurring and qualitatively distinct biological races. Among these expressions of Afrocentrism, he finds that the explanation of social and psychological patterns is couched in terms of biological determinants that replicate the principles of social Darwinism and are reminiscent of the racial determinism that legitimized white supremacy. Blakey also illuminates the opposition of Afrocentric thinkers to social theories that root inequalities in economic relations and their resistance to social programs seeking to ameliorate those inequities. He finds that the intended audience of the Afrocentric movement is composed mainly of educated, middle-class North Americans who accept the terms and logic of the dominant discourse. He also recognizes that the movement depends on the identification and valorization of its singularity, a device which asserts ownership, denies commonalities, and inhibits the development of alliances with other communities.

Partha Chatterjee, a key member of a group of Indian scholars responsible for the journal *Subaltern Studies*, examines in chapter 10 a common thematic thread that emerged from the seminar's discussion of marginalization: the imposition of the categories and analytical frameworks of the colonial library. The colonial library is not only the documents collected by and for the colonial state but also the categories, questions, and concepts used to collect and organize that information. The colonial library goes beyond the documentation created by the state to include, in some cases, many generations of historical analyses that accept the categories and assumptions which structure such archives. Chatterjee shows how nationalist history in India was written in the nineteenth century using Enlightenment concepts such as the decline from a golden age and the collapse into barbarism.

Chatterjee's examination of modern Indian historiography shows that when local intellectuals in colonial India began to write histories of that state, they did so in terms of Enlightenment categories concerned with the emergence of modern nation-states. These nineteenth-century accounts were framed in terms of lineal sequences of periods that accepted what happened in the West as normal and eliminated cultural differences that did not fit Enlightenment categories. Chatterjee discloses the processes of distortion historians use in the context of a state that suppresses cultural and historical diversity in order to create a state-centered identity which appears legitimate and rational. An important aspect of the analysis is his focus on the dialectic between the nineteenth-century intellectuals who were creating history for the colonial state and those creating a counteridentity for the nationalist state—both laboring in a colonial setting and using the concepts of the colonial library.

Alison Wylie places the intellectual capstone on this volume in the last chapter, where she shows that recent developments in the philosophy of science, as well as challenges from the history and sociology of science, have undercut the nineteenth-century distinctions between science and history. Recognition of the hermeneutic dimensions of science—that theories outstrip evidence, that interpretations are underdetermined, and that facts and data are theory laden—carries with it the corollary that the ways in which empirical science undergoes paradigmatic transformations are similar to the ways in which interpretations in history tend to change with each new generation of historians. Our awareness or self-knowledge of the affinities between empirical science and history sets the stage for the debate between monolithic science in archaeology and the practice of history within archaeology, whether in the Third World or elsewhere.

Wylie's reprise of the seminar sets out the legitimacy of a historically informed archaeology while at the same time affirming that such an enterprise emerges out of cultural and political conditions that equally influence the formation of scientific theories. Because of this shared foundation, she reasons, it is to be expected that the generational instability experienced by historical interpretation parallels the transformational changes experienced by science (such transformations having been witnessed in archaeology several times since about 1965). Wylie sees that the alternative histories discussed in this volume arise out of similar conditions—usually colonial or neocolonial domination—in which deliberate attempts are made to erase or marginalize the historical identity or even the historical presence of various groups whose historical consciousness may lead to claims to land, resources, and distinctive identities, all substantive challenges to colonial ownership, privilege, and production of historical knowledge. Within the context of Wylie's argument, for example, the intellectual domination of historical archaeology by an almost exclusive emphasis on the material manifestations of European colonialism can be seen as a form of ownership that prevents access to alternative histories struggling to be heard in resistance to colonial domination.

Wylie's exegesis of standpoint theory (Harding 1991) draws from feminist theorists who insist that continuous, reflexive analysis of the various conditions of knowledge production be accompanied by detailed empirical inquiry. She sees that the contributors to this volume operate within a similar frame when they call for "systematic empirical inquiry" to understand "at a second-order, reflexive level the limits of these accounts." Thus Wylie also opens the way for the application of empirical science in non-Western contexts under standpoint theory, a position that she feels—correctly, we believe—is not inimical to non-Western views. The Nigerian philosopher-critic Irele Abiola, for example, also sees that while the refutation of any colonial thesis is conducted within the frame of colonial concepts (the master's tools), nonetheless a positive quality results when the counterdiscourse "creates a collective introspection that fulfills the conditions of historical reflection" (Irele 1991:62; Schmidt, this volume).

Continuing the Dialogue

Negotiating the tensions between the use of systematic empirical inquiry and the reflexive questioning of the sources and presuppositions of that inquiry, as suggested by Wylie, allows us to listen and learn from the intellectual contests about history in the Third World, where there is much greater clarity and consciousness about the political consequences of such contests. The challenges heard in the seminar and in this book offer hope that there are alternative ways in which to go about the business of history making. Furthermore, those challenges suggest that there are many interpretive historical problems of significance heretofore ignored by historical archaeologists and archaeological theorists that demand our attention.

The seminar and this book represent a dialogue among people unfettered by the current limiting conditions of "scientific" archaeology. This dialogue, seen here as a necessary, continuous process, offers opportunities for enriching everyone's archaeological practice by accounting for the diversity of the experiences and views of scholars working under the constraints of neocolonialism. If we fail to open ourselves and engage experiences and ideas similar to those encountered in the seminar and this book, then we set our own practices outside the gaze of critical reflection.

The Theme of the Indigenous in the National Projects of the Hispanic Caribbean

JALIL SUED BADILLO

The twenty-first century will find many Caribbean peoples overwhelmed by a new and profound crisis of identity. Defining collective symbols of identity and adjusting them to existing political projects have been continuous processes since the beginning of the nineteenth century. While the revolutionary experience in Cuba nurtured political discourse, encouraged discussion and historical investigation, recaptured the particularities of various racial and ethnic components, and aired their contradictions, something very different occurred in the Dominican Republic and Puerto Rico. In both countries, although unequally, foreign capital eroded long struggles to harmonize claims of modernity with meaningful cultural inscriptions. Local or popular representations were always derided in favor of "universal" or "Western" values and symbols. Intellectuals' attempts to reformulate traditional popular values are making some gains today. They are trying to recapture a truncated historical memory and create a new symbolism that permits people to experience the country in a different way. They are challenging the symbols of class and the ways of life imposed by colonial dependency. These efforts are combated by the old cultural elite, still firmly entrenched in educational and cultural institutions, and by the North-Americanized sectors that control mass communications.

Cracks in contemporary cultural discourse suggest that profound modifications are already in motion (Quintero Rivera 1983; Rivera-Medina and Ramírez 1985; Sued Badillo 1978). In Puerto Rico, for the first time the debate is moving away from traditional views that sustained the distinctiveness of Puerto Rican historical identity toward a position that will promote its dissolution into North American society. The keynote of this "neocolonial" stance is the interpretation of the Puerto Rican colonial situation as a domestic problem within the "nation," meaning the United States, reducing the conflict between the two countries to a question of minorities within the United States.

Historically, Puerto Ricans distinguished themselves from other immigrant groups in the United States by their conviction that they would persevere as Puerto Ricans and that their stay in the host country would be short. To migrate was a tragedy, not a welcomed adventure. Now a new group is emerging in the island that promotes permanent relocation abroad as an ideal rather than as a short-term option, as well as insisting that the quality of life is better across the ocean. Annexationists (those who support U.S. statehood), opportunists, and *independentistas* (those who support an independent state) who accept the formulations of the majority parties have deformed the vision of reality experienced by Puerto Ricans and have not provided ways of filling the emerging cultural vacuum.

Two events in 1992 underscore the uneasiness Puerto Ricans feel regarding cultural identities and historical interpretations: a plebiscite with quickly improvised symbols of cheap patriotism and the quincentenary celebration of the conquest of the Americas. Both exaggerated the supposed Hispanic identity of nationality as an antidote to North American annexation. But the remedy may be more deadly than the disease, because people's tolerance for official, ruling-class, Hispanophile, pro-white interpretations of Puerto Rican identity has reached its limits. For the first time in a century, the dominant cultural myths are not having the desired political effects on the mood of the Puerto Rican people.

As Albizu Campos observed years ago in a speech: "The nation belongs to those who assert it, not to those who deny it." Since there is always an intimate relation between historical consciousness and political projects, we may ask, What occurs when most of the population is removed from forging its collective identity and channels itself, consciously or unconsciously, toward its own dissolution? Progressive forces have repeatedly emphasized just how important the study of history is to the success of emancipatory projects, but Puerto Rican patriotic sectors today do not seem to recognize the importance of this lesson. The quincentenary celebrations, which showed that colonialism could not be both defended in the past and combated in the present, forced Puerto Ricans to become intellectual accomplices to Spanish imperial violence in the past and, at the same time, to destroy an idyllic image and mythical component of their own identity.

The recreation of what is indigenous in Puerto Rican culture has been a historical given (Alvarez Nazario 1977; Corchado Juarbe 1985; Rouse 1992; Sued Badillo 1978:1–32). There is not a town that does not boast of finding and celebrating the vestiges of some Taino chieftain in its local history. This consciousness expresses the uncontested idea that the reality of Puerto Rican identity is rooted in its mythical geography, a sacred past that is Amerindian in origin and meaning and geographic in its present attributes. Simultaneously, it expresses a profound sense of loss and an intuition that life was better in the mythical past. As the poet Juan Antonio Corretjer (1970:10) said with great sensitivity: "Why then is there constant literary evocation of the Indian and the indigenous? Do the resonances point to romanticism? No. It is that the sacrifices of our last free countrymen secretly touches all of us. Our nostalgia for the Indian is the nostalgia of freedom."

The state teaches that Puerto Rican identity is the historical product of the convergence of three races (Indian, European-Spanish, and African) and that the biological takes precedence over the cultural. Discussions of the symbolic elements of Puerto Rican identity insist on their juxtaposition and the maintenance of their integrity rather than on their fusion.

Mestizaje (the mixing of races), which can support the idea of European-white supremacy, is the cultural and racial ideal of the social elite. In this view, the Indian, by being extinct, is insignificant; the African, by being foreign and undervalued, is strange. In mulatto Caribbean societies, official allegory penetrates deeply into popular loyalties. Therefore, managing what is viewed as indigenous at popular levels acquires particular importance because existing practices have stressed racial and social aggregation rather than racial and cultural exclusion. Such management of identity entails administering the historical continuity and integrative capacity of contradictory symbols (e.g., the insignificance of the Indian and the strangeness of the African), as the social sector that initiated liberation struggles in the Caribbean in the early nineteenth century clearly understood.

The Indigenous Past in the *Independentista* Projects of the Nineteenth Century

Since the early 1800s, Caribbean intellectuals have debated how symbols of the pre-Hispanic past provide an alternative to Spanish identity. Enrique Florescano (1988:262) has suggested that, unlike their contemporaries in Peru or New Granada, the creoles of New Spain appropriated the indigenous past to legitimate their own claims to political leadership and to separate that past from the one claimed by the peninsular Spaniards. The first step in their struggles for independence was to rebaptize the colonies, giving them indigenous names that recognized a historical continuity the Europeans had only interrupted. This rite of restoration began in 1804 when patriots called the first black republic in the Americas "Haiti." By the 1820s, separatists in Cuba called their island the Republic of Cubanacan, and creoles in Puerto Rico and the colony of Santo Domingo on Española (Hispaniola) revived the names Borincanos and Quisquellanos—local communities whose names had come to identify resistence—to distance themselves from the Spaniards (Arrom 1971; Betánces 1975:11; Sevilla Soler 1986:161).

As liberation struggles developed, the indigenous past provided an alternative history that united Puerto Rico, Española, and Cuba. The main exponents of the idea of the West Indian Federation began their literary careers with novels dealing with themes of the indigenous Indian. The foreign-educated creoles of the Greater Antilles became aware of sources about their ancient history in metropolitan archives and libraries —sources that were banned in their own countries. The most important discovery was Bartolomé de las Casas's *Breve relación de la destrucción de indias.* Under its influence, the names of the West Indian chiefs were converted into themes in poems and novels as well as given to newborn infants. The clandestine revolutionary press reproduced and circulated the new history among the peasants in the rebel camps, and the revolutionary clubs of the exile community adopted indigenous symbols. Although repression often tamed the political content, it could not control the elaboration of the new themes and cultural symbols (Llorens Torres 1967). *Indigenismo* took different paths during the nineteenth century, depending on the class sector that managed it. There is no doubt, however, that the island creoles had embarked on a profound reevaluation of their histories and on the assertion of new collective identities.

In this new history (Sued Badillo 1978), the Spanish state was a usurper and the colonial governments illegitimate. Only the legitimate successors of the original owners of the island had the right, by virtue of cultural inheritance, historical solidarity, shared conviction, and suffering, to represent the nation and its political projects. But who were they? Puerto Rican revolutionaries called them the "Children of Agueybaná the Brave" and "the Jíbaros of Borinquen." The peasantry was the class that continued the resistance and valor of the ancient chiefs. That identity was more than a political convenience, for it recognized that the political and racial unity of all social sectors could be organized only in that class. Only the peasantry, integrated racially and oppressed, could break the state of an apartheid-like system imposed by the dominant groups.

In the second half of the nineteenth century, island writers used *indigenismo* to promote West Indian confederation. *Indigenismo* was simultaneously a symbol of racial unity in a society divided by color and an acknowledgment that the peasantry had been integrated racially in the course of its historical development (Rosa 1989:4). This new historical identity was a political wisdom that threatened the colonialists, and the Spaniards repressed its expressions as vehemently as they had quashed religious heresy. It was the first time a political project was carried out with a symbolism that oppressed people accepted, understood, and reproduced as their own.

The claim of being indigenous had a binding and potentially revolutionary mystical power. That power was deactivated over time and forgotten by the generations of creoles who followed. Massive immigration, political repression, the allotment of lands, and finally the new North American owner (the United States) in Puerto Rico transformed *indigenista* nationalism into Hispanic nationalism and projects that at their foundations were antinationalist. Both *independentistas* and colonialists, however, recognized a fact that is forgotten today: loyalties are learned and cultivated; one is not born with them. The schoolteacher, the press, the political theorist, and the writer had the task of creating an identity and history alternative to that of the colonial. They expressed the experience accumulated by the popular classes.

The Track of the Indigenous

Modern historiography concluded that indigenous societies of the Greater Antilles perished under the blow of the conquest (Cassa 1992; Chaunu 1973; Elliot 1987; Wilson 1990). To the degree that those social formations were disarticulated and ceased to function in traditional ways, that conclusion is correct. Possibly 90 percent of the population perished in the first few decades. But that same historiography also recognizes that small groups and numerous individuals survived; they reproduced and merged with other survivors. Our understanding of their historical development is clouded, however. Consequently, it is essential to track down those who survived the conquest, the hell of the mining camps and *encomiendas* [an institution granting labor service in return for "civilizing" those under its protection—Eds.], the new diseases, and the profound anguish that the holocaust produced. The survivors had much in their favor. Many remained in their native lands and retained ancestral cultures whose resilience and efficiency had not been lost as colonial society emerged.

Cuba

The economy of Cuba was oriented toward cattle raising and the production of foodstuffs rather than toward mining or sugar. Consequently, slavery was not as intensely and continuously developed there as on the neighboring islands. Cattle raising did not require a large work force, and its organization provided space for the existence of rural social units with diverse histories and compositions. Besides native inhabitants, these social units included indigenous people brought as slaves from all of the lands surrounding the Caribbean; they were granted freedom and left to fend for themselves after the New Laws of 1542, enacted to prevent enslavement of Indians, were enforced (Simpson 1966; Sued Badillo 1987, 1992). Colonial officials did not distinguish foreign from native Indians during the second half of the sixteenth century, and the immigrant indigines were slowly integrated into existing or emergent ethnic groups.

In 1574, the *cabildo* (city council) of La Habana established corrals and farm plots in Guanabacoa, the countryside around the city where 2,000 or so indigenous people lived (fig. 2.1). Its reason for conceding farmlands to the indigenous groups was to promote the production of foodstuffs—pigs, cassava, maize, tobacco, and rice—for consumption in the city and to provision the fleets that arrived seasonally. Some of the land grants were held by Indocuban communities and others by individuals including free blacks and recent freedmen who, even though they were legally distinct, also lived in Guanabacoa and shared common experiences with other residents. The first militia units composed of Indians, mestizos, and freedmen from La Habana and Guanabacoa were organized in 1582, providing work for Indians and mestizos as support personnel, lookouts, and salaried laborers (Marrero 1972–75 II:65–78, 466). This inclusion did not diminish the racial discrimination that marginalized them in other social spaces such as the bureaucracy, established military units, and the clergy.

Land grants were also issued to indigenous people in Bayamo at the other end of Cuba before 1568. Reference was made in 1612 to 160 indigenous people near Bayamo who were "outside the church" on the margins of the colonial community. By the end of the seventeenth century, the Indomestizo community of Bayamo resided in five localities,

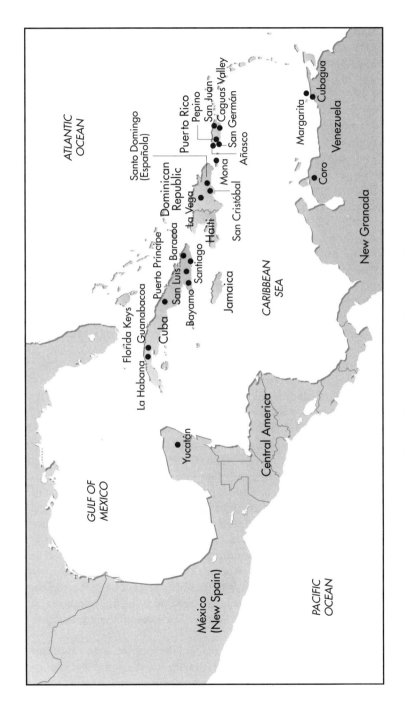

Figure 2.1. The Caribbean, showing major places discussed in chapter 2.

and indigenous residents of Port Príncipe lived in an urban barrio called Triana. New Indian communities were also discovered in widely separated parts of the island: in the depopulated area of Macuriges in 1576 and in the hills near Baracoa in 1607 (Castillo Meléndez 1987:45–6; Marrero 1972–75 II:45, 468, III:57). The latter communities were described as consisting of "Indian people, though Spanish"—that is, mestizos who "count differently from the Spaniards" because they constituted an autonomous community (Macías 1978:19).

A few "poor" Indians were also reported in San Luis de los Caneyes near Santiago, the colonial center of the island. Although many had abandoned the town for nearby forests, the community actively defended its communal privileges throughout the seventeenth century (Castillo Meléndez 1987:47; Marrero 1972–75 III:225, V:24). In 1655, its cacique wrote the Crown accusing the hacienda owners of abuse and of encroaching on the Indians' lands. His accusations—so clear in their exposition, class consciousness, and sense of ethnicity—reveal that more than a century after the conquest, indigenous people kept alive the memory of their past, their sense of ownership of ancestral lands, and their sense of historical placement. The Indians and mestizos of the community were a living segment in the new social formation. They claimed not their past but their rights in the new social order.

A large mestizo segment was also the bearer of traditional culture and ethnic identity. Differentiating mestizos arbitrarily from Indians obscures the real path of cultural transmission and continuity, but censuses distinguished them for legal reasons. Indians were wards of the state, which granted them special protection and communal lands. This condition was not transferable unless, in some manner, their descendants remained pure. Admitting miscegenation meant automatic exclusion from communal grants, a situation the state encouraged in order to lessen its responsibilities. Thus, while the state promoted the disappearance of Indians, mestizos reaffirmed their Indian identities. Consequently, the dynamics of official classification simply did not agree with the reality of fluid categories. For example, in 1604 the Indians of Santiago constituted 12 percent of the total population (Macías 1978:21–22; Marrero 1972–75 III:23, 59). The 1605 census of the whole island listed the indigenous population at 1,027 inhabitants, or 6.5 percent of the total. This suggests that if the first census included only pure Indians and not also mestizos, then there was a population decline—an unlikely possibility without corroborating evidence.

Historians have chronically undervalued the mestizo sector in census data. They associate it preferentially with whites and assume that the indigenous cultural inheritance was erased by *mestizaje*. However, the marginalization encouraged by racial discrimination kept the mestizos closer to their ethnic origins and traditional customs than is usually acknowledged. They were more freely integrated into groups that could not easily dispense with their services and knowledge. Mestizos were the cultural solvent in a world of poor whites and free blacks whose economic disadvantages and lack of options pushed them toward creolization.

New contingents of indigenous people from the exterior began to arrive in Cuba toward the end of the seventeenth century. The first immigrants, who came from the Florida Keys, sought employment in agriculture, the ports, and domestic service (Marrero 1972–75 IV:163). Other groups arrived throughout the eighteenth century. During the nineteenth century, slaves and convicts from Yucatán and Mexico came to work on fortifications and then remained in the islands. In the late nineteenth century, the governor of Yucatán sent slaves captured during the Caste Wars to landowners in Cuba. Indian hunters in the American West also provided occasional victims for the insatiable Cuban sugar market. Because of their social condition, these indigenous outsiders were assimilated into the poorest sectors and eventually adopted the ways of life of their mestizo counterparts.

Española

The slave-based economy of Española quickly passed from mining to sugar production. By the mid-sixteenth century, Española was the commercial center of the Caribbean, the main sugar exporter in the Americas, and supplier of food for the expeditionary forces and dozens of new settlements in the region. The value of its leather was second only to that of New Spain. In addition, this production was duplicated in the clandestine economy, whose real work force was never reflected in official estimates (Sued Badillo 1992).

Neither the continued exploitation of the native population nor the introduction of Indian slaves from the outside was prevented by the implementation of the New Laws of 1542. A native center that survived precariously in the Bahoruco mountains of Española was led during an insurgency by a chief known to the Spaniards as Enriquillo. In 1533, he and the remnants of his group obtained lands and grants in exchange for their pacification (Peña Battle 1948; Utrera 1973). A group of encomienda Indians in the region of La Vega attempted to establish a town at the end of San Cristóbal de Manabao, but they were dispersed "to serve according to their conveniences and the chiefs remained without a town and without Indians" (Utrera 1973:484). Four Indian communities were discovered in the northern part of the island in 1555, and two more were reported in the 1580s (Deive 1980 II:562; Rodríguez Demorizi 1970:16). Similar groups probably existed elsewhere as well. During the sixteenth century, powerful plantation owners, bothered by the high cost of slaves, never permitted the formation of Indian towns. Many Indians, swindled or intimidated, ended up working in the cane fields. Others maintained their freedom by moving from place to place, and numbers of them ended up in the northeast, where sugar plantations did not dominate the landscape. The Indian peoples of Española did not prosper like the indigenous communities in Cuba.

There were close relations between the Indians of Bahoruco and the black *marron* (escaped slave) communities in the sixteenth century. Some sources indicate that the indigenous community was destroyed by marrons; others claim they were allies (AGI, SD, 49, 109). In 1610, the inhabitants of the town of Boyá complained to the Crown about harassment by large landowners who sought grants to their lands (Gil-Bermejo 1983:105).

Most of the Indians in Española during the second half of the sixteenth century were probably foreigners. There was an intensive trade in native slaves; Caribs seized throughout the basin were sold in Coro, Cubagua, and Margarita and were brought to the island as a cheap alternative to African slaves. In 1573, the Council of the Indies granted licenses to capture them "with women and boys who could not be enslaved and bring them to the island where they are bred and converted to Christianity" (Utrera 1979:124). In 1587, the Crown demanded that the chronic abuse of indigenous people by planters be remedied (Rodríguez Demorizi 1945:53). Some may have been released from servile work, after which they intermingled with and became integrated into marginalized groups of blacks, Indians, mestizos, and mulattos.

Portuguese dealers also supplied indigenous slaves to the Antilles. In 1550 and again in 1569, Dominican authorities requested permission to purchase Brazilian Indians legally, but their petitions were denied. In 1615, a cargo of 100 Brazilian Indians was confiscated, and the authorities hurriedly distributed them among the leading citizens (Gil-Bermejo 1983:93). Thus, Indian slaves, even if they were a minority in comparison with those from Africa, were maintained in Española during the seventeenth century.

Contraband was already emerging as an alternative to the sugar economy by the end of the sixteenth century. Smuggling was rampant in northwestern Española, encouraged by the herders and farmers of the region and by the growing number of poor who had moved away from the sugar plantations and urban centers. Indians and mestizos, free blacks and escaped slaves came to the region and created the first free territory in the Americas. The colonial state was unable to exercise effective control over that remote region, and the arrival of foreign smugglers helped to convert the northwest into the space that marginalized people needed. This explains the absence of Indians and mestizos in the urban censuses of the early seventeenth century and their supposed disappearance. The mistreatment they received on the sugar plantations and the limited opportunities they found in the towns, where African slaves predominated, pushed them toward cimarronization and clandestine activities (AGI, SD, 51).

The state was moved to transform the free poor population into workers, which would benefit large landowners, and to exert control over the flourishing subsistence economy of the small peasants. The colonial governments, however, never gained effective control over peasant communities, who transformed patches of forest into swidden fields yielding crops for food and profit. Tobacco was incorporated into clandestine commercial cultivation—the farming counterculture—to acquire cash "to fulfill their religious and civic obligations and to acquire their basic necessities" (Baud 1991:31). In 1605, the governor described a peasantry that was far from egalitarian and expressed his concern over the ascendancy of the "common people" over the "honored" segments (Rodríguez Demorizi 1945:26). This unexpected economic mobility in the hinterlands apparently had no racial or cultural associations, as the rise of rich mestizos and mulattoes mentioned in the sources illustrates. The cultural distance between white small landholders and their black, mulatto, mestizo, and Indian counterparts vanished with the same rapidity as did color differences.

The collapse of the sugar plantations provided small producers with an economic space that frankly benefited the mestizos and free mulattos. However, traditional historiography has preferred to see the total disappearance of Indians and mestizos in periods when circumstances were more favorable to their social and cultural reproduction. At the same time, it ignores their capacity to adapt and change like their poor white and free black counterparts.

The seventeenth century witnessed the emergence of a creole group in Española: the transformation of Indians, Africans, and Europeans into a new social product—children of the land, new natives. These new identities arose in the countryside and originated with all the internal conflicts that the racist, colonial framework encouraged: the sense of superiority and preponderance of whites even though they were poor, the stigma of blacks even though they were free, and the resentment of Indians and mestizos because they were the original, legitimate inhabitants. These conflicts took time to quiet. But to the degree to which each generation repeated the rite of miscegenation and to which caste lost out to class, tensions were quieted, contradictions were weakened, and creole identity was affirmed.

Creole identity encompassed a geography and a way of life that emerged in confrontation with what was official, urban, and foreign. The dominant elites, whether in Havana, Santo Domingo, or San Juan, could not claim paternity of the popular identities that emerged beyond their control during the seventeenth and eighteenth centuries. Racial whitening, the usurpation of peasant cultural spaces by the state, and colonial social control were accomplished long after insular popular identities were forged. In that long process, in which all groups native to the islands became indistinguishable or "indigenous," the roots of nationhood would begin to take hold—as Juan Bosch (1970:147) keenly observed for Santo Domingo.

Puerto Rico

By 1520, Puerto Rico had begun to produce more gold than Española, and it became the port favored by the armed slave-raiders who brought thousands of distraught natives from their continental homelands to toil in hell (Otte 1977; Sued Badillo 1989). The shift from gold mining to sugar production led to the intensification of slavery. Because of the high cost of African slaves, however, landowners kept alive the option of using indigenous slaves in their projects. Although the New Laws of 1542 forbade the enslavement of indigenous people, clandestine shipments continued. Official correspondence concealed this trade and portrayed the native population as being insignificant in numbers (AGI SD 172 #11; 94 #14).

The church delayed the implementation of the New Laws and concealed the reality of continued aboriginal servitude. Because it depended upon tithes on production, it maintained an unusual interest in the well-being of the sugar-producing and herding sectors of the economy. Moreover, both the church and its officials as individuals were important slave owners who were also susceptible to pressures from the powerful mining and sugar-producing elite of the island (BHPR 1921:105; Sued Badillo 1986).

In the mid-sixteenth century, Indians throughout the island continued to be exploited and were slowly but inexorably incorporated into the colonial society. However, communities of free Indians—one intention of the New Laws—were not created in Puerto Rico because of colonial policies that gave plantation owners control over their members (AGI, SD #155). In the 1560s, Governor Bahamón de Lugo was accused of having Indian slaves. He responded that he was merely doing his job as "Protector of Indians and Mestizos." His admission is all the more remarkable because the bishop of San Juan had claimed there were only 60 native Indians on the island in the 1540s.

Governor Bahamón also mentioned the existence of an Indian community whose members were small farmers in the Quebrada de Doña Catalina near the capital (AGI Justicia 98). The community charged that it was being harassed and mistreated by white landowners, especially the *provisor* (a colonial official), and that the governor was not attending to the complaints of its Indian, free black, and mestizo members. Both the dispute and the colonial office of protector indicate that indigenous communities were viable social sectors who fought to defend their resources and space in the new society. The community in question occupied fertile lands near the capital and struggled to prevent large landowners from forcing them into remote areas. Poor peasants with diverse backgrounds spontaneously formed the community of Doña Catalina in response to the land dispute (Caro Costas 1971:131–32). It appears that most Indians, natives or not, and the first generations of mestizos were scattered by the large landowners, who forced them onto marginal lands. They resettled in areas beyond the control of the state, landowners, and church (AGI, SD 168). This does not mean that they sought shelter in the mountainous interior, which remained largely uninhabited until the eighteenth century, but rather that they moved to the hilly terrain of the piedmont overlooking the coastal plain. At a time when the population was small, unpopulated areas existed a few miles from the urban centers (Moscoso 1984).

These marginalized groups created a culture that opposed the urban colonial way of life and provided an alternative to it. Their exodus, together with the high cost of African slaves, aggravated the labor crisis at the end of the sixteenth century. The state launched and repeatedly pursued coercive measures during the seventeenth century that were designed to prevent marginalized peoples from becoming independent peasants (AGI, SD 164, 168; Sued Badillo and López Cantos 1986).

There was also a correspondence of forces affecting the different castes constituting the marginalized groups at the end of the sixteenth century. The white sector decreased considerably and experienced neither immigration nor exodus. Slaves experienced high rates of mortality on the sugar plantations. Mestizos and free mulattos increased in numbers and established a mestizo way of life that characterized both groups during the next century. Consequently, the policies of the state and the landowners, which sought to prevent the emergence of a poor peasantry, were unsuccessful. Even though numerous mestizos and wage workers toiled in the towns, this does not mean they had abandoned their rural plots, for there were local and foreign markets for cash crops. Thus, Indians and mestizos participated continuously almost from the beginning in the circuits of clandestine capital that grew as Spain lost control over the Caribbean. Thousands of peasants sold ginger, cassava, and wood while the island elite marketed sugar and hides.

The Indians, mestizos, and free blacks integrated into the spaces forged by this mestizo way of life lived on the margins of ideological control of the church, its racist canons, and legality (Pagden 1982). Excommunication was the penalty for smuggling, and the bishop of San Juan lamented openly in 1577 that this alternate way of life with "rebel freedom" threatened colonial culture and the established social order (AGI, SD 172). The cultural management of the state failed in vast regions of Puerto Rico, as it had in northwestern Española and much of rural Cuba. The social order was hierarchical and rigid in the towns and on the sugar plantations, reproducing the metropolitan estate structure with its great social and racial barriers. Furthermore, it maintained narrow ties with populations fresh from the exterior. On the sugar plantations, African slaves made up the most significant population group, but they quickly died off under an intense exploitation and deculturation that forced them into styles of life determined by the production of sugar. The few who received manumission had stopped being Africans, for their identities had been transformed like sugar cooked up in the kettles of the sugar boiling-houses.

Neither the creation of the creole cultural system nor the fusion of races occurred on the sugar plantations. By the late sixteenth century, colonial officials were already complaining about the spread of indigenous religious practices among the Spaniards and mestizos (AGI Justicia 70; Tío 1961:485). As Indians disappeared, they only gave rise to mestizo descendants who, along with the other mixed groups, created an emergent culture strongly rooted in the indigenous tradition. References to mestizos and their social position also become more abundant toward the end of the century, as are notices of interracial unions showing that Indians intermarried with whites and blacks. The *mestizaje* of indigenous people and blacks is not dealt with by the traditional historiography.

Most "Indians" were in fact mestizos, marginalized and subordinated by racial discrimination, who lived in rural areas on the edges of the large ranches and haciendas. The economy of this peasant society, however, was far from egalitarian, and cultural contrasts were accentuated from one century to the next. The large landowners constituted a social elite even when they shared a material culture and habits of eating, dressing, and living with the subaltern groups. During the eighteenth century, the local elites believed they belonged to a social class superior to that of their neighbors, even though their view of reality "was not sustained in a concretely economic manner" (López Cantos 1985:8). Humboldt observed the same phenomenon in Cuba: "A barefoot white riding a horse imagines himself to be from the nobility of the country" (Marrero 1972–75 XIII:63). Thus, within the mestizo way of life, there were class differences as well as distinctions within the same class.

The Indigenous Community of Mona

Mona Island, equidistant between Española and Puerto Rico, passed into the jurisdiction of the latter in 1511, when it became a Spanish Crown property. Subsequently, the more than 100 workers who toiled on the royal estate producing food and clothing did not suffer the pain of mining (Sued Badillo 1989; Tanodi 1971). In 1519, the island and its Indian population were leased to an entrepreneur, and their production, mainly cassava and other foodstuffs, was used to maintain the pearl fishermen of Cubagua (Otte 1977). Thus, soon after the arrival of the Europeans, the Indians of Mona gained experience producing for the Caribbean trade and dealing with foreign merchants and transport workers. Because of its location, the island was an inevitable port for ships, many of which engaged in smuggling. Ship captains recognized the utility of treating the island's inhabitants with respect because of the help the captains received during their voyages.

The Indians of Mona had a large amount of freedom. In 1578, the bishop of San Juan began to recommend that they be resettled in Puerto Rico with grants of land and tribute exemption. He repeated this recommendation five years later, because it was difficult to supervise the population and because French vessels marauding in the region used the island as a port (AGI, SD, 172, 2280). In 1594, the community was charged with bootlegging—buying goods from the French and then selling them on the northwest littoral of Puerto Rico (AGI, Escribanía 1333; Gelpi 1993:217). It was linked with the mestizo contraband circuit of the larger island. The Indians of Mona were resettled before 1685 in the hills of Añasco and San Germán in Puerto Rico, where they lived at the beginning of the eighteenth century.

The resettled Indians intermarried with Spaniards, blacks, and mulattos who lived in the hills. "In this way, the Indian caste of the island became extinguished" (Abad y la Sierra 1966:77) and a "new population, whose inhabitants were dedicated to the cultivation of ginger, cacao, indigo, cotton, and livestock" formed (Abad y la Sierra 1977). *Mestizaje* continued and the small landowner reappeared as a mode of production. In 1828, the municipalities of Añasco and Pepino were the principal cassava producers on the island. By that time, the importance of cassava had diminished because of heavy Spanish immigration during the second half of the eighteenth century. For that reason, cassava's continued popularity in particular regions can indicate only the persistence of a mestizo tradition in which the crop was grown for local consumption or sale (Córdova 1968).

Censuses taken from 1775 to 1803 listed a large indigenous population but did not specify who they were or where they came from. In 1776, Indians constituted 2.3 percent of Puerto Rico's 70,335 residents. Their numbers remained more or less constant until 1803, when the census category ceased being used (Padilla Escabí 1985:120). Traditional historians have used these censuses to confirm the survival of Indian communities (Alvarez Nazario 1990; Brau 1972a; Fernández Méndez 1976; Tío 1966); more recent historiography has sought Indian origins outside the island (Silvestrini and Silvestrini 1987). Although it is difficult to relate these communities to the Indians of Mona, two possibilities exist regarding their origins outside. The first points to Venezuela. In the late seventeenth century, the governor of Cumana, Venezuela, was instructed to relocate rebel Caribs, allied with the French, to Puerto Rico and La Habana (AGI, SD 875, in Bentivenga de Napolitano 1977, vol. 7; Real Díaz 1968:223). The other possibility points to New Spain. In 1697, the Royal Audiencia of Mexico sent men to Puerto Rico to build infantry quarters in the capital. Three years later, it shipped a larger number of "vagabonds and convicts to serve as soldiers on the island" (Reales Cédulas, vol. 44, FA 53). Many were Indians or mestizos from different parts of Mexico. When the convicts completed their terms, they were granted land in the new settlements to remedy the lack of labor in the fields and to stop the evils that a destitute man could commit. Thus, year after year, hundreds of ex-convicts were incorporated into the native society, reinforcing the poorest strata.

At the end of the eighteenth century, the mestizo population was concentrated in the western region of the island. Its members had diverse origins and arrived as a result of diverse circumstances. They may have included the descendants of the people relocated from Mona Island. The censuses do not indicate place of residence or occupation. Smuggling, however, was always lucrative in the western region, especially around Añasco and the littoral. This region was also attractive to small cultivators and workers because it was a watering place for the seasonal Spanish fleet. Thus, what was indigenous for the creole rebels in Puerto Rico in the early 1800s was not only an intellectual fantasy but also an important historical process in the social formation of their country.

The Mestizo Way of Life

Efforts to understand West Indian social order before the nineteenth century are relatively recent. Primary documents disappeared into distant Spanish archives, and Puerto Rican historiography was built on a small but varied pile of documents. Historians have just begun to remedy this situation, and investigations of the socioeconomic conditions that prevailed in the period when national identities were forged are now appearing (Carrión 1986; Duany 1985; Moscoso 1984; Picó 1979, 1984, 1985, 1986a, 1986b, 1990; Quintero Rivera 1973, 1987; Scarano 1989). Although significant differences in method and appreciation exist among the exponents of the new historiography, their work is already having an impact on the generalities that underlie cultural discussion. These writers recognize the need to integrate local histories, insulated from one another for centuries, into wider discussions of Caribbean history in order to specify both the similarities and the particularities of the islands.

The peasant population acquired its personality over the centuries on the margins of slavery and the institutions of the state. The dominant mode of production and marker of peasant culture in Puerto Rico, Española, and Cuba was the stock-owning *latifundio* (large landed estate) that appeared after 1550 as a step on the road from gold mining to sugar production and cattle raising. Land, rather than slaves, became the major means of production. The latifundio system became dominant in the seventeenth century after the collapse of sugar and the market economy. Small subsistence producers—the poor, racially mixed peasants— also underwrote the new social order and met the labor needs of the large landowners. The latifundios generated an independent "superfluous population" even as they limited access to land and restricted its agricultural potential (Moscoso 1984).

The diverse cultural modalities that appeared among the poor peasants reflected differences of origin, race, occupation, and relations with other social sectors of the island. There were also class differences within the creole peasantry. Through time, the contours of a common culture were widened in the course of everyday life. Everyone used the same natural resources, confronted the same environment and threats from the state, ate the same foods, and wore the same clothing. Many material and nonmaterial elements of the emerging culture had their origins in the ancient pre-Hispanic social formations; these elements survived, were reproduced under new circumstances, and were incorporated into the new colonial social order. This process was cultural, not racial.

The history of the races was important when they also represented particular ways of life, as they did in the sixteenth century: whites were synonymous with what was European, blacks with what was African, and Indians with what was American. But *mestizaje* broke that cultural equivalence. The most interesting result of our investigation is the simple fact that one racial sector, the Indian, which was believed to have been eliminated very early, persisted for a sufficient time so that its associated cultural repertoire functioned as a solvent in many spaces of the emerging culture. Mestizos became the bearers of knowledge about the land and its resources, and, in the context of an economically and demographically precarious colonization, transculturation favored the autochthonous or indigenous more than the foreign, at least in the formation of the peasantry.

The different cultural groups that came into contact because of the conquest did not do so under equal conditions. Spaniards and Africans could impose their customs only to the extent that their demographic and economic resources permitted them to do so. They were at a disadvantage initially because both were strangers to the land. For this reason, colonial domination was linked to the small urban centers, to the sugar plantations, and partially to the herding economy. But these were no more than isolated forts in a peasant world the colonists could neither dominate nor subdue. To the degree that the rise of the latifundio coincided with the withdrawal of the commercial and cultural metropoles, their capacity to widen the zone of colonization was weakened.

White immigration slowed during the seventeenth and eighteenth centuries. Distinctions within the white metropolitan world, based on class as well as ethnicity and region, were complicated in the Antilles by the arrival of persons disaffected from state and church and by continued contact with foreigners who smuggled and who were mostly Protestant. The effects of these pluricultural influences on the process of creolization and on the official culture have not been studied, but they obviously eroded the supposedly hegemonic "Hispanic" culture that counterfeited primary identities.

The poor peasants, forced to distance themselves from selected lands bordering the urban areas, opted for a standard of dispersed settlement. Quintero Rivera (1987) interprets this as the defensive retreat of a weak and insecure social sector. However, the complaints launched against the poor peasants by ranchers and royal officials reveal the colonists' own dread and insecurity. The dispersal ought to be seen as a defensive measure against the state and as a countercultural statement.

Life on the littoral, not seclusion and obscurity in the mountainous interior, was the setting in which creole peasant culture formed. Only fugitives, or *cimarrones,* and mestizo hunters looking for stray animals or occasional game went into the interior. The persistence of an indigenous toponymy in the interior, however, reinforces the idea that it was mestizos who used the area. There were no significant centers of population there. At the end of the eighteenth century, 90 percent of the population of Puerto Rico lived on the coast, 4.5 percent in the Caguas Valley, and 4.5 percent in the mountains (Padilla Escabí 1985:126). Small agriculture developed on the littoral and in the piedmont in association with smuggling.

The various modalities of creole peasant culture developed under conditions of low population. Cuba, for example, had a total population of about 50,000 around 1700; Española's population had declined to 6,000 in 1737; and Puerto Rico had about 27,000 residents in 1750 (Gil-Bermejo 1983:81; López Cantos 1984:100; Marrero 1972–75 III:18, 64; Padilla Escabí 1985). Low or declining population must have been one factor neutralizing class conflict over land; there was always sufficient space to accomodate the claims of one group or another. It also partly explains why many elements of creole culture were appropriated from the dominant culture of the antagonistic landowning class (Quintero Rivera 1983:27). The important class contradictions that existed within the peasant social formation simply did not prevent the emergence of a shared culture and social identity.

It is in the context of demographically small groups that we should investigate the origin of the Jíbaro and Boricua, identities that existed before the nineteenth century and were subsequently transformed. The Jíbaros of the eighteenth century were not the timid and anemic personages of nineteenth-century literature. They were peasants who evoked dread because of their "rebellious freedom," their valor, and their knowledge of the illegal. The original Jíbaros, whom the *independentistas* of the nineteenth century identified as heirs to the indigenous tradition, were neither racially pure nor the bearers of the Hispanic ancestry that was attributed to them a century later. Etymologically, the nickname is an indigenous term that originally referred to the least yielding, least docile, and poorest sector of the peasantry. The Jíbaros were the peasantry with historical continuity—the cultural and racial mestizo who had a firm identity before the arrival of new sectors that also settled in the country-side during the eighteenth century.

Small agriculture was the most characteristic activity of mestizo culture. Slash-and-burn agriculture, digging sticks, and the primary products—cassava, *yautías,* maize, cotton, and tobacco—had their origins in pre-Hispanic social formations. New techniques and plants, which never displaced the old ones, were slowly incorporated and enriched agriculture. There was little valorization of property in land because the poor peasants were itinerants who burned new forest swidden patches and sowed their maize fields for the time when they would bear crops. It was the white immigrants, not the creole peasants, who were driven to possess the land as property (Buitrago Ortíz 1976:29).

The mestizo way of life represented an accumulation of very ancient knowledge that recent arrivals could adopt without scrutinizing the tradition of work that guided their lives. Many of the products they made and used retained indigenous names that point to their cultural origins. These products and techniques represented a deeply valorized alternative to the urban colonial culture. The varied inventory of mestizo culture helps us understand how poor peasants were inserted into the social order and what made them indispensable: their knowledge, their labor power, and their excellence as artisans.

Let us reflect briefly on some statistics: in 1824, there were 31,710 housing units in Puerto Rico, 19,648 of which were Amerindian-type huts (*bohios*). The log cabin of North America, which represented the reproduction of the urban way of life with all the uncertainties of abandonment, never had a counterpart in the island. With modifications, the concept as well as the form of life was indigenous. For many years to come, most of the population would sleep in hammocks, eat with their fingers, and travel in canoes.

The mestizo mode of life was also characterized by two activities that had both historical continuity and deep effects on the process of identity formation: contraband smuggling and military service. One confronted the state and the other integrated it. Smuggling as a formative experience, and one that continues to the present, has had more influence on creole identities than has official religion. And the defense of the island has long been organized on the shoulders of poor peasants. Local militias were more prominent than the Spanish army in the face of foreign incursions. After 1765, their organization was class-based and racist, since their officers came from the elite sectors of the society. Military service was also intimately bound to privateering—an avenue of social mobility and an area in which many creoles distinguished themselves. Thus, different class sectors were combined in both smuggling and the military, as likely in collaboration as in conflict.

A creole culture which was neither Spaniard, Taino, nor African, and which I prefer to call mestizo, was articulated and defined by the beginning of the nineteenth century in the rural areas of the Spanish colonies in the Caribbean. It was not egalitarian but was divided into classes that shared a historical experience and a community of symbols and values that distinguished the creole classes together from urban, elite colonial culture.

The first national projects in the Caribbean, apart from Haiti, stemmed from the creole urban middle class, which had strong ties to the traditional, mestizo peasant culture. Its members produced the first *independentista* groups and the first alternative interpretations of history and culture. Racially and culturally mestizo, they refined their liberation projects in ways that distinguished and distanced them from the estranged white elite. In the face of colonial political authoritarianism, they hoisted the postulates of liberalism. In the face of racism, they became abolitionists and proclaimed racial equality. In the face of an austere and repressive Catholicism, they proclaimed the freedom of cults and secularism. And in the face of a Europeanized cultural model, they promoted nativism and *indigenismo*—both of which were part of the peasant historical experience.

The first nationalist outbursts would be suffocated in the political currents of the nineteenth century because the class sector expounding them, the poor peasant, at least in Puerto Rico and Española, was not the hegemonic sector with the strongest creole culture. The native landowners, their cultural kin, deformed the symbolic content of their nationalist drive by sheer political opportunism (Quintero Rivera 1987). Puerto Rico was recolonized in the nineteenth century by heavy European immigration and, politically, by the United States. There was selective, intensive white immigration; the militarization and spiritualization of the society; intellectual repression and the exile of the most radical *independentista* sectors; and the proletarianization of the peasantry. Forced from their ancestral spaces to the misery of servile labor, the peasants progressively lost the characteristics they had at the beginning of the century. In spite of this, they inspired the first movements for political freedom, even as literary genres caricatured and distorted their true history (Brau 1972b; Cruz Monclova 1964; Meléndez Muñoz 1961, 1963). The ingenious mestizo who impressed the writers of the eighteenth century became the anemic and brutalized Jíbaro who was ravaged on the sugar and coffee plantations.

The landowning class Hispanicized creole identity at the end of the last century. It invented a nationality and associated national symbols based on the urban, colonial ingredients required by its political Manichaeanism (González 1980; Quintero Rivera 1979). It continues to make a pretense of fighting the vortex of North Americanization with a symbolism that is both ahistorical and alienated from its indigenous roots. Although there is no longer a peasantry in Puerto Rico, I hope to have shown that there exists the capacity to recuperate a historical memory that can help us develop political projects which affirm the identity of our people rather than marginalizing or tearing them apart.

The Perception of History and Archaeology in Latin America

A Theoretical Approach

IRAIDA VARGAS ARENAS

H istory and archaeology face a critical situation in Venezuela. They confront similar situations elsewhere in Latin America and in the Third World in general. This is because of the conceptual distortions "official history" introduces into the definition and analysis of its subject (Chatterjee, this volume).[1] Official history—as well as the teaching of history at different educational levels and the perception and teaching of archaeology in most university departments—is rooted in positivist or neopositivist perspectives (Kolakowski 1969). These perspectives simultaneously naturalize and universalize contemporary capitalist social relations and practices, argue for the historical and cultural uniqueness of the social systems of given epochs and national states, and advocate technical or instrumental types of research instead of theoretical analyses that would challenge their self-proclaimed scientific neutrality (Third World Network 1993).

Official histories—such as the accounts found in virtually all of the history textbooks used in primary and secondary schools in Venezuela and the United States—mask the real causes of historic change. They communicate to the younger generation the idea that history is a lineal, chronological accumulation of events, names, and dates unrelated to everyday life. They portray everyday life as the continuous efforts of autonomous individuals to optimize or maximize their circumstances as they adapt to the existing sociopolitical order rather than seeking to change the conditions of that order or those of the increasingly global system of which they are also a part.

Official histories manipulate the knowledge of history, that is, the objective processes lived and experienced by peoples, which constitute the only way to understand and explain present-day social conditions in dependent countries like Venezuela and, more generally, those of Latin America and the Third World (Stavrianos 1981; Vargas and Sanoja 1990: 51). Given today's sociopolitical conditions, knowledge of objective history is essential for promoting and preserving the real independence of a dependent country as well as its historic and cultural identity. Official histories, however, do not provide students with the information and tools they require to clarify and develop a critical, theoretically and empirically informed perspective on the internal dynamics of society.

From the perspective of official history, the task of schools and universities is thoroughly instrumental: to prepare students so they can fulfill the needs of socioeconomic development (Alatas 1972, 1977; González Casanova 1984; Rahman 1983). The goal of teaching history in the educational system is defined in terms of the interests of ruling oligarchies and political bureaucracies, which function increasingly as the local agents of global power structures such as the World Bank and the International Monetary Fund. The interests of these local agents become defined as the national interest. The elementary school, the high school, and the university are vehicles for reproducing the conditions of everyday life produced by dependent capitalism and the system of transnational institutions that has been promoted throughout the Third World by the mechanism of foreign debt (Bonfil Batalla 1989:183–86; Cueva 1989:23–37).

The explanations offered in official histories often obscure the importance of daily life in understanding sociohistorical processes, historical variables, and movements of social creativity and change. They freeze historical facts by cementing them into self-contained and self-explained temporal blocks of events that are connected neither to the past nor to the present. These blocks are filled with personal trivia, symbolic events and objects, and enduring transcendental values—such as Simon Bolívar's drive to free Latin America, the Chaco War, the Liberty Bell, and American exceptionalism. When history becomes official, it also becomes stereotyped and loses a vital function as an axis of social life. When the power of history is weakened, distorted, and trivialized, the processes underpinning historically constituted identities are eroded and ultimately broken. This paves the way for imposition of neocolonial visions of the future and reconstituted understandings of both the present and the past.

In official versions, the history of the nation is often portrayed in terms of a series of more or less disconnected periods such as the pre-Columbian, colonial, republican, and modern eras used to depict history throughout Latin America. Each era has its unique characteristics that distinguish it from the others. Historical changes in one period and their consequences are only tenuously connected with what happened in earlier or later epochs; as a result, official histories of the colonial period provide, at best, superficial discussions of the linkages between their subject and what happened in pre-Columbian times, and works by archaeologists rarely consider what happened after A.D. 1500 (Cruxent and Rouse 1961; Morón 1971). Once past history is frozen into slices, past social experiences add little to understanding either the present or the future, except as they are called upon to provide mythic charters or backdrops against which progress can be measured.

Unfortunately, official histories often teach people the negative images that have been associated with their social origins: for example, the savagery and laziness of the Indian, the slave heritage and vulgarity of the Negro, or the untrustworthiness of the Spaniard (Baralt 1975; Dupouy 1958:7; Montero 1984; Ocampo López 1989; Stepan 1991; Vallenilla Lanz 1961:123–47). These negative images become embedded in people's daily consciousness through formal and informal education; they reinforce the processes of neocolonial domination as well as the programs of cultural interference coming from the First World metropolis (e.g., Dorfman and Mattelart 1975; Tomlinson 1991; UNESCO 1982).

There are several reasons why official history is promoted at the expense of the kind of social history advocated in this chapter and why many anthropological inquiries end up cementing theses that actually support alternative viewpoints onto foundations established by official history (Asad 1987; Fahim 1982; Pathy 1981; Rodríguez 1991). Official histories are sustained by the material and social conditions of national states and by local financial resources for research and cultural projects — for example, museum exhibits, which are typically managed by those linked to state or professional bureaucracies, who are usually uninterested in theoretical debates.

Consequently, it is difficult to publish or disseminate ideas that challenge the existing hegemony (Karp and Levine 1991). Furthermore, to the extent to which these bureaucratically linked groups control the purchase of journals for libraries, it is also difficult in countries such as Venezuela to locate journals or books with alternative viewpoints that do not follow the lines established by official history. As a result, the process of discovering critical perspectives on social theory and practices undergirding history and archaeology is a slow one.

To the degree that historians and archaeologists neither effectively understand the strengths and weaknesses of various paradigms nor recognize the significance of their differences, their research faces the dual dangers of becoming steadily more descriptive and of providing increasingly less effective explanations of social processes. At the same time, the concepts they teach to younger generations become continually more dated and out of touch with the intellectual currents that agitate and propel the world of social theory, as well as those that underpin history and archaeology. In a milieu where there are few mechanisms for systematically transmitting knowledge and critical understanding, the already existing trends derived from official history thrive. These circumstances have also permitted a number of historians, archaeologists, and anthropologists to achieve postmodernity without ever having seriously confronted either modernity and the modernist ideas they claim to reject; they consider it appropriate to devise a polysemic vision of society that eclectically mixes different perspectives by juxtaposing words, concepts, and analytical categories yanked randomly from theoretical frameworks. However, unless there is access to the financial resources required for research and the dissemination of ideas (Schmidt, this volume), it will continue to be difficult to assert, through empirical studies of social and historical realities, the validity of scientific hypotheses that stand in opposition to those of official history or its postmodernist shadow (Liprandi and Casanova 1991).

The social sciences are constrained in significant ways by the historically constituted states in which they are practiced (Longino 1990). Many studies concerned with the teaching of the social sciences point out that the ruling classes of underdeveloped or Third World countries such as Venezuela are unaware that they have greater, more important needs in the social sciences than in the hard sciences (e.g., Alatas 1972; Rahman 1983). They can always import a chemical laboratory, a petrochemical plant, or a technology to build houses and make them function in their new context. But a country cannot import its own history or its own social explanations because those are not interchangeable. The raw materials for understanding them and for solving the problems they refract must be sought first in the particularities of each historically constituted country and the way in which those particularities articulate into wider global realities.

The historical development of the Latin American countries reflects the intersection of forces that must be understood in terms of how they affect the development of human society in general, the development of the region as a historically constituted entity, and the development of each country in its particularity (Frank 1969). Thus, it is essential to develop a theoretically informed understanding of the social changes underlying the formation of the nation itself and setting in motion those historically contingent, uniquely national processes that have affected Venezuela in one way and Mexico or Peru in others. This claim has a number of implications. It means that historical, archaeological, and anthropological analyses must take into account those sociohistorical processes that led to the formation of particular nations and states in the context of historically constituted regions now encompassing more than one country. It means that the academic corpus of history, archaeology, and anthropology must also be restructured to incorporate theoretical perspectives and practices addressing this issue. The organization of that academic curriculum should be one in which the basic or instrumental subjects provide students with critical, theoretical, and methodological tools organized around a framework of assignments that require them to explain the working objects of social scientists: the history of their own society and the formative processes of their own nation (Sanoja 1990; Sanoja and Vargas Arenas 1989; Vargas Arenas and Sanoja 1993a).

At the present time, there is enough empirical information about the Caribbean to formulate explanations that integrate the various levels. Julian Steward's "circum-Caribbean hypothesis" (Steward 1948, 1950, 1955; Steward and Faron 1959; Steward et al. 1956), based on the concept of a macroregion, was such an attempt. An explanation alternative to Steward's, however, would view the Caribbean as reflecting both the historical influence of the center-periphery relationships of early class-based societies in Mesoamerica and the central Andes and the particular dynamics of uneven historical development promoted by social structures that emerged in different parts of the Caribbean basin, as well as their differential articulation with Spain and other European colonial states (Sanoja and Vargas Arenas 1989).

In such a perspective, the processes involved in the conquest and colonization of the aboriginal American ethnic groups in the area, which undergirded the formation of nations and nationalities in the eighteenth and nineteenth centuries, were not uniform. The various pre-Hispanic peoples did not share the same level of sociohistoric development. Populations in Mesoamerica and the central Andes had long been organized into class-based states. In the Caribbean area, people who were organized into territorial entities with state-type, stratified social relationships coexisted with egalitarian tribal societies whose members continued to practice forms of gathering, fishing, and hunting resembling those of the continent's earliest populations. As a result, the processes of conquest and colonization yielded different rhythms of development, the consequences of which are still felt in everyday life in contemporary Caribbean countries.

In those regions of South America and the Caribbean where egalitarian tribal societies predominated, the struggle against European intrusion was long and bitter and led in many instances to the total destruction of entire populations. In the Venezuelan case, the processes of Spanish conquest and colonization lasted until the beginning of the nineteenth century. Subsequently, the *criollos* (individuals with legal claims of European or Venezuelan national descent) have continued to reduce by force or to acculturate the remaining aboriginal groups surviving in the peripheral areas of the country. Similar processes have occurred in Brazilian Amazonia, Colombia, and the countries of Central America. In areas where hierarchically organized tribal societies existed—such as northwest Venezuela, the mountain valleys and plateaus of Colombia, Panama, Costa Rica, and Nicaragua, and the southern periphery of Mesoamerica—conquest and colonization as well as the development of Indohispanic culture were rapid and lacked the destructiveness of conquest seen among the more egalitarian communities; this was due partly to the state structures and exploitative social relations already in place.

In circumstances in which nonhierarchical societies were found, the egalitarian sociopolitical structures of the aboriginal societies were completely incompatible with the class-based social relations of the Castilian conquerors. As a result, Indians could be assimilated only as individuals, not as groups, or they had to be physically destroyed. Where there was already some degree of social inequality and political organization manifested in the structure of dominant lineages, the processes of conquest and colonization were initiated at a relatively low social cost to the aboriginal groups, as, generally, the dominant lineages were assimilated and incorporated into the structures of colonial power. Their leaders were transformed in the process, becoming intermediaries between the colonial state and their kin and neighbors, who were simultaneously transformed into Indians.

The social and cultural consequences of conquest and colonization—as well as the qualitative condition of the aboriginal groups who, together with the Europeans, would form the social base of the colonial order—were also influential in the formation of national states. In Venezuela and elsewhere, the provincial oligarchies composed mainly of *hacendados* (owners of landed estates) that developed between the sixteenth and early nineteenth centuries often resisted the centralizing power of the colonial state in order to preserve their political leverage. The hacienda laborers—mostly Indians, blacks, and mestizos—formed the cannon fodder of private and national armies that fought among themselves for almost a century, for the sole benefit of the warlords who organized them. It was only in the early decades of the twentieth century that modern state structures could be organized.

The Formation of the Nation and the State

Among the precapitalist societies in the Americas, there were two centers with high core-periphery political tensions: the central Andes and Mesoamerica (Sanoja and Vargas Arenas 1989). These societies were state-based, multiethnic, and multicultural political systems that resolved antagonisms through cyclical displacements of the centers of power and the reordering of social relations with groups on their margins. In contrast, the center-periphery relationships among less stratified tribal societies were resolved through political and military alliances among dominant lineages and through relationships of cooperation that included war as a form of the cyclical interchange of people and as a reaffirmation of territorial rights. Regions were historically constituted through both processes, and their boundaries were more or less stabilized by the expansive capacities of their constituent communities, which were defined by their origins, composition, character, and place in the regional network (Bauer 1979:10–119).

The processes of conquest and colonization initiated by the Spaniards in the sixteenth century did not begin—as many official historians pretend—with the occupation of an empty territory by Europeans. Although judicial statutes were necessary to organize the European domain, the particular sociohistorical conditions of the aboriginal societies produced a set of variables that shaped certain forms of the incipient nations (Sanoja 1990). That Spain could organize viceroyalties so swiftly only in areas where the aboriginal societies were state organized was not accidental. The aboriginal ethnic groups and communities who formed the flesh and blood of those viceregal institutions had already been organized politically into states long before the fifteenth century; the central Andes and Mesoamerica encompassed politically defined territories that included communities of origin, shared or contested destinies, official vernacular languages, and sets of social and political institutions that attempted to regulate the daily life of every individual.

In areas occupied by tribal social formations and communities, such as Venezuela and the eastern and western Caribbean, the Spanish colonial regime resorted to violence in order to integrate and reduce most Indian groups and to define the political boundaries of provinces and

53

capitanias (a group of people controlled by a captain) in a loose way, since the tribal territories were rarely defined in objective terms. As a result, the political boundaries of colonial entities defined on the margins of the former pre-Hispanic states refer to historical regions that had been defined first by hunting-gathering bands and later by tribal societies (Vargas Arenas 1990).

The imposition of Spanish rule on the diverse social formations that coexisted in Latin America did not produce a monolithic social and cultural unity in the new territories, as official historians often claim (Bonfil Batalla 1989:73–74; Gil Fortoul 1961; Silie 1992:249). To the contrary, regional differences were accentuated. The colonial powers isolated the provincial areas from one another, a process in which different kinds of social relations based on inequality and political dependence were formalized in each of the regions. Different processes of social and cultural synthesis occurred within the matrix of regional isolation and inequalities; these processes underwrote the consolidation of ethnic groups among the embryonic nationalities that were developing simultaneously in the Spanish colonies. These processes in the Latin American colonies were different from the national processes unfolding inside the Spanish kingdoms of the Iberian peninsula, which, like others elsewhere in Europe, were also being influenced by the development of capitalism (Bartolomé 1985:39–50).

The historical processes culminating in the consolidation of the Latin American states began long before the sixteenth century; they were already present in the initial class-based societies of Mesoamerica and the central Andes. Nationalities began to develop in most parts of Latin America after the sixteenth century. Nationalities are political identities constructed around ethnic components that tend to lead to movements of self-determination because they have been integrated into a state-determined territory that is neither recognized nor acknowledged as theirs by the colonial or metropolitan state. Once this tendency is set in motion, the aim of the national group is usually to create autonomous nation-states and to impugn ties with the former metropole (Díaz Polanco 1985:27).

The thesis just outlined concerning the historical formation of Latin American society and states is a valid theoretical position widely accepted by social scientists in Latin America. It is denied, however, by official history, which holds firmly to the belief that history equates with written documents. As a result of this belief, official historians cannot and do not take into account events and processes that occurred before the sixteenth century in their explanations of state formation and the development of national identities (Cero et al. 1980; Meléndez 1983; Monge 1976; Morón 1971).[2] Moreover, given the intellectual division of labor promoted by official history, considerations of precapitalist social formations become almost exclusively the domain of anthropologists, whose business, as seen through the reductionist lens of the official historians, consists entirely of stone tools, old pots, and Indians, especially dead ones (Bonfil Batalla 1989). Within this view of history, the concept of dead Indians becomes particularly important; it serves as fuel for the rhetoric of patriotic speeches while objects of the Indians' material culture make their way into national and international markets for stolen cultural goods.

The explanations of national history provided by official historians are not constructed solely for consumption by elites. They also provide the ideological underpinnings of the pedagogical programs that are training people to teach history in both public schools and universities. This kind of training and the discourse it reproduces perpetuate the deformed perceptions that children already have about themselves, their national identity, and their nation (Colmenares Goyo 1989).

Defining the Object of Study

Studies of ancient and contemporary indigenous populations have an important place in the strategy for explaining the formation of nations and states (Fonseca 1989; Sanoja 1990; Vargas and Sanoja 1990). Unlike the processes of conquest and colonization in anglophone North America, which originated with the immigration of organized communities of British subjects, the processes in Latin America were carried out mainly by male immigrants. These men had extensive sexual relations with Indian women and with African women brought to the Americas as slaves (Rosenblat 1954:20–21). As a result, a dominant and diverse mestizo population appeared throughout much of Latin America; its members lived side by side with African American communities whose members worked as slaves on plantations and with the remnants of Indian communities whose members remained isolated in territories already dominated by *criollo* society and the colonial administration (Acosta Saignes 1984).

Through the nineteenth century, the indigenous population seems to have been the major ethnic component in most regions of the continent. In the Antilles, however, most of the indigenous population was exterminated and replaced by Africans and mulattos (but see Sued Badillo, this volume). Since the nineteenth century, the demographic trends seem to have had different rhythms, producing basic differences in the character of the new nations. In Venezuela, Colombia, Brazil, Panama, Costa Rica, and possibly Nicaragua, the numerical and territorial expansion of *criollo* national culture has accelerated the ethnic and cultural dissolution of most of the independent or reduced Indian groups. Their members were assimilated and employed as *peones* (agricultural workers), artisans, or domestic workers. In countries with large pre-Hispanic states—including Mexico, Guatemala, Peru, Bolivia, and Ecuador—the rural Indian communities, which always constituted the majority of the national population, continued to live, for the most part, in their ancient pre-Hispanic territories, to speak their own languages, and to preserve their own cultural and social organization while *criollos* and mestizos dominated the urban spaces. A similar trend occurred in northern Central America. Some countries—Cuba and Puerto Rico, for instance—saw their European populations augmented during the nineteenth century with the arrival of immigrants from Spain. Other countries, such as Argentina, witnessed abrupt changes in their ethnic composition during the nineteenth century as massive waves of immigrants arrived from the Mediterranean world (Bartolomé 1985).

Differences in how the various national societies and cultures were formed—the object of historical, archaeological, and anthropological inquiry—helped to cast and mold the social sciences in different ways in the countries of Latin America (Patterson, this volume). A ruling class's perception of ethnicity was an important element of the political strategy its members used to consolidate power in the region during the nineteenth and twentieth centuries, to guide their relationships with the dominated classes, and to adopt and promote the appropriate national cultural stereotypes (Gamio 1960; Gil Fortoul 1961; Sarmiento 1947; Vallenilla Lanz 1961).

The *criollos* offered various explanations of the formation of national society in sociohistorical contexts that were preserved until the middle of the nineteenth century. Their theses constituted a proof of the legitimacy of the political and economic power exerted by the national bourgeoisies. That legitimacy was based on the claim of historical continuity for the civilizing process initiated by the Spanish Crown in the sixteenth century through its agents, the incipient *criollo* bourgeoisies, and continued by the *criollo* bourgeoisies of the independent states, whose members consider themselves to be the direct heirs of that will to civilize (Bate 1984; Salas 1908:45).

An alternative thesis concerning the origin of the nation was developed during the first decades of the twentieth century, about the same time that archaeology, ethnohistory, and ethnology were constituted as scientific disciplines in several Latin American countries. This thesis was a consequence of the popularity of Marxism among middle-class intellectuals, who considered past and present Indian cultures as well as the cultures of blacks and mestizos to be basic elements in the construction of national identities (e.g., Acosta Saignes 1954, 1984; Hewitt de Alcántara 1984; Mariátegui 1952; Patterson 1994). According to this thesis, which was supported mainly by populist parties in Latin America, Indian and peasant societies were considered an important part of class struggle. The proponents of the thesis and the political parties with which they were associated undertook the task of recovering and restoring these communities in order to ensure their incorporation and integration into "democratic" society—aspects of the civilizing process that legitimated the political power of the state (Britto García 1988:27–36; Cuevas Molina 1989:39–45).

By the 1940s, political alliances had already formed in many Latin American countries between the state bureaucracies, filled with members of the populist parties, and the new oligarchies composed of tradesmen, bankers, industrialists, and professionals. These alliances provided the institutional foundations for a scientific anthropology that found its expression in the ethnopopulism of the *indigenista* movement. Its advocates attempted to preserve what they viewed as the authentic, autochthonous cultures of Indian and other minority communities, whose members had been separated from their lands as they were incorporated into or marginalized by the national political process. They also wanted, however, to keep these communities tied to the political establishment and bureaucracy by creating parallel and similarly constituted Indian bureaucracies representing the political and economic interests of the ethnic groups (Aguirre Beltrán 1957:48–63; Veloz Maggiolo 1984).

A third, alternative thesis has been proposed in recent years, again by anthropologists influenced by Marxist social thought. They are concerned with and support movements of national identity based on the autochthonous character of the historical processes involved; however, they consider indigenous societies to be ethnic components in existing class structures. As a result, the processes underlying the formation of particular identities must be explained in terms of the political antagonisms of the national society and resolved in light of the conditions and balance of forces they have created (Díaz Polanco 1985, 1987, 1988).

In spite of recent developments, most of the traditional archaeological and ethnohistorical studies reflect the cognitive blurring or lack of focus about the past that exists in Latin America anthropology. In the beginning, the intention of the anthropologists and ethnohistorians was to

vindicate the aboriginal cultures. Implicit in their inquiries was a theoretical perspective closely related to that of ethnopopulism. The historical past of a particular indigenous community was seen as a chronological
block disconnected from both the pre-Hispanic social reality and that
of the national culture. This view fused two positivist tenets: the reductionist assertion that the parts can be studied separately from the whole,
and the claim that sensory experience is the only source of knowledge.
Because of the cognitive ambiguity that resulted, researchers perceived
the indigenous communities as if they stood outside civilization—both
the pre-Hispanic historical reality and the modern national one. Since
they were not part of the civilized world, they must therefore be part
of nature. This cognitive blurring echoes the interests of official history
(e.g., Morón 1971).

Because particularistic studies using a culture area approach have
dominated the study of archaeology and ethnohistory, the pre-Hispanic
past has become a relic: a dead body that can be partly recovered but
never completely revived. It is a reminder of the better times enjoyed
during a golden age whose existence is only hinted at in those lifeless
museum displays of archaeological objects used to present chronologies
or demonstrate cultural diversity (Vargas Arenas and Sanoja 1993b). In
private art collections, archaeological and ethnological objects are even
further reduced to the economic values assigned to them by the pre-
Columbian and Indian art market. Thus, instead of exposing the processes involved in the formation of national societies, the positivist explanations provided by archaeologists and ethnohistorians actually mystify
the conditions of economic and cultural dependence by portraying historical reality as a series of disconnected fragments. So long as archaeologists and ethnohistorians are concerned exclusively with the recovery
of material objects, their research contributes nothing to explanations
of the contemporary realities of Latin American countries (Bullen and
Bullen 1972; Cruxent and Rouse 1961; Porras 1975).

A similar claim may be made about folkloric studies focused on the
persistence of pre-Hispanic or peasant technologies and sociocultural
forms in modern society. While there is no doubt about the scientific
honesty and the utility of the work of folklorists who salvage those
cultural traditions, there are questions concerning their theoretical approach, which is best characterized as survivalist. In this approach, folkloric traditions are viewed as fossilized behaviors of dead societies. They
are exotic relics rather than living forms of popular creativity that manifest themselves as the phenomenal or material components of ethnicity
or of the culture of given social classes, which, in the present situation,

include peasants, urban workers, and marginal people as well as sectors of the middle class who assert their feelings of otherness through ethnic cultural expressions (Vega 1959; Veloz Maggiolo 1984:53–58).

Linguistics has become, in a general way, a technique for studying Indian languages or *criollo* dialectical forms, and it has contributed much to the development of bilingual intercultural programs oriented toward the acculturation of Indian groups (Díaz Polanco 1983; Krisólogo 1976; Lizot and Mattei-Muller 1981:143; Mosonyi 1966). Although these programs have helped revitalize ethnic consciousness among Indian groups, their underlying ethnopopulist idealism has been shattered by the socioeconomic realities of the Latin American countries (Aguirre Beltrán 1967; Bonfil Batalla 1977; Cuevas Molina 1989; Díaz Polanco 1979). In Peru and Guatemala, where they constitute a majority of the national population, Indian communities have undertaken more active and violent actions to recover their human, social, and economic rights.

With regard to physical anthropology, most of the positivist-influenced studies conducted in Latin America have created an object of study—the individual—that can be understood only in terms of morphology, genetic makeup, or adaptation to particular environmental milieus. The object of many of these studies seems to be to describe different dimensions of human variability and the evolution of both pre-Hispanic and modern populations. While these objectives are valid ones, physical anthropologists have generally expressed little interest in either social theory or the implications their studies have for contemporary communities in Latin America (Fleury 1953; Gómez 1947; Herrera Fritot 1964, 1965; Jaén, Serrano, and Comas 1976; Kohn and Méndez 1972; Pretto 1947).

What Can Be Done?

Up to the present, Latin America has been a testing ground for anthropological theories emanating from First World universities, particularly those in the United States. Most U.S. anthropologists, for example, have appeared more interested in promoting their own academic careers than in developing accurate understandings of contemporary social problems in Latin American countries and contributing in meaningful ways to their resolution. Given the weak institutional support they receive in their own countries, many Latin American anthropologists participate in the research activities of foreign scholars in order to reap the advantages of their funding; consequently, they often end up pursuing the same avenues of research as their foreign colleagues. Social scientists in Europe and the United States, however, long ago began to deconstruct anthropology and look for a rationality proper to their own societies (Andah, this volume; Schmidt, this volume).

Anthropologists in Latin American countries can no longer afford to import shopworn ideas from the outside and uncritically operationalize them at home, because those ideas neither clarify nor help to resolve the problems they confront. Growing levels of poverty make it abundantly clear that First World remedies have not worked in the past and are not working now. As a result, Latin American anthropologists must begin to lay the foundations for new understandings of the rationality of development and change occurring in their own countries. This is an urgent task, for the poverty gap between the First World and the rest is increasing rapidly. To understand and alleviate the conditions developing in Latin America and elsewhere requires more than applying remedies advocated by First World social scientists and politicians.

As scientists and members of the academy, we must reckon with the complexity of these and related problems in Latin America. Many of them reflect the institutional conditions in our countries, in our educational systems, in our universities, and in our museums and institutes of anthropology. This is one area of our daily activity; we feel the pressure to reconceptualize anthropology, especially archaeology, and to revise the traditional approach of official history. Our universities must begin training social scientists who have a critical awareness and appreciation of the new sociohistoric conditions emerging in their countries and how these are related to developments in other countries (Contreras Alvarez 1990; González Casanova and Bonfil Batalla 1968:41–43; Licha 1991). That training begins as the discipline asserts a healthy intellectual autonomy in the various regions and countries and its practitioners stop mechanically and uncritically adopting every idea that emanates from First World social scientists.

Answers to the question of what can be done have followed two avenues. In one, archaeologists and anthropologists from a number of Latin American countries have developed social archaeology. This effort has involved an ongoing dialogue since 1970 in which concerns common to the entire region as well as the particularity of their manifestations in different countries have been explored. In the other, archaeologists and anthropologists have responded to the circumstances prevailing in their own countries while keeping in mind the general problems confronting the region and their colleagues elsewhere. In Venezuela this avenue has led to the creation and elaboration of the integrated museum. With regard to the production of knowledge, there is a dialectical tension as we move from the general region to the specific country and from the specific to the general.

The Theory and Practice of Social Archaeology

Archaeology is important because of its potential for creating historical consciousness among people. It reveals the processes that energize and integrate history. This means, however, that archaeologists must have an organic theory concerning the historical formation of different societies, which are the working objects of the various national archaeologies in Latin America. This organic theory must form an integral part of teaching, research, publication, and the dissemination of knowledge.

Up to now, most Latin American archaeologists have adopted cultural-area approaches and functionalist theories—or their new and improved versions—to understand the historical reality of their own countries. Given their positivist and neopositivist underpinnings, however, those theories involve a partitioning of historical reality, a point I argued earlier. In the technical division of labor that results, archaeology deals mainly with societies viewed as products of adaption to environmental forces. Human labor invested in creating and improving those conditions which allow the reproduction of society is conceptualized as the effort exerted by individuals to tie themselves increasingly to the yoke of the environment via the processes of adaptation. Thus, in accordance with those theories, the history of society is perceived as a permanent interplay between environment and society, where changes are related to magnitude, not quality.

The environment-society contradiction is dominant in societies with a low development of productive forces. From a dialectical perspective, however, the dominant contradictions are not stable throughout the entire history of a society, and the poles of the contradictions are not always qualitatively the same ones. In every historical time and society, the environment-society contradictions are solved by the development of productive forces. As this solution is achieved, inter- and intracommunity social relationships are transformed and become increasingly complex in order to protect the group from environmental contingencies. This transformation involves the development and reorganization of the labor force as well as the qualitative and quantitative expansion of all the other material and nonmaterial factors of society. Intensification in social relations manifests itself in the intensification of social contradictions. When the level of social contradictions is low, historical change proceeds slowly; as it intensifies, the rate of historical change accelerates.

In an earlier book (Vargas Arenas 1990), I tried to develop an approach to the study of society that retained the classic categories of "mode of production" and "socioeconomic formation" but conceived of them in a redefined or reformulated way. The first is understood as the sphere of reproduction of the material life of society. The second, the conceptualization of society as a concrete totality, is a category that permits us to define the changes impinging on the sociohistorical conditions of a society at a given time. To these categories, which refer to the macronarrative of history, I have added others in order to apprehend the concrete expression of reality in microhistory: the mode of life, the mode of work, domestic space, and daily life. The mode of life refracts the mode of work, which expresses the materiality of daily life, and it mediates the creative processes shaped by the dynamics and the continually shifting social relations of the socioeconomic formation. Taken together, these categories provide an analytical framework that is valid for human societies at all times and places. They open a common semantic space of shared meanings that facilitates the integration of perspectives derived from other disciplines into the social sciences. They undermine the self-contained blocks into which history has been divided by the culture-area and functionalist approaches and also by the universalized model of adaptation.

What Is Social about Social Archaeology?

Social archaeology reconceptualizes history as a continuous process that does not exhibit divisions between the pre-Hispanic and the post-Hispanic (Fonseca 1988; Vargas Arenas 1990). Similarly, social archaeology contributes, via formal and informal education, to the construction of an alternative to official history by creating real historical consciousness. For instance, formal education should express, through texts and pedagogy in the classroom, the objective contents of the historical process that led to formation of the Venezuelan nation, without the distortions that have been introduced for the convenience of a single dominant social class against the interests of the majority with whom they are inextricably linked by a shared but contested history.

In Venezuela, the late nineteenth and early twentieth centuries marked the beginning of a national project whose foundations, elaborated by the *criollo* oligarchy, were established by an alliance between the large *hacendados* and the commercial bourgeoisie. The goals of their project were to modernize the social and political structures of the country and to create a centralized state power based on a shared national consciousness. Once the project was set in motion, the oligarchy began to manipulate the collective historic consciousness by forging and disseminating a fragmented concept of history. This official history recognized the existence of a past connected to the present only through the legacy of negative traits among the Venezuelan population: laziness, passivity, indolence, insolence, and brutality, among others (Morón 1971). These attributes, claim the official historians, are atavisms linked variously with Indians, Negroes, and Spaniards. Because of them the Venezuelan people are disorganized and unruly. They have inhibited the country's socioeconomic development. As a result, the only way the country can reach an acceptable level of sociopolitical and economic development is to be guided by the force of an iron fist.

Contrary to the claims of official history, the research contributions of social archaeology show that indigenous peoples first, and then the mixed population of Indians, blacks, and Spaniards, all contributed positively to the formation of Venezuelan society. Environmental knowledge, traditional technology, continuous and creative work, and the arts and crafts of the mestizo population constituted the base upon which the modern nation-state emerged (see Sued Badillo, this volume). Yet from the inception of the modern state an official history was needed that would respond to the interests of the ruling class and allow for its social reproduction and expansion. This need was filled by ideological manipulation aimed at destroying the mechanisms that fostered the creation of historical consciousness—such as cultural and historical identification with the past. The official historians did this by arguing that the historical subjects had no positive qualities (Gil Fortoul 1961). Today the ruling class, which is linked to transnational power blocs, continues its work of material dominance with a neocolonial ideology built upon neoliberal economic models, the denial of utopias, and the end of history (Hueck Henríquez 1993).

Thus, social archaeology constitutes a challenge to neocolonial proposals. It reclaims the power of national states and it uncovers the historical mechanisms that in the past promoted a cultural and economic integration among nations respecting regional and national particularities. Social archaeology constitutes a scientific practice: the knowledge it produces about reality is not merely contemplative but of a fundamentally transformative nature. At the same time, it rescues the knowledge of daily life, true and genuine—as well as that of the extraordinary—by recognizing that daily life is the space where history develops, where routines are repeated and reiterated, and where monotonous routines are also transformed and the spontaneous is created (Heller 1985).

A process of social transformation involving this kind of archaeological practice implies abandoning science linked only to the academic world. It requires instead forming relationships between archaeologists and communities—relationships based on the idea that archaeologists are not only social beings but also members of the society in which they work. It also requires the production of texts that can be used by social scientists and teachers in formal educational institutions, as well as active participation in the creation of museums that provide alternatives to the views of official history.

The history of a community is a process connected to the regional and national historical process and cultural heritage. The regionally integrated museum represents an effort to blend domestic daily life with the community's collective or public daily life without fragmenting history into unrelated periods or giving precedence to one developmental phase over another. To make an integrated museum a reality, it is necessary to study the community—be it a village, a town, or a city—in order to discern the diverse historical reference points and cultural components necessary to contextualize the museum's subjects.

Such a study could have a number of objectives, among them (1) to formulate plans for territorial use or management, which requires knowledge of the physical environment within which the community is located and its evolution in order to identify elements that are or could eventually become natural resources; (2) to define the characteristics of the cultural landscape, such as the number and distribution of dwellings, the forms and loci of productive activity as well as of the distribution, exchange, and consumption of products in places like markets or shrines, and the kinds and availability of institutional services such as schools or health clinics; (3) to provide historical and structural analyses of the community's spaces and structures, including archaeological sites and colonial buildings; (4) to determine the interconnections of property arrangements and various work processes; (5) to elaborate a distribution map that defines and categorizes the urban area as well as the hierarchy of living spaces and activity areas; (6) to specify the domestic tool kit; (7) to determine the shifting demography and structure of domestic groups by examining, for example, family histories, religious forms, and oral literature; (8) to develop an appreciation of the aesthetics of domestic life and how it is revealed in art, furniture, patios, kitchens, or commercial shop windows; and (9) to understand attitudes toward outsiders, both national and foreign.

This sort of research, which also includes probing written sources, makes it possible to move into a second phase in the development and realization of an integrated museum: members of the community come into contact with realities that are different from those of their own daily surroundings. This goal entails disseminating in various ways information about the contributions of popular knowledge to the wider society—for instance, local alternatives to "Western" technologies and the destruction of myths that contrast "true," "formal," or "scientific" knowledge with "local" or "popular" knowledge. Experience of such information expands the horizons of the community and challenges negative stereotypes received from and reinforced by the official histories. Thus it forces community members critically to confront negative self-perceptions as well as their own sense of worth and self-esteem.

In sum, the integrated museum is an institution whose creators try to understand and project the holistic, organic, and authentic nature of a community and who attempt, at the same time, to design tactics that foster the attainment by individuals of consciousness of themselves as social beings, as well as to help outsiders understand and grasp the everyday life of others (Crew and Sims 1991:159–75).

The community museum is, for lack of a better term, a kind of subproduct of the integrated museum. Whereas the integrated museum is concerned with consciousness raising, the community museum serves as a base from which personnel can construct information modules using various media that depict the life of a whole community or of one of its sectors for both local residents and outsiders. Furthermore, it is a place for sharing information in the community by providing a forum for both local and outside storytellers, artisans, oral historians, and musicians. The community museum rescues what is considered important by the community: its heroes, its events, and its creativity in relation to what has happened and what is taking place in other communities.

Why This Approach?

The early 1990s in Venezuela witnessed events that shattered many people's hopes for a future based on social justice, freedom, and social equality (Departamento de Investigaciones 1994; Licha 1991; Ruiz Zúñiga 1991; Sorman 1993). The end of history has been declared for those not belonging to the First World, to be replaced by a neoliberal conservative "revolution" that preaches the end of national states and the intermingling of their economies in a global economy answering to the agenda of finance capitalism, its transnational government, and its demands for more efficient exploitation of the material and human resources of the poorer countries (Cueva 1987:24; Hueck Henríquez 1993). The consequences of this revolution for people in Latin America and elsewhere in the Third World are a dramatic loss of their national independence, a reduction in the quality of their lives, and even the loss of their lives.

There is resistance to this revolution, however—for example, in Chiapas and Brazil. Adherents of these resistance movements simultaneously cling to national values as symbols of their freedom and oppose the ideas espoused by their governments and ruling classes. In this context, historical reality once again reveals itself as a strategic asset opposing the false consciousness created by neoliberals who view the world market economy as the final solution to the problems of humanity.

Since neoliberal theory provides no adequate explanation for the social and economic problems such as poverty, homelessness, and unemployment that ravage all the developed First World countries, the jobless masses of Third World people confront a contradiction after moving to the United States or Europe to escape the poverty traps of their own countries. As they search for work, they find themselves in competition with the unemployed or underemployed citizens of the host countries for jobs (Cueva 1987:22; Derrida 1994:55–61, 77–94). This competition has spawned neo-Nazi and racist movements in various countries. The rhetoric of neoliberal politicians and policymakers in the First and Third Worlds, proclaiming the "end of history," the "clash of civilizations," or the "collapse of civilization," fans people's hatred and attempts to discourage the majority from preserving their social and human rights (Fukuyama 1992). In spite of neoliberal efforts to implement economic and political integrationist policies—such as the Caribbean Initiative, NAFTA, and GATT—the historical subjects in Latin America have become increasingly radical. Microregionalism based on ethnic, geographical, and national identities is developing increasing strength within the framework of everyday life, which is the center of microhistory.

NOTES

1. A sample of official histories includes Jorge Basadre's twelve-volume *Historia de la República del Perú* (Editorial Universitaria, Lima, 1961–68); Lorenzo Meyer's *México y Estados Unidos en el conflicto petrolero, 1917–1942* (Colegio de México, Mexico, 1968), Héctor Aguilar Camín and Lorenzo Meyer's *In the Shadow of the Mexican Revolution: Contemporary Mexican History, 1910–1989* (University of Texas Press, Austin, 1993); the

fourth edition of Guillermo Morón's *Historia de Venezuela* (Ediciones Rialp, Madrid, 1967); and *Venezuela independiente, 1810–1960* (Fundación Eugenio Mendoza, Caracas, 1962), by Mariano Picón-Salas, Augusto Mijares, Ramón Díaz-Sánchez, Eduardo Arcilla Farias, and Juan Liscano. Official history in the United States stresses consensus and exceptionalism. Daniel Boorstin's three-volume work *The Americans* (Random House, New York, 1958–73) is among the most widely read of the U.S. official histories. Michael Apple (1990) provides an overview of the contents of curricula in U.S. schools. Linda Gordon (1994) and Sundiata Cha-Jua and Robert Weems, Jr. (1994) expose the limitations of U.S. consensus histories, while John Higham's (1989) lament about the collapse of consensus is also a call to restrengthen it. The authors writing for Byron Shafer's *Is America Different? A New Look at American Exceptionalism* (Clarendon Press, Oxford, 1991) point out the diverse underpinnings of this doctrine. — Eds.

2. Mejía (1970) and Arancibia (1985) illustrate how, in discussions of the history of Honduras, if indigenous peoples are mentioned, they are reduced to "Mayas" but no connection is made between the ancient Mayas and contemporary populations.

Archaeology, History, *Indigenismo,* and the State in Peru and Mexico

THOMAS C. PATTERSON

The critique of nationalist discourse must find for itself the ideological means to connect the popular strength of those struggles with the consciousness of a new universality, to subvert the ideological sway of a state which falsely claims to speak on behalf of the nation and to challenge the presumed sovereignty of a science which puts itself at the service of capital.

—Partha Chatterjee, *Nationalist Thought and the Colonial World*

C rises rocked Peru and Mexico around the turn of the twentieth century. In Peru, the breakdown occurred after the War of the Pacific (1879–83). In Mexico, unrest festered for years before exploding in the Revolution (1910–17) and the events that followed in its wake. The immediate cause of both disruptions was that large numbers of the poorer classes were armed and angry and did not see state institutions and practices as serving their interests. The underlying cause was the decomposition and re-formation of class and state structures—the withering of the old nation-states with their colonial legacies and the emergence of new ones better suited to the demands of international capitalism. This class formation provoked new kinds of capitalist production relations, internal migration, attempts to integrate rural communities and new groups of urban poor into the social fabric of the nation-state, and the need to forge new identities and understandings of the present in order to shape perceptions about what was possible in the future.

Both crises had an important culture-historical dimension: Who were these armed, angry, and potentially dangerous people? What was their place in their nation? What role should they play in the future? This was the Indian Question, and the turn of the century was not the first time people's identities had been closely inspected in the two regions. The examination process had been set in motion by the European invasions of the sixteenth century, but the contours of the problem—what issues were appropriate, what lines of argumentation were acceptable, and, conversely, what was excluded—changed through time. In both regions, the terms of the arguments were set by the ruling class and managed by agents in the state apparatus who, in their attempts to resolve social issues, historicized and homogenized the interests of people with diverse understandings and experiences of everyday life.

The Indian Question acquired a recognizably modern form in Peru and Mexico around the turn of the century with the almost simultaneous appearance of the new capitalist relations of production and the incorporation of positivist, idealist, and materialist views into contemporary social and political debates. The injection of positivism, with its empiricist claim that knowledge is based exclusively on observable or experiential phenomena, provided the foundations for essentialist understandings of the Indian. The category of Indian was reified, and Indians were variously defined by their physical attributes, place of residence, powerlessness, capacity to learn, or lack of organic connections with the capitalist sectors of the national economies (Knight 1990; Pike 1967: 159–236; Powell 1968; Stabb 1959).

What distinguished the twentieth-century debates from earlier ones was that the state agents were archaeologists, historians, and anthropologists. They wielded archaeology and history not as narrow disciplinary practices but rather as historical social sciences that articulated the study of material remains with written and oral traditions. The agents of the state framed the Indian Question in terms of Enlightenment analytical categories and the colonial encounter. They depicted the pre-Columbian societies of the two regions as civilizations conquered by the Spaniards in the sixteenth century and either said nothing about contemporary Indian communities or portrayed them as unruly peasantries. They typically saw education as the vehicle for the actualization of the Indians' potential, for their social and economic recovery, and for their integration into the fabric of the modern nation-state. This emphasis legitimated the centralizing tendencies of those states and incorporated their expressed aims and intentions (Chatterjee 1992).

Because the goals of states, however, are always malleable when new pressures exert themselves, the views of the first generation of state intellectuals to use archaeology and history were challenged by their opponents and by other groups whose members typically had different relations with the state apparatus. Critics questioned the utility of the earlier understandings and the programs based on them in light of the effects they had. The consequences of those programs became increasingly apparent after World War II: massive urban migration, monolingual public education, and the states' inability to promote social justice and adequate economic opportunities. The critics phrased their message primarily in political-economic rather than in cultural terms; their understanding no longer revolved exclusively around the Indian, whose designation and identity they viewed as problematic at best.

Many of the critics did not see integration as something to be achieved, because they believed it had already taken place in the sixteenth century. They questioned views portraying the Indians as a distinct, backward sector of the nation-state and focused instead on the social and cultural foundations of the class structures that formed during the colonial and national periods and on the profound political-economic and social changes that occurred during the first half of the twentieth century. They offered alternatives to state-supported schemes granting primacy to political centralism and national integration. Consequently, the accounts of pre-Columbian history provided by archaeologists and ethnohistorians figured differently in their arguments about the origins and resolution of contemporary social problems. Their critiques — along with their understanding of history, ethnography, and class formation — have sometimes been appropriated and modified or transformed by Indian and political movements in the Andean countries and Mexico.

Historically, archaeologists in Peru and Mexico have played a variety of roles — agent of the state, critic, and silent spectator. This chapter compares the linkages between the positions archaeologists have held, how they have conceptualized and practiced their discipline in the two regions, what they have said about historical development and what this implies for understanding contemporary social relations, how their views have been appropriated and deployed by the state, and what currency their ideas and practices have in indigenous communities and political movements. I hope this comparison will illuminate the purposes and interests served by various contemporary perspectives on the rise of civilization in the two areas.

The Indian Question in Peru: Archaeology, Folklore, and History

Debates over Indian identity have passed through various stages since the 1890s (Bonilla 1982; Favre 1982; Rama 1975, 1982). The argument that developed after the War of the Pacific was shaped by the opposition of rural and urban poor to the Chilean forces during the war, armed insurrections in some rural communities resulting from the repressive acts of landlords and state officials, the end of the guano and nitrate economies, the emergence of new linkages between the old landowning aristocracy and foreign-owned export firms in the south, and the consolidation of political power by the largely immigrant (Italian, German, English, and U.S.) agrarian capitalists of the coast (Mallon 1987; Spalding 1980). In the 1890s and early 1900s, the Indian Question was an aspect of integration: the restructuring of class relations, the securing of legal rights, and the formation of a nation-state which, by force of circumstances, had to include new sectors of the population. The debate focused on the incorporation of the Indians into the nation-state through education and on cultural *mestizaje,* an attempt to link the bourgeois values of the Peruvian upper classes with those of Europe and with what they viewed as the enlightened despotism and virtues of the Inca nobility who ruled during the fifteenth and early sixteenth centuries.

Cultural *mestizaje* resonated with the views of the export capitalist farmers who controlled the Peruvian state at the turn of the century. Many members of this group were immigrants with close ties to their homelands and with settler-colonist mentalities. Max Uhle, the German archaeologist who directed the Museo Nacional de Historia between 1906 and 1911, was a leading advocate of this perspective; his worldview had been shaped by the agrarian and nonindustrial sectors of the German middle class, who saw agriculture, not industry or commerce, as the basis of civilization (Patterson 1989:38–40). Uhle studied the pre-Columbian history of the Andes—Inca civilization and its predecessors—and accumulated archaeological objects and documentation to build museum collections. His understanding of pre-Columbian history incorporated both evolutionist and diffusionist elements: civilized people farm and primitive ones do not; and civilization was brought to the Americas by Asian immigrants in the late second millennium B.C. (Uhle 1910, 1913, 1940). His views provided historical support for the self-perceptions of the agrarian capitalists: immigrant settler-farmers introduce civilization to primitive Andean peoples and become legitimate rulers.

The agrarian capitalists' control over the government waned when finance and the extractive export industries, centered in the highlands, emerged as the dominant economic sectors after 1912. This shift is mirrored by the political fortunes of Augusto Leguía, who was president for 11 years before being overthrown in 1930. During this period, Julio C. Tello, his client, emerged as Peru's leading archaeologist and became an established state functionary: professor at the Universidad Nacional Mayor de San Marcos, advocate of curricular and other university reforms, director of the national museum, and senator. Tello extolled the capacities of the Indians and saw education as the vehicle that would allow them to achieve their full potential and facilitate and their integration into the national society; he was convinced Indians had suffered because of emphasis on the economic development of the coast at the expense of the highlands (Patterson 1989:40–45).

Tello rejected Uhle's view that the impetus for Peruvian cultural development came from the outside. He argued instead that archaic Andean culture developed autochthonously and first achieved its highest forms in the north highlands before spreading to other highland areas and finally to the coast, where it developed distinctive features after the initial radiations weakened. These coastal cultures were ultimately influenced by the Incas—the last great wave of creativity to roll out of the mountains (Tello 1923, 1929:24–25, 1930). For Tello, the philosophical romantic, each culture had its own particular laws of development and character that directed the energies of individuals and led them to participate in the common tasks of the community. Human capabilities could be enhanced only when they followed the lead of an intellectual and artistic elite whose creative genius was immortalized in the architectural monuments and elaborate objects that expressed their religious fervor (Tello 1940:626). As a result of his emphasis on creativity, Tello gave positive valuations to the unconscious, to the legendary or mythical, and to the importance of the contemporary rural folk cultures as the true repositories of Andean tradition.

Tello's emphasis on the achievements of the pre-Columbian societies of Peru appealed to the sensibilities and expressed the protest of well-educated, ambitious individuals who were largely denied opportunities for promotion by the propertied classes dominating the state (Bourricaud 1954:169). In opposing the *hispanismo* of propertied contemporaries such as José Riva de la Agüero and Víctor Andrés Beláunde, Tello and others challenged an attachment to the colonial past that traced Peru's roots to the Iberian peninsula and virtually excluded its Andean legacy. They found validation for their identity in the pre-Columbian cultures revealed in the archaeological record—a validation that was largely denied to the *castas* and members of Indian society during the colonial and republican periods. In the process, they used the Spanish language to create an essentialist national identity that complemented the one constituted in the same language by the *hispanistas*. The identity they constructed was nativist in the sense that it recuperated a time when the problems of the present did not exist. For *indigenistas* like Tello, the failures of Peruvian national character were a consequence of the Spanish conquest; for the *hispanistas*, the present problems existed because the

Indian population either was not or could not be assimilated and integrated into modern Peruvian society. Together, *indigenistas* and *hispanistas* framed the Indian Question in a way that provided no exit and no opportunity for resolution or closure.

Indigenistas and *hispanistas,* however, were not the only groups examining the Indian Question in order to use history during and after the 1920s. Activists such as Hildebrando Castro Pozo (1924, 1946), José Carlos Mariátegui (1928), and Luis Valcárcel (1927, 1981) also brought archaeological and historical information to the debate. They focused on the communal organization of the economy during the Inca empire, praised the judgment and organizational skills of Inca rulers for developing the agricultural productive forces and retaining the communal social relations of the indigenous peoples, and condemned the Spaniards for destroying the indigenous economic structures and relations during the colonial period. They concentrated on rural class structures rather than ethnicity and emphasized the capacities of kin-organized communities rather than those of elites whose members constituted the state apparatus and carried out its programs. These activists took cognizance of the agrarian question and of recent and ongoing events in the Soviet Union and Mexico.

Valcárcel (1943:19–28, 1948)—an organic intellectual, in the Gramscian sense of the term, who occupied various positions both inside and outside the government during his long career—portrayed Peruvian society as a totality. Historically, it was a unity of the ancient period—Inca society and its predecessors, known from archaeological, traditional, and historical testimony—and the period of written history that began in 1532 and is known from historical accounts, official documents, and ethnological reports. Geographically, it was a unity composed of the continually shifting and varied connections among diverse coastal, highland, and tropical lowland communities, none of which ever acquired sufficient independence to develop a distinctive culture uniquely its own. This representation of the Peruvian reality was very different from those proposed by the *indigenistas* and *hispanistas,* who gave precedence to either the indigenous or the European elements in the state's heritage, and by archaeologists, who separated the pre-Columbian and later periods and gave priority to the inhabitants of one region or another in their interpretations of pre-Columbian social development.

From the mid-1930s onward, various *indigenista* writers also participated in debates over the Indian Question. The most influential was José María Arguedas—novelist, poet, folklorist, and ethnologist—who was concerned with the liberation of subordinated communities under the historically and socially constituted peculiarities of Peruvian national culture and political economy; his perceptions of the Peruvian reality resonated with those of Mariátegui, Valcárcel, and Castro Pozo (Rama 1975:xv–xvi, 1982; Rowe and Schelling 1991:155–56, 213–15). He viewed the world dialectically: the whole was more than the sum of its parts, and only an understanding of the complex interrelations of the whole and its parts permitted authentic, concrete knowledge of the Andean world (Arguedas 1975, 1989:18–20). He associated *indigenismo* with integration, and integration with the acculturation of indigenous, rural Andean communities to Western norms and the Spanish language. He saw culture and language as the contested terrains in the struggles between the Indian and Peruvian classes; between coast and highlands in a context shaped by road-building, modernization, mass immigration to the cities, and erosion of traditional communal ties; and between Peru and the imperialist states (Forgues 1989:440; Rowe and Schelling 1991:59).

Arguedas (1935) dealt with the conflicts and ambiguities between the antagonistic worlds of the Indian and the *mistis* (whites) in his first novel. He subsequently showed how this socioeconomic struggle was waged in cultural terms and how culture afforded the means for working through and resolving the contradictions (Arguedas 1941:1958). He continually provided examples of what might happen when traditional and modern communities confronted each other in new circumstances and when new social and cultural forms were created—for example, when Quechua syntactic structures were incorporated into Spanish or when a rural community adopted modern technology and deployed it in terms of traditional communal relations rather than capitalist ones. Rather than providing a detailed plan of action imposed by an outsider, his examples were intended to provoke and stimulate creative thinking about what might happen when the ambiguities and contradictions of the Andean reality were juxtaposed, worked through, and resolved in different ways (Forgues 1989:412–31). His examples were also reflections of the new realities being created every day as monolingual Quechua speakers moved to the cities and became part of new, increasingly bi-cultural neighborhoods at the same time that their ties to their natal communities were changing.

While Valcárcel, Arguedas, and others were arguing that contemporary indigenous communities could not be understood if they were extracted and isolated from the socioeconomic contexts and contradictions that defined their very existence, a number of archaeologists adopted cultural evolutionism (Patterson 1989:45–47). They had various reasons for embracing a perspective that understood development in terms of a succession of stages, each characterized by a particular economic base and by functionally related sociopolitical institutions and ideas. Rafael Larco Hoyle (1948), the influential agrarian capitalist from the north coast who formulated the model, believed that expanding the productive forces—that is, having the state build large-scale irrigation systems on the north coast—would promote economic growth for the affluent; he supported a coup d'etat in 1948 to prove his point. Some archaeologists adopted the model because of its widespread use by professional archaeologists in North America and Europe during the 1950s; others recognized echoes in it of the Second International. Their actions reconstituted narrow disciplinary practices, professionalism, and a technical division of labor that once again separated indigenous peoples from their pre-Columbian history. For these archaeologists, Andean history stopped when the Spaniards arrived, and they had no interest in examining the colonial societies that followed in the wake of the pre-Columbian civilizations they studied.

A few archaeologists and historians—for instance, Luis Lumbreras (1974) and Alberto Flores Galindo (1988)—have studied the historical development of social relations in ways that neither rely so exclusively on the increasingly specialized technical language and discourse of professionalism nor give so much weight to political centralism and the primacy of the state in resolving crises. They demonstrate a willingness to frame understandings of past societies and social processes in ways that have affinities with the current concerns and sensibilities of the less powerful rather than with the more narrowly defined, purely professional interests that ultimately refract in complex ways the views of the state. For them, the issue of whose interests are supported by particular interpretations of the past is a meaningful question. They acknowledge the existence of communities and classes whose voices are too often muted and whose contributions to the Peruvian reality are downplayed or denied altogether. Instead of imposing their views, they present them in ways that potentially provoke and promote critical thought among these groups. They appreciate the common concerns and diverse circumstances of indigenous communities in the Andean states. They understand the multiple dimensions of struggle and constraint in a terrain where race, ethnicity, class, and the state continually shape the tensions of everyday life and political practice. Most importantly, they recognize that the members of these communities, having read histories and ethnographies describing their circumstances, are using these data to construct their own understandings of their place in the Andean reality and to enter into arenas such as the courts where their voices were excluded or marginal in the past (Albó 1987, 1990; Mayer 1991; Poole and Renique 1991; Santana 1982; Stern 1987).

Archaeology, History, and the State: The Indian Question in Mexico

The Indian Question also passed through various stages of debate in Mexico (Bataillon 1982; Keen 1971). During the dictatorship of Porfirio Díaz (1880–1910), when nationalism and positivism dominated education, history validated heroes and patriotism, and archaeological monuments provided vivid testimony of the existence and achievements of the ancient civilizations in central and southern Mexico. Anthropology was centered in the museum, and its practitioners were concerned mainly with accumulating facts and objects. Historians produced compilations of documents providing accounts of the colonial and indigenous legacies of the Mexican state. Together they separated the pre-Columbian societies from contemporary communities whose members spoke indigenous languages (Suárez Cortés 1987; Vázquez León 1987: 148–94).

The anthropological perspectives consolidated during the Mexican Revolution (1910–17) were not produced by foreigners but rather by the civil war, the consolidation of the nation-state and capitalist production relations, the demand for agrarian reform, and two episodes of military intervention and prolonged interference by the U.S. government (Rivermar Pérez 1987). There was a shift from the positivist-inspired "collection of facts" program that dominated the waning years of the Porfiriato to the action-oriented, integrationist, and developmentalist position that crystallized in the early years of the Revolution.

Officials of the revolutionary state apparatus were acutely aware of the intensity with which Indian communities—the Yaquis in the north and the Mayas in the southeast—had resisted the demands of their predecessors. They were concerned with providing the historical foundations for a nation-state that identified the leading elements of the society as white and relegated its Indian legacy to pre-Hispanic times revealed by ongoing archaeological investigations. They also supported a liberal political strategy implemented by Columbia University–educated Manuel Gamio, whose family had extensive landholdings in Oaxaca, Veracruz, Puebla, and Santo Domingo and lost its fortune during the Revolution. Gamio became Mexico's premier anthropologist and one of the state's leading intellectuals after the Constitution was ratified in 1917.

He claimed (1916) that Mexico's indigenous cultures reached their highest levels of development before the conquest and that the customs of the various contemporary Indian communities reflected the degeneration of those traditions. The backwardness of the contemporary Indian cultures, he argued, doomed them to ever-increasing levels of poverty, impeded their integration into the mainstream mestizo culture, and ultimately blocked the formation of a truly progressive national culture. Modernization and rural education programs directed by enlightened outsiders would be the vehicles for overcoming these obstacles (Hewitt de Alcántara 1984:10–15; Médina 1988:719–21; Vázquez León 1987:154–56).

As head of the Dirección de Antropología in the Ministry of Agriculture between 1917 and 1925, Gamio (1922) carried out extensive studies at Teotihuacán: exploring and reconstructing its ancient architectural monuments and studying the lifeways of its impoverished inhabitants who eked out a livelihood on nearby haciendas. In his view, it was essential to study the rural Indian communities in order to recognize and correct the problems created by their backward folk cultures. His plan of action involved education, confronting alcoholism and other social problems, and introducing beekeeping and pottery making to Teotihuacán; it did not extend to the inhabitants' petitions for land reform (Hewitt de Alcántara 1984:10–15; Vázquez León 1987:155–56).

The Dirección de Antropología was dissolved in 1925 and replaced by two subdirectorates: one that shaped the inquiries of archaeologists working with pre-Columbian cultures and another that directed the efforts of ethnologists, linguists, and historians studying colonial society and contemporary cultures. This technical division of labor allowed narrowly defined disciplinary practices to resurface, it provided no means for linking the results of increasingly distinct kinds of anthropological inquiry, and it effectively nullified Gamio's vision of anthropology as a holistic field of study. There was no archaeology of the colonial or national periods, and there was no ethnology of the pre-Columbian societies.

Columbia-educated Moisés Sáenz—who belonged to the power bloc dominating Mexican politics in the 1920s—emerged as a leading state intellectual when he became subsecretary of public education in 1925 (Hewitt de Alcántara 1984:14–16; Rocha 1987:142–47). His aim was to develop an integrated program of education that would promote social and economic change in all rural communities, regardless of whether they were called Indian or peasant. These programs focused on health, literacy, and the economic circumstances of rural communities rather than on their cultural particularities. He increasingly advocated economic development and cultural pluralism in the countryside rather than the acculturation and integration of rural communities into some homogenized national culture. He also proposed the formation of a Department of Indian Affairs "which would coordinate the development efforts of all public agencies working in indigenous areas and adapt them to the particular requirements of each group" (Hewitt de Alcántara 1984: 15). Mexico could be integrated, according to Sáenz (1939:xi–xii, 232), by constructing a multicultural state whose diverse communities would be linked by a fair and equitable economic system. This position contrasted with Gamio's view that the communities were parts of a larger, historically constituted whole that incorporated both pre-Columbian and colonial societies. President Lázaro Cárdenas (1934–40) supported the efforts of Sáenz, who served as director of the Instituto Interamericano Indigenista (III) (1936–41).

Archaeological investigations, which languished during the late 1920s, were revived partly through the efforts and organizational skills of Alfonso Caso—a lawyer who served briefly as the official mayor of the Federal District in 1921 before entering the Ministry of Industry and Commerce. Caso's interest in archaeology was piqued when he visited archaeological sites in Michoacán with his friend and future brother-in-law, Vicente Lombardo Toledano, in 1920. His understanding of Mexico's pre-Hispanic past grew steadily during the decade, and in the mid-1930s he launched a series of archaeological investigations in Oaxaca and Michoacán that were supported by President Cárdenas, the Ministry of Education, the Panamerican Institute of Geography and History, and the Carnegie Institution of Washington. Caso's research reflected the desire of Cárdenas and others in the state apparatus to obtain new revenues from tourism. He excavated large pre-Columbian centers, restored buildings, and deciphered royal genealogies (España Caballero 1987:252–53, 269–71; Téllez Ortega 1987:310, 319).

The state-subsidized Instituto Nacional de Antropología e Historia (INAH) was created in 1939, largely through the efforts of Caso, who served as its director until 1944. His goal was to bring the various kinds of anthropological research being carried out in Mexico under a single institutional umbrella in order to ensure their continuity despite fluctuations in the policies of the state. INAH sustained anthropological research and promoted the ethnohistorical investigations of Miguel Othón de Mendizábal, Paul Kirchhoff, and others who studied the economic conditions of pre-Hispanic Mexico and how they were transformed by the conquest, and who used the writings of Marx and Engels to create a more sophisticated appreciation of the political-economic and social transformation of tribal societies into state-based societies with class structures and private property (Keen 1971:466, 472–79, 488–94). During the 1940s and 1950s, Caso constructed a culture history of Mexico that was informed simultaneously by cultural evolutionism and functionalism and that emphasized the role of elites in the historical development of pre-Hispanic Mexican society (Caso 1953; España Caballero 1987:270–71; Téllez Ortega 1987:310).

After the restoration of the Street of the Dead in Teotihuacán in the early 1960s and completion of the new National Museum of Anthropology in 1964, the state began to reduce its financial support for archaeological investigations. This cutback was occurring at the time of the Tlatelolco massacre in 1968, when the state murdered students demonstrating at the Plaza de las Tres Culturas (Lantz 1985:139). People were outraged by the institutionalized violence and repressive actions of the state. The outpouring of antistate sentiments that erupted in its wake coincided with the appearance of professional criticisms of the kinds of archaeological research that had been supported earlier—that is, the construction of museums and the restoration of buildings in the ceremonial centers of pre-Hispanic state-based societies. At times, the two seemed to fuse. Critics argued that the state had supported the wrong kinds of projects and that the funds available should be shifted to new forms of archaeological practice. What was needed was an archaeology that was more rigorous in providing and using documentation. It should have purely scientific aims rather than providing tourists with places to spend money. Research should be initiated outside the areas where tourists ventured; these inquiries should incorporate new methodological advances; and any restorations should be accurate and well documented (Méndez Lavielle 1987:416). As these largely internal, purely professional and technical debates took up increasing amounts of time and space in publications, the state made steadily less use of the capacity of archaeology and history to create a national heritage that would ultimately sustain and legitimize its own practices and institutions.

The state's support for archaeology increased briefly after 1978, when an elaborately carved monolith associated with the Templo Mayor was discovered in Mexico City. Rescue excavations were conducted to salvage the monument, and then more extensive excavations were conducted by Eduardo Matos Moctezuma (1979), who criticized the preceding generation's pyramid archaeology as well as its acquiescence to the nationalist sentiments of the state and its demand for tourist revenues. Matos also responded to criticisms of his work by linking it with earlier investigations and by pointing out that the archaeological materials and context of the Templo Mayor indicated the political-economic and religious control exercised by the Aztec rulers over their own people and subject populations; it was the place where Aztec military leaders manipulated ritual practices and sacrificed victims for political ends. In subsequent publications, the sacrifices became a magical ritual practice that ensured the survival and triumph of the Aztec society—that is, the state. However, the museum texts describing the pyramid simultaneously extoll the achievements of Aztec society and condemn the barbarism of both the Aztecs and the Spaniards who succeeded them (Lantz 1985:47–49, 86–94). By presenting both views, the state effectively subsumed the views of its critics at a major tourist attraction in the capital city.

The economic crisis of the late 1960s also added significant new dimensions to the construction of anthropological perspectives of rural Mexico. In the 1950s, the Instituto Nacional Indigenista (INI) established a pilot project in highland Chiapas to study processes of regional integration and domination and to devise strategies that would promote development. Indian culture was portrayed as a subjective feeling, a psychological state, and an Indian community was any group whose members felt that they were Indians. Thus, the institute viewed indigenous communities as aggregates of individuals, and its programs focused on their cultural development as individuals—that is, learning Spanish and scientific rationality in place of native languages and traditional understandings. This would facilitate their incorporation into a national society which the state characterized as multicultural. At the same time, however, the state seemed intent on eliminating the cultural diversity of the rural communities, especially those elements that would allow them to retain some degree of independence and autonomy in face of exploitative social relations and state control (Hewitt de Alcántara 1984: 40, 49–50; Téllez Ortega 1987:302–304).

The Chiapas Project, according to Gonzalo Aguirre Beltrán (1953, 1955, 1957), showed that Indian communities were the creation of national society and that all the inhabitants of provincial or regional cities benefited from the exploitation—that is, control over the disposable labor and goods—of the surrounding communities, whose identities were typically expressed in racial and/or ethnic terms. Aguirre clarified how the rural social structures and cultures of multicultural regions such as Chiapas were constituted historically. He also understood how exploitation worked at the regional level, but his evolutionary functionalism prevented him from conceptualizing how it worked at the level of the national state. His goal was to modernize the regional cities in order to eliminate their inhabitants' need to exploit the ethnic minorities in the surrounding villages (Hewitt de Alcántara 1984:52–57). This approach encouraged Gamio's incorporationist perspective without sufficiently questioning its assumptions: political centralism and the equation of progress with political integration and cultural homogenization (Arizpe 1978). The uprising in Chiapas in January 1994 and subsequent statements by Sub-Comandante Marcos of the Ejército Zapatista de Liberación Nacional (EZLN) provide eloquent testimony to the failures of this project and the policies of the Mexican state (*Anderson Valley Advertiser,* August 3, 1994).

During the late 1960s and the 1970s, the dependency theorists— for instance, Rodolfo Stavenhagen (1969), Pablo González Casanova (1969), and Guillermo Bonfil Batalla (1987)—challenged the functionalist understanding of *indigenismo* as ethnic identity and focused instead on the creation and development of rural class structures and systems of exploitation and domination. By examining the interconnections of ethnicity and class structures, their investigations shed light on power relations within the Indian communities and on the institutions and practices involved in resisting exploitation by city residents and by the state. Their argument that exploitation, not ethnic identity, was the real problem echoed the anti-incorporationist perspective of Sáenz in the 1930s; it shifted the focus back to political-economic issues from ones of ethnic and/or cultural identity. In their view, Indianness was simultaneously a class position, a means of resistance, and a point around which subordinated indigenous peoples could mobilize politically.

The Mexican ruling class has always viewed the National Indian Institute with suspicion. For many years, anthropologists in the institute and the Department of Indian Affairs steered a precarious course between advocating Indian rights, on the one hand, and promoting the *indigenista* policies of the state, on the other. Beginning in the mid-1970s, however, state functionaries with less appreciation of *indigenista* politics gradually expanded their influence in the regional centers as the number of bilingual teachers grew. This shift heightened the already existing contradictions between the state, which has sought to control *indigenista* programs and politics, and the Indian communities, whose members have struggled since the the First Interamerican Indian Congress at Pátzcuaro in 1940 to determine the direction of the movement under the continually changing circumstances created by new forms of agrarian capitalism, urban migration, emigration to the United States, and the concomitant reappearance of Indian communities in regions where there were none

20 or 30 years ago. The technicians and bilingual teachers who toil in the regional centers have provided the inhabitants of some areas with the means for talking to the Spanish-speaking state apparatus, but not with the message; whether the voices of their students were heard, however, is another issue. With the heightened sensitivity to linguistic and cultural differences promoted in the 1970s and 1980s, *indigenista* politics has taken two forms: a social movement whose members use analyses of rural capitalist development in Mexico, and ethnic movements whose adherents demand autonomy and proclaim their separateness from the problems of the Mexican state (Bonfil Batalla 1987; Díaz Polanco 1987, 1988).

Writing History in Peru and Mexico: A Discussion

Perspectives on how oppressed regions should articulate with the state may differ significantly from one country to another and from one historical phase to another in the same state. Although Peru and Mexico are both located in a geographical area called Latin America, capitalist development and the relations between powerful and oppressed regions have exhibited quite different trajectories in the two states. In Peru during the twentieth century, hegemony has resided in the capital city and has been extended into the highland regions when the demands of their inhabitants threatened existing power relations. On those occasions— the early 1930s, 1959–65, and the 1980s—the state has consistently sent the army into regions whose residents challenged its hegemony and has ignored events in other areas, such as Putumayo during the rubber boom at the turn of the century, where its influence was weak or had not been threatened. In contrast, the Mexican state was consolidated along different lines by 1920. The state attempted to incorporate oppressed or marginal regions rather than suppress them. Debates centered on the formation or construction of a national culture, whether and how the indigenous peoples of backward regions like Chiapas or Quintana Roo should be integrated into it, and whether they should be viewed as distinct from the remainder of the rural population.

Indigenista intellectuals in Peru—Pozo Castro, Mariátegui, Valcárcel, and Arguedas—were either oppositional figures or had intermittent and usually brief associations with the state. They exhibited a good deal of critical skepticism about either the capacity or the willingness of the state apparatus to create conditions that would facilitate the emancipation and empowerment of Indian communities. They linked political economic concerns with the issues of class struggle being contested in cultural arenas. They attempted to create conditions that would provide

Indian communities with an array of options from which their members could draw for their own emancipation and empowerment. They argued that changes must originate within the Indian communities rather than be imposed by technicians from the state apparatus or by intellectuals whose primary allegiances were to the ruling class, the state, and the historically constituted power blocs for whom they were spokespersons.

This situation contrasts with that in Mexico, where, from the Revolution until the 1970s, most *indigenista* intellectuals were part of the state apparatus, and at least one—Moisés Sáenz—had close ties to its inner circle of power. Their intimate relations to the state had two obvious consequences. First, these intellectuals often viewed themselves as advocates—virtually representatives—of the Indian communities, giving voice to the Indians' sensibilities and understandings and translating them for the state and its ruling classes. They tended to view social and cultural change as something that originated within the state and the ruling elite; technicians and teachers introduced ideas, and the communities adopted them. They waged their struggles on behalf of the Indian communities in Congress and the various ministries when they sought financial appropriations and support for the programs they devised and desired to implement. Second, by virtue of their integral positions in the state apparatus, the Mexican *indigenista* anthropologists, much more than their counterparts in Peru, were attracted by and sympathetic to writers such as Max Weber who were concerned with the relationship between intellectuals and the state, the iron cage of bureaucracy, and the legitimacy and legitimation of state institutions and practices.

Neither the Peruvian nor the Mexican state has succeeded in creating conditions wherein its rural populations enjoy reasonable standards of living. Indeed, they have failed miserably, especially during the last 20 years, as increasingly large numbers of people have lost their lands and immigrated to the cities to eke out a bare existence. More than 70 percent of the population of each country lives in poverty. The Chicago-style, neoliberal economic agendas and legislation of the 1980s probably aided no more than a few hundred individuals in each country, all of whom were already intimately linked with the inner circles of power and benefited from those associations.

Indigenous and rural communities in the two countries are acutely aware that their standards of living have declined, often dramatically, during the last 20 years. Consequently, one of the last things members of rural communities want to hear at the present time is how intellectual elites—who, according to archaeologists and historians, have always constituted state apparatuses in civilized societies—will help them progress to a new and higher stage of social development. They understand clearly that these very same intellectuals, the bureaucracies they staff, and the laws they have promulgated to promote capitalist development have precipitated the miserable conditions in which many rural people now live. The uprising in Chiapas in January 1994 and subsequent statements by the EZLN provide eloquent testimony to the complete failure of the policies of the Mexican state.

The accounts provided by archaeologists and historians who repeat the old story—that economic development is driven by the intellectuals who help the masses elaborate their productive forces and construct markets for commodities—provide no insights, either for communities or for state bureaucracies, into the processes of class formation, the power relations, the uneven development, or the cultural wars that shape everyday life in the 1990s. To write a new story, they must first recognize the existence of communities and classes whose voices have been muted and muzzled by the very states that employ them. Once this reality is acknowledged, they must consider how their managers and masters have influenced the stories they tell about the rise of civilization. They must situate hegemonic groups, themselves, and indigenous communities in terms of the complex webs of social relations that characterize society today. They must also historicize the operation of their views, recognize the historical specificity of their claims, and consider closely whose interests are ultimately served by claims that exploitation and oppressive social relations are the natural and inevitable outcome of human history.

Confronting Colonialism

The Mahican and Schaghticoke Peoples and Us

RUSSELL G. HANDSMAN AND TRUDIE LAMB RICHMOND

The fact nevertheless remains: archaeologists have no informants. We cannot see the past from the ancients' cultural perspective because they cannot tell us what that might have been.
—Lewis Binford, *Data, Relativism and Archaeological Science*

We have been discouraged from remembering anything but what the missionaries wanted us to remember. But it's time to read between the lines of the white man's history books.
—Dorothy Davids, *Mahican historian*

More than 40 years ago, in July of 1951, James Davids, together with his wife and four of their five children, traveled from Bowler, Wisconsin, to Stockbridge, Massachusetts, to visit the homeland of his ancestors. During their stay, they spent several hours in the historical room of the community library gathering information about Mahican Indian history. They made visits to traditional burying grounds and to the graves of respected clan leaders. The Davids family also toured the Mission House museum on Main Street, where they discovered in a back room, carefully protected under glass, a two-volume English bible originally given to the Mahican people of Stockbridge in 1745 by Sir Francis Ayscough, chaplain to the Prince of Wales (*Berkshire Eagle,* 31 July 1951) (fig. 5.1).

When forced in the 1780s to relocate for some 30 years among the Oneida Iroquois in New Stockbridge, New York, the Mahicans who had decided to leave their homeland took their bibles with them. For the next 150 years, as they journeyed westward along what is now remembered as the Stockbridge Trail of Tears, the books went along, well cared

Figure 5.1. One of the Mahican bibles at the Mission House museum in Stockbridge, Massachusetts. "When we saw our bibles again, there was a happy, happy feeling." —*Arminta Chicks Hebert. Photo by Joel Librizzi, the* Berkshire Eagle, *courtesy Charles Bonenti.*

for and kept in an oak chest. At each new campsite and settlement, in Ohio, Indiana, Illinois, and Wisconsin, the bibles were taken up and read from, a visible reminder of the Mahicans' constant struggle to survive and of their continuing cultural identity. Too, the bibles served to connect the Mahican community in their diaspora to the ancestral homeland in western Massachusetts. The Mahicans' reverence for their bibles was mentioned by a visitor to their 1830s community on the Fox River in Wisconsin: "I saw yesterday a Bible in their church, which is saved in a kind of ark of the covenant and is one of the finest Bible exemplars I ever saw" (*Stockbridge Bible*, p. 13).[1]

The bibles were looked after continuously over the next century, even as Mahican communities fragmented, relocated, and rejoined in response to local racism, acts of violence, and shifting federal and state policies. Sometime after 1911, the bibles were placed for safekeeping in a local Presbyterian church in Wisconsin. In 1930, this church's dwindling and predominantly non-native congregation voted unanimously to sell the bibles and an associated pewter communion set for $1,000. The buyer was Mabel Choate, who was establishing a museum in Stockbridge, Massachusetts, as a memorial to her parents and to John Sergeant, one of the founders of the 1730s mission to the Mahican Indians. Choate had restored and then lived in the house once inhabited by Sergeant's family; in 1948 she deeded the house and all its contents, including the bibles, to the Trustees of Reservations, who own and operate the Mission House museum today.

The Mahican community living in and around Red Springs and Bartelme townships, Wisconsin, in the 1930s knew nothing of the sale of their bibles. During the Great Depression years, which saw the dramatic decline of the state's logging industry, many Mahicans were unemployed and threatened with foreclosure on their houses (Mochon 1968:206). Some elders remembered and spoke of the bibles; others lost track of where they had been placed, assuming they were in a bank vault in nearby Shawano. It was even rumored that the Smithsonian Institution had them. So when James Davids returned from Stockbridge with the news of his discovery, his neighbors responded with excitement and anger as well as many unanswered questions. Decades later, in the 1960s and early 1970s, other Mahican families made the trip east to visit the ancestral homelands. Each group returned talking of its excitement and happiness at seeing "these books that our ancestors used over and over through their tedious and dangerous and bitter years of having to leave home after home" (*Stockbridge Bible*, p. 12).

"And we're going to get our Bibles back"

The Stockbridge Mahican Tribal Council wrote to the directors of the Trustees of Reservations in 1975, formally requesting the return of the bibles and communion set to "their rightful owners." In reply, the organization stated that custody of the Mahicans' cultural patrimony could not be relinquished without a court decree because the bibles had been given to the trustees by Mabel Choate to be held for "the benefit of the public." Throughout the next 15 years, as Mahican people continued their efforts, the validity of their claims, as well as the moral responsibilities of the trustees, was debated and written about in both communities.

Even as final resolution drew closer, some Mahicans remained understandably cautious, impatient, and skeptical. It was obvious to them that their bibles would be repatriated only because their claim of ownership was supported by clearly incontestable and legally compelling evidence. An inscription inside the first volume reads, in part, that the bibles were given for "the use of the Congregation of Indians, at or near Housatonnoc in a vast wilderness . . . and [are] to remain to the use of the successors, of those Indians, from Generation to Generation" (*Stockbridge Bible*, p. 1). Without this explicit language—suppose the inscription had been lost or destroyed as the Mahicans were continually displaced?— their legitimate ownership could easily have been dismissed as a traditional belief or story and thus made to seem inadmissible in court.

Imagine that such a legal struggle did take place and that historians and anthropologists were called upon to testify about the continuities in Mahican traditions, the contested meanings of the bibles, and the cultural survival of native peoples in New England. What might have been heard? Considering what has happened in similar circumstances (see Clifford 1988) and what has been written to date, some authorities would have talked about acculturation and assimilation instead of resistance, positing the idea that the Stockbridge Mahicans had "abandoned many aboriginal cultural patterns" long before the 1730s (Mochon 1968:213). Or they would have spoken of factionalism instead of persistent efforts to maintain a native identity (Brasser 1978; Mochon 1968). Few would have been willing to admit under oath that colonialist practices, sometimes based upon wrongheaded anthropological and archaeological models, continue to marginalize and misrepresent the lives and experiences of Indian people. There might also have been witnesses who insisted that the traditional histories of native peoples are seldom "factually" supportable or "truthful" (in Washburn's words [1987]). In effect, the long-term existence and cultural integrity of the Mahican people would have been disputed and quite possibly undermined. Thus, their desire to have the bibles returned might have been represented as a spurious and ingenuine act undertaken by people whose claims to an Indian identity were at best, in the words of James Clifton (1990), a "recent cultural invention."

Seen in this way, the Mahicans' persistent effort toward the return of their bibles becomes yet another chapter in an almost 500-year history of prejudice and alienation. This sort of struggle is well known to the Mahican people and their kin, as are the cultural memories through which they preserve and share a knowledge of how their ancestors survived colonialism, maintained and enriched living traditions, and nurtured an enduring identity in place after place, homeland after homeland (Lamb Richmond 1994; Mochon 1968). It is their words and voices that can tell us what might have happened and that will teach us how to see and confront the interpretive silences between the lines of history and a rigorously written scientific archaeology.

What follows is an initial effort to think and write alternative, unofficial "counterhistories" of and against colonialism in New England. Our goal is to illuminate the lives and experiences of native people while challenging how those same lives and experiences are so often still misrepresented. We use, necessarily, a critical, confrontational voice because these misrepresentations are much more than mistakes to be corrected or failures to be forgiven. The writing of history and the doing of archaeology continue to affect (and disrupt) the lives and futures of native people and thus to impact everyone committed to building more open, culturally democratic communities.

"After the chuh-ko-thuk, or white people, settled amongst them"

Beyond the bibles themselves, the conflict just sketched encompasses history and alternative histories: New England history (and anthropology), for generations written almost exclusively by non-native people, and traditional histories written and remembered for far longer by Mahican people who, it seems, have always had to contest a dominant history and its misrepresentations—they call it "reading between the lines." For instance, a 1991 article in the popular *Berkshire Magazine* (Ericson 1991), although appropriately titled "The Latest of the Mahicans" (thereby correcting the myth of extinction nurtured by James Fenimore Cooper and later by Hollywood writers), dismissively characterizes eighteenth-century native society as disrupted, disoriented, and politically unstable (see Brasser 1974, 1978 for a scholarly confirmation of this story). Considering this historical background, the article continues, it is not surprising that Mahican Indians so willingly participated in John Sergeant's "novel experiment" to build a "civilized," bicultural Christian community in a six-square-mile village called Stockbridge. There, the writer enthuses, native people were to be "protected from further corruption" while being taught by white families the "skills they would need to prosper in an irrevocably changing world" (Ericson 1991:21).

By ignoring obvious evidence of Mahican resistance to and persistent concerns about their being missionized and resettled (Axtell 1985: 196–204; Mynter 1987), Ericson implies that the Indian people of Stockbridge willingly participated in the colonialist efforts while renouncing their traditions and beliefs. Moreover, because John Sergeant's character and sociopolitical purposes are left unexamined in the article—he did, after all, speak incessantly of the need to "root out their vicious habits" and "promote humanity among them" (Sergeant 1743)—the dark and disturbing forces of colonialism remain hidden from contemporary view.

With these silences, Ericson's article remains faithful to the ways in which histories of Berkshire communities and other Massachusetts towns have been written for more than 150 years. Beginning in 1829 with a county history compiled by an association of Congregational

91

ministers and continuing for the next century (see Jones 1854; MacLean 1928; Smith 1869; Taylor 1882), Stockbridge missionaries are celebrated for their successes in Christianizing and educating the Indians and thus transforming them into "respectable and industrious citizens" (Taylor 1882:67). At the same time, the hard work and self-reliant individualism of the colonial settlers, mostly men, are pointedly praised, often by contrast to the character of the Indians, who are usually stereotyped as "savage, uncivilized, and lazy" (Smith 1869:43–45) or as speaking only in a "parrot fashion" because of "limited brain power" (Sedgwick and Marquand 1939:1–24).

Baneful representations like these were common in the community histories written throughout western Massachusetts during the later nineteenth and early twentieth centuries. A study of such histories in the Connecticut River valley, east of the Berkshire region (Handsman 1991b), reveals a set of adjectives used redundantly to describe Native Americans: warlike, treacherous, lazy, thieving, quarrelsome, constantly drunk. Consistently Indians were portrayed as people unable to profit from the benefits of civilization brought to them by men like John Sergeant of Stockbridge.

Many of these histories were written after 1850 as the communities of western Massachusetts were urbanized and industrialized (Merchant 1989). Between 1860 and 1900, for example, the population of Great Barrington increased almost 100 percent while that of Pittsfield grew more than 150 percent. By 1895, both towns had become commercial and industrial centers (Wilkie and Tager 1991:35–36). At the same time, the cultural landscapes of western Massachusetts became increasingly diverse as large numbers of immigrants came to work as unskilled laborers and skilled craftsmen in Berkshire manufactories. Foreign-born workers accounted for more than half the labor force in the region's paper mills by 1870; 10 years later, almost one-third of such workers were native-born of foreign parents (McGaw 1987:290–93). Prejudice against these newcomers was common. W. E. B. DuBois wrote of his African-American childhood in Great Barrington as a time when the Irish, their Catholicism, and their "dirty, stinking slums" were the target of everyone else's jokes and ridicule: "The racial angle was more clearly defined against the Irish than against me," he remembered (DuBois 1986 [1940]:563).

Nevertheless, these newcomers persisted. As their numbers and wealth grew throughout western Massachusetts, they increasingly challenged the political power and social status of the white middle class, affluent gentry farmers, and wealthy factory owners. In response, this elite turned to the past and made obvious the "bravery and contributions" of each town's early colonial settlers, in order to legitimize their class positions and policies. Beginning in 1844 with the Berkshire Jubilee (Birdsall 1959:314–22) and continuing into the 1930s, when many communities celebrated their bicentennials through historic pageants (Glassberg 1990), the elites systematically glorified the colonial past while making explicit their genealogical connections to those who lived then. In a supplement to the history of Great Barrington (MacLean 1928), for example, biographical notes about an early colonial aristocracy were inextricably mixed with those of their descendants—the merchants, manufacturers, and bankers who wanted to control the town's economic destiny. Indeed, the chapters concerning "notable citizens of the past" spoke only of men who were native-born, old-time New Englanders.

As the identity of the elites was now explicitly joined to that of the colonialists, it was necessary for them to do more than simply honor their ancestors. They also felt compelled to defend, or at least explain away, the colonists' more reprehensible actions. The result was that the histories of Mahican peoples in the Berkshires were hidden and denied. Some writers, for example, arrogantly insisted that the Native American presence there was impermanent and sparse, beyond even the "ordinary meagreness of Indian populations" (Smith 1869:43). Saying the same thing differently, a 1926 history of western Massachusetts confidently described pioneer Berkshire County as an unbroken wilderness of dense, undisturbed forests (Lockwood et al. 1926). Some historians, however, told a somewhat different story (Taylor 1882).

Charles Taylor of Great Barrington (1882), himself a dedicated avocational archaeologist, stated that although there were few Indians in the Berkshires at the time of colonial settlement, their numbers "formerly had been quite numerous." Furthermore, he argued, Indian peoples had dwelt here "for a very long term of years," as evidenced "by their many places of interment" and by the "great numbers of their utensils" that are still found by local residents. The pottery fragments, numerous burials, a bedrock corn mortar and stone pestle, and the stone fishing weir preserved near a local factory were all unquestionable evidence for him of the prehistoric existence of a "very considerable Indian population" (Taylor 1882:50–52). According to Taylor, however, none of these archaeological sites could have been occupied and used by Mahican people because their presence did not substantially predate that of the colonists. He insisted, in fact, that there were only eight or ten Mahican families in the entire southern Berkshires when the Stockbridge Mission was founded in 1734.

By thus underrepresenting the number of native people, as well as denying their early and continuing presence, Berkshire County's historians argued that their colonial ancestors settled lands only sparsely occupied and scarcely used. And because there were so few Mahican Indians living there in the early eighteenth century, or so they argued, the effects of colonial settlement on native people were assumed to have been both negligible and short-lived.

This same, seemingly trustworthy argument had been used somewhat earlier by Charles Allen, attorney general of Massachusetts, in his 1870 *Report on the Stockbridge Indians*. Writing in response to a petition from Stockbridge Mahicans living in Wisconsin, Allen (1870:3) dismissed their request for an allowance, declaring that the state had already, and for a long time, aided the Mahicans "by its watchful guardianship." The state must not make itself responsible for land deeds given earlier for which little or no consideration was paid. It did not really matter, Allen argued, that the country was never rightfully obtained. After all, long before the colonial settlement of the Berkshires, the Mahicans "had become reduced in number and scattered" (Allen 1870:23).

Significantly, such nineteenth-century misrepresentations are now being corroborated and thus made to seem more scientifically valid and objective through two archaeological models of late prehistoric and postcontact land use and settlement proposed for the Berkshires. In one study (Shaw et. al. 1987), early Mahican peoples are redefined as Connecticut River Algonkians who occupied and used the lands of the Berkshires only on a seasonal basis for hunting and gathering. The second model tries to interpret the undeniable and highly visible historic Mahican settlement around Stockbridge as a recently arrived community of native people whose purpose was to procure beaver pelts for sale at trading posts along the Connecticut and Hudson rivers (see project summaries in Hasenstab 1989:5–6).

Among Mahican peoples, counterhistories, both oral and written, have existed for a long time. In 1734, as John Sergeant traveled north to begin his work in Stockbridge, his Mahican Indian interpreter-guides stopped along the Housatonic River somewhat north of the Massachusetts border. There they walked into the woods until they reached a "large heap of stones," already, according to Sergeant, more than ten cart-loads in size. As was their custom, the Mahicans placed more stones on this memorial pile every time they passed (Butler 1946). When questioned by Sergeant, they explained that "their fathers used to do so, and they do it because it was the custom of their fathers" (Hopkins 1753:11; Taylor 1882:44–48).

Somewhat later, in the 1790s, another body of Mahican oral tradition was recounted to Hendrick Aupaumut, himself a Stockbridge Mahican, presumably by elders then living among the Oneida Iroquois (Belknap and Morse 1796). These stories told of the ancient origins of the Mahicans and spoke of how their ancestors came to the traditional home- lands in eastern New York and western Massachusetts a long time ago. There they found abundant game and fish and rich planting fields: "They seldom felt much want and were very well contented." After "the chuh- ko-thuk, or white people, settled amongst them," the story continues, "they were subject to many disorders and began to decay" (Jones 1854: 15–16). Unlike the town histories written so frequently after 1850, the Mahican traditions make obvious and confront the catastrophic effects of colonialist policies of expansion and occupation. The very fact that such oral histories and cultural memories continued to exist and to be passed on to succeeding generations also means that the Mahicans had not renounced or repudiated their traditions as desired by John Sergeant.

Illuminating the Hidden Histories of Homelands

Although the colonialist image of an occupied and untamed wil- derness persists today, in reality there were a series of ancestral Mahican homelands spread along the entire length of the Housatonic River valley in the seventeenth century. The numerous burials and communal ceme- teries frequently disturbed by nineteenth-century farmers and house builders in Great Barrington (Nicholas and Mulholland 1987:22–33; Tay- lor 1882:50–54) indicate that the core of one such homeland was located along the river between that town's center and Stockbridge. Additional homeland cores, including that associated with the Weantinock Indian homeland in New Milford (fig. 5.2), are situated along the river in north- western Connecticut and were the focus of the Fort Hill project, a long- term archaeological study undertaken by the American Indian Archaeo- logical Institute between 1987 and 1992 (Handsman 1990, 1991a).

As happened in the Berkshires, the long-term presence of Indians in northwestern Connecticut was denied by nineteenth-century histo- rians, who, using John DeForest's imagery (1851:45–68), characterized the region as a wilderness frontier. The misrepresentation endures today (Handsman and Silberman 1991). Two 1987 maps showing "tribal loca- tions" in 1625 still leave this part of Connecticut empty and uninhabited (Eisenhardt 1987; Lavin 1987). In addition, a recent archaeological study in Canaan, midway between New Milford and Stockbridge, insists that the area was "little used by various groups of Indians" in later prehis- tory (Connecticut Archaeological Survey 1989). Yet archaeological signs

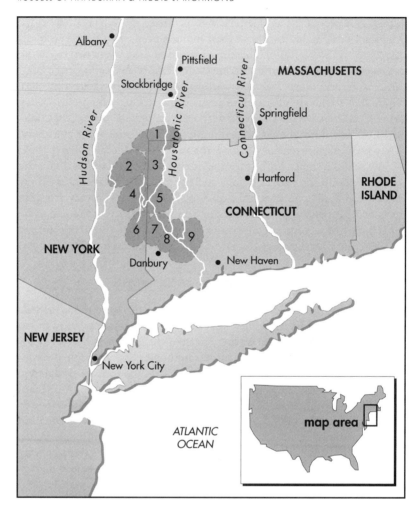

Figure 5.2. Some of the traditional Native American homelands along the upper Housatonic River. Key: 1, the Mahican homeland, where Skatehook was, around Sheffield, Massachusetts; 3, homeland of the Indian people of present-day Sharon and Salisbury, Connecticut; 5, the ancestral Schaghticoke homeland around Kent, Connecticut, where the Schaghticoke reservation is located today; 7, the Weantinock homeland, focus of the Fort Hill project; 8, one of the Pootatuck Indian homelands in present-day Southbury, Connecticut, where the traditional settlement of Pootatuck Wigwams was located. The other homelands were occupied by Mahican and Paugussett peoples, kin of the Schaghticoke and Weantinock.

of long and enduring settlement traditions are common throughout the region. The Edward H. Rogers collection from greater New Milford, once housed at the American Indian Archaeological Institute, contains numerous triangular points of chert and quartz, drilled and incised pendants, and clay pipes recovered from plowed fields earlier in the twentieth century. Together with the cultural memories of the valley's First Peoples and clues gathered from archival documents, these archaeological assemblages are helping make more visible the ancestral homelands of the Weantinock and their Mahican kin.

Typically, the core of each homeland was more than ten square miles in extent and contained one or two important settlement places, often located at long-used fishing sites. There, clan ceremonies and elders' councils were held. Extensive cornfields were nearby, as were sacred sites such as cemeteries, memorial piles, and sweat lodges used for curing (Butler 1945). Throughout the core area and surrounding spaces of each homeland stood dozens of wigwams, alone, in pairs, or in small hamlets not very different in size from a traditional meeting place (Handsman 1990).

The people who lived in a homeland were joined to one another and to their kin in other homelands by enduring social and economic relations organized and mediated through a system of matrilineal descent (Brasser 1974:6–9). The principles of matrilineality were still central to Mahican everyday life in the eighteenth century and were therefore commonly observed, though not well understood, by John Sergeant. For example, after seeing one family quarrel, he reported that "the parting of man and wife is a very common thing." In such cases, "tis their law [the Mahicans'] that the children and all household stuff belong to the woman. . . . The man, according to their custom, has no right to the children, any more than any other person whatever" (in Hopkins 1911:45).

Among the Mahicans, and presumably among all their kin along the Housatonic River, there were three matriclans—the Bear, the Wolf, and the Turtle—whose social connectedness was, in the words of Hendrick Aupaumut, "ever united as one family" (Jones 1854:22). In every homeland, each clan was probably represented by localized segments: a dozen or more households, with members from perhaps all three clans, would have inhabited larger settlements while smaller groups of wigwams might be lived in primarily by one clan. Thus clan relations were localized within and around homelands as well as regionalized well beyond each homeland. An extensive network of paths linking people belonging to the same clans was used, for example, by those living in the Weantinock homeland to visit kin and participate in clan ceremonies in Mahican homelands in eastern New York and western Massachusetts.

John Sergeant himself recognized the importance of the enduring relations within and among clans when he reported that "it is a custom among the Indians not to proceed in any affair of importance [such as the decision to permit Sergeant to settle with them] till they have the consent of the several Clans belonging to the Nation" (quoted in Mochon 1968: 192). Through such close and enduring clan relations and the political alliances nurtured by them, it was both symbolically and actually possible for native people to communicate up and down the length of the Housatonic River. There is a long-standing tradition among the native people of the Housatonic Valley that describes this practice: "The Indians of New Milford were on friendly terms with the Schaghticokes of Kent, the Pomeraugs [the Pootatuck] of Woodbury, the Bantams of Litchfield, and the Weantanaugs [a local Mahican group] of Salisbury. It is said that by a system of calls that could be heard from one mountain-top station to another and repeated, an alarm could be conveyed down the [upper Housatonic] river in three hours" (quoted from a traditional story reprinted in the *New Milford Times,* 2 October 1924).

The origins of many traditional homelands and the clan relations that wove them together lie in the distant past. More than 3,000 years ago, native people throughout southern New England began to settle into some areas more permanently than they had previously (a pattern of increased sedentism) while intensifying trade networks and formalizing social relations across the region (Bernstein 1990; Dincauze 1990). Long-used locations on the landscape, such as traditional fishing places, became sites of sacred activity as communal cemeteries were created and then used by successive generations (Handsman 1991b:16–21). Caches of finely chipped bifaces, sometimes made from "exotic" lithic materials, were often placed with the dead or deposited in nearby freshwater springs to mark the symbolic importance of these places. The caches themselves were continually exchanged between clans or clan leaders to cement their social obligations and political alliances (Loring 1985). Somewhat later, these sacred sites and traditional meeting places became the cores of ancestral homelands that are remembered and visited today.

Metichawon, located along the falls at the junction of the Housatonic and Still rivers in the Weantinock homeland, was used as a traditional fishing site and sacred place long before the coming of white people. Archaeological evidence suggests that this locality began to be visited, at first perhaps on a seasonal basis, more than 3,000 years ago. Over successive millennia, settlements became more permanent; by the seventeenth century Metichawon was the residence of one of the Weantinocks' important clan leaders. Today, this long-term pattern of settlement and sacredness is represented by an extensive archaeological record covering more than 50 acres (Handsman 1991a).

The archaeological visibility of places such as Metichawon, like that of the memorial piles built across Indian New England, is evidence of how the cultural meanings of homelands have survived for thousands of years. Yet despite the enduring importance of homelands to Indian people, their cultural meanings and historical presence are often obscured or ignored by regional archaeologists. For example, when New England archaeologists study the late prehistoric period (between 1,000 and 1,500 years ago), they rarely write about ancestral homelands. Instead, one reads stories about decreased mobility, changes in the utilization of habitats, or the intensification of trade networks (Feder 1984; Lavin 1988; McBride and Bellantoni 1982). Indian people themselves are rarely mentioned. Indeed, the language of scientific analysis and interpretation is so dehumanized that it becomes easy to forget that the archaeological record represents the memories and heritages of living people.

> I wish I could think of a better term to provide for gathering. Because when people think of gathering, well, we're going to gather berries or we're going to gather nuts. . . . And it's not given the importance that it should be given, because in terms—I mean, the women were responsible for the gathering of plants; they had to know a great deal. . . . My grandmother had a lot of knowledge, for example, about plant life and how they were used in terms of medicines and foods and things. And I know some of these things.
> —Trudie Lamb Richmond[2]

That very same archaeological language can also prevent or inhibit the exploration of continuing traditions of settlement and land use in ancestral homelands. Archaeologists normally assume that Mahican peoples and their kin, including the Schaghticoke and Weantinock, lived in centrally located, nucleated villages of between three and sixteen bark-covered long houses and dome-shaped wigwams; population levels varied between 45 and 260 people (Brasser 1978; Snow 1980: 88–90, 319–35). Such settlements are understood to be well above the threshold of archaeological visibility. Yet New England archaeologists have only rarely discovered late prehistoric villages (Thorbahn 1988), and their maps of regional site densities strongly suggest that many interior regions in southern New England were either unoccupied or used solely on a seasonal basis between 1,000 and 300 years ago (see Thomas 1976 for an important exception).

But in the Weantinock homeland there were no large nucleated or stockaded villages. Instead, numerous small hamlets, paired wigwams, and isolated houses were present everywhere. Even the traditional meeting places located in the homeland's core were small, consisting of a few wigwams and one long council house inhabited by a respected clan leader. One of the conceptual and methodological challenges of the Fort Hill project was to develop a systematic approach to the archaeology of these almost invisible settlements. Excavations in 1986 at the late prehistoric Weantinoge site along the Still River in Brookfield clarified the issue of size and spatial organization (Handsman and Maymon 1987). The artifact density there was low, and an initial sampling interval in excess of 10 meters would have missed the site. Features uncovered during block excavations, including pits, ash lenses, and post molds, suggested that between one and three wigwam floors were present in less than 600 square meters. The Weantinock homeland once contained dozens of such settlements.

Fieldwork in 1990 provided an additional opportunity to study the archaeological scale of Weantinock Indian wigwams. By excavating closely spaced lines of test pits across a terrace of the Still River, a previously unknown, late prehistoric settlement (site 96-026) was discovered. This site is represented by thin-walled, well-fired pottery sherds, chert and quartz tools, and features including post molds and charcoal stains. Shovel testing at site 96-026 was conducted in two successive phases, during which the sampling interval between transects was reduced from 10 meters to 5. This resulted in the identification of a second wigwam floor or group of floors, suggesting that even a "tight" testing interval of 7 to 10 meters may not ensure the discovery of such settlements (Handsman 1990). Unless New England archaeologists revise their conceptual models of Native American settlement and the field methodologies reflected by them, our maps will continue to misrepresent traditional homelands as wilderness areas, scarcely occupied and barely used.

By the early eighteenth century, affordable land in many parts of colonial New England was becoming scarce as affluent merchants and farmers continually enlarged the size and value of their private holdings. Wealthy landowners, often acting in concert with speculators as well as with scarcely propertied people, petitioned the General Courts of Massachusetts and Connecticut for permission to explore poorly known "frontier" regions (Akagi 1924). Although the colonists' maps of these areas did not show native settlements, most would-be explorers realized that these lands were already occupied. So long as the petitioners could show evidence that they had incontestable "deeds" from Native Americans, however, colonial courts routinely permitted them to form groups of proprietors who would then decide how the lands of each new town were to be divided and used.

In reality, the documents the colonists (and later historians) referred to as deeds were often carefully worded agreements to share the use of homelands and resources. In them, native people consistently reserved for themselves the rights to collect firewood, hunt and fish, use their planting fields, and even build wigwams on the colonists' common pastures (Handsman 1991b:19–21; Wright 1905). In a 1724 "deed," Mahican people in the southern Berkshires agreed to allow colonists to use a "certain tract upon the Housatonic River" while reserving some lands for themselves, including the locality they called "Skatehook," a traditional meeting place and sacred site (Taylor 1882:15–16). Almost 40 years later, many of the same Mahicans sent a petition to the Massachusetts legislature protesting a 1762 act that had authorized the formation and public sale of 10 new townships in the Berkshires. "They were the owners of the lands in question," the Mahicans insisted, reminding the colonists that neither "they nor their ancestors had ever been at war with the English or dispossessed of said lands" (Taylor 1882:72; also see Wright 1905:116–19, 184–87). A committee was appointed to "inquire further into the Indians' title"; its report said the Mahican Indians could not offer "sufficient evidence" to support their claims. A recommendation was made and it was so ordered that a sum of 1,000 pounds be made available to keep the Indians "quiet and in good temper" (Taylor 1882:73). In this way the proprietors and settlers of the Berkshires hoped to persuade Mahican peoples to forget and abandon the homelands where the bones of their ancestors were buried.

Similar histories of colonialist appropriation and native resistance were being played out almost simultaneously in the homelands of the Weantinock and their kin along the Housatonic in northwestern Connecticut (Handsman 1990; Wojciechowski 1985). For example, in 1737 the colonial legislature authorized the establishment of six new towns in northwestern Connecticut. Fifty shares of each town were then sold at public auction to speculators as well as to those who planned to resettle (Akagi 1924:197–99; Grant 1972). In less than five years, local Mahicans—long-time, permanent residents of the region—began to complain that they were being defrauded of "their reserved and unsold lands," of which they were the proper owners. After a visit to northwestern Connecticut, a legislative committee reported that there had been no deception involved; the Indians had simply "misunderstood the bargain." Although 50 acres were subsequently reserved for native use, the conflicts continued for almost 10 years. In 1751, colonial settlers in the town of

Sharon wrote to the General Assembly expressing their concern over the uneasiness of some Mahicans who were "very angry with those [colonialists] who are the rightful owners of the land" (Sedgwick 1898:36–40).

Earlier, in the beginning of the eighteenth century, the first colonial settlers had arrived in the Weantinock homeland in New Milford. Soon after, in 1702–1703, a deed was signed in which the Weantinock people reserved for themselves "the use of their present planting field and a privilege of fishing at the Falls," the place known traditionally as Metichawon (Wojciechowski 1985:135–36). Even after they were dispossessed of much of their homeland, Weantinock people continued to travel to Metichawon to fish for eels and shad, using the privilege they had reserved for themselves. In the 1770s, local residents formed the Cove Fishing Company. Shareholders were guaranteed a place along the river for spring fishing. Native people were not shareholders; nevertheless, they continued to fish at the falls until 1877, when the building of a dam in the lower Housatonic irreparably injured the shad fishing upstream. The settlement of damages between the Housatonic Water Company and the Cove Fishing Company never mentioned the rights of the Weantinock and their kin (Handsman 1991a:6).

In the early eighteenth century, the Weantinock planting fields covered dozens of acres along the Housatonic; today the fields are a well-preserved archaeological site opposite present-day New Milford village (Carlson and Handsman 1993). Used primarily for corn, these extensive fields probably were worked by both clans and local communities according to traditional calendars based on the lunar cycle. Native people would have set the corn seed in late spring, formed the hills in early summer, celebrated the arrival of the newly ripening green corn in late summer, and harvested the crops in early fall, storing large surpluses for exchange and ceremonial feasts (Butler 1948; Lamb Richmond 1989; Thomas 1976). In the fields, Weantinock elders would have reminded their children of the communal values of working together and sharing, telling them the story of how corn had once grown from the body of a loving woman:

Glooskap and the First Mother

After the first man and woman became husband and wife a long time ago, there came a famine. The woman asked her husband to take her life and draw her body around an open field. He was hesitant, but after talking with Glooskap, the great teacher, did as she said. The man drew her body until the flesh was worn away, and in the middle of the field they buried her bones. When seven moons had gone by and the husband came again to that place, he saw it all filled with beautiful tall plants. The fruits of the plants tasted sweet and he called it *Skarmunal,* corn. (Anastas 1973:12–14)

Soon after the signing of the 1702–1703 deed, the Weantinocks' planting fields began to be taken away. In the first decade of colonial settlement, the proprietors subdivided the better-drained floodplain soils into tiers of four-and-a-half–acre to five-acre lots. Fifteen acres, ironically called "the land improved by the Indians," were reserved for native use. But even this parcel was soon appropriated and divided into 20 individual pieces, each smaller than an acre. Before 1730—less than three decades after initial colonization—the Weantinock and their kin no longer had access to their ancestral planting fields.

Throughout southwestern Massachusetts and northwestern Connecticut this history of colonialism was repeated over and over as the eighteenth century continued. As they were alienated from their traditional planting fields, as mills and dams were built, disturbing long-used fishing sites, and as pigs and cattle were allowed to graze freely in marshes and groves of nut trees, native peoples were being forced to abandon their homelands.

"According to our law and custom"

That Native Americans sometimes consciously decided to continue living in their ancestral homelands is a fact seldom mentioned in town histories or in the writings of colonial historians today (Merrell 1989). Yet even as parts of Mahican and Weantinock homelands were appropriated, surveyed, divided, and fenced, some native people resisted by making themselves less visible, resettling their families and communities beyond the fringes of colonial settlements (Handsman 1989). Less accessible settings such as the tops of ridge lines and small upland valleys became new home sites. Often such places were in disputed areas along the borders between the colonies of Massachusetts or Connecticut and New York, far removed from administrative centers. Because, at least initially, no one colony had systematic knowledge of or control over these lands, or access to the resources in them, those who lived there—Native Americans, African Americans, and others who were dispossessed—often survived as cohesive multicultural communities into the twentieth century (Feder 1994; Wetherbee and Taylor 1986).

Such localities had long been familiar to Indian people; their paths had traversed them for centuries, linking hamlets in the valleys to locations where raw materials (stone outcrops), food resources (groves of nut trees and sugar maples), or medicinal herbs had been gathered for generations. In these newly occupied places, Native Americans could continue to live within or close to ancestral homelands without making their presence known—unless they so desired.

The existence of such historic communities cannot be documented with any certainty from the records and maps of the colonialists. Similarly, material signs of their presence are either unrecognized or misinterpreted today by those who continue to assume that Native Americans were not an integral part of New England's social landscape after the early 1700s. Yet archaeological sites representing just such enduring traditions of settlement have already been excavated and can be used to aid in the recognition of further evidence. For example, the limited assemblage recovered from the Pootatuck Wigwam site (130-27), located along the Housatonic River in Southbury, Connecticut, includes native-made ceramics, well-worn quartz tools, pieces of cut-up copper or brass kettles reshaped into pendants, gun flints perhaps reused as scrapers, and European ceramics (primarily salt-glazed stonewares and lead-glazed red earthenwares from broken cups and mugs). Normally archaeologists would assume that this assemblage represented a prehistoric lithic scatter overlain by and mixed with historic artifacts redeposited from nearby colonial farmsteads. Oral tradition and a wealth of archival documents, however, make clear that Pootatuck Wigwams was a well-known traditional meeting place and a sacred site (like Metichawon) occupied by clan relations of the Weantinock people in the late seventeenth and eighteenth centuries (McBride 1989). According to Cothren (1854:108–109), "in the 19th century, an elderly native woman, then living among her kin at the Schaghticoke reservation, would travel to Southbury to visit the site of Pootatuck Wigwams and the graves of her ancestors. As she stood along the riverbank with tears on her face, she would say, 'There, there is Pootatuck.' "

At the Wigwams site, Pootatuck people continued to live and work as their ancestors had, at the same time interacting with colonial farmers, traders, and trappers who had been a steadily growing presence in the valley for almost a century (Wojciechowski 1985:46–48, 113–31). When seen in this context, the site's supposedly mixed archaeological assemblage actually represents evidence of periodic contacts with colonists and the selective acceptance and integration of modified colonial artifacts into everyday life (see Rubertone 1989). Examples include the cutting up of trade kettles to provide raw materials for pendants and the re-use of gunflints as woodworking tools. The numerous quartz tools were probably made and used predominantly by Pootatuck women and elders, whose interactions with colonists were much less frequent. Indeed, this tool assemblage could even be seen as representing a strategy of resistant accommodation in which some Pootatucks consciously turned away from the colonists' world—modifying locally available stone cobbles for knives and scrapers instead of acquiring metal tools to use—while others maintained contacts necessary for economic survival. Seen this way, the archaeological record at Pootatuck Wigwams cannot be read as a history of gradual social assimilation and cultural loss. Instead, the site can be interpreted as an important and highly visible center for native resistance and the continuation of living traditions, a place whose significance was well remembered by later generations.

Significantly, very similar assemblages have been recovered from the nearby Weantinock homeland along the route of a recently constructed gas pipeline. At least eight sites located in three adjacent towns produced artifact inventories reminiscent of that from Pootatuck Wigwams, including quartz and chert tools, Native American ceramics, and pieces of lead-glazed stonewares (data abstracted from Cassedy et al. 1991). Without hesitation, the project archaeologists interpreted these assemblages as representing prehistoric campsites or lithic reduction stations mixed with "scatters of historic refuse associated with the agricultural use of the land" (quoted from the summary of site 270A-4-1 in Cassedy et al. 1991). Some of these sites, however, can undoubtedly be interpreted as eighteenth-century homesteads or wigwams occupied by Weantinock people who refused to leave their homeland despite the losses they had suffered.

Other Native Americans did leave, moving to other homelands to live with their kin, often in places of long-standing traditional importance. As native communities in these places slowly increased in size, they became more visible to colonial governments and land companies, who, in turn, wanted to implement policies of assimilation and resettlement. In 1734, John Sergeant began missionizing in one of the Mahican homelands centered along the Housatonic River in southern Berkshire County, Massachusetts. Although later community historians paternalistically celebrated his efforts to bring civilization and Christianity to the Indians, both Sergeant and his financial backers (the New England Company) knew better. Well aware of the interconnectedness of Mahican peoples in the Berkshires and eastern New York, they hoped to extend their influence and that of the Massachusetts colony into disputed territory while establishing economic hegemony over the region's resources and lands (Mandell 1982:5–11). John Sergeant himself argued in 1749 that the educating of this "barbarous, uncultivated people" would prove to be a "means of engaging them more firmly in the British interest" (quoted in Hopkins 1911:148–49).

When John Sergeant first arrived, some of the Mahicans inhabited two small meeting places, each identified with a respected clan leader, and others lived dispersed throughout the homeland in hamlets consisting of three to five wigwams and a small garden. For the next 15 years, until his death, Sergeant continually railed against this tradition of settlement, which did not permit him sufficient control over or daily contact with the Indians. No sooner had he arrived, in fact, than Sergeant (see Hopkins 1753:9–10) insisted that the Mahicans "come together in one place" in order that the Sabbath be better attended and native children "taught on week days." Although a "public house" was built and then encircled by "small huts" (wigwams), Mahican people did not forget their customary obligations or repudiate their traditions. They insisted on "retiring to their own places" in late winter to do maple sugaring and again in late spring to plant and nurture their corn (Axtell 1985:198; Brasser 1978:207; Hopkins 1911:23, 25, 28). Native men were absent more frequently, hunting and trapping in distant parts of the homeland and working on Dutch farmsteads. The food acquired when hunting and the goods men received from their furs or labor, combined with what was grown, caught in the rivers, and gathered by others, provided adequate support for many Mahican families. They in turn could preserve some degree of social separation and cultural autonomy despite the missionary's efforts.

It soon became obvious that Mahican traditions were going to persist, so in 1735 John Sergeant and others developed a plan to establish a mission settlement (the Stockbridge Indian Mission) "in the great meadow above the mountain," where all the Indians could live and work as farmers together (Hopkins 1753:43–51). In order to accomplish this, it was necessary to effect transfers of lands involving Massachusetts colonists, Dutch settlers, and the Mahicans. At a meeting in April 1735, a clan leader expressed some concern: his people could not show clear title for some of the lands being considered for exchange. "If anyone should insist upon anything more than the testimony of living witnesses," Umpachense confessed, "they could prove no title at all." However, he went on, "their [the Mahicans'] titles were good, according to their law and custom in such cases" (Hopkins 1753:49). Despite assurances from Colonel John Stoddard, who, when he died in the 1750s, had become one of the region's wealthiest merchants and gentleman farmers (Sweeney 1984: 233), the Mahican leader was not convinced. What would happen in the future, he wondered, if the children of the colonialists forgot the land "was in great measure given them" and assumed a "superiority over" native people? "What security," he asked, could the Mahicans have "that their children would be free?" (Hopkins 1753:50).

His concerns proved real. Although Mahicans made up a clear majority of Stockbridge's population well past 1760, colonists had gained political control of the town and its elected offices by 1750 (Mandell 1982:20–30). Legislation was passed in the 1760s by the General Court of Massachusetts permitting the English settlers of Stockbridge to tax themselves "exclusive of the Indian inhabitants," thereby sanctioning the division of Sergeant's bicultural community into two unequal parts (Mandell 1982:28). During this same period, as moneys once received from the New England Company and other supporters diminished and as their traditional sources of income and food were denied them, the indebtedness of Mahican peoples rose dramatically (Canning 1894; Mandell 1992:240–44). Increasingly they were forced to sell their lands to discharge debts. Between 1762 and 1772, one-half of all the Mahicans' land in Stockbridge was acquired by colonists (Mandell 1992:245). By 1783, there was little land left to return to after the American Revolution, in which half of Stockbridge's Mahican men lost their lives fighting for the patriots.

The conflict between the indigenous tradition of living apart in homelands, while being woven together by clans, and the colonial aim of resettling Indian people and thus bringing them under control was central to the cant of conquest and resistance in eighteenth-century New England. Connecticut's colonial government attempted to terminate the enduring tradition through legislation. A 1717 act for the more "effectual well ordering" of Indian peoples declared, "Measures shall be used to form villages of the natives, wherein the several families of them should have suitable portions of the land appropriated to them, so that the said portions shall descend from the father to his children, the more to encourage them to apply themselves to husbandry" (reprinted in Kittrie and Wedlock 1986:28). Their purposes, almost identical to those of John Sergeant and his associates (Axtell 1985:196–204; Jones 1854:62–66; Sergeant 1743), were obvious: to redefine and destroy customary communal matriclan relations and to nurture and intensify dependency relationships by creating settlements that would become instrumental to the establishment and workings of formally recognized reservations (Kawashima 1969). Yet such villages were already being created by Indian people in Connecticut and, ironically, were destined to become centers of resistance and cultural survival.

The place known to the Mahicans as Pishgachtigok or Scaticook, along the Housatonic River just south of present-day Kent, Connecticut, was probably an important meeting and fishing site before the early 1700s. As Weantinock and other native peoples living in the so-called "Western Lands" were alienated from their planting fields by the colonists, some families resettled at Scaticook, joining kin who had lived there for generations. Pishgachtigok was at the center of a traditional homeland which overlapped that of the Weantinock (see fig. 5.2). By the early 1740s, the still growing native community there had attracted the attention of Moravian missionaries, who built stone churches at Scaticook and in several nearby Mahican homelands (Beaver 1988:432–33; Brasser 1974:34–35). The Moravians were strangers to New England and thus could rightly claim to be innocent of earlier acts of dispossession and genocide. They were welcomed by traditional leaders, including a man named Gideon Mauwee, especially because they seemed more intent on quietly bringing their beliefs to those who were "disposed to hearken to them" than in converting and "civilizing" entire communities (Axtell 1985:265; Orcutt 1882:132–46).

For almost 20 years, Moravian missionaries preached the gospel at Scaticook, even as the native community continued to maintain and nurture its living traditions (Lamb Richmond 1987, 1994). On numerous occasions, evening services in the church were canceled or poorly attended because traditional ceremonies were being conducted in nearby sweat lodges. As happened at Stockbridge, Schaghticoke people were often absent from the settlement, living beyond the "missionary gaze" in winter hunting camps or visiting kin in nearby Mahican homelands. A series of paths linked the Schaghticoke and Moravian community at Pishgachtigok to other such mission settlements to the west and north, including Shekomeko (near Pine Plains, New York) and Wechquadnack (on Indian Pond near Sharon, Connecticut), where their Mahican kin continued to live. These same paths were used by John Sergeant when he traveled south to preach among the native people in Sharon and Salisbury in northwestern Connecticut, as well as by Schaghticoke people when they went north to attend clan ceremonies and council meetings in Massachusetts. In 1756, after a land sale threatened to cut off one of their traditional paths "into ye Woods" and beyond, the "Chief Sachem and others of the Scaticook Tribe" petitioned the General Assembly to appoint a committee to look into their claims, "that all our grievances may be redressed." They wrote of their patriotism and peacefulness, reminding the government of how they had willingly "encouraged the settlement of English near us by selling our lands for very trifling sums" (quotations from the petition in Wojciechowski 1985:146–47).

Sometimes the Moravians sought to interfere with and disrupt native traditions. The missionaries suggested, for example, that the Schaghticoke organize their labor differently. Instead of entire families moving into the woods to build canoes, perhaps only a few men should go while others gathered raw materials needed for making splint baskets and brooms. For the most part, these ideas were rejected because the Schaghticoke "had always worked together" (Lamb Richmond 1987:135).

In the decades following the establishment of the Moravian mission, the colonial presence in Kent increased substantially; by 1777 there were almost 300 more adult men living in the town than in 1739–40. During this period, many farms began to produce surpluses for resale in local and regional markets (Grant 1972:31–54). Agrarian land uses intensified, as did mining, milling, and lumbering activities. A traveler in 1780 observed, "I have never traveled [in Kent] three miles without meeting a new settlement." Yet "four years ago one might have traveled ten miles in the woods without seeing a single habitation" (quoted in Grant 1972:40). The emergence of agrarian capitalism in Kent and surrounding towns meant that native people now had less access to their traditional fishing sites and planting fields and to the woods where they once hunted and trapped.

These problems were not entirely new. In the early 1750s, the Schaghticoke wrote to the General Assembly complaining that they did not have enough planting ground, their ancestral fields having been appropriated by Kent settlers for use as common pasture: "Your petitioners [the Schaghticoke] have been possessed of a considerable quantity of land of which the white people have got from them and of late the county has surveyed it in Order as [we] apprehend to dispose thereof. [We] have at present for Eighteen Families but a small piece fit for planting which lies between the Haustenick [Housatonic] River and Pachgatgoch Hill which is not sufficient for them to raise corn upon" (1752 petition in Wojciechowski 1985:145, brackets ours).

These changes were also apparent to the Moravians, who encouraged Schaghticoke and Mahican people to manufacture useful household items such as wood-splint baskets, brooms, and wooden bowls (figs. 5.3, 5.4), arguing that their sale would provide additional income necessary for survival (Brasser 1975). In addition, the income would permit native people to become less dependent on their colonial neighbors, whom the Moravians considered intemperate and unscrupulous.

But the production and exchange of wood-splint baskets had another meaning for the Schaghticoke. When given as gifts, in the way caches of finely chipped bifaces were once exchanged, baskets became a way for native people to build and sustain connections with kin who now had to live apart, dispersed throughout the Housatonic Valley (Handsman and McMullen 1987). The mission records from Pishgachtigok (Fliegel 1970)

Figure 5.3. Mahican wooden cup. Carved from an apple tree knot, this cup belonged to "Old Siacus," a Schaghticoke or Weantinock Indian who lived in northern New Milford. After some of his kin moved to the traditional settlement of Scaticook in the 1730s, he continued to live in his people's apple orchard along the Housatonic River in full view of colonial settlers (Heye 1921). Collection of the National Museum of the American Indian, New York City.

contain numerous references to canoe loads of baskets and brooms being paddled down the river. Along the way, native people would stay over with their clan relations, stop at old meeting places now unused, and visit sacred sites where the bones of their ancestors were buried. Some went as far as Stratford, Connecticut, to the mouth of the Housatonic, where today their splint baskets are preserved in the collections of local historical societies.

The Schaghticoke traditions of making and exchanging splint baskets continued through the nineteenth and into the twentieth centuries (Lamb Richmond 1987). Eunice Mauwee (fig. 5.5), a well-known basketmaker and descendant of the eighteenth-century community leader Gideon Mauwee, lived at Scaticook for most of her life. In 1852, at more than 90 years of age, she spoke of her strong attachment to that place,

Figure 5.4. Early nineteenth-century wood-splint baskets made by Jacob Mauwee, Schaghticoke (top), and Molly Hatchet, a Paugussett from farther south on the Housatonic River. Native basketmakers used distinctive techniques of weaving and decoration to represent group and community identities. Collections of the New Milford Historical Society and the American Indian Archaeological Institute.

Figure 5.5. Eunice Mauwee, Schaghticoke (1756–1860). Those who live on the present-day reservation remember Eunice Mauwee as "the grandmother of us all," because the main Schaghticoke families today can all trace genealogical connections to her and her descendants.

saying that she did "not wish to leave it for a single day."[3] Her grave-stone still stands in the small cemetery along the River Road, part of the Schaghticoke Indian reservation in Kent, Connecticut (Handsman and Williamson 1989:33–34).

"That's why it means so much to be a part of Schaghticoke"

In March 1953, the judiciary committee of the General Assembly of Connecticut held public hearings in Hartford concerning a proposed bill whose stated purposes were "to end the second class citizenship of the state's few remaining Indians" and thus "reduce the administrative burden" of state agencies. In response to questions, Clayton Squires of the state welfare department explained why his agency wanted a mandate to redistribute reservation lands. "We have more and more demands," he said, "from people [of color, whom he refused to acknowledge as Indians] to be allowed to build on these reservations and from my investigation they are not the type of citizens we want."[4] If passed and signed into law, the bill would have authorized the dispersal of communally owned lands reserved long ago for native peoples. Some parcels would have been sold at public auction, others incorporated into state forests and parks. The cultural assimilation of the indigenous Indian peoples of Connecti-cut would thus have been hastened (Bee 1990:194–96). As the hearing ended, the bill's supporters remained seated. The 25 or so non-Indians in opposition stood, joining the Schaghticoke, Golden Hill Paugussett, and Mashantucket Pequot people at the rear of the room. The Indians had lis-tened silently as others dismissed their heritage and traditions, declaring that their presence on ancestral lands was no longer relevant, affordable, or meaningful. The bill died in committee.

Some 37 years later, across the street from the state capitol, the Supreme Court of Connecticut heard arguments in 1990 in a case in-volving the Schaghticoke people. What began as a local dispute over log-ging and consensus politics within the reservation community became a highly visible and closely watched legal struggle. Connecticut's then attorney general asked the Supreme Court to overturn an appellate de-cision and restore the state's authority to regulate what happened on the reservation. Although they did not participate in the proceedings, the Schaghticoke wanted the decision to stand, insisting it supported their struggle to achieve sovereignty. The attorney general stated that "there [were] no facts in the record" to support the contention that "a bona fide Schaghticoke tribe has existed since 1790"; nor was there any evi-dence of "cohesiveness" or "common interests" within the community.

Neither had the Schaghticoke people petitioned the federal government "to acknowledge they exist." In an earlier appearance before the appellate court, the attorney general had argued (wrongly) that the Schaghticoke had no permanent place of settlement until 1752, when the colonial government reserved some land at Scaticook for native use.[5]

After review, the Connecticut Supreme Court, in March 1991, remanded the case to the appellate court and then the original trial court, with clearly stated instructions that the judges involved must determine whether the "Schaghticoke Indians are still a tribe" and whether "they have in the past and presently continue to exercise some form of tribal sovereignty." "The record is devoid of evidence," the justices wrote, "as to whether the tribe is still, or has ever been, a cohesive ethnic unit."[6] Thus in 1991, as in 1953 and the later nineteenth century, the Schaghticoke people were told they could have no identity save that given to or forced upon them. Nor could they have any pasts save the ones written and remembered by others. Their living traditions and their cultural memories and stories about resistance would have no legal standing. Their voices, speaking of the place once called Pishgachtigok, would be denied and marginalized as they continued to make a new place for themselves and for their histories.

> Schaghticoke is a harmonious balance of mountainous terrain, thickly forested hills and swamplands; of rocky ledges and streams. And everywhere there are healing plants just waiting for those who know where to look. At one time the air was filled with the sounds of the pounding of ash logs for basket splints. It takes a lifetime to make a basket; a lifetime of growing, of creating and of sharing, to shape what is in your heart; a lifetime filled with customs and traditions. That knowledge is not always visible to the eye. It is so deeply buried in the past. But sometimes only a heartbeat away. There are rare, precious moments when I am privileged to glimpse some of this. That's why it means so much to be a part of Schaghticoke. (Trudie Lamb Richmond, Schaghticoke, quoted in Handsman and Williamson 1989:34)

Conflicts like those between the Schaghticoke Indians and the state of Connecticut or between the Stockbridge-Munsee people and the Trustees of Reservations are often viewed as involving only indigenous people and "the law." But nowadays, struggles for equality and against systematized prejudice increasingly involve the domains of science, cultural politics, knowledge, and writing (Gordimer 1988; Said 1985). In these struggles, which will continue long after 1992 and the supposed "end of history," there is both space and need for scholars to take responsibility for their work and actions and for the consequences of them. Rather than continuing to declare our innocence, we need to see and confront the ways in which our words and actions contribute to the silencing and dispossessing of other people.

Working against colonialism in the future means that we have to interrogate, challenge, and break apart the emerging ideology of cultural difference. This ideology of difference obscures and deflects our critical gaze so that relations between different cultural traditions are not easily seen as matters involving hierarchy, alienation, domination, and control. Instead, the ideology implies that the very real inequalities in power between peoples in the Americas are simply a matter of differing points of view, requiring that we need only learn to be more respectful and tolerant of the "stories" others wish to tell.

As we confront the ideology of cultural difference—the political philosophy of colonialism today—we who are archaeologists will also be helping to open new understandings of Native American history. Archaeologists can help map and thus make visible the cultural landscapes and social relations of ancestral homelands. We can, for example, help document the persistent presence of Mahican peoples in their homelands, countering the myth of abandonment and cultural extinction by exploring historic wigwam and house sites while searching for all the wood-splint baskets that undoubtedly remain hidden and unrecognized in museum collections throughout the Berkshires (Handsman 1994). By learning to do archaeologies of resistant accommodations and living traditions, we will help create a much-needed long-term perspective for understanding the significance of the Mahicans' struggle to get their bibles back.

Some people in Stockbridge, Massachusetts, today dismiss that struggle and the continuing visits by Mahican people from Wisconsin as the work of activists who only recently decided to remember their Indianness and reclaim their heritage. For a long time, they insist, Mahicans were uninterested in their own pasts and histories. There is little truth in these words. In the early nineteenth century, two Mahican Indians "from the far west" came to Stockbridge to visit "the graves and hunting grounds of their ancestors." While there, they visited the mountain where John Sergeant and the Mahican guides had stopped in 1734. The ancient memorial pile could no longer be seen, having been thrown down and desecrated in the late eighteenth century. Nevertheless, "after standing for some time thoughtfully and in silence," each of the Mahicans "cast a stone upon the spot and turned away" (Taylor 1882:47–48).

Today, when Mahican families travel to Stockbridge, they always visit this place on the mountain. They leave behind piles of stones they have brought from their new homelands in Wisconsin. And they gather stones to take back west, where they are placed on coffee tables and mantles and used as doorstops in their homes. Others of these stones end up in the Arvid E. Miller Memorial Library and Museum, where they can now be seen next to the Stockbridge bibles, which have been returned.

NOTES

We want to acknowledge the patience and support of Peter Schmidt and Tom Patterson, who organized the seminar in Santa Fe. We will never forget the experience or those who made it so memorable. Trudie Lamb Richmond dedicates this work to the memory of her Schaghticoke and Mahican ancestors, who struggled to survive the impact of colonialism. Their voices can finally be heard and their histories known. Russ Handsman wishes to thank the staff of the local history rooms at the Stockbridge Library and the Berkshire Athenaeum in Pittsfield for their help. The collection from Pootatuck Wigwams was borrowed from Kevin McBride of the Public Archaeology Survey Team, Anthropology Department, University of Connecticut, and was analyzed by Polly Fiacco, then a research and curatorial assistant at the American Indian Archaeological Institute. Handsman also thanks Trudie Lamb Richmond and Lynne Williamson.

1. The quotation and related background information concerning the bibles' history and the Mahicans' struggle to have them returned are from *The Stockbridge Bible* (1981), a collection of oral histories, extracts from newspapers and correspondence, and selections from books, compiled and published by the Stockbridge-Munsee Historical Committee, Stoughton, Wisconsin.

2. The testimony by Trudie Lamb Richmond is from an oral history interview, "Native American Gathering," collected and transcribed by Jeremy Brecher for Connecticut Public Radio in January 1989. A copy of the transcription and taped show are on file at Connecticut Public Radio, Hartford.

3. From David T. Lawrence's "Biographical Sketch of Eunice Mauwee" (1852), manuscript collection (81808) of the Connecticut Historical Society, Hartford, Connecticut.

4. The testimony of Clayton Squires and background information on the 1953 bill can be found in Minutes of the Hearings before the Judiciary Committee, 1953, volume II, pp. 423–27, Connecticut State Library, Hartford. Relevant newspaper clippings and correspondence are in records of the State Welfare Department, Record Group 19, Box 4, State Archives, Connecticut State Library.

5. The background and legal arguments related to the Schaghticoke case can be found in the following documents: for the appellate review, see (1) "Schaghticoke Indians of Kent, Connecticut v. Keith Potter et al. (7919)," a 1989 consolidated brief and related appendix filed by the attorney general, state of Connecticut, and Leslie A. Carothers, commissioner of environmental protection, with the Appellate Court of the State of Connecticut, Judicial District of Litchfield; and (2) the majority opinion in the above-named case written by Judge Lavery, released on May 16, 1990.

For the State Supreme Court review, see (1) "Schaghticoke Indians of Kent, CT v. Keith Potter et al. (14005)," a 1990 consolidated brief and related appendix filed by the attorney general, state of Connecticut, and Leslie A. Carothers, commissioner of environmental protection, with the Supreme Court of the state of Connecticut; and (2) consolidated brief and related appendix for the above-named case written by William R. Breetz et al. as amicus curiae, Supreme Court of the state of Connecticut. Newspaper accounts include "Connecticut Indian Land in Legal Quandary," *New York Times,* 10 July 1990; "State Power over Indian Tribe in Kent Is Challenged in Ruling," *Litchfield County Times,* 13 July 1990; "Court to tribe: It's all yours," *News-Times of Danbury,* 15 July 1990; and "Day in Court Nears for Kent Indians," *Litchfield County Times,* 2 November 1990.

6. The text of the Connecticut Supreme Court decision in "Schaghticoke Indians of Kent, Connecticut, Inc. v. Keith Potter et al." can be found in *Connecticut Reports,* volume 217. See *Connecticut Law Journal,* 5 March 1991.

Using Archaeology to Remake History in Africa

PETER R. SCHMIDT

A major intellectual concern of African as well as some Africanist scholars since about 1965 has been how to liberate historical knowledge in Africa from the paradigmatic constraints of European historiography and the colonial library (Mudimbe 1988). Attempts have been made to develop new avenues of inquiry, new sources of historical evidence, and new theoretical perspectives. Each of these developments, beginning with an emphasis on African oral traditions and oral history and more recently finding expression in Marxist critiques of African history, has led to important new ways of constructing the African past. Each in its own way, nonetheless, is constrained by theoretical or analytical frameworks that arise out of European epistemologies or that remain bounded by evidence contained within the colonial library.

A prominent paradox in African historical studies is that archaeology's potential for developing alternative histories has not been fully realized. Because most of ancient African history is accessible only through archaeological approaches, there is compelling reason to refocus attention on archaeological constructions of the past as a means to build an independent, authentic, and distinctly African history. At the same time, archaeology is a distinctly Western activity. Its governing paradigms and epistemologies often conflict with African historical needs, views of the past, and ways of structuring time and space. Thus the paradox unfolds: a repertoire of techniques and approaches that promise significant ways of recuperating African pasts heretofore obscured is accompanied by theoretical assumptions that are often out of tune with African sensibilities, needs, and structures. One goal of this chapter is to explore the role archaeology might play in developing alternative histories in Africa and, at the same time, to examine the range of constraints that so far have inhibited this development.

Achieving this goal entails an analysis of the tensions between Western academic archaeology and African academics and folk who both live and make their histories. Is a resolution of the paradox possible? Can African scholars transform archaeological methods to fit their own theoretical positions? Is it possible to chart new pathways along which such developments could occur, and if so, in what domains of inquiry might these new pathways be found? Does Western scholarship have the capacity to listen to and learn from such African departures?

These concerns arise out of my more than two decades of extensive archaeological research and teaching in Africa, primarily in Tanzania but also in Gabon and Cameroon (fig. 6.1). As an American academic, I brought to my first African research in the late 1960s a grounding in history as well as training in the "new" archeology with its logical positivism and regional approach. Although these were my initial intellectual predispositions, my work with oral traditions, indigenous cosmologies, and symbolic systems in Africa profoundly affected my scientific attitude from the beginning of my first fieldwork experience. These experiences inevitably transformed my thinking, taking me beyond processual and postprocessual concepts and leading me naturally to an "angle of vision" from which I aim to deconstruct "taken-for-granted" interpretations of the African past. My approach emphasizes the importance of African contexts and distinctive values of time and space in negotiating interpretations of the African past while it also searches for archaeological signposts that point to common paths of experience—that is, it remains an anthropology concerned with cross-cultural patterns.

It is also important to ask how African and Africanist archaeologists might come together in the development of an archaeology that meets scientific standards yet also conjoins with African values, knowledge, and concepts of time. This essay will emphasize practice and agency as well as discuss some of the problems practitioners of archaeology have confronted in Africa during the post-independence period. Although some imperial and colonial practices of archaeology have been discussed by others (Posnansky 1982; Robertshaw 1990; Trigger 1984, 1990), the issues are worth reexamining inasmuch as African archaeology continues to accept colonial relationships and many Africans and Africanists continue to think and practice in colonial paradigms.

My discussion also includes a short history illustrating how the potential for alternative histories through archaeological agency has been

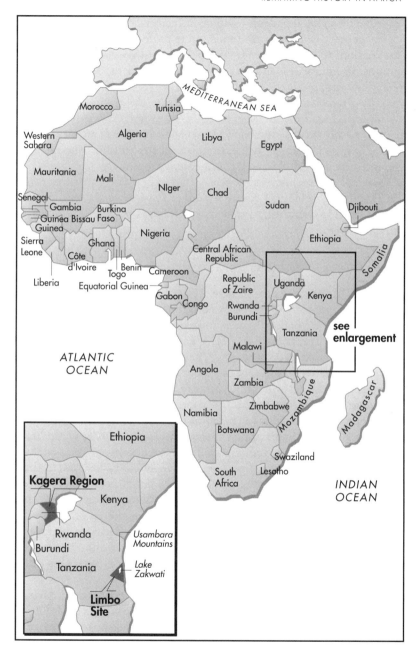

Figure 6.1. Africa. The enlarged area shows regions discussed in chapter 6.

impeded by colonial underdevelopment, financial constraints, and ideo-logical debates. And I examine other, more profound contradictions: the domination of archaeology by history, archaeology's use and abuse in nationalist enterprises, and archaeology's potential to overcome inter-pretations arising out of the colonial library—yet its suppression, in one case, by a radical group of historians. Because my knowledge of these dynamics is based on direct experience in eastern Africa, my analysis focuses mostly on that region. The struggle to establish archaeology in Tanzania is one example that illustrates well the tensions among vary-ing interests in a developing African country, but it also highlights the considerable successes that have been achieved in making alternative his-tories from archaeology. I discuss several of these successes, ending with what I see as an arena for possible rapprochement between Western and African archaeologists.

Defining the Problem

The Nigerian literary theorist Abiola Irele has refocused attention on the dilemma facing historical and other scholarship in Africa today: how to find independent expression while working with the Western scholastic tradition (Irele 1991). He speaks of an ideological imperative within the context of "objectivity." The search for an independent voice in Africa that makes important contributions to the modern world must develop, he reasons, from "the necessity to take charge of the knowl-edge that has been produced and continues to be produced on and about our continent, to take charge of this knowledge in [an] autono-mous discourse" that contributes to the continent and to the world (Irele 1991:58). Irele's recent thinking on this issue acknowledges a debt to earlier African historians whose work on indigenous history and institu-tions repudiated the colonial thesis (1991:59). This process of refutation, nonetheless, was often conducted within the frame of the colonial ex-periment. Although the counterdiscourse restricts the vision of a truly authentic African voice, Irele sees in it a positive quality: when the West functions as subtext, the process of refutation creates a collective introspection that fulfills the conditions of historical reflection (Irele 1991:62).

One impediment to the development of an independent African historical and archaeological science is the economic marginality of Afri-can scholarship in the whole of intellectual and scientific inquiry in the world today. Irele (1991:64) sees this sort of marginality as character-ized by a dependence on the Western frame of inquiry and on a scientific protocol determined by the Western tradition. But the roots of this marginality and dependence are profoundly related to the absence of sufficient wealth for the production of *African* knowledge and the dissemination of that knowledge throughout the world. More profoundly, until conditions change, African historical scholarship will remain dependent upon validation by the Western academy for its legitimacy. This issue is magnified in the case of archaeology, a form of inquiry that demands a significant material base capable of sustaining multidisciplinary research and publication.

The issue of economic dependency in the practice of archaeology in Africa is central to the questions addressed in this chapter. That economic conditions will change sufficiently to support a flourishing African scholarship and dissemination of knowledge is highly improbable in the near future. What alternatives arise in the face of this improbability? One step, Irele suggests, is to move toward full collaboration between Western and African scholars, a collaboration reaching beyond the role of the African as native informant. The African scholar, precisely because he or she is so familiar with Western theory and concepts, is uniquely placed to influence the reconfiguration of theory.

Before action can accompany this idealized program, we must overcome more fundamental and debilitating conditions of dependence and absence of equity in African archaeological inquiry. Such conditions of dependence are largely economic but are also manifested in a derivative psychological disposition arising out of a long tradition of Western scientific dominance that goes unacknowledged. Most archaeological research in Africa remains dependent upon funding from foreign investigators and sources. This legacy is part of a colonial syndrome well illustrated by the major role played by outside funding in the Leakeys' "early man" investigations.

The Leakey enterprise at Olduvai Gorge demands reflection. First, the impact and influence of generous funding on research at Olduvai brought results that altered remarkably the very structure of thought about the origins of humans. Money applied to science produced historical knowledge of enormous importance, but under conditions of some mystification for African populations.

The important and highly visible Leakey investigations assured the dominance of colonial archaeology in postcolonial eastern African and served as a powerful model of how archaeology should be funded for much of the continent, a model that influenced how African governments treated and viewed archaeology in subsequent decades. Archaeology became the preserve of large, European-dominated expeditions funded from abroad, replete with a confusing array of exotic names for new finds. While some expeditions created a new view that Africa was the womb of humankind and new governments scrambled to identify the discoveries with their nationalist agendas, the project itself remained distinctly alien to most Africans.

Archaeology came to be regarded by the African elite as an endeavor requiring the participation and usually the leadership of foreign institutions. The identification of archaeology with both nationalist agendas and colonial institutions created a peculiar kind of continuity in the status of archaeology from the colonial era to the postcolonial. This model also gave rise to the notion that African governments need not invest in constructing pasts, because funding was available from other sources. Dependence on external funding came to be accepted as natural, a condition that assured low priority to governmental funding of studies of the ancient past, especially in the face of other growing development concerns. Internal priorities such as health and agriculture have continually required heavy investment, leaving little money for museums in many African countries. Meanwhile, international economic crises, especially the impact of oil prices, have ravaged African economies (Musonda 1990). The tradition of foreign research money, combined with internal economic failures (many of which were also related to mismanagement of centrally controlled economies), has created a milieu of dependency that subjugates African initiative.

National versus Ethnic Tensions: The Politics of Archaeology

While the current distribution of resources militates against the development of an independent African archaeological voice, archaeology's methodological focus itself creates tensions that sometimes obscure its historical potential. This process can be seen clearly in South Africa, where the political implications of archaeological research provide a cautionary tale, ironically, for other regions of sub-Saharan Africa. One reason archaeology has not been high on the agendas of many African governments and their political parties is that it has not been seen as compatible with a nationalist program or with a particular political ideology.

In South Africa, archaeology has presented powerful but poorly disseminated contradictions to apartheid-related claims that Africans had not settled much of the southern part of the continent long before Boer settlement (Hall 1990). Archaeological documentation of settled ways of life by Bantu-speaking peoples in the first half of the first millennium A.D. has defeated part of the Afrikaner ideology that underpinned claims to land and superiority. Archaeology's social impact, however, has been partially offset by its application among specific ethnic groups, further differentiating ancient as well as recent histories and making each ethnic group easier to distinguish on cultural and historical grounds. This process of separation and differentiation was easily exploited by the apartheid state: it fit neatly with the divide-and-rule policy of apartheid and the creation of homelands for each ethnic group. Martin Hall (1984a, 1990) has directed attention to some of the practices of white archaeologists in South Africa, such as the use of a culture-area approach (see Maggs 1976; Mason 1986), that inadvertently contributed to and amplified a political policy of ethnic separation. The absence of self-consciousness among otherwise well-intended, liberal white archaeologists in South Africa also led to serious logical errors easily exploited by the apartheid state. For example, the projection of contemporary and historic ethnographic configurations onto archaeologically determined segments of the past creates a false picture of an unchanging, static past, forming an illusion of primitive continuity (Hall 1984a; Schmidt 1983a).

Some African countries, such as Tanzania, have held a conscious policy of national integration based on common history and language. Tanzania's Swahilization policy has been a remarkably successful unifying device. Tanzania has also stressed its recent nationalist history—the common fight against colonialism and the growth and success of the first nationalist political party. This is a history that all peoples of the country have in common. It is easy to understand that, in the search for commonality and national unity, any history focusing on regions and idealizing ethnic accomplishments could be perceived as a threat to nationalist goals.

One expression of such concerns can be read in the removal of ethnically oriented museum displays in Tanzania's national museum during the early 1970s (Bertram Mapunda, personal communication 1992). Ethnic emphasis in the context of a national museum was seen as contrary to the nationalist (and socialist) project. Such a strict interpretation can easily set up political tensions with archaeological research that focuses on particular regions to build regional culture histories. The construction of culture histories for previously unresearched areas and the increasing use of ethnoarchaeology inevitably identify archaeology with specific ethnic groups. Thus it is easy for archaeology to appear to elevate ethnicity at the expense of national unity. Archaeologists and their work are also subject to being manipulated in interethnic jealousies and conflicts. Foreign archaeologists may be vulnerable if their research does not fit the silent ethnic agendas of those who wield power over research, and African researchers may be particularly vulnerable to unscrupulous superiors who have an ethnic ax to grind.

If there are tensions over ethnic and national identification with archaeological research in African countries that reached statehood in the 1960s, these tensions are not new to the arena of African history. An early example is the contradiction that arose when nationalist history created kingdoms and empires as new "myths" of African identity and unity intended to counteract the primitivist constructs of the colonial past. The idealization of the kingdom as a symbol of complexity and accomplishment obscured relationships of dominance and exploitation in the past. At the same time, the identification of the people with rulers in the historical past set up an attractive model easily appropriated by the political elite in the postcolonial era (Neale 1985; Temu and Swai 1981: 83). This nationalistic agenda sometimes created bizarre contradictions, compelling at least one student of history to question, "Was [the site of Great] Zimbabwe really an appropriate symbol for the freedom fighters of Rhodesia?" (Neale 1985:47). Neale's question discloses the contradiction between a symbol replete with royal attributes and hierarchical characteristics and its appropriation by democratic freedom fighters.

The question about Great Zimbabwe, however, ignores an even more serious historical problem: the identification of the ruins of Great Zimbabwe with the majority Shona people. Contradictions inherent in the inequalities of past state(s) at Great Zimbabwe pale in comparison with the contemporary ethnic tensions that the Great Zimbabwe monument, as a symbol, brings to the surface. The appropriation of this archaeological monument as a symbol of state and nation-ness in Zimbabwe masks—while simultaneously heightening—the enormously divisive role that ethnicity plays in contemporary Zimbabwe. Conflicts between the Shona and Ndebele figure prominently in recent and contemporary political life and create questions about national unity and the legitimacy of the state. Martin Hall's exegesis of interpretations of Great Zimbabwe, first by imperial interests and later by various nationalists, brings to light the political volatility of this site's different representations (Hall 1984a:464). Interpretations of Great Zimbabwe's indigenous origins and development again came under attack when white nationalists of the UDI regime (Unilateral Declaration of Independence from Great Britain by the white elite) charged that archaeologists sympathetic with such views were politically aligned with the black opposition.

Once the black opposition took power in 1980, there was a reaction to such white nationalistic prejudices. Hall quotes a poignant commentary attributed to Zimbabwe's president by the journalist K. N. Mafaka, to the effect that it would be "a mockery of our culture to ask a white man to interpret the Great Zimbabwe" and that "whenever the white man's interpretation of Great Zimbabwe differs from that of our black scholars we will take our own" (Hall 1984a:464). Hall remarks that this is the mirror image of the earlier white nationalist sentiment, an interpretation that appears to have ignored local rights to construct history and therefore one that merits further scrutiny. If the issue is examined from the perspective that the interpretive history of the site, like the archaeological record of Zimbabwe, has been confused by Western imperial agendas, colonial speculations, and other Western ideologically informed "scholarship," then it is altogether reasonable to suggest that successive Western constructs should be discarded as useless and irrelevant cultural baggage. Until independence in 1980, Africans played no role in the interpretation of Great Zimbabwe, and even more recent cultural interpretations of Great Zimbabwe based on ethnographic accounts and structuralist models (Huffman 1981) continue to alienate Zimbabwe's history and affirm the incapacity of Western thought to represent local needs and sensibilities. In this context, Mafaka's account captures a declaration to take back Zimbabwe and to Africanize its historical interpretations. This is hardly a mirror image of white nationalist sentiment, which was an anti-African colonial enterprise.

Because many of the archaeological deposits of the central portion of Great Zimbabwe have long since been destroyed by "mining" activities and by archaeological quests remote from African history, few deposits remain from which African archaeologists may construct alternative views of areas such as the Great Enclosure, which, because of its impressive stone architecture, has elicited the most inquiry. The archaeological record is so limited that there is little room to negotiate a liberation from the idea of Great Zimbabwe as a royal site. One possible resolution of the contradiction inherent in employing a royal site as a symbol of national unity lies in evidence for "folk" culture held in the unexcavated outer precincts of Great Zimbabwe. These areas may contain evidence that would provide important insights into the majority of ancient Zimbabwe's population—the non-elite residents, craftsmen, traders, and functionaries. The remaining archaeological evidence and its likely socioeconomic associations may fit well with a nationalist and socialist agenda in Zimbabwe. It is virtually certain that future excavations at Great Zimbabwe will again follow an ideological program, but this time one determined by indigenous African scholars.

The Politics of Archaeology: Power over the Production of Knowledge

I want to return to the underdevelopment of African archaeological inquiry that I examined earlier within the East African setting and how it is linked to both nationalist history and the later growth of critical history. The contrast between East and West Africa in the development of an indigenous archaeology seems to parallel differences in the degree of their reaction to colonialist historiography. In West Africa, Nigerians led the way with a school of historical interpretation that spoke with much greater self-confidence and without a preoccupation with conferring legitimacy on the nation (Neale 1985). In eastern Africa, particularly Tanzania, the tone of historical discourse was defensive in posture, justifying in tone.

Part of this difference, Neale (1985) suggests, may result from a stronger educational history in the west and a correspondingly greater need in the east to establish an intellectual identity. Whatever the cause, it is instructive to observe that in anglophone West Africa, separate archaeology departments were established relatively early in three different locales: Legon, Ghana (1963), Nsukka, Nigeria (1963), and Ibadan, Nigeria (1966) (Nzewunwa 1990). In contrast, archaeology in East Africa remained underdeveloped until 1985, at best a small and subsidiary part of history departments. What accounts for such a remarkable difference?

The reasons for underdevelopment in Kenya appear to be political and ideological. Since the Leakeys' pioneering expeditions during the late twenties and early thirties, archaeology in Kenya has come to be equated with paleoanthropology; it has continued to be seen in the same way under the leadership of Richard Leakey. Inquiry into the past has been predominantly the domain of white Kenyan prehistorians and their European collaborators working under the aegis of the state-supported National Museum. This alliance between the state and a white-directed paleoanthropology fits nicely with Kenya's internal problems with power and ethnicity. The Kenyan state is a fragile instrument, always under severe threat from competition for power among several large ethnic groups. Any element that tips the balance toward one group over another is potentially a threat to the state.

Archaeology, if allowed to flourish at a regional level, can easily be identified with an attempt to valorize the history (which in Kenya can readily underwrite land claims) of one ethnic group at the perceived expense of others. The state's deep investment in the white intellectuals' pursuit of ancient human ancestors has been an ideal way to neutralize regional histories. It uses an easily co-opted white minority, eager for local legitimacy, in an enterprise that is extra-ethnic: it focuses on a "population" devoid of ethnicity—indeed, devoid of humanness. State investment in this perspective creates a national identity from a period of history so remote that it imitates mythological time. Using a belief that is globally endorsed, the state can draw on the neutrality of ancient nonhumans to provide Kenya with a new universal myth of origin. This powerful new myth serves the Kenyan state well, and it is certain that no Luo or Kikuyu or Kamba archaeologist will be allowed to deconstruct one of the most important myths of the contemporary world. We can expect that the mutual advantages accruing from this alliance will persist until such time as political change creates a need for a new Kenyan history. Until that day arrives, we can expect that archaeology will remain firmly in the control of whites, who will develop clients who are either loyal to this project or are partially disabled by inadequate training abroad.

Any hope that archaeology will find an independent base in Kenya is unlikely so long as the current power alliances prevail. Though archaeology was instituted as a subsidiary course in the history curriculum at the University of Nairobi in 1970, it has remained in an underdeveloped state since then, capturing a few undergraduate students who have later studied abroad for higher degrees. The development of a fully constituted archaeology department is not in the interests of colonial institutions such as the National Museum and the British Institute in Eastern Africa, formerly known as the British Institute of History and Archaeology in Eastern Africa.

The British Institute is a curious colonial legacy, conceived by Sir Mortimer Wheeler and the British Academy just at the time when East African states were gaining independence. After its founding in 1960, the institute operated out of Dar es Salaam between 1961 and 1964, when it moved its headquarters to the comfortable "colonial" neighborhood of Choromo in Nairobi. In 1966 it established the journal *Azania,* which is devoted to publishing research primarily in East African archaeology and ancient history.

With its European-dominated agenda, colonial setting, European membership (until recently payable only in foreign currency), and almost completely European contributorship to *Azania,* the British Institute is a palpable symbol of the contradiction between a disenfranchised African population not enabled to construct its own ancient history and a foreign institute on African soil that studies African history and continuously produces knowledge satisfying mostly the European academy.

African participation in the research mission of the institute is rare, nor has the institute made an effort to change its mission so that it might incorporate training and collaboration with Africans in archaeological research (also see Okpoko 1991).[1] Although its research results have added much to empirical evidence for ancient history in eastern Africa, the British Institute's mission has been a colonial one that speaks to diffusionist goals (e.g., the Bantu Studies Project, which focused on Bantu migration) or goals that satisfy the historical research agendas of foreign academics (e.g., long-term British interests in the royal earthworks of Uganda). Africans, if they appear in the process at all, are peripheral, sometimes participating only to legitimize the research.

Some investigators associated with the institute have reflected on the contradictions inherent in this production of knowledge. One of the first expressions of a conscious effort to break from the colonial paradigm is seen in the 1966 publication of *Prelude to East African History,* a small book edited by Merrick Posnansky that developed out of a 1962 conference sponsored by the institute. According to the preface written by the institute's director, this work explicitly sets out to create a new perspective in African archaeology, one separate from a strictly colonial approach. Acknowledgments are made, for example, of the importance of historical linguistics and oral traditions in the construction of later "prehistory," although no chapter in the book illustrates how these new approaches are to contribute to the writing of history.

The importance of this book is its expressed goal to write an ancient history that appeals to local people. In this respect it indicates a consciousness of the need to accommodate the British Institute's archaeological mission to the changing political configurations in Africa. *Prelude* represents a transitional phase in that it is the first liberal view of a new role for African archaeology (Mapunda 1992), a view that has remained mostly unrealized and distinct from the paradigmatic trajectory that the institute itself was to take in subsequent years. Despite the ideas expressed in *Prelude,* a liberal view did not interpenetrate historical thinking or research at the institute. And the hegemony of the British Institute and the National Museum assured that archaeology in Kenya remained underdeveloped, with very limited opportunities for African participation.

The reasons for the underdevelopment of archaeology in Tanzania are different from but also similar to those in Kenya. The Kenyan expeditions to Tanzania's Olduvai Gorge were exclusively Kenyan and European affairs, so the several Tanzanian archaeologists who received higher-degree training outside Tanzania during the 1970s pursued their careers independently of the concession granted to the Leakeys at Olduvai. Archaeology was initially introduced at the University of Dar es Salaam by John Sutton as an optional course within the history syllabus, and it was never offered as a separate course of study. Archaeology's minor role as a subsidiary part of history complemented the prevailing attitude of the 1960s that archaeology was a handmaiden to history. As Sutton was to argue later, archaeology was "an historical technique" (Sutton 1973a:1); it added historical facts to diffusionist constructs coming out of Europe, such as those promoted by the Bantu Studies Project of the British Institute, which focused on Bantu expansion or migration. Although Sutton saw in 1973 that archaeology was drifting and in danger of underdevelopment, he nonetheless concluded that it was best that Tanzania not attempt to develop archaeology within the university but that the university instead seek cooperation with the government's Antiquities Division and the National Museum (Karoma 1990; Sutton 1973a, 1973b).

Sutton's observations (1973a) included the ideas that staff should be kept to one or two archaeologists, that training of archaeologists would need to be undertaken partly in foreign universities, that there was no justification for creating internal research facilities, and that student attachment to foreign projects could help supplement the students' local exposure. Paradoxically, Sutton noted that other universities in Africa were making progress in creating departments of archaeology and training their own archaeologists. He saw this contrast with the situation in eastern Africa as "serious," but his recommendations contradict that assessment. Moreover, his suggestion that archaeology in East Africa be established as a regional venture at the University of Nairobi in the context of colonial domination is curious.

Sutton's perspective on the underdevelopment of archaeology may have indirectly assured archaeology's further stasis at the University of Dar es Salaam. The then-prominent nationalist school of history found Sutton's recommendations for marginality congruent with their mission, which was proving that Africa had as glorious a history as Europe and that Africans had resisted European colonialism from its very beginnings. Archaeology had little immediate relevance in this agenda of reaction to colonial historiography, and its marginality suited the needs of this group.

Another important faction of the history department at the University of Dar es Salaam was engaged in demonstrating the authenticity of African voices in oral histories as alternatives to the colonial library (Kimambo and Temu 1969). There, following the lead of Vansina and Oliver, who were advocating the utility of archaeology in verifying oral sources (Schmidt 1983a, 1990), archaeology was seen to have a supplementary role to play, but in fact it was a role that was never given more than lip service. Thus, the negotiated ideology of the times incorporated the legacy of the Leakeys' well-established position, Sutton's ambivalence and diffusionist perspectives, and the nationalist assumption that archaeology was a handmaiden to African history and another way to affirm the authenticity of African oral history. This negotiated position led to a cultural hegemonic view that consigned archaeology to the periphery, accepting it as historical but perceiving it as a mysterious and little-applied technique (Beaudry, Cook, and Mrozowski 1991; Bennett, Mercer, and Woolacott 1986; Sutton 1973a).

The ideological peripheralization of archaeology had profound consequences during the decade after 1973. Recommendations for developing archaeology at the university level were adopted during a 1973 meeting of Tanzanian archaeologists and were presented to the university repeatedly by the Antiquities Division, but no action was taken. When, after Sutton's departure, the only Tanzanian archaeologist in the university, N. J. Karoma, pursued the question and advocated the development of archaeology there (Karoma 1977), he was greeted with derision and challenged on the grounds that archaeology was not relevant to the socialist experiment.

By the late 1970s, a radical school of historians had come into prominence alongside the nationalists. Archaeology's position as marginal had already been negotiated when Karoma (1977, 1990) began to argue that the national interest deserved comprehensive training of students in archaeology. His arguments had been preceded by strong recommendations from the Antiquities Division for a full-fledged training program in archaeology and paleoanthropology. University colleagues turned a deaf ear, and Karoma was challenged in a departmental seminar by a Marxist historian who demanded: "Will archaeology feed the people?" (Karoma, personal communication 1990). The debate was acrimonious and attempted to portray archaeology as too resource-intensive—too consuming of the precious resources of the peasants—and as an overly empirical discipline. It was argued that the collection of material data or myriad "facts," which were themselves theoretical constructs, was a bourgeois enterprise antithetical to attempts to build a socialist society (see Temu and Swai 1981:111–52).

The reaction of the Dar es Salaam radicals may well have arisen out of their perception of archaeology as the collection of facts which themselves are produced under the aura of "science" and therefore take on a false objectivity (Bernstein and Depelchin 1979:24)—yet another expression of bourgeois historicism. Given the strong empirical foundations of African archaeology until the 1980s and its modes of production, it is understandable that archaeology could not escape the condemnation of this new hegemonic ideology. Even when it inquired into such unknown domains as technology and the history of power struggles over, say, the control of iron production, if such inquiry emphasized innovation and achievement, then it could be characterized as "counterideological" and as taking its "terms of reference from the enemy" (Bernstein and Depelchin 1979:25). The opportunity for archaeology to negotiate a place within this prevailing consciousness was remote. Even if ideologically radical questions were asked, they were illegitimate because they were posed within a "bourgeois historiography" and lay outside materialist history (Bernstein and Depelchin 1979:36).

Such characterizations of archaeology betray some serious misunderstandings of its potential to operate in fresh intellectual territory. But the late 1970s, particularly in Africa, had not yet seen a self-conscious critical archaeology, although there was a radical archaeology that focused on ancient African culture with the aim of overturning the ruling paradigms that continue to dominate the structure of thought about ancient Africa (Schmidt 1978; Schmidt and Avery 1978). Unquestionably, a critique of theory-laden empirical archaeology in Africa, although not specifically articulated in print, was accurate and pertinent. Any quick review of publications—for example, in *Azania*—shows page after page of tables, drawings of ceramics, and esoteric discussions of artifact attributes and comparisons, mostly in the service of diffusionist constructs and local cultural histories.

Although such details make sense to the archaeologist, who sees them as essential parts of conventional archaeological reporting, format, implicit interpretation, and esoteric technical language, they converge to mystify historians and lay readers. Archaeologists of Africa have failed to acknowledge their theoretical groundings. Equally troubling, they have often failed to communicate with anyone other than a very small number of their own kind. In this respect, archaeological knowledge has little affected the historical thinking and perceptions of Kenyans, Cameroonians, or Tanzanians about their own pasts. The most significant impact appears to have been in Nigeria (Afigbo 1986; Okpoko 1986), where more popular accounts have been published and more attention paid to integrating archaeology into school curricula. Neglect of communication, however, has been the case in most African countries, suggesting that the production of archaeological knowledge fails to change the present and or to promise a better future.

These are some of the problems facing the construction of archaeology in Tanzania. Some critiques by the secular Marxists at the University of Dar es Salaam were predicated upon an incomplete understanding of archaeology yet accurately captured the empirical predilections that were a legacy of most British practitioners. Other issues point out contradictions compelling some self-reflective dialectical analysis. Let us return to the Dar es Salaam group's assertion that attempts to "recover or reconstruct" precolonial history are counterideological and take their terms of reference from the enemy (Bernstein and Depelchin 1979:25).

Bernstein and Depelchin elaborated on this position to argue that opposition to denigrating colonial representations leads to romantic responses or to emphases on African achievement in reaction to claims of lack of achievement, but that both results are counterideological projects and must be confronted. I believe, however, that we have moved beyond the era when African historians romanticized kingdoms and empires, overlooking their conditions of domination, poverty, and exploitation. Archaeology in Africa has long been sensitized to these issues and rarely participated in such hyperbole, the case of Engaruka being one exception (Leakey 1936).

Bernstein and Depelchin (1979:40) hold that a counterassertion of achievement works from a European standard arising from social evolutionary theory, which assumes the retention of primitive survivals in Africa. Any assertion of equal or greater complexity, therefore, accepts the efficacy of this theoretical frame. This position initially appears to pose a dilemma. But the assertion itself is an ideological finesse meant to obscure a more profound problem: how can negative and pathological constructs arising out of the application of this theoretical base be deconstructed? Subsidiary dualities arising out of evolutionary theory, such as complex/simple, literate/illiterate, subject/object, civilized/savage, and scientific/intuitive, so deeply interpenetrate assumptions about the ancient African past that they must be disabled before it is possible to develop a liberated archaeology of Africa, an archaeology with its own theoretical niche compatible with Africa.

I have related elsewhere how historians of Africa accept and think of African technological inferiority (Schmidt n.d.). These unconscious, taken-for-granted notions were, ironically, also expressed in the thought of some Dar es Salaam radicals, who were preoccupied with why and how African technologies fit into capitalist relations of production in the colonial and postcolonial eras and how that fit contributed to the absence of innovations since precolonial times. Absence of innovation under capitalism can be assessed, however, only if precolonial innovation has been documented, a historical requirement obviously ignored. This failure to document early technological life was, at the same time, accompanied by vague and unsubstantiated acknowledgments that Africa had contributed to technological advance (Temu and Swai 1981:156). Such disregard for the history of precolonial technology accepts the thesis of antecedent inferiority.

Archaeology has a demonstrated capacity to overcome different forms of this received knowledge, with its underlying assumption of inferiority. For example, a challenge to this intellectual position was mounted by researchers studying iron technology in northwestern Tanzania, studies that lay outside the paradigms of reaction or "reconstruction" (Schmidt and Avery 1978). Such projects recognize the fallacy of "reconstruction" and replace it with an active, self-aware *construction* of the past. The effect of such studies is to make new histories that independently collapse part of the dichotomous structure of Western thought—now also the thinking of many Africans—by presenting histories that not only contradict received knowledge about African technology but also have their own local integrity and theoretical expressions.

Those who engaged in attempts to establish the teaching of archaeology in Tanzania simultaneously took on the effort to remake historical thinking about ancient Africa. This project recognized the profound transformations caused by colonization of the historical mind of Africa, transformations reaching so deeply into contemporary historical thinking, self-perception, valuation, and interpretation that much more is required to counter them than the application of historical materialism to the colonial and postcolonial libraries. The absence of a self-reflexive critique by the Dar es Salaam clique meant that they did not realize that they themselves were trapped deeply in reaction and recovery (see Temu and Swai 1981), a perspective that afforded no new pathway.

After the initial debate over archaeology erupted at the University of Dar es Salaam in 1977, several events occurred that were to alter the development of archaeology in Tanzania. First, ethnoarchaeological and archaeological research that I had conducted over the previous decade in northwestern Tanzania had produced observations and discoveries that overturned several dominant interpretive paradigms of the history of African technology. This research demonstrated the development of an indigenous science that solved technical problems and conducted experiments within a mystical, ritualized setting that masked its scientific principles from all observers, especially those from the West.

International and domestic publicity surrounding these findings in the fall of 1978 affected the way African technological history was represented, which in turn impacted local and international perceptions of the African past. The Tanzania National Scientific Research Council took an immediate interest in the research, seeing in it a way in which Tanzanians could be sensitized to the relevance of science and technology in the present and future. The ministry concerned with culture also took a keen interest, using the findings as a means to increase awareness that archaeology fit into a national education plan. But official action did not coalesce until the leaders of these institutions visited China during late 1978 and observed firsthand the power of antiquities in building a national socialist state, particularly through Chinese emphasis on the contributions of worker-artisans to remarkable royal sites (Trigger 1984). This experience illustrated the possibilities for archaeology in Tanzania, and the leaders of both institutions returned to Tanzania determined to push the development of archaeology within the university.

For the next two years, historians in the university continued to oppose archaeology, mostly behind the pretense of expense. During this time, however, an alliance between the leaders of the ministry and research council, on one side, and local and foreign archaeologists, on the other, led to the formation of an independent, nonprofit organization designed to recruit the financial backing necessary to establish archaeology at the university. The university was pushed by the ministry to create a plan to implement the teaching of archaeology. By 1986, a full curriculum was in place. This short history brings to light the political and intellectual forces engaged in the struggle for power over the production of knowledge about the ancient past.

Archaeology held demonstrated power to create new and socially responsible knowledge unconfined by the colonial library and also germane to creating new interpretations challenging the interpretive paradigms arising from the colonial library — the context in which historians exclusively worked. Archaeology was thus poised to co-opt the agenda of the radical group. Concern arose among the radicals over how this threat could be contained and countered.

The question "Does archaeology produce food?" was a legitimate query in the political milieu of Tanzania in the 1970s. But if the question is asked of other domains of production of historical knowledge, then we must recognize the failure of historical practice in Tanzania to provide new histories leading to changed identity and self-perception. In this respect, the once-vital nationalist school of history and its heir, the "Marxist" school of history at Dar es Salaam, have disappointed. The latter radical group provided an important auto-critique and an essential refocusing on questions of class and social relations of production in the colonial era, but it failed to go beyond this refocusing to produce history that serves the people, creates awareness of the causes of contemporary inequalities and injustices, and creates a sense of potential betterment in the future.

Alternatives for Making History in Africa

One idea that holds hope for the future is archaeological inquiry into scientific and technological accomplishments in African settings, with the goal of understanding how and why distinctive technological innovations and variations arose out of the African environment. Innovation need not be measured relative to events and developments in other world areas; it must first be comprehended within its own cultural and historical contexts. Only archaeology has the techniques required to document ancient processes of innovation and scientific experimentation. The importance of this project lies not in potential revelations that might impact modern science. Rather, it lies in the recognition that it is possible to unearth original African contributions to science and, as Irele (1991:68) put it, that "the fund of positive knowledge available to our traditional societies has yet to be seriously investigated and made available to the world." Irele sees this project as an African contribution to human knowledge about the past in which Africa takes neither a dominant nor a subordinate place but contributes in a way that revalues and recuperates that knowledge.

The revaluation of African scientific experience is one way to remove the science/intuition dichotomy and its science/ritual variant that perpetually diminish the African experience. Revaluation focuses on the pragmatic lessons that can be learned from the ways in which stress and difficulties were overcome in the past and from understanding what "inherent scientific values" underlie and unify successful experimentation with the natural world. It discovers a confident socio-scientific posture in the past that offers a model of success which in turn can help people confront the contradictions of the present (e.g., development failures attributed to insufficient technological know-how) and meet the challenges of the future.

This perspective was one of the guiding principles behind the development of archaeology in Tanzania. Another important principle was that an African archaeology should produce its own historical knowledge under the leadership of African scholars who value the search for an archaeology appropriate to Africa. This requires the training of undergraduate students working on African problems at the B.A. level within an African setting, a goal also pertinent to higher-degree training that is currently met at only a few African institutions. It also requires a focus on research problems that have the potential to address important historical issues, issues that challenge interpretations about the past of African science, trade, technology, urbanization, environmental relationships, symbolic life, and so forth. The curriculum at the University of

Dar es Salaam incorporates a strong program of archaeological research design and implementation from the first year on, so students start early in their training to "think theory" and experience its relationship to field methods, laboratory analysis, and interpretation.

One proven way to proceed with student training was to continue making inquiries into the development of technologies that followed innovative tracks in Africa. The development of the preheating technique in iron smelting, for example, is a remarkable African contribution to technological innovation that demands to be understood more completely (Schmidt and Avery 1978). Techniques that overcame the presence of phosphorus in iron are another of the many aspects of ancient iron technology that invite further inquiry elsewhere in Africa (Childs 1995; Schmidt and Childs 1995). Archaeological evidence for the development of economic systems that degraded forested environments 1,000 to 2,500 years ago provides views reshaping previous ideas that African civilizations changed because of movements of ethnic and language groups. Such new views of the past encompass practical lessons to be learned from the early successes and failures of human societies to manage different environments and offer antidotes to nationalist tendencies to glorify complex societies in the past.

University-related research that first addressed these concerns in Tanzania took place in 1986 in the western Usambara Mountains, a locale suggested by students who observed similarities between the environment required for an early Iron Age technology as documented in western Tanzania and the well-watered Usambara Mountains of eastern Tanzania. Field research was structured so that students found most of the sites, among which was an early Iron Age iron-smelting site on the western and highly degraded slopes of the mountains. These finds were important in demonstrating that an early technology using preheating principles was also practiced on the opposite side of the country, in the area of an ethnic group (the Shambaa) that is close to and has some affinities with two of the most prominent ethnic groups (the Chagga and Pare) of eastern Tanzania (Schmidt 1988; Schmidt and Karoma 1987).

These initial research results, obtained under University of Dar es Salaam sponsorship, led to a perceptible softening of earlier subtle ethnic opposition to archaeology, with scholars from northeastern Tanzania taking particular interest in this trans-territorial phenomenon that linked widely separated parts of the country. The "national" characteristics of these discoveries, also represented in the ethnic diversity of the students pictured in a newspaper photo of the excavations, created for the first time an image of archaeology as a national enterprise with the power to make history that was African.

The success of the first research season was followed in the second year by research in an archaeologically unknown part of Tanzania's coastal zone, an area spurned by colonial archaeologists who were interested in the monumental sites of the littoral. The monumental sites, long known for their remarkable tombs, mosques, and coral houses, had come to be identified with the advent of urbanization and civilization along the East African coast. The growth of these complex communities was attributed to the arrival of Shirazi and Omani immigrants from the Persian Gulf during the first half of the second millennium A.D. This diffusionist explanation holds that Islam and trade were among the most important cultural forces leading to economic as well as community organization and coherence.

The history of archaeological research that incorporated this diffusionist package shows a steadfast fixation on the exotic, the imported, and the Islamic. Extensive archaeological investigations along the coast by Kirkman (1963) and Chittick (1974, 1984) at important urban "medieval" sites such as Kilwa, Manda, Mombasa, and Gedi had revealed evidence for earlier, first-millennium populations who also lived on these sites. But evidence of the earlier settlement was reported in very summary form, the ceramics were assigned pejorative labels such as "kitchen ware," and interpretation of the ancient remains was omitted (Chittick 1974, 1984)—an archaeological approach that effectively erased such communities from the landscape (see Handsman and Lamb Richmond, this volume). Whatever interpretation did occur denigrated these early communities through negative naming of artifact categories. No questions about socioeconomic organization, population size, political organization, affinities with other settlements, industry, or diet—all conventional questions of the era—were asked about these indigenous communities. The only germane research goals were those of explaining the influences of foreign populations on trade conducted by these communities and of elaborating histories by explicating the few written historical accounts that touched upon them.

The "foreign civilizing" paradigm, while offensive to the sensibilities of African populations (Trigger 1990), nevertheless was still very much in vogue for the East African monumental sites and in no danger of collapsing when the second year's research under the university's new archaeology program began in 1987. Student researchers and instructors selected a "dead" zone that they thought would not soon capture the attention of investigators: low-lying hills with several small lakes approximately 10 to 20 kilometers from the Indian Ocean and located about 100 kilometers south of Dar es Salaam. The results from that season are significant from several perspectives. They revealed for the first time that during the late first millennium A.D., large communities with trade goods and practicing a local industry such as iron fabrication and possible fabrication of copper goods were located in the immediate hinterland adjacent to the littoral. These communities bore close affinities to the long-ignored communities buried under the coastal monumental sites and also found elsewhere along the coast (e.g., Chittick 1974, 1984; Kirkman 1963).

This research was also significant because it took place in an area in which there has been tremendous ethnic fluidity over the last century, with many ethnic entities located on the same landscape. The ethnic pluralism of the region and its significant change in ethnic makeup over the last century, when combined with the transformation of the landscape wrought by cashew farming, contributed to an erasure of history from that landscape. These characteristics meant that the archaeology could not be identified with a particular ethnic group and therefore could not easily be co-opted by any group. This in turn meant lessened political tensions over the development of ancient history for an area in which history had been mostly silenced.

Other research of consequence to making alternative histories in Tanzania occurred during the same year (1987) with the excavation of the Limbo site, an early Iron Age iron-smelting site located about 25 kilometers from the Indian Ocean. The Limbo site contains an enormous amount of industrial debris relative to other sites of similar antiquity in Africa (other than the famous factory site of Meroe in the Sudan, which dates to the early first millennium A.D.). Never before had evidence of very early iron production been uncovered within 50 kilometers of the eastern African coast, though several other sites, such as those in the western Usambara Mountains and in the Teita Hills of Kenya, fall within the 100- to 200-kilometer range. Excavations at Limbo have yet to uncover any furnaces used to smelt iron, but the industrial debris and other evidence indicates that this activity occurred at the site about A.D. 100–250 (Chami 1988a, 1988b, 1994; Schmidt and Chami n.d.).

Perhaps more important is the settlement context in which Limbo was situated. Survey in the same zone showed a light density of early Iron Age occupation sites, suggesting that the surrounding countryside supported sparse early Iron Age populations. A sparse population engaged in the production of large quantities of iron at the Limbo site suggests either that Limbo was the only iron-production site in the area or that iron produced there was in excess of the needs of the local population.

When these archaeological observations and interpretations are juxtaposed with historical interpretations of the ancient East African coast, the importance of Limbo and its surrounding sites becomes clear. Early historical accounts of the coast have stimulated two millennia of speculations and false constructs about the economic history of this region, asserting that it produced "natural products" (rhino horn, ivory, etc.) and consumed manufactured products from abroad. How did this misunderstanding come about? Greek accounts made during the first few centuries of the historical era by authors working with secondhand reports have since been reworked and reiterated so often that the depictions found in the very early historiography of the coast have been accepted at face value and have gained widespread currency. Historians' readiness to accept these early accounts has been amplified by the material inventory of trade provided by these early histories, an attribute that confers a false concreteness to the "evidence."

This story of bias and transformation begins with *Periplus of the Erythraean Sea,* written in the first century A.D. (Casson 1989; Kirwan 1986). The *Periplus* is poor on descriptions of people but strong on descriptions of goods exchanged between local people and foreigners. The most important interpretations of the document made by historians of the twentieth century dwell on the lists of goods, particularly those made of metal—hatchets, daggers, awls, and lances: "These tools would mostly have been of iron, and indicate that the inhabitants of Azania had little or no knowledge of how to smelt this metal" (Chittick 1968:106; see Oliver and Fagan 1978).

This unsubstantiated assertion has been repeated in scores of subsequent publications along with the rest of the interpretive package, which includes the idea that the local populations lacked the knowledge and skills to produce iron (Kirwan 1986:104). This characterization of the East African coast as an economic and technological backwater has retained remarkable vitality and has remained unquestioned for as long as archaeologists have focused on monumental sites and the influence of foreign cultures. It is also an example of how the amplification of bias in the historical record can erase local histories—a process that Sued Badillo (this volume) captures for Puerto Rico. Because there is no historical evidence until the tenth century that contradicts this early portrait of East African economic capacities, the idea that the coastal areas and their immediate hinterlands were receptor areas for goods, ideas, and civilization has gained widespread acceptance.

This uncritical depiction of East African economic development and sociopolitical organization during the first millennium A.D. is not based on substantive archaeological evidence but on one ancient hearsay "historical" account and its myriad repetitions. When this construction of history is considered against the Limbo site excavations and regional survey, a different and more compelling interpretation of hinterland history becomes possible. First, the volume of iron-smelting slag in the excavated portions of Limbo suggests a level of prehistoric iron production far in excess of that in well-known iron production sites dating to the early first millennium in western Tanzania (Schmidt 1983c; Schmidt and Childs 1985). The Limbo technology does not appear to be related to the Mwitu iron technology found elsewhere in East Africa at the same time (such as in the western Usambara Mountains). Its dating to the first two centuries A.D. suggests that it was contemporaneous with the other technological systems yet geographically isolated from them.

Settlement data for the area surrounding Limbo add an additional thread of evidence for an emerging interpretation that threatens the conventional history. We found only two small sites with apparently brief settlement histories contiguous to Lake Zakwati, east of Limbo (Schmidt et al. 1992). The poor, sandy soils and light density of settlement suggest that the primary productive focus of residents during the Early Iron Age was the economic activities seen at Limbo. Because Limbo shows a production capacity beyond what might be expected to serve local needs, we believe it represents iron production oriented to the early Indian Ocean trade (Schmidt and Chami n.d.). The Limbo industrial evidence defeats the idea that early populations lacked skills in iron production and shows that large iron-smelting sites were located close to the coast, well positioned to take advantage of the early documented coastal trade.

Historical interpretations that attribute the fabrication of early iron goods to people in Yemen using iron from sources in Europe and then distributing their goods into eastern Africa are questionable in view of this new evidence. The alternative view presented here fits nicely with later historical observations that raw iron was exported from the mainland to offshore markets, including Madagascar, for fabrication (Shephard 1982).

The later export of raw iron to Madagascar and possibly to the Comoro Islands in the ninth and tenth centuries (Wright 1984) suggests that the history of East African production of iron for commercial trade in the Indian Ocean originated as early as the first or second century, when the *Periplus* was written. Thus these archaeological results produce substantive new knowledge about ancient technology and economy that fits with later Arab historical accounts recognizing East Africa as a source for iron in the early second millennium A.D. The tying together of these various threads helps explain where early traders were obtaining the raw products later reworked into tools, possibly on the Arabian peninsula, and redistributed to Africa. A historiography originating in hearsay accounts illustrates the selective emphasis and omission of details that significantly biased later historical characterizations and effectively erased from history the economic life of a large region of Africa. This research illustrates the value of an angle of view that sets out to use archaeology to deconstruct negative historical interpretations of Africa. It hardly uses the enemy's own terms.

The success of this project, however, does not depend on any explicit ideological agenda. Rather, it depends on the substance of the archaeological findings and the inferentially derived interpretations that enrich their meaning (Wylie 1992b:220). In this instance, a political-ideological position pushed us to pursue inquiry into a "void" zone marked by its negative characterizations, its lack of monuments, and the erasure of a visible past. The results achieved came unexpectedly and in a form completely unrelated to the political-ideological consideration or design that motivated the research. This example captures the power of archaeology to overturn false constructs that negatively impinge upon contemporary self-perceptions. The production of historical knowledge through archaeology at the University of Dar es Salaam has surprised many of its critics and has demonstrated that research free of the colonial library has a unique power to make histories that are accessible and refreshingly different from the evolutionary, diffusionist ideas imposed on the African mind for generations.

In Africa today, the influence of positive, accomplished pasts revalued in the present is essential in the face of economic demoralization and loss of social capital in the development experiment. Goran Hyden's (1992) recent findings about the loss of trust and mutual cooperation—of what he calls "social capital"—in Tanzania suggest the unfolding of a crisis of social confidence that may well trace its beginnings to deleterious images of an insufficient and inadequate economic experience in the ancient and recent past. The alarming erosion of social capital cannot be arrested solely by making a new economic history on the partial archaeological evidence just discussed. But a positive history can play an active role in the mentality of African economic development, helping to revitalize a base for the reclamation of social capital in the future.

The Search for an Indigenous Archaeology

I want to return to the question of making histories that provide hope for a better future and that open African capacities for development. Much of the research just discussed touches on these issues, and they are also addressed by Bassey Andah, whose agenda clearly includes questions about control, identity, liberation, and the future (Andah 1990a:2):

> Authentic excavators of African cultural history need to descend into the burrow of Africa's invisible silent times . . . and strive for control of the text of our experience. Such excavation is thus motivated by the need to have the power to force others to recognize our African presence and rights to be Africans and to own what God has given us: namely, our African continent and identity as Africans.

The language Andah uses in this text (1990a) emphasizes power and control over identity while also stressing that identification with "significant ancestors" is liberating, that it reveals how and why the past exists in the present and the value this has for a "future meaningful existence." Andah sees the key to constructing an Africa with "an enlarged future" as lying in the process of regeneration, wherein Africans "*return* or journey back to our African homes, natural, social and spiritual, of our yesterdays [so] that our present will accede to merge with our past, and to emerge from the past in an enlarged future" (Andah 1990a:3).

We have seen in the language of both Andah and Irele an emphasis on revaluation, regeneration, and return. Irele, though not an archaeologist, echoes his fellow Nigerian's concerns with the past and with a fundamental renegotiation of ideological relationships and languages of power to reclaim and recuperate the past for Africa. For Andah, this journey back depends on the strength of "spiritual" bridge building, an assertion apparently contradictory to his hope that a revolutionized historiography will result from a history transformed from storytelling into a vigorous scientific search for the truth through anthropology (Andah 1990a:4).

The contradiction between spiritual bridges and scientific searches is momentarily disorienting, yet if I understand Andah properly, his message lies in the language he uses—metaphors of ritual grounds in the past, spiritual journeys, identity with ancestors—all drawn from the deep wellspring of African life, sensibility, and history. Andah is recasting the archaeological discourse so that it is reconfigured to fit African mental constructs, a bold departure that promises to threaten those who control the production of knowledge about the past in Africa. Andah's program gives notice that there are now groups prepared to challenge those who control the production of knowledge, inevitably leading to negotiation for a new language of hegemony. As he observes, power depends on language.

Elsewhere Andah argues that there is a history of Africa that is distinctly African and that those who study it need to be uniquely equipped to unravel it. Andah explicitly argues that for any African history or archaeology to be relevant to an African audience, it must resonate effectively with an African cultural ethos. This view is more than the perspective that archaeology practiced in Africa must be aware of the historical sensibilities of the people among whom it is practiced (Schmidt 1983a). Andah wants to push beyond this perspective to suggest that African archaeology needs to incorporate other "rich sources" with the goal of "re-enacting African cultural history" in such a way that it departs from "an archaeological discipline that often tries to create what may not have existed, rather than discovering and describing people, what they did and what happened to them" (Andah 1987:vii). We see here a view that resembles a "folkways" approach intended to construct a more animated narrative of everyday African life.

Andah's exploration of alternative methodologies assumes a commonality in the African experience, or an "African ethos." Although some will argue that making this assumption risks reducing rich variability in cosmology, belief systems, and historical experience among African peoples to a simple commonality, such a reaction would miss the importance of Andah's position. Though he fails to take his argument about what constitutes an African ethos farther, he makes clear that he thinks the cultural frames of reference in (most) reports and books written by Westerners about Africa assume that the "European cultural experience constitutes the image of universal man. As a result the framework is largely irrelevant for communicating the normative aspect of African cultural experience" (Andah 1987:viii).

Thus Andah's concern—as an African archaeologist—is the search for a normative African epistemology of time and space to which African practitioners of the discipline can subscribe. What room is there in which an Africanist archaeologist can operate successfully under these conditions? It is abundantly apparent that Andah is not arguing for a relativist view that assigns distinctive meanings to each archaeological region. The most important understanding arising from his discourse is that inferential interpretations in Africa, if they are to be assessed as pertinent and meeting criteria of reasonable fit, must be based on deep cultural understandings.

Foreign investigators are on difficult ground here, for they lack socialization in African languages and cultures. I believe, however, that there are domains of inquiry that may reveal important new paths allowing the merging of Western methods with African experience. Here I take inspiration from Irele as well as from a challenge Mudimbe (1988: 198) sets out when he suggests that there be a "reconceptualization of scientific method and the relationships that 'scientific knowledge' might have with other forms or types of knowledge." How then might we proceed to develop a science of archaeology that incorporates African ways of living and seeing?

Consulting with the ancestors and revisiting sacred ritual grounds, as Andah puts it, are essential components of African cycles of change and continuity that must be integrated into an African archaeology. For example, ritual events ordered by rhythmed time often leave behind clear and powerful physical signposts that are clearly remembered in the oral histories of African peoples. Such events are often remembered longer than events that may once have had a linear order, say, in clan genealogies, because such important ritual moments are marked by mnemonic devices such as sacred groves or trees that are preserved in the landscape today. Thus a royal shrine tree where a king was buried in a beer boat, or where a king was ritually buried during his installation rites, preserves the memory of the transformational event long after the waning of other oral records. Mnemonic systems present an enormously important extant record of rhythmed time in African cultures (Schmidt 1978). In many cases these indigenous African archaeologies are accessible to Western techniques of investigation. We must understand, however, the dynamics of social life that create the nonlinear characteristics of African ritual time, and our archaeology must be sufficient to account for a flow of events as rhythmic pulses that mark significant social and political transformations.

These ideas complement Andah's position and pose a challenge to both his fellow African archaeologists trained in the principles of Western archaeology and to those of us Westerners who have been exploring our own comprehensions of and reactions to African systems of thought and knowledge, insofar as they transform and inform our practice of archaeology on the continent. How do we respond to Andah's call for a new language within the African past? How can we carry out his more pragmatic suggestion that the past can inform African people about lessons the past holds for environmental management and appropriate ideologies of governance? The second question is more easily addressed than the first. Some archaeologists, including Africanists, are doing so by redirecting their study of past environments toward affecting management policy in the present and future (Marquardt 1994; Schmidt 1994).

But the question of a new language of archaeology, like that of a memory that returns to the African past, is an issue few archaeologists are prepared to face. Our distance from such issues is significant, even within the Africanist community. One measure of that distance is seen in the separation between Africans and Westerners that continues in the production of knowledge. While Andah and his colleagues struggle to produce the only continuous indigenous journal of archaeology in black Africa, white archaeologists have recently joined together (Robertshaw 1990) to write a history of African archaeology that includes a contribution by only one black African archaeologist (see Okpoko 1991). This is symptomatic of widely differing access to global information systems, but more disquieting, it also signifies the de facto peripheralization of Africans in the writing and dissemination of their own histories. Until we overcome such fundamental problems, the possibility for Western archaeologists to be able to read, understand, and accept African archaeologies remains distant.

NOTE

1. At the Xth Congress of the Pan-African Association of Prehistory and Related Studies held in Harare, Zimbabwe, in June 1995, David Phillipson announced that an Institute project at Axum, Ethiopia, was incorporating training of African postgraduate students.

Studying African Societies in Cultural Context

BASSEY W. ANDAH

As recently as 1991, P. R. Willoughby (1991:71) asserted that archaeology provides the bulk of our information about African societies prior to the availability of documentary sources and the earliest oral traditions. According to this view, archaeology has done much to reveal the long history of human settlement on the continent, dating back at least two million years. In Africa, too, archaeologists are in a position to examine the origins of technology and the nature of initial human adaptation to the environment. This view holds, moreover, that because hominids and the earliest tools both appeared first in Africa, we can reasonably claim that humans and their cultural mode of adaptation are African inventions. Not only does Willoughby see the unbroken prehistoric record on the continent as offering detailed information about how people responded to environmental change and population stress in the past, but she also suggests that such information may offer clues for evaluating similar problems today.

These are reasonable and attractive propositions. But as Willoughby herself admits, if archaeology is perhaps the one historical science best positioned to contribute so much to our understanding of African peoples, it seems, ironically, to have added very little to African peoples' own understanding of their cultural history from earliest times. Indeed, most Africans hardly care to relate to archaeology in its current form and are more likely to dismiss it as being irrelevant for present-day Africans and Africa. This is so despite the fact that archaeological research in Africa is quite old and the majority of Africans are not unaware of it. Why this paradox? One can identify several reasons to explain why such a dichotomy should exist between Africans and archaeology.

The Paradox of African Historiography

Perhaps one major reason for the paradox is that archaeologists working in Africa, like anthropologists and to a large extent historians of precolonial Africa, tend to address their subject matters in general/universalist and, at best, ecological and materialist (i.e., economic) terms rather than in sociological, area- and time-specific terms. Archaeologists subsume their concept of culture under technology and/or economy. Many seem also, as a matter of course, to employ methods and theoretical models that tend to obscure rather than illuminate their subject matters. Moreover, workers in all these fields, especially those examining prehistory, cultural evolution, and human biological origins, usually create the impression that the remarkable finds and findings come from the midst of an uninhabited African wasteland and bear no links with present-day African peoples. It seems, at the same time, that there has been a concerted effort to make African studies the exclusive preserve of the Western world. Especially among Western paleoanthropologists, Africa has served as the platform for all kinds of "acrimonious debates" (Willoughby 1991) and for self-gratifying autobiographies and accounts that have little or no place for Africans and their historical experience, except, of course, that of mythical, "primitive" Africa.

According to Willoughby (1991), Africans' awareness of the lack of practical value in archaeology led to an explosion of interest in the precolonial period—a period seen by Africans to yield hard, factual, and reasonably unquestionable data about the nature of precontact African societies. This new thrust, Willoughby argues, has made it possible for scholars to begin to correct the false perception of African peoples as backward or primitive and to examine closely the nature of societies and their *degree* of social complexity—and to examine, as well, who determines what complexity entails.

If indeed it is true, as Willoughby argues, that as a result of this explosion of interest, "African Iron Age" research has, by choice or by default, become integrated into the larger African studies context, the question arises whether it is an African studies that is truly at home in the continent or one that is more relevant to the Western world than to Africa. This, of course, is part of a much larger question having to do with whether there in fact exists a truly African historiography—a historiography attempting to deal with historical issues and questions of direct relevance to modern Africans. The answers to these questions must address recovering African cultural self-identity and utilizing it to build a meaningful, purposeful, fulfilling future for present-day Africans and generations yet unborn.

P. M. Martin (1988:539) asserts that a historiography of Africa does exist and that it came into existence in 1960 with the first issue of the *Journal of African History*. Martin may well be right. But if so, does this historiography indeed qualify as African? Here I examine the question critically from the standpoint of archaeology, focusing on (1) who controls and determines what is studied, (2) the nature of what is studied, (3) the methods normally employed, (4) the substance of the story derived from the evidence, and (5) the relevance or utility of such studies in the quest for identity and development by Africans.

By *usable* past I refer to a past that does not merely instill pride but also helps Africans build sociopolitical units equipped to fight "cultural poverty" and negotiate justice at both national and international levels precisely because they have their roots solidly in history and have learned the right lessons from their historical experiences.

African Studies: Who Directs the Center, and What Do We Study?

At present, Western scholars are very much in control of African archaeology, as they control all other fields of African studies, largely as an outcome of Africa's recent colonial experience. For about 200 years, the West has controlled both African affairs and African studies. The "experts" in African affairs and the various fields of history, anthropology, and other social sciences are Europeans. The sources students are expected to consult—museum collections, libraries, archives, and so forth—are also overwhelmingly European. In sum, the documented history of Africa is found in sources that are European, not African.

One major problem with this situation is that both research and publications remain, by and large, European instruments of propaganda. Africa is a breeding ground for Ph.D. students from Europe and North America in all the social sciences and in historical sciences such as geology, geomorphology, and ecology. Africa also seems to be the Western world's laboratory for testing its ideas on just about anything in the field of economics, psychology, technology, medicine, politics, and welfare demography. Therefore, not only are the authors of standard archaeological, historical, and other social and natural science texts and articles on Africa invariably European—or, at the very least, Western-tutored Africans—but also the subject matters usually studied hold greater interest for Europeans than for African peoples.

In the case of archaeology, subjects of interest revolve largely around chronology and chronological frameworks, particularly the dating of what are considered to be important sites, places, artifacts, ecofacts (domesticated and cultivated animals and crops), environmental events, and so forth, rather than people and what they actually did. And where people are the subject matter, issues of cultural symbols and practice are obscured by the formulation of problems such as the Early Iron Age or the spread of the Bantu (see Huffman 1982:133). Moreover, the dynamics of cultural phenomena such as migration are simply assumed rather than hypothesized and systematically examined.

The progression in African archaeology has been from chronology to paleoclimatic change and thence to economy. The concept of culture is imposed rather ill-fittingly on African cultural materials, essentially through techno-economics within what turns out to be for Africans a puzzling cultural time frame at best. According to this frame, early African peoples apparently did nothing else but make tools and search for food. They had no social life and no social thought. Regional reviews and continent-wide texts are usually written from this angle (e.g., Klein 1983; McIntosh and McIntosh 1983). In all these presentations, paleoclimatic change is extremely important, if not central, to interpreting cultural behavior, not just for the earliest phases but right up to the present. African "man"—no matter which version—has always, after all, been subject to his environment, never dominating it (McIntosh and McIntosh 1983: 217–18). He adapted to periodically deteriorating climatic conditions by migrating, by modifying his subsistence base, or by becoming more mobile. Although the McIntoshes admit that monocausal or deterministic explanations of prehistoric change are to be avoided, they apparently cannot be avoided in West Africa because, according to McIntosh and McIntosh (1983:218), "the influence of major palaeoclimatic shifts on human populations in large portions of West Africa is undeniable." In any case, in their review of West African prehistory, the McIntoshes confess to following the chronological conventions observed in the *Cambridge History of Africa* (Clark 1982), which hardly account appropriately for the African cultural context.

One might argue that for the "Stone Age" there is really nothing else to study. If so, what about the post–Stone Age, if we retain these rather non-African concepts? Archaeological narratives concern industries, plants, and animals—not humans. Their questions are about domestication—about plants and animals, not domesticated people (e.g., McIntosh and McIntosh 1983:238–39)—as if the story of farming were only about domestication of these elements. Or rather, it is as if the beginning of farming had to do with the beginning of plant and animal domestication rather than with their cultivation. Thus, little is known about the development of cultivation of indigenous crops, primarily because investigators are attuned to looking not for evidence of cultivation but for biological changes in plants and animals. The impression given is that drastic morphological changes in plants and animals have direct bearing on, and lead to, what is a social and not a biological phenomenon, and that there is a universal regularity to these biological (morphological) changes—regardless of the specific nature of the crops and animals and the locale at which the interaction between humans and other species took place. Is the nature of the interaction such that we can understand culture from these changes? Even if farming is seen solely as an economic activity, which it is not, would it ever fit into this biological model in which domestication equals the beginning of farming?

Another limit on knowledge about the African past stems from the obsession with origins—the origins of agriculture, of metallurgy, and so forth. Of course, the origins of anything are extremely elusive. This line of inquiry is ideal for proving that Africans could not have initiated farming or metallurgy or urban life or anything significant on their own. The impression given is that social change (sociological phenomena)— any social change whatsoever, be it as complex as the discovery of metallurgy or the change from hunting and gathering to farming—is a univariate (or rather, monocausal) phenomenon. Again, this impression arises from the reducing of cultural behavior, which influences social and economic institutions, to mere technology and economics. This practice reverses the normal order of cultural dynamics by putting the machine (technology) and the body (economics) as superior to the human mind and spirit. Are humans by nature social animals or simply slaves of tools and food needs? Clearly either Marx, on the one hand, or the initiators of reformation and capitalism, on the other, were very wrong in their reading of cultural humans, or else their adherents have not in their different ways been entirely fair interpreters of their thoughts.

In this light it seems clear to me that the culture-chronological schemes imposed on African cultural phenomena through time, including the classic ages (early, middle, and late Stone Age, Pastoral Neolithic, Early and Late Iron Age), have been far from adequate if not extremely inappropriate. Workers excavate sites and unthinkingly locate unit levels in these "age" compartments as soon as they find the supposedly diagnostic artifact—usually a distinctive stone tool for the Stone Age levels or a style of pottery decoration for later levels. Other artifacts are apparently unimportant, regardless of how very different they may be at intersite or interregional scales. Even when a range of artifacts is present, the variation it shows (in an Early Iron Age site, for instance, the types of iron-smelting furnaces and their locations), the associated artifacts and waste products, or the intensity and nature of artifact distribution (e.g., where iron slag, *tuyeres,* and pottery are concentrated and why, what they were used for, where they were found, or how they were made) are similarly unimportant.

Ironically, even though the prehistory of most regions of Africa is poorly known, this lack of information appears not to have hampered workers from knowing in advance, or predetermining, the framework or outline form of the final narrative. A result of assuming that the framework is well known is that workers are often constrained to search for specific things in specific time periods (e.g., Acheulean sites and nothing else). Not only are these specific things often mirages, but also the possibility of discovering features and entities that are characteristic of and clearly unique to the tropical regions (e.g., the predominance of wooden artifacts, not stone, and not Acheulean stone tools, for that matter) is ruled out. But so it has to be. From the Acheulean we are taken on to the middle Stone Age and the Sangoan—despite our protest about the rather loose use of the conceptual term *Sangoan* in the bid to apply it to West Africa (Andah 1973)—and thence to the late Stone Age: aceramic and ceramic in the Sahara and late Stone Age in sub-Saharan regions. The scheme at best blindfolds its users. The worker is subtly guided or lulled into looking not for anything and everything but only for something specific and often unreal. This perspective obviously represents a very closed cultural system. Yet so far as I am aware, neither African nor non-African culture constitutes a closed system so long as it is a *human* product.

While we insist on imposing a European culture framework on Africa, Africans of the past—certainly those of West Africa, given its poor preservation conditions—will continue to elude our blind eyes. Similarly, review articles, especially those on African archaeology, will be riddled with European catch-phrases: little is known of this and of that (McIntosh and McIntosh 1983:239), or a particular entity (such as the Acheulean) is poorly represented or absent (McIntosh and McIntosh 1983:226).

Western social scientists also pursue an unbelievably disproportionate interest in the odd relics of Africa, such as relic peoples, rather than features pertaining to mainstream Africa. In this regard, there seems to have been a graduation from studies of the sexual lives of African primitives and of magic and witchcraft to relict, preindustrial hunter-gatherers such as central African Pygmies, the San of the Kalahari, and the Hadza of northern Tanzania. If one depended on anthropological literature for an introduction to Africa, one would almost think that the bulk of present-day Africans were hunter-gatherers. Such a skewed picture justified continued European "colonization," domination, and oppression of Africa—a relationship that brought with it an ill wind even for the colonizer, at least in the long run. Africa, for many American and European anthropologists, is at best a classic laboratory for studying human origins, early prehistoric cultural evolution, and, especially, Pleistocene hominid foraging.

What the Experts Say They Do and What They Do

Subjects that are of central importance for understanding African cultural history and dynamics have thus usually held little or no interest for the experts. For specific time periods, such subjects would include (1) the language and biological character of the people; (2) the structure and function of the specific people's family and household systems, on the one hand, and its sociopolitical systems, on the other; (3) the people's technologies, crafts, and production and exchange systems—including farming, herding, and hunting practices, land use, and land tenure systems; (4) the people's religious and social beliefs, norms, and practices—especially those concerning birth, marriage, death, planting, and harvesting over long periods; (5) patterns and trends in language, biological and social attributes, and characteristics of defined groupings, human-land relationships, and interaction in specific cultural regions; and (6) distinctiveness and diversity at the lateral (synchronic) sociospatial level as well as changes in social arrangements at the vertical (temporal) level (i.e., through time).

Though Western traditions of scholarship on Africa often claim as central the study of African cultural dynamics, very few scholars actually embrace the realities—what the Africans themselves make of this subject. Even when they attempt to do so, little of the network and dynamics of social, cultural, or historical relationships of Africans filters through. Historians and archaeologists, for example, usually compile a culture trait list from which efforts are made to ascertain which cultural traits in the area of study are typical of the people or state and how and when such traits (e.g., paleonegritic characteristics) gained entrance among the African people (Fisher 1987:283).

For the precolonial period, Western scholarship often sought to ascertain the influence of Arabs, Persians, Indonesians, or other "civilizing" groups on Africans, or the influence of the "Arabized" Africans (now civilized), such as the Mande of the western Sudan hinterland, the Swahili of the East African coast, and other, more remotely located African peoples. This tradition of African historiography viewed Arabs and, more recently, Europeans as civilizing influences rather than as destroyers of African civilizations and cultures. The African continent was seen as composed of very large, culturally monolithic regions, including the Sahara, the Sudan, the Guinea forest region, and central, eastern, and southern Africa.

Alongside the tendency to see Africa in monolithic terms is a tendency which, for lack of a better term, I call the *fragmentation syndrome.* African peoples and societies and their histories were fragmented with regard to time depth, cultural wholeness (or integrity), and even the person. Not only were experts unable or disinclined to view African societies contextually, but they also made little or no effort to search for and understand the various frames of meaning African peoples employed to express themselves culturally. The normal research practice was to picture Africans from the smallest possible pigeonhole—micro-time and micro-person for historians, a small community and small (synchronic) time bracket for ethnographers, and, for archaeologists, a small hole within a site and spectacular artifacts rather than a cultural region.

Fragmentation was a tool employed by colonial powers (Europeans and Arabs, in the African case) to maintain an economic stranglehold on subject peoples and to help foster the right type of historiography. With the help of their historians, geographers, anthropologists, administrators, and priests, these powers created the myth that African peoples have no history, no wealth of traditions they can draw on to cope with problems of living; they must, therefore, depend on the "benevolent" mother country. On the practical side, local technologies, productive systems, and cultural expertise (including expertise in governance) were systematically dislodged to make way for products, inventions, and institutions from the colonizing mother country. Educational institutions were usually geared toward indoctrinating Africans into a captive mentality (Andah 1985). Africans are still, by and large, pictured as undeveloped, primitive, and uncultured, apparently because they have had no educational systems of their own for fostering improvement (Andah 1985, 1988).

Western Philosophical Frames for Studying Africa

To perceive Africa in this light, Western scholars have usually relied on untested, preconceived ideas, and on the study of cultural traits and their distribution. In this way it was possible for any cultural achievements evident in the African record to be credited to outsiders: breakthroughs in food production, metallurgy, state building, trade, architecture, medicine, and so on. The general tendency was to collapse several, if not all, of the pasts of African peoples from various regions (be they Akan, Baoule, Yoruba, Edo, Mande, Bantu, or Zulu) into one not-too-creditable and very short past, devoid of pre-Arab African civilizations, that was climaxed by the gun-powder and slave-trade era that gave birth to ethnic politics.

Such thinking, rooted in nineteenth-century European epistemology, has been expressed differently by various schools of thought. For evolutionists, Africans represent the unitary savage stage of human progress or are considered a throwback from the medieval and dark ages of Europe (Hart 1985). For structuralists and functionalists, Africans have no history but are essentially unilineal descent societies formed primarily through kinship and marriage ties (Andah 1988). Underlying European thought is a false, racist, unilineal theory of evolution with European civilization representing the apex. Various devices were invented to cope with social complexities not accommodated by the picture of Africa as made up of stateless societies in which social organization owed everything to the lineage. This perspective was largely responsible for marginalizing works like Nadel's (1942) *A Black Byzantium* (about the Nupe kingdom of Nigeria), and it is seen in virtually all European thought from Plato to Marx, with the European edifices constituting "God's own kingdom" (Andah 1985).

Even the supposedly radical (essentially Marxist) schools that claim to have rid themselves of assumptions of unilineal evolution have bequeathed to African societies their own share of specificities said to be characteristic of the Third World. For them, Africa is characterized by a lineage mode of production, belongs to the underdeveloped world, and is peopled predominantly by peasants. Neo-Marxists and structural Marxists postulate that scientific practice, as purely theoretical reflection (theory of theories), is entitled to immediate political influence, that scientific knowledge (meaning Western science) must occupy the central place in transforming the world, that this knowledge is positive in character, and that rational thinking must hold primacy over the social actor's consciousness (Jewsiewicki 1989:14).

Western anthropologists, generally Europeans, thus reacted (rather than responded) to the inevitable unfolding of the complex nature of African societies through the ages by going materialist (Hart 1985). British scholars stressed kinship, domestic cycle, and economy, while the French stressed the operation of the African mind in abstraction. Where the structural functionalists saw Africans as perpetual creatures of their environments, the Griaulle school was incorrigibly idealistic, ahistorical, and unconcerned with the details of practical existence or the significance of ordinary speech in its quest to understand the African mind (Hart 1985). Western political scientists were no different in their orientation to Africa.

Similarly lacking in historical knowledge about Africa—the main models of the nation-state derive from the West—other writers presented parliamentary and presidential democracy as the goal that Africans needed to achieve (Apter 1963; Cohen and Middleton 1970). Simultaneously, economic development meant (and still means, falsely in my view) transforming the mythical African peasant farmer and replacing the supposedly small and peripheral "precapitalist" African markets with Western markets and capitalist principles.

During the 1960s, there was an explosion of historical research on Africa; precolonial African kingdoms began to be recognized and studied. They were studied, however, not to find models on which to base future political development but to obtain some picture of national or regional histories to teach African schoolchildren. As might be expected, most of these studies lacked depth of both time and substance, and the stories of these kingdoms focused mostly on slaving.

Perhaps the most important thing to happen during the 1960s, from an African standpoint, was the emergence of an indigenous anthropology through the efforts of creative writers, primarily novelists and playwrights. These people brought a new perspective to the study of African cultures and societies. They showed clearly the interweaving and linking between cultural symbolism and cultural practices and often successfully described the dynamics of changes, something European and Western-trained African anthropologists had never been able to achieve.

Thus, directly or indirectly, Western social science, including archaeology and history, has been and continues to be an extension of a power system that imposes its ideology and its socioeconomic system as the only valid cultural system for the world. Western scholars usually have had an unequal relationship with their African subjects of study (directly in history and anthropology, indirectly in archaeology). Information from local ethnographers, oral historians, and other informants is seldom obtained in a fair and open climate devoid of pressure. The Western-trained researcher usually occupies the driver's seat rather than the learner's seat, guiding and shaping what informants, living or dead (e.g., sites and artifacts), reveal.

When concepts of culture, time, history, or anything else differ from those of African informants, the Western scholar usually determines what is valid and what should be discarded (Grosz-Ngate 1988:501). Privileged to come from a "scientific" culture, she or he (not the often illiterate informant) is qualified to separate "real and precise" facts from "vague and confused" local traditions. The knowledge of these "others" has to be "evaluated, appropriated and classified by a representative of a voracious and systematizing Western power/knowledge" (Grosz-Ngate 1988:501). Regardless of the particular chord they strike or tune they sing, virtually all purveyors of this knowledge system believe it is their sole business (or rather, responsibility) to construct the cultural beliefs, social structures, and history of Africans and not to concern themselves about how Africans represent their own history or culture, because "these others" know precious little about representation in any case.

Even when Western study of African ways of thinking, speaking, and acting has been well intentioned and broadly conceived, the outcome has usually been essentializing and reductive. It has to be so if the task of describing such a vast variety of cultures, societies, and civilizations is to be manageable and the results useful for policy formulation by their home countries. For this reason, the principles underlying indigenous customs are pressed into categories derived from Western social reality. This categorization has led to the creation of dichotomies between Africa and the West in the realms of cultural and social forms such as property, contracts, marriage and the family, social organization, urban and rural, civilization, the state, religion, and cultural values.

A Glimpse at Archaeological Methodology

In a comprehensive survey of aspects of surface archaeology in Africa, Bower (1986) suggests that for real progress to be achieved in African archaeology, the following requirements must be met: (1) precise definition or delimitation of the region surveyed; (2) determination of the intensity of surface coverage; (3) determination of the extent to which geomorphological processes have masked or removed surface material; (4) establishment of appropriate models for drawing socioeconomic inferences from settlement patterns; (5) deciding where surface data need to be supplemented with test excavations; and (6) sustaining long-term research programs.

Bower (1986) has also singled out site definitions, collection strategy, and the determination of the meaning of material distribution as being among the more ubiquitous methodological problems of intrasite surface archaeology in Africa. These problems may, in fact, be central to all of African archaeology—not just surface surveys, but intensive site, intrasite, and regional studies. But perhaps the most important of Bower's requirements is the proper study of settlements so as to discern socioeconomic patterning and make socioeconomic inferences. What do investigators make of such parameters as the nature and extent of settlement (living, work, industrial, or burial sites), the types of artifacts these contain, their location, spread, and density? How do they define site and regional boundaries of cultural entities or the collection strategies for retrieving samples? How do they interpret the meaning of material cultural and noncultural remains? All these questions have a direct bearing on how close to—or far away from—the actual African cultural contexts a researcher is able to get.

Where the region delimited does not in fact fit with the cultural complex it purports to represent, everything else done in the resulting study will yield at best only skewed results. This, to my mind, is the Achilles heel of much of what passes today as African archaeology. The delimitation of cultural regions, where it is attempted at all, often has no real bearing on the sociocultural entities or groups being investigated. Perhaps because Africans themselves—the social actors producing culture—have not been the central concern of investigators, the delimitation of cultural boundaries that would define Africans has been done arbitrarily by relying on Western concepts of culture, on natural geographical features, or, at best, on the surface spread of artifacts thought to have distinctive styles of manufacture or decoration.

Despite claims to the contrary, most archaeological studies of African sites and regions have utilized a culture-normative rather than a culture-processual frame to characterize their findings. The trend is to define cultural entities in terms of purportedly typical artifacts and assemblages retrieved from sites thought to be typical and believed to have been replicated more or less in their entirety from nearby sites in contiguous geographical regions. This approach not only resorts to a series of assumptions—selected artifacts and their stylistic traits equal a cultural entity—but it is also easily manipulated to portray prehistoric and historic peoples of Africa as able to adapt only to environmental changes and crises. Sometimes these cultural constructs were equated with ethnic identity, as in the cases of Nubia (Wendorf 1968) and the Early Iron Age of central and southern Africa (Huffman 1982). Migration and diffusion were freely used to account for the history of large regions. For central and southern Africa, the cultural past has been so formalized and Bantu peoples and their environments depicted as so unchanging and unchangeable that one need look only at the Nguni- and Sotho-Tswana–speaking peoples of today—their religion, politics, economics, social norms, and settlement types—to visualize Early Iron Age cultures of 2,000 years ago. A projected ethnographic present is also used to understand and explain the early Zimbabwe culture (not civilization) and state (Huffman 1982:133–50). Such studies are typical of much research that has been and continues to be done in various parts of Africa.

In his investigation of the settlement behavior of foraging peoples who may have lived in the Lake Chad region prior to 3000 B.C., for example, Connah (1981, 1984) preferred to relate the spatiotemporal distribution of their sites to possible climate fluctuations rather than to any hypothesis derived from the behavior of known historic or ethnographic examples from the region or from regions nearby. Although a sophisticated array of resources may be brought to bear, many European- or American-initiated archaeological studies in Africa have been more concerned with narrow, preconceived questions about how food production must have been *introduced into* the area than with finding answers to more central questions about the lives of African peoples.

An example of such a study is that of the central Sudan region east of the Nile Valley undertaken by the Italian Mission to Kassala Province and the Joint University of Khartoum/Southern Methodist University Butana Archaeological Project (Fattovich, Marks, and Mohammed Ali 1984), which claimed to be concerned with elucidating the culture history of the eastern Sudan and to emphasize the relationship between environmental change, economic adaptations (including the introduction of food production), and settlement systems (Bower 1986:32–33). The main findings in this case were that the people who lived in eastern Sudan from about 5000 B.C. to the first half of the first millennium A.D.—whoever they may have been—made pottery (designated Atbai) under conditions of increasing aridity. All we learn of the entire developmental sequence of this "tradition" is that it represents a series of adaptations to a regional drought with the resultant environmental opportunities and constraints. The focus of interest in such studies seems to be not man but the environment. Humans, for their part, seem to do little else in African habitats other than adjust to their environment, erecting settlements and keeping animals only when the environment allowed them to do so. African peoples would seem to have no special techno-economic or social capabilities.

Archaeological reports are primarily technical volumes for specialists with little useful to say to Africans about ancient peoples, their social relationships, and their relationships to their environments but with much to say about artifacts, architectural features, and the like (see Schmidt, this volume). For instance, the report on Tegdaoust III (Babacar 1983), described by Fisher (1987:282) as a "magisterial volume executed under magisterial leadership" (how typical of the power-knowledge relationship), is principally a study of artifacts. It devotes 50 pages to ceramics, 67 to decorated *fusaioles* (spindle whorls), and over 200 to stratigraphy and architecture. Against this there is a little more than one page on the paleobotany of this important town site and no direct evidence from excavations or other relevant sources on the people and their network of relationships—that is, no interpretive commentary on the social matrix in which the artifacts were used. Establishing socioeconomic models that allow confident interpretation of surface and excavated remains has also been problematical in studies of earlier cultural entities such as hunter-gatherers, pastoralists, and early farmers.

The Not-So-Traditional

Compared with the methodologically loose work that seems to predominate at present, there have also been some important, forward-looking, and imaginative studies that have had great import in African archaeology. For early prehistory, Glynn Isaac (1977, 1984, 1986) did what may be described as pathfinding work in his study of the site of Olorgesailie, his social models of hominid behavior, home bases, and food sharing, and his study of site-formation processes and human behavior in Koobi Fora, east of Lake Turkana in Kenya (see Gifford 1980). There have also been important studies of vertebrate taphonomy (e.g., Brain 1981) in eastern and southern Africa. And in Nigeria, the archaeology department of the University of Ibadan is studying the rate and nature of decay through graded time periods of various artifact and settlement features in an abandoned village (located at the International Institute of Tropical Agriculture) under the vegetation and climatic conditions of the humid tropics.

In this connection, off-site studies such as Foley's (1981) of the Amboseli Basin also have some importance for African archaeology, especially insofar as such studies recognize that the spatial limits of their research areas need to be more or less equivalent to the cultural "home range" being studied, be it hunting or herding groups (e.g., the later Stone Age and Pastoral Neolithic cultures of this southern Kenya basin). Whether or not such pathfinding researchers actually succeeded in their bid to assemble information about the surface occurrence of cultural persons and materials within their appropriate cultural boundaries (rather than simple bounded ecosystems), and whether or not the correct meanings were inferred from the "background scatter" of artifacts within and between the sites of the cultural regions are entirely different questions.

The study of Jenne-Jeno by the McIntoshes (1980, 1984) is another worthy example. The researchers selected an area of about 1,100 square kilometers thought to represent the diversity of land forms and vegetation found in the region directly associated with the origins and growth of the city of Jenne-Jeno. One could take issue with the underlying assumption that only one town or city developed and was functionally the center of this region, but the important point is that the definition of the research area was directly related to the cultural problem being investigated. All relevant sources, oral, historical, and ethnographic, were consulted to decipher the evolution of the city. I would also note that to study the origins and growth of Awdaghust, another Sahel town, using the same approach, one would need to look at the archaeological remains in the context of the historical growth of Mauritania's central Adrar-Tagrant region, because its growth appears to have been critical to that of the town (McDougall 1985:2).

Works that directly address prehistoric human behavior from a practical and multipronged standpoint have much to contribute to our knowledge of African economic and social history. They shift the emphasis away from artifacts to settlements and burials in well-defined cultural regions. How much of this kind of work is actually under way in Africa at present? What are the best methods for achieving such results?

Archaeologists committed to scientific methods must acknowledge that past social behavior is what they are supposed to examine, through preserved material remains, in any part of the world, including Africa. This assertion raises the problem of inference in all archaeological modeling that attempts to create knowledge of the past (Larson 1984). Aware of the gap between the archaeological record and prehistoric society, archaeologists have turned to contemporary life for analogies (Larson 1984). Yet how observations of contemporary phenomena can inform us about the nature of past behavior remains a serious problem (Sullivan 1978:184), and possible answers to questions of methodology directly affect the acceptance of theories. One way in which the inference problem has been dealt with in African archaeology is through the application of an anthropological outlook, which I now examine briefly.

Ethnoarchaeology and the Reconstruction of Cultural Variety

Ethnoarchaeology has been proposed as one answer to the strictly methodological question (Agorsah 1990; Atherton 1983; Schmidt 1983b). Models applied to the study of cultural activities in sites of various time periods have increasingly been derived from the study of contemporary spatial distributions, that is, the structuring of artifacts, dwellings, and other physical remains across space. But does ethnoarchaeology, as presently conceptualized, provide the breadth and depth necessary if we are to reconstruct the varied and complex cultural realities of African peoples through time? This question is pertinent because many of the cultural pasts studied by archaeologists date to times far removed from the present; in some cases the "cultural" entities are associated with hominids that were not *Homo sapiens*.

A recent overview of African ethnoarchaeology (Agorsah 1990) suggests that present methodological problems can be overcome if ethnoarchaeologists are more careful and more theoretical in their orientation. Agorsah proposes three necessary steps in ethnoarchaeological research. First, ethnoarchaeologists must clearly define the cultural problem being investigated and from the outset construct testable hypotheses in the formal statement of the problem. Second, they must detail the possible tests and test implications of these hypotheses and proceed with the testing through problem-oriented collection of data. Third, after having collected and analyzed data along these guidelines, they are to derive theoretically framed generalizations from the empirical evidence. A practical example, if offered, might have shown the validity and feasibility of this scheme.

The most important flaws in Agorsah's otherwise laudable scheme are its overemphasis on theory in the study of human behavior and the narrow place of "living societies" from which ethnoarchaeological models are to be drawn. First, Agorsah and others err in thinking that theoretical considerations can, by themselves, dictate which methods to use to effectively address the question at hand. Second, ethnoarchaeology need not explain the behavior of past societies on the basis of analytical models derived from observed behavioral or cultural phenomena of living societies. An orientation toward an explicitly well-defined interface between models drawn from modern (traditional) behavior and those of the past (Agorsah 1990:192) is one possible approach, but it is not the only alternative. Other approaches derive from the historical particularities of the local case being studied. An approach sensitive to a whole cultural context as well as to site formation and transformational processes points the way to a scientific method more open than closed.

Why Ethnographic Models Are Inadequate

To rely on ethnographic data to generate models of prehistoric social or economic behavior in Africa is to be blind to a great variety of social and economic changes. Colonialism, first Arab and later European, disrupted relationships that had developed between and within political and socioeconomic groupings in various regions (Berry, Campbell, and Emker 1977:83–91). Among these changes were shifts, or accelerated shifts, in the focus of trade. With the arrival of Arabs, trade shifted from the West African savanna-forest hinterland northward across the Sahara. The Europeans' arrival on the coast in the sixteenth century shifted trade from the hinterland southward toward the coast. As a result, former centers of trade and production were steadily reduced to serving as sources for primary goods.

Moreover, as a result of a process of colonial subdivision and "nation building," many parts of the African interior were progressively dispossessed of their distinctive cultural character and importance and were relegated to the periphery. These areas are now poorly integrated into the regional economic system. Colonial policies aimed at suppressing indigenous initiative and ensuring cash crops for a world market certainly had disruptive effects on Africans practicing subsistence and craft production. This disruption of social systems weakened the efficacy of many local social mechanisms for coping with and overcoming regional ecological hazards and problems. The most recent example is the drought phenomenon in the Sahel, which either would not exist or would not be so severe if the time-honored conservation programs of local people had been treated with more respect by the "advanced" technological powers. These cases point out that when ethnoarchaeologists rely solely on contemporary African societies for their models, changes introduced by colonial agents would provide the basis for distorted interpretations of earlier African groups.

Not surprisingly, Agorsah and others attempting to appraise the field have not specified how ethnoarchaeology builds theories and for what kinds of cultural situations and settings they are appropriate. It is apt here to warn against theorizing about culture at the expense of studying actual historical peoples in order to discover rather than impute their behavior. Excursions into abstract "cultural" realms assume objectivity: "facts" can be collected in a systematic fashion because of the "objective" social and cultural categories of tribe, peasant, farmer, ethnic group, and so forth, allowing comparison of recent and ancient society. A recent study of ABO blood groups among the Yoruba has shown that there is no such thing as a pure Yoruba strain (Adekoya 1994). Where Agorsah is right is in asserting that ethnoarchaeologists in Africa will need to redefine and if necessary reject social categories such as band and ethnic group. This is one way to counter the Western-dominated evolutionary concept of culture as a closed system with a finite number of social organizational types, graded from simple to complex, each with its characteristic economic mode and technology.

Comparison assumes the existence of known and knowable social/cultural universals, which in turn assumes that there are biological determinants of human culture and society (Cohn 1980:21). This approach discards, along with subjective field methods, a central discovery of anthropology, namely, that people lead meaningful lives and these meanings can be discovered only within the context of those lives. Meaning cannot be imputed to past lives (as is blatantly done by many Western scholars in their study of African and other non-Western societies) on the basis of models derived from ahistorical and non-African contexts.

Common to most historical and social science studies in Africa is an intellectualist strand that often resorts to notions, implicit or explicit, such as etics, emics, and representations and rules. The idea here is that universal rules and conventions of cultural classification and representation have been discovered and must be adopted by all who write "standard"—that is, acceptable—scientific ethnography, history, or archaeology. These universal conventions, it is assumed, have been discovered and validated by the intellectual scientific mainstream of the Western world.

The distinction between etics and emics, first employed by the linguist Kenneth Pike, extended the etics of phonetics and the emics of phonemics to ethnolinguistic analysis (Stoller 1989:118–19). The notion was later taken up by anthropologists such as Marvin Harris to undergird a cultural-materialist view of society in which the analyst uses emics (what the other knows) to refine etics (what the researcher knows or thinks he or she knows). Local knowledge (emics) thus becomes data for Western social scientists to use in refining theory (etics). Whose theory? As Stoller (1989:119) aptly notes, "Western social scientists think that by considering etics, they are protected from buying into the natives' system of knowledge." Objectivity thus ensured, they are enabled to discover real culture and cultural universals.

Significantly, the assumption on which the separation of emics and etics rests is at best, as Stoller maintains (1989:119), "a pernicious one: Europeans take other people's explanations of what they know, yet they use their own (European) theories to uncover the real meanings of other people's historical experiences." Yet this emic-etic distinction is the cornerstone of scientific anthropology, including archaeology, in North America as well as in Africa, whether it is practiced by Europeans or North Americans.

A Western anthropological tradition with something potentially positive to contribute to African historical studies is the phenomenological school. Although it is a long way from conceptualizing the study of African cultures, this school at least advocates a "return to things themselves." It sees this return as providing the foundation for a radically empirical approach to anthropology, one that considers intellectual understanding, emotional experience, and behavior to have equal value. Such an approach embraces the full range of human perception, taking into account people's external and internal realities. It explores individual as well as social histories, the extraordinary as well as the ordinary, what people say and what they do.

It also admits that, far from the Enlightenment ideal of deciphering right and wrong in other people's worlds, anthropologists can perceive only cultural text (not context) and that doing so captures only fleeting moments of what is (Stoller 1989:116–18). According to Stoller (1989: 118), the best the outsider can do is to "strive to represent sensually and fully the indeterminacies of the multiple realities of social worlds," because lying beyond the politics of representation (which shapes interpretation) is "the utter contingency of language and social relations . . . which blurs the putative 'eagle-eyed' vision of analytic philosophers and positivist anthropologists" (Stoller 1989:116). More importantly, adherents of this school treat informants as real people with personalities, strengths, weaknesses, confidence, and fears—as people who think, speak, and act for themselves.

What Do We Do with Ethnography?

If ethnographic and ethnoarchaeological models are to be credibly applied to the interpretation of evidence from prehistoric societies, then for each problem identified there must be an extensive set of precisely formulated linking arguments or observations and postulates derived from a careful study of as many appropriate ethnographic cases as are available. Multiple sources of information, such as ecological and historical (especially oral) sources, are needed to link ethnoarchaeological observations to the past—that is, a level of complexity in bridging arguments is needed that will allow assessment of the applicability of the data being considered. Success of such a strategy will be dependent upon preservation; what is preserved and then recovered archaeologically is only part of what was originally extant (Schiffer 1987). Only after elements within each of the multiple domains have been properly defined can they be articulated into a larger-scale archaeological analysis of settlement, social organizational, land-use, and tool-making patterns, and of the relationships of these to one another (Newell and Dekin 1978:10). Obviously, both ethnoarchaeology and archaeology in Africa are still far from building and utilizing models in more finely textured and less restricted manners. The conventional tendency is to let models get the better of us. They become abstracted from history and bear no relation whatsoever to local historical peoples, their settings, cultural values, and products.

To arrive at reasonable reconstructions of the cultural habits of African societies of past times, by either inductive or deductive means, we clearly need strategies based solidly on the premise that the variety of settlements people own and use contain artifacts produced and/or abandoned as a result of behavior specific to the people living in and relating to a particular place. These behaviors occurred at locations marked by the distribution of artifacts (unless, perhaps, the sites have been disturbed postdepositionally); the spatial attributes of the artifacts take on meaning only in relation to local, not universal, nuances and practices.

If, methodologically, the partitioning of artifact loci into meaningful behavioral units and the interpretation of these units through comparison with sociocultural models (settlements, communities) is the most crucial aspect of archaeological research (Newell and Dekin 1978:8), then we can query the approaches used by many archaeologists working in Africa. How representative is the evidence, and how pertinent are the questions asked? Excavated units often are not representative of a regional cultural picture, and, especially in West and central Africa, reconstructions of prehistoric life patterns have relied too heavily on surface scatters with few features and little evidence for structures or stratification. Even with ample data, interpretation has tended to be too abstract and unrelated to the African cultural setting and context.

If these components of human behavior and associated natural processes are to be understood for any period and for any area or region in Africa, ethnographers, historians, archaeologists, and historical geographers are obliged to study with as much temporal depth as possible all available related local behavior, with attention to social changes that took place and the sociohistorical factors responsible for those changes. The questions then are, What has been the case for African archaeology? What direction has African cultural history taken and with what results? The following is an appraisal of the results of African archaeology to date.

Africa's Cultural History: The Story Told to Date

The evidence indicates that African archaeology is relatively weak in its grasp of subject matter and in the methods and theories under which data are collected and then translated into cultural interpretations. The relative dearth of substance and method allows researchers to force whatever cultural, historical, and sociological "knowledge" is available from the continent into temporal and sociocultural frameworks that have little or no relationship to real African cultural forms and dynamics. Reliance on untested, preconceived notions and concentration on the distribution of cultural traits have credited cultural achievements evident in the African record (e.g., breakthroughs in food production, metallurgy, state building, trade, architecture, and medicine) to outsiders. This practice often involves collapsing several pasts of various regions in Africa into one very short past, the climax of which is seen in gunpowder and the slave trade, an era that gave birth to ethnic politics.

Connah (1975), in his study of Benin, Nigeria, from limited rescue excavations, characterized Benin history as stretching back not more than 1,000 years. He saw social relations prior to the slave era as being essentially like those of the slave period, characterized by bloodshed and human sacrifice. The ancient states and city-states of western and central Sudan and the coastal city-states of East Africa are also usually characterized by scholars as dating back to just before A.D. 1000 and resulting primarily from an Arab civilizing presence and trading interests. There were apparently no pre-Arab African civilizations or societies worth speaking of.

In southern Africa, scholars like Huffman (1970, 1986), Kuper (1980), and many before them have found it convenient to equate the history of Bantu-speaking peoples with the Iron Age, largely by equating "ethnic" groups with lithic and/or ceramic assemblages and matching these with ethnographic peoples viewed as having "equivalent" technologies—a phenomenon discussed by Schmidt in this volume. Viewing cultural traits as related through time to "natural" ecological zones rests on the culture-area concept. To further confuse matters, some scholars of Bantu history (e.g., Huffman) see ceramic classification and description as the basis for a form of cultural structuralism that seeks universal processes of human mental organization, rendering the past ahistorical. Such a perspective is no doubt attractive in a political environment that calls for stasis, not change, in the pasts or presents of indigenous African societies.

The end result is that we really do not have a reliable picture of the earlier parts of Africa's pre-Arab and pre-European past. A second and equally important fact is that presently, except for a very few cases such as those of the Mande of West Africa and the Swahili of East Africa, enormous gaps exist in what is generally known of the cultural histories of the societies in virtually all of the language groupings of Africa.

Similarly, little is known about the beginnings and growth of complex forms of society and their settlements (towns, cities, and states) and political systems in most regions of Africa. Often, part of the problem is an over-reliance on dubious Arabic and European sources (Fisher 1978: 96) or a reluctance to investigate all relevant sources. There seems to be little recognition, for example, that archaeological surveys and investigations carried out in concert with the examination of local records can greatly help in sorting out the tangles of political history, such as the precise relations between Songhai and the cities of Gobir, Katsina, Zaria, and Zamfara. Certainly, this approach can result in better understanding of the economic, technological, and social facets of the developmental history of Hausaland and other regions such as Dhar Tichitt, which is shown by archaeological work to have had an agricultural civilization between 2000 and 500 B.C., but which then seems to disappear from the archaeological record for almost a millennium (McDougall 1985).

Relying on oral evidence, McDougall suggests that this cereal agricultural civilization, located in the valleys and wadis of central Mauritania, had settlements that were probably as old as those of the Soninke kingdom itself, which, according to oral tradition, could be several centuries. Of course, the precise location and character of these Gangara settlements and their history are subjects for the discerning archaeological spade. What is less obvious is that the oral evidence at least provides data to help us formulate hypotheses that can be tested archaeologically.

Spear (1989), addressing from a broad-range perspective the problem of gaps and incongruities in historical knowledge of the Mijikenda people of East Africa, raises points that hold more or less true for most other African societies whose cultural histories are similarly little known. As with the Dhar Tichitt region, for example, so also with the Mijikenda: archaeological data leave unexplained gaps. In the Mijikenda case, the gap extends nearly fifteen hundred years, from the first evidence of iron working in the area in the second century A.D. up until the "initial" Mijikenda settlement sites of the sixteenth century. This gap simply does not correlate with any of the other evidence and cannot do so as long as the settlements are not studied archaeologically.

In some cases, even the evidence from language history appears to be of little help. Spear (1989) informs us that there exists a good genetic classification of the Mijikenda dialects and related languages, which has made it possible to relate language development to other evidence. But as for many other African peoples, little documentary evidence for the Mijikenda pre-dates the mid-nineteenth century. In this instance, oral traditions appear to jump directly from putative origins to the nineteenth century, while ethnographic information dates largely to the early colonial period. Until archaeology is employed to help out, it has been possible only to reconstruct the broad outlines of socioeconomic change in the late nineteenth century and, in the face of conflicting evidence, put together a very confused picture of events of the preceding two centuries.

To explain the gap and incongruity, Spear (1989) suggests that for peoples like the Mijikenda, and the Meru and Arusha peoples of Mt. Meru in northeastern Tanzania, a situation exists that is the reverse of that on the Swahili coast. The archaeological remains in these areas, such as they are, are not obvious, permanent, or attractive; the languages and cultures have not remained homogeneous; and the settlements, which like those of the Swahili are widely scattered, have not been linked into a single highly mobile maritime culture. Spear's observation raises the problem of how we tackle the cultural history of peoples and groups (and there are many such in the forest and savanna woodland regions of West Africa) who have suffered serious splits and fragmentation as a result, largely, of disruptions brought on by the transatlantic and Arab slave trade and related phenomena. As I see it, there is clearly a need to develop the right methods for handling the oral lores and traditions of such African peoples, so that we can perceive the distinct social and cultural landscapes otherwise obscured by these disruptive recent historical events.

Fortunately, the African past is rich in sources for dealing with the problems outlined here. Unique opportunities and challenges await disciplined yet imaginative collaboration, and a few perceptive workers in several disciplines are beginning to respond. African societies of iron-working and later times present genuine opportunities for collaboration between archaeologists, historians, oral historians, geographers, and linguists. The ongoing revolution in our knowledge of early food production in regions of Africa south of the Sahara, and of the early cultural history of language groupings such as Mande speakers in West Africa and Swahili speakers in the east, is one result of a reasonable and effective response to the opportunities for interdisciplinary African cultural history.

The Need for an African Approach to Investigations

For African archaeology to provide deeply textured history, archaeologists need to investigate cultural questions with people at the center. Studies must be committed to using all information available for a cultural landscape, including a wide range of sources such as oral traditions, ethnography, linguistics, ecology, and remote-sensing imagery. Only when absolutely necessary should archaeologists use statistical devices borrowed from locational geography, such as site catchment or nearest-neighbor analyses and central place theory, to try to decipher cultural meaning in the spatial distribution of people's activities.

If archaeologists are to achieve a more meaningful and representative reading of past African cultural landscapes, they must adopt an approach appropriate to the problem being investigated. As a general "rule," however, such an approach would have as its point of reference not a site but a cultural region that was inhabited by an actual people or group of peoples, and within which are found a suite of related sites that were inhabited and/or used by these peoples. The size of such a region is normally determined not arbitrarily but, first, according to the character of the entire culture and, then, according to whatever facet of the culture is being studied. The researcher would need to visualize at the outset the regional spread of the cultural set and subsets, using all the relevant background material available, and in particular the people's concept of their cultural homeland as inferable from ecological, linguistic, oral traditional, or other ethnohistorical and/or ethnographic evidence.

Such a scalar, hierarchical approach also demands important reorientations in our use of ethnographic, historical, and linguistic sources to understand social change as expressed spatially and temporally at micro, median, and macro levels. This demand is premised on the fact that the common cultural language that normally knits a society together is not a closed scientific construct. Whether the common cultural ties are ideals, values, beliefs, attitudes, or ways of thinking, speaking, and doing things (e.g., eating, dressing, marrying, living, dying), they are usually manifested in differing ways in various spheres of life (social, political, economic, technological, spiritual). The distinctive features of a people's common cultural language at any point in time and its inventive usage by the various groupings of the social community are normally deduced through a historical or sociological, not a physical or mathematical, process. This point has important implications, some of which are examined here, for the use of ethnographic, linguistic, and oral data in constructing African cultural history.

Ethnographic Data and Language

As Langley (1975:98) has pointed out, a group's perception of its natural and social environment, as revealed through semantic study, is a primary (but not sole) source for understanding the relationships between social structures and organization of space. Yet practitioners of orthodox African archaeology have rarely examined the oral lore and ethnography of African societies (see, however, Schmidt 1978, 1983b) to determine what insights these sources offer into the methods various historical groups use to elaborate and express knowledge not only of production techniques and spatial organization of the habitat but of the underlying concepts and conceptual frameworks that shape these activities, including the movable forms (e.g., artifacts, spatial units, settlements, markets, burials), ideological units, and structural units of time and of life in general. European and American archaeologists seem unaware of this; however, such concepts, explanations, and reasonings have always been commonplace in the daily lives and traditions of all categories of Africans—rural farming and pastoral folk as well as urban dwellers. The imposition of Western (European) concepts such as band, ethnic group, and village prevents researchers from getting at the roots and nuances of the social and cultural concepts of African peoples, their social, political, and popular science traditions, and the appropriate use of such information in the reenactment of their cultural histories.

Properly approached, ethnographic data reveal that concepts in many African cultures have an ecological basis and character. This applies particularly to the dominant modes of production, ways of constructing settlements, how spatial categories are precisely defined, and how the structures of languages relate to natural and temporal spaces. As Langley (1975) observes, the very structure of every language is partly a product of the natural space inhabited by the social system and the use made of it. It is important to note that descriptions in African languages often do not have European-language equivalents, and it is consequently difficult to translate such concepts directly by a single word. Langley (1975) cites several pertinent examples from West Africa and Zambia.

Only by digging into the conceptualizations of rural and urban African societies, especially as expressed in ethnographic and oral historical sources, can we gain entry into the fabric of African knowledge systems—not just for present-day cultural landscapes but for the often very different landscapes of earlier (e.g., pre-slave trade) times. Understanding those knowledge systems is a firm basis for learning the social and environmental plans and designs of past populations and for formulating actions for social and environmental planning today.

Such ethnolinguistic (lexical) studies, whether of basic geographical and environmental terms or of technological, economic, and socioeconomic terms, can yield such understanding only when, as Richards (1975: 106) observes, "We begin to consider complete terminologies. When for example we look not at isolated words for rocks, soils, and plants (vegetation), animals, and the cultural facts and artefacts derived therefrom, but at whole sets of terms and complete taxonomies covering the biological and social cultural domains." A study, for example, of the naming and classification of natural and social elements of the environment makes it possible to understand how a local hunter, farmer, pastoralist, or metal worker conceptualizes the world and the ways in which different worlds interrelate to constitute one world (see Richards 1975:106). Understanding the classificatory principles of the people should also give insights into the fundamental process of linguistic and symbolic coding that permits a society either to replicate or to change its social structure and culture from generation to generation.

Oral Traditions

Archaeologists working in Africa know that oral traditions can be effectively decoded only when the social environment in which the oral historian/local consultant lives and its symbolic and structural contents are understood. We also know that the ways in which these traditions can be useful as history (see Schmidt 1978) are very different from the ways in which scholars employ written narratives. From oral data we obtain various strands of symbolism—both dominant and underlying patterns. Often emphatically contradicting each other, these strands offer more than a hint about essential social transformations that took place in the past and are connected with contemporary society. A researcher can trace such contradictions to earlier forms of contemporary institutions and sometimes even to their gender aspects.

Broad patterns of history are also obtainable (Binsbergen 1987) with the help of rigorous historical and anthropological methods. The periodization of such patterns can at best be only relative, but with greater time depth one may find difficulty drawing sharp boundaries between mythical and historical time. Telescoping often occurs in oral transmission, especially in genealogical renderings of history. Properly approached, oral texts allow sensitive observers to perceive, among other things, the processes linked with whatever relative time ranges are discerned, such as the processes of farming, metal working, and state formation, all of which can be expressed as hypotheses to be tested archaeologically.

Archaeologists must remember that with the advent of Islamic influence (and later Western colonialism), many African societies constructed legendary genealogies and derivative origins from, for example, the socially prestigious Near East or the north. This is true of many peoples in West and East Africa. The Habe legend of Hausaland (Nigeria) and the Shirazi of East Africa (said to come from the Persian Gulf) are examples. R. L. Pouwells (1984:254) correctly sees the Shirazi not as representatives of literal migrations but as representing the Swahili construction of genealogies. He also sees the Shirazi as a countermyth born of the radical oppositions and tensions inherent in historically immigrant communities. As a term of identity, it served as a countermyth to the origin myths and genealogical links of Arab immigrants, being both Islamic and culturally equal to, yet different from, Arab pretensions. A similar phenomenon may have appeared in parts of West Africa with the advent of Muslim traders (especially in west and central Sudan, but gradually spreading southward and, with the spread of Mande trading groups, reaching into Sierra Leone, Ivory Coast, and Ghana).

Hausaland, located in a relatively dry grassland in present-day Nigeria, is the source of another cautionary example. The Habe (Hausa) legend of "Abuyazidu" suggests that indigenous peoples and their culture were altered by successive waves of migrating Berbers between A.D. 500 and 1500. This peaceful fusion is said to have taken an unknown period of time to run its course, but one manifestation of it was the emergence of the Habe language. Habe legend also suggests that these Berber immigrants brought a higher civilization that ultimately advanced the indigenous sedentary people. There is little evidence, historical or archaeological, to support the Habe legend. On the other hand, works by noted Arab scholars, as well as orally transmitted myths, traditions, and chronicles—especially the Kano Chronicle (Johnston 1967:9) —suggest that the people of Hausaland, like the pre-Islamic, African, Bantu-speaking peoples of the coastal regions of East Africa, were fairly sophisticated in the smelting and working of iron for at least 500 years, and probably more, before the advent of the Arabs (Johnston 1967:4). Archaeological evidence at Nok and Taruga suggests significant cultural development more than 1,000 years before the period referred to in Habe legend. People in the region had developed agriculture, trade, cities, and a system of government based on chieftainship (Smith 1960:4).

Oral traditions generally document the narrator's identity, world view, and historical perspectives. Because oral traditions are structured, the historian must understand what the structure represents in order to reconstruct history from them. These traditions usually are more than simply charter myths and structural presentations of people's world views and social arrangements. Not only do they often preserve historical information, but even their structure is a reflection of people's perception of their historical development.

The incorporation of oral histories into archaeological inquiry is beginning to reveal, for example, that African farming and pastoralist communities were not tied to specific types of environments, as many non-African workers tend to assume (e.g., pastoralism is assumed to be restricted to drier areas, and crop farming to more humid areas). For South African history, such use of oral histories is showing that there have been no specific groups or societies that were tied down to specific forms of subsistence through known historical time (Maggs and White-law 1991:3–24). For instance, there now seems to be no basis for the popular belief that the San have always been hunter-gatherers and the Khoi pastoralists (see also Wilmsen 1989).

A historically based approach should help show that the character of the landscapes of most parts of Africa from the late seventeenth through the nineteenth centuries was atypical, those landscapes having suffered heavy depredations by slaving and colonial powers. The perceptive archaeologist has in oral traditions an important source of information that discloses sharp contrasts between the land-use styles of conservation-oriented locals (even the herders) and the exploitative, intensive styles of colonial governments and settlers (hunting, plantation agriculture, and concentrated herding of cattle, sheep, and goats). An important reason for adopting a flexible scalar frame of thinking and a compatible methodology with which to conduct archaeology in Africa is that doing so has the potential to free us from the tyranny of grand theorizing. This approach allows real people, now long gone, some room to speak to us and even to dance for us. It may enable us to encounter real (rather than mythical) African peoples and to discover from them how they coped with and transformed their real (not mythical) environments, how they dealt with the tasks of living with social selves and neighbors at specific times and over long time periods, and what technological, economic, and social measures they devised in their drive to find answers to what they perceived to be their problems.

General Discussion

There is a common impression that archaeology is a neutral historical science that makes available incontrovertible sociohistorical facts from material remains. Thus disguised, this ideologically loaded historical social science has thus far served as an important vehicle for psychologically tying colonized (that is, oppressed and suppressed) peoples in Africa and other parts of the world to the colonial state, so that they can continue to be exploited economically and in other ways. In the first place, Arab and European colonial powers played major roles in disrupting the social and political African entities and unities that existed prior to their arrival and which resisted their incursions for as long as they could. In their place, arbitrary units have been imposed under the pretext that there were no such complex entities previously. At the same time, the more credible versions of Africans' oral traditions and archaeology have been encapsulated to ensure the endurance of the saga of mythical African peoples. In keeping with the Lévi-Strausian position, the constructs are concerned with global transformation, and social structure is seen as an end in itself; people's kinship relationships and ties are treated with a logic that denies them real existence in both social space and sociohistorical time.

I hope it is clear from the foregoing that for African archaeology to begin to provide a true history, archaeologists would need to engage more in the investigation of cultural questions that not only have African peoples as the centerpiece, and their cultural regions and time spans of occupation as the context, but also are alert to discerning the high- and low-water marks that indicate major changes in the cultural configuration of the landscape. It follows that there is an urgent need to reconstitute the historical social sciences so that they relate directly to the desire of African peoples to achieve total liberation, both mental and material. For African archaeology to play a key role in this total societal liberation, it would need to be seen and practiced as a liberating historical and educational discipline whose central concern is to recover and produce knowledge regarding the social dynamics and realities of past African cultural landscapes. It would have to sift out and transfer relevant facets to appropriate agencies so that they might serve as educational tools for directing the restructuring of African societies, and in particular the reinvention of sociopolitical and economic systems for the benefit and improvement of all parts of society, not only the dominant class or gender.

A prime goal for these types of African archaeology and history would be to develop appropriate tools for unearthing as fully and as properly as possible all previous African cultural landscapes, especially those that have been deliberately suppressed by colonial and neocolonial historical orthodoxy and whose suppression has kept African peoples from taking a firm hold on their own sociopolitical and economic states. A major task of such historiography should be to point out how these former African social entities worked and what led to their demise, especially when faced with the Arab and European threats. A related task would be to identify what lessons contemporary African countries interested in establishing (rather than creating) regional unities and continental unity should best learn from these.

Clearly, European scholarly traditions are far from well positioned to cultivate a genuine African historiography, simply because of their specifically European interests and perspectives. No matter how well intentioned or conceived, these interests are tangential to real African needs and interests (Jewsiewicki 1989:8–9). It also seems that postcolonial governments in Africa are not well positioned to assist in this project because experience has shown that no matter how radical their postures, these states still constitute, through either reaction or response, extensions of the colonial state model.

Radical African intellectuals, too, seem to have little to contribute to a genuine African historiography. Reacting against the colonial experience, African intellectuals cling to entrenched myths which, paradoxically, are rooted in the colonial ideology of Africans' having no history. Being more concerned with the state than with the nation, their perceptions of social and political life and problems of society are often far removed from the social, historical realities of African peoples. Considering their grave misreadings of the histories and lives of ordinary Africans, it is not surprising that these radicals have failed to provide realistic answers to African peoples' real and vital need for ideologies (in the sense of moral community).

Thus, the much-maligned ordinary Africans are best placed to direct the course of African studies for the cultivation of a genuine African historiography because they are the principal historical and social actors. In my view, a history that reduces historical research on people or periods to a scientific or documentary technique or to an ethnoscience cannot unravel African cultural history because it obscures the very questions we should be addressing. Similarly, history that turns "people" into empty formulas and constitutes their histories in terms of forms or types of early stone tools (Sussman 1991), modes of production, underdevelopment, peasants, slavery, and so forth, also obfuscates.

Because they continue to react against rather than respond to the colonial and neocolonial threats, national and pan-national African histories and historiographies usually have served as useful vehicles for the visible political struggle against colonial rule. However, they have been less than adequate as ideological vehicles for holding African social groups together. Theirs have been tales of woe principally because they usually simply incorporated the same or other romanticized versions of the African past and of African social systems, while actually depending for their strength on European Enlightenment ideologies that were by and large alien to African social and historical realities. In differing ways, this is what constitutes the Achilles heel of the Nkrumah, Sekou Toure, and Nyerere versions of African socialism and of Leopold Sedar Senghor's negritude and the pan-nationalism of Cheik Anta Diop.

Official versions of the histories of African peoples are usually carefully cultivated by these colonial powers and their successor neocolonial governments, and even by their radical Marxist enemies. These were and are then used to indoctrinate the colonized and thereby keep them under control. Oral traditions, the written word, and much more recently archaeology have been important vehicles for this exercise. The maxim here has been that those who control the educational tools rule the people's minds. This has worked quite well to date for both colonial and neocolonial powers.

An African history that aspires to dig up and recover Africa's usable past has to be one that reverses the tendency to exclude the ordinary African from the past. African Marxist interpretations, as rightly pointed out by Jewsiewicki (1989:10–11), cannot bring about such a reversal because in their concern for structures and societal models they often lose sight of historical reality and of social actors. "National" and ethnic interpretations of history are not well placed to effect such a reversal because they are not particularly concerned with getting at the real historical facts, as Schmidt observes elsewhere in this volume.

Although social scientists of various leanings tend to ignore ordinary African social actors, those actors hold the key to the proper constitution of African history and historiography. In spite of the depredations of the slave trade and colonialism, African people have not ceased to recount history, making use of specific ways of remembering to help create and maintain identities and solidarities (Jewsiewicki 1989:10). To represent properly African experiences and performances, we need this perspective. Researchers need to shed their superiority and meet with ordinary people, not as equals but as students. This is the only way to overcome the false belief in Western society as the model for social science and the development of humans. A starting point is recognizing the necessary relationship between concepts and the real world: that concepts have social and historical roots (Carr 1986).

Conclusion

To liberate itself from the shackles of colonialism, African archaeology must become a historical science that distances itself from an discipline that studies mythical entities and reduces human beings to pieces on a chess board, part of the organic world totally under the control of physical and mathematical laws of science and nature. It must be an archaeology firmly founded on the premises that historical, not mathematical or other scientific, awareness is the only form of self-knowledge, that history is open to constant reinterpretation in a universal quest for useful precedent (Ajayi and Ikara 1985:6), and that history is an anvil of identity on which distortions are readily beaten by those in power. We need an archaeology that recognizes and actively seeks to counter tyrants, whether in colonial regimes or their successors, who "are terrified at the sound of the wheels of history . . . so [if] they try to rewrite history, make up official history, put cotton wool in their ears and in those of the population, [then] maybe they and the people will not hear the real lessons of history," lessons of struggle and change (Ngugi Wa Thiongo 1987:xiii). It must be constructed as a social historical discipline, recognizing that much of Africa's written and unwritten history has taken the part of its rulers rather than its people (Lonsdale 1989) and proceeding unambiguously to correct and counter this inexactitude.

As soon as we begin to do this, we will start to see that the historical past for Africans is not solely the entire time span from human origins to the present, but that within such a time span African history is neither singular nor simple but rather as multiple and complex as the functions of human memory. To discover and represent this multiple and complex historical Africa and its inhabitants requires new anthropological, historical, and archaeological usages in a language drastically different from the disciplinary languages we presently use.

Archimedes once said, "Find me a fulcrum and I will move the world" (Andah 1985). I do not know if we will ever be allowed to use this fulcrum when we find it, but that does not deter me from pointing to it as we try to construct an authentic cultural history of Africa. For archaeology to yield "inside" history and an authentic African biography such that the ordinary African is enabled to rediscover a true historical self (individual, social, and cultural) and thus a sense of history and creativity, its practice in Africa will need to be drastically rewritten. The focus of study must remain the people—their daily activities, their social life and institutions, and their scientific and literary explorations, as preserved and recounted by them historically.

This means that African archaeology cannot and must not be reduced to the nonhuman sciences of geo-, bio-, and chronostratigraphy. Such sciences must be seen for what they are: tools to help us gain a better understanding of cultural stratigraphy—in its vertical (temporal) and horizontal (sociological/ecological) expressions. Rather, the focus has to be on human societies living in Africa and interacting on the basis of shared meaning. Through the ages, African peoples, like others, have lived in defined territories and interacted with one another and have, of necessity, devised social forms and cultural products to meet their basic requirements. As it did for other peoples, this direct experience served as the substratum for their philosophizing and political thinking, a substratum that accounted and continues to account for the recurrence of certain questions in the history of their political thought, questions about what type or manner of political system to adopt and who should control it and why. As a discipline, African cultural history should be concerned with studying, on its own terms, the complex forms of social change, interaction, and synthesis that characterized identifiable cultural regions. Indeed, it is largely concerned with precisely those facets of life which other (especially experimental and theoretical) sciences attempt to eliminate from their field of vision by isolating the phenomena to be studied under laboratory conditions or by formulating theories of extreme generality that are abstracted from the irregularities and special cases of the real world rather than from the regular and the typical.

I argue that there is an urgent need for a vigorous alternative to the present tradition of archaeology in Africa and a new course that such an alternative should chart. For archaeological and anthropological education to be beneficial and fruitful to any people, it must be thoroughly self-reflexive and other-critical. Distancing ourselves from the dominant paradigm is a politically vital—not a dubious—strategy, especially in an age when Western imperialist archaeology is bent on swamping the cultural identities of peoples under its political and/or economic sphere of influence. Through this process of distancing, African peoples are able to see their cultural performances and productions for what they really are, and thus are able to identify the modes of thought which their own cultures posit.

African History: Past, Present, and Future

The Unending Quest for Alternatives

AUGUSTIN F. C. HOLL

T he subdivision of time, be it human or physical, is based to some degree on the image of an arrow—a unidirectional flow. And in different social systems, conceptions of time are more or less internalized or externalized. In the internalized situation, conceptions of time may lead to a cyclical framework of social time that may include, for instance, the dynamics of environmental systems and their interaction with social systems at different levels. In the externalized situation, conceptions of time may lead to an increasing degree of instrumentation, with consequences such as the development of machines to divide time into meaningful units increasingly less connected to obvious natural phenomena such as night, day, moon cycles, and seasons (Pomian 1984). The variability and diversity of modes of ordering time suggest that time is more than a framework for action; it is intimately linked to the very nature of human social systems and consequently to their evolutionary pathways. Worldviews are thus better considered as sociotemporal constructs.

Both internalized and externalized conceptions of time are present to varying degrees in every social system, and the nature of their combination depends mostly on the dominant mode of social dynamics: segmentation or integration. There is, therefore, a long continuum with mostly internalized concepts of time at one end and mostly externalized "time-views" at the other. The emergence of history, as a structured set of techniques always in the making, is itself historical and depends on a combination of symbolic, social, and economic factors. At the simplest level, that of individual historians, we may consider it axiomatic that the production of comparable historical accounts has to be based on a shared concept of time—that is, schools of thought are based on a consensus among some scholars about what is relevant. An emphasis on variable, culture-specific concepts of time is, of course, a relativist proposition, which is inescapable when one is dealing with social and historical sciences in general. But this does not mean that it is out of the realm of scientific investigation, which does not need to be based on only one dominant worldview. The theory of general relativity did not lead to generalized relativism among physicists; rather, it has generated sounder scientific investigations of the cosmos. I am convinced that the same thing may be achieved in the social sciences if, and only if, social scientists wish it to occur in the future.

In principle, history may be considered an account of past events. This minimal definition raises difficult problems in setting the boundaries between past, present, and future. If the present is viewed as the intersection between two planes, the past and the future, it does not itself have any temporal depth. Consequently, it is individuals and, more generally, social groups who "decide" to widen or narrow the temporal extent of the present according to cultural and wider social needs. History, both oral and written, is a contextual product of human minds: the past in itself is not yet history; it is mostly virtual history, which starts to emerge as explicit history through the efforts of humans who select, transform, and transmit what is considered to be important for the present:

> For me, history does not correspond to any kind of pre-established truth, everlasting, "pre-written," which has to be discovered by the historian after an ineffable treasure hunt; it is constantly reworked and rewritten according to the specific time, habits, and societies of reference. As Marc Bloch said a long time ago in *Apologie pour le métier d'historien,* each period reconstructs the past according to its own preoccupations. Being a historian thus means, beyond the techniques and methods, being able to evaluate as honestly as possible the conditions determining the requirements and prohibitions that, within the historian's own society, constrain the making of history. (Devisse 1988:325, my translation)

Historiography, or the history of history, is of paramount importance if we wish to grasp the extreme complexity of the making of history. Whether in Africa, Europe, or elsewhere (e.g., Boahen 1988; Boubou Hama and Ki-Zerbo 1980; Devisse 1988; Fage 1980; Fall 1988; Finley 1987; Momigliano 1992; Sahlins 1985), there are different degrees of diversity within traditions of historical scholarship, and it is only during certain segments of time and social circumstances that their internal diversity is reduced. The colonial period is such a segment, one in which historical scholarship concerning conquered territories was based on the denial of any historical depth and socioeconomic achievement on the part of past African societies.

Historical Science as an Evolutionary Process

Without variation, conceptual change would be impossible, and it is amazing how some of us who have been trained to be scientists abhor variation and diversity. The process of knowledge seeking is characterized by tensions and paradoxes (Kuhn 1990; Popper 1991). This simple statement will be the cornerstone of my discussion. What appears as history in the world of learning emerged in different times and places and was shaped by different aims and purposes. The histories written by professional historians have emerged in specific social circumstances. Academic or scientific history, with its endemic theoretical and methodological debates, its organization into competing "demes," or "schools of thought," and academic "curricula," starts to become intelligible if considered in evolutionary terms (Hull 1988:15).

Many disciplines belong to the large domain of the historical sciences. In this chapter, I focus mainly on archaeology and history as practiced in West Africa during and after the colonial period. The situation in archaeology (De Barros 1990; Holl 1990; Robertshaw 1990) is relatively simple in comparison with that of history, in the sense that precolonial African societies had not developed a concern about archaeology per se, while historical knowledge transmitted from one generation to the next was extremely important in different social circumstances (Boahen 1988).

African archaeology and professional history, in the modern sense of the terms, are offshoots of the colonial enterprise; they have been shaped in the academy by their role in either supporting or countering dominant assumptions concerning Africa's past. Changing truths, theories, and explanations are often interpreted by professional scientists as signs of progress in the basic issues of their disciplines. This attitude has been challenged by many scientists and scholars (Bourdieu 1984; Hull 1988). Kuhn (1970), for instance, has convincingly argued that paradigmatic changes in scientific explanations result from complexes of interacting factors and not merely from progress in interpretation:

What occurs during a scientific revolution is not fully reducible to a reinterpretation of individual and stable data. In the first place, the data are not equivocally stable. More important, the process by which either the individual or the community makes the transition from one theory to another is not one that resembles interpretation. . . . Given a paradigm, interpretation of data is central to the enterprises that explore it. This enterprise can only articulate a paradigm, not correct it. Paradigms are not corrigible by normal science at all. (Kuhn 1970:121)

Clearly there are many advantages in studying the histories of archaeology and academic history in Africa as a selection process. First, we will be in a position to realize that archaeology is not simply a straightforward record of discoveries, and history is not a simple account of past events. Second, we will find that the data recorded in both fields of knowledge are variable mixtures of empirical facts and social and ideological assumptions. Third, we will be in a position to understand why scientists challenge certain tenets and take others for granted. In this regard, the reconstruction of the past must be considered neither as an unattainable "past in itself" nor as a series of "pasts-as-known" but mainly as dependent upon the scientists' minds and the intellectual and social framework within which their aims and purposes are conceived.

The past can therefore serve multiple purposes: it can be "past as charter" or "past as bad example" (Wilk 1985:319). Far from being an escape from the present, the past assumes specific roles in the present in social and political spheres. As members of fields of research committed to studying the past, archaeologists and historians assert firmly that there is a connection between past and present and that this connection is relevant and important. There is no need for archaeologists to be defensive about explicitly or implicitly drawing on their personal, cultural, and political experiences in their professional work (Hall 1984b; Wilk 1985). Richard Wilk (1985:319), for example, has convincingly argued that it is important "to acknowledge that there is no neutral, value-free, or non-political past" and that we should drop any pretense of absolute objectivity.

For the sake of simplicity, at this point I consider two grand traditions: the "Western historical tradition," on one hand, and the "African historical tradition," on the other. The African side of the Western historical tradition, which may be termed colonial history or "official history" (Vargas Arenas, this volume), was an offshoot of the national histories of colonial powers after the "scramble for Africa" that took place after the Congress of Berlin in 1884–85. From its Greek origin, the Western historical tradition followed different evolutionary pathways through the Romans, the Middle Ages with their ecclesiastic historical subtradition, and the emergence of the National school of history after the fifteenth century (Momigliano 1992). History making was always controversial. In the nineteenth century, the nature, characteristics, and aims of history were strongly debated, and the emergence of revolutionary ideologies such as Marxism added complexity to an already complex issue (Hegel 1965; Kolakowski 1987). For Hegel and his followers, adhering to the dialectic of the master and his slave, history was the manifestation of the progress of the mind from an ahistorical and primitive stage to civilization. For Marx and Engels, who attempted to translate the Hegelian dialectic into less ambiguous social models, history was a result of the struggle of contradictory and conflictual modes and systems of production of material goods; their approach is called historical materialism (Kolakowski 1987).

Science being a selection process, colonial history was based upon one subtradition—the Hegelian one—selected from among many equally probable worldviews available at different times of the colonial regime. In a series of lectures given in 1822, 1828, and 1830, published in German in 1955, and translated into French in 1965, Hegel formulated his conceptions of history and the development of mankind. His ideas about Africa's past were endorsed by many generations of researchers in history, anthropology, and the social sciences generally. For Hegel (1965: 246–47), Africa was composed of three parts that had to be considered differentially: northern Africa, from the Sahara to the Mediterranean Sea, which was linked to Europe; Egypt, in the sense of the Nile basin, which was the center of an autonomous and great civilization connected to Asia and the Mediterranean area; and finally, sub-Saharan or black Africa, which was out of the realm of history.

After a long and vivid description of the environmental conditions of Africa and a consideration of the different patterns of behaviors there, Hegel constructed an archetype of the Negro: "It results from these different traits that the pattern which determines the characteristics of negroes is their 'unbridled-ness.' Their condition is not susceptible to either change or education. They have always been as we happen to see them today" (Hegel 1965:268–69). Concluding his presentation of Africa, he set the tone on Africa's place in history:

> It has, properly said, no history. We leave Africa at this point without further mention. It does not belong to the historical world; it shows neither movement nor development, and what happens to occur there, that is, in the north, belongs to the Asiatic and European worlds. Carthage was an important but passing element, but it belonged to Asia as a Phoenician colony. Egypt will be considered

in the context of the passage of the human Mind from the East to the West, but it does not belong to African Spirit. What we subsume under the word Africa is an undeveloped, ahistorical world, entirely prisoner of the natural Spirit; its place is still at the threshold of universal history. (Hegel 1965:269, my translation)

All the arguments of European superiority are present in Hegel's lectures: African childishness, backwardness, and lack of cultural achievement, and the disconnection of Egypt from the mainstream of African history. Researchers such as Leo Frobenius (1987) took these proposals for granted. Even if he was in sympathy with Africa in general, and more specifically with its cultural traditions, Frobenius initiated his expeditions in order to discover cultural patterns of the childhood of mankind, which he thought were still preserved in Africa and definitely lost in materialist Europe. These views were congruent with and supportive of the *mission civilisatrice,* or the "white man's burden," which aimed to bring the light and achievements of civilization to the poor and unfortunate African Negroes.

The clash between the Western and the African historical tradition occurred during the conquest of Africa and the installation of colonial regimes, and it happened that the *mission civilisatrice* had to be implemented by weapons and coercion. What was termed "pacification" by the colonial powers was "resistance" to African leaders and later intellectuals and historians (Boahen 1985, 1988; Boubou Hama and Ki-Zerbo 1980; Fall 1988).

The African historical tradition is a complex of different kinds of histories. Two components may be distinguished: one composed mostly of professional historians, teachers, and researchers, the other composed of official and unofficial "historians" attached to particular segments of the native African societies. Both components have internal variations and diversity. The emergence of professional historians is linked to the development of colonial regimes with their different academic and educational systems. The second component is much more diversified and may include heads of families who are engaged in disputes over land and who may use historical information, mostly transmitted from generation to generation, to support their claims; officials of state whose function is to keep alive the memory and genealogy of members of the royal families or clans; and official historians attached to specific rulers—for example, Ahmad Ibn Furtu (Lange 1987), who has written a chronicle of the Borno expeditions of King Idris Alauma (1564–76).

In general, in native African societies, history is experienced and conceptualized as social time, and knowledge is power. These features are much more obvious in centralized political systems:

> In African societies with centralized political regimes, the most important social position is that of the king or the ruler. In general, members of only one family have access to the throne. But in the majority of cases, whatever the kind of descent rules — matrilineal or patrilineal — it is the vote and not only the order of birth that decides the successor. It is thus important for the candidate to the office to convince the voting members of the councils that make kings of their qualities as genuine heirs. The legitimation of their titles and claims can be based solely on historical arguments. (Boahen 1988: 256, my translation)

It thus appears that it was not the lack of history per se that was instrumental in the development of colonial history but the alterity, the violent clash with other peoples and their histories. The cornerstone of this tragic misunderstanding was the absence of written records, which were, for nineteenth-century European historians, the sine qua non for the making of histories. The incredible violence of the colonial powers in their use of physical constraint, political domination, economic exploitation, and cultural alienation was differentially resisted from the beginning to the end of the colonial period. But colonialism went beyond the use of violence to appropriate the ancient histories of the colonies through the practice of an archaeology that was an arm of the colonial enterprise.

The Colonial Trauma: Research Problems and Explanatory Frameworks

The majority of the earliest archaeological reports from West Africa were concerned with stone artifacts collected at random (De Barros 1990; Holl 1990). Data from these artifacts were used to construct typological charts similar to those for France in order to build an approximate time scale. Another major concern was with monuments and impressive buildings. The data collected were used to locate ancient political centers and the capital cities of West African empires of the first half of the second millennium A.D. that were mentioned in the Arabic historical record (see Delafosse 1916; McIntosh and McIntosh 1983).

Many of the people who played important roles in the emergence of French archaeology as a self-contained discipline actively participated in colonialism. Ernest-Théodore Hamy, who was a medical officer in West Africa, published about 12 papers between 1877 and 1907 and edited several volumes in the series *Matériaux pour servir à l'histoire de l'homme* from 1864 onward. He was also the editor of the journal *Revue d'ethnographie* in 1890 (Mauny 1968). Maurice Delafosse was governor-general of the French colonies of West Africa; it was his duty to enforce French colonial policy. Delafosse was not trained as an archaeologist, historian, or ethnologist, but he was a scholar who used different kinds of available information in order to provide accounts of the past, the process of peopling, and the emergence of "civilization" in West Africa. His publications (Delafosse 1900, 1916) are therefore among the best illustrations of the colonial attitude toward the West African past (Fall 1988). In both history and archaeology, the pioneer phase of research was characterized by the publication mostly of short notes. In history, people like Yves Urvoy (1949) and H. R. Palmer (1936) published works that are no longer considered to be genuine history. In archaeology, the first Pan-African Congress of Prehistory, organized by L. S. B. Leakey and held in Nairobi in 1947, can be considered the major event that brought genuine change in the nature of archaeological investigation in Africa.

In both history and archaeology, the explanatory framework adopted during this pioneer phase to explain the development of African societies of the past was simple and straightforward: this was the golden age of diffusionism. In the 1880s, F. Ratzel, the founder of cultural-historical studies in German anthropology, argued that only real historical descent can explain the similarity of form between objects found at places hundreds or thousands of kilometers apart. He promoted a theory of culture contact—the migration theory—according to which the driving forces behind dynamic historical processes are migrations. Ratzel, who shared Hegel's views on Africa, published classifications of African peoples based on both their cultural achievements and their economies. The culture-based list included, from top to bottom, Arabs and Nubians, Ethiopians, Berbers, peoples of the Sahara, peoples of the central Sudan, and the Fulani and the "dark" peoples of western Sudan (see Zwernemann 1982:29).

According to Ratzel, where older cultural traits point to sources outside Africa, they point east; thus iron, cattle, pigs, chickens, the cultivation of millet, the vertical loom, and the simple bow came from the east. Frobenius (1987) shared Ratzel's point of view. The presence of white people everywhere in West Africa was considered a precondition for cultural evolution and technological change: "It seems that we owe to those movements of peoples iron metallurgy" (Pedrals 1950:112). Much evidence from material culture, such as the use of stone as building material and the erection of megaliths, was seen as proof of migrations of people and diffusion of culture traits from the Nile Valley and Egypt to the rest of the continent. The white man's burden was therefore validated; colonial systems had simply to continue the onerous task of their white forerunners and bring the light of civilization yet again to "backward" Africa.

In the 1950s, a slight change occurred in the milieu of the colonial historical and social sciences. Professional researchers began to take up appointments in various research institutions. Institutions of higher education were already present in some British colonies, and the first museums were founded in modern Ghana and Nigeria (Shaw 1978). The Institut Français d'Afrique Noire (IFAN) was founded in Dakar, Senegal, and published a journal beginning in 1939 in place of the *Bulletin du Comité d'Études Historiques et Scientifiques de l'Afrique Occidentale Française* (1916–38). The first Pan-African Congress of Prehistory and related disciplines, which took place in Nairobi in 1947 (the second one was in Algiers in 1952), gave professional archaeologists the opportunity to compare and contrast their methods and results. The resolutions of these congresses aimed to achieve methodological clarification and a common terminology.

Major research problems of the pioneer stage of West African archaeology were not completely abandoned, however; researchers were still confined within the framework of a cultural-historical paradigm. "Raciology"—the definition of racial classifications—was still a focal point of investigation, using a series of anthropometric indices to uncover racial types from skeletons. So was the problem of the origins of material-culture items such as stone tool complexes, the Levallois technique, blade technology, microlithic complexes, pottery, food production, and metallurgy. Change was manifested mainly in greater emphasis on archaeological artifacts, on the description of sites and finds, and on typology, with only very brief discussions of origins and attempts at a contextual interpretation of the archaeological record. Instead, the construction of chronological charts was the main aim of the first generation of professional archaeologists. Monumental textbooks on African prehistory, unequaled today, were published in French in the 1950s (Alimen 1955; Balout 1955; Vaufrey 1955—remarkably, all three in the same year). The process of selection of relevant sources of information and ideas was at work; references to Frobenius and his associates of the cultural-historical school all but disappeared from the literature.

Some research topics, however, were still couched in crude diffusionist terms. This was the case with topics related to the emergence of iron technology in West Africa. According to Mauny (1952, 1953), iron technology diffused from Carthaginian North Africa to West Africa through contacts with proto-Berbers. Mauny's discussion is, in fact, very similar to the arguments of the cultural-historical school (see Zwernemann 1982:50). He first considered the technological complexity of iron production and the manufacture of iron implements, and then stated that technological processes are such complex phenomena that repeated independent invention is improbable. From these premises he concluded that iron technology was developed elsewhere and later diffused to West Africa.

In history, the paucity of local written sources relevant to the history of African societies generated serious methodological problems: first, the writing of highly speculative histories (Pedrals 1950); second, an uncritical and literal use of Arabic sources; and third, difficulties in the use of alternative records of the past transmitted orally from one generation to the next. The early colonial historians who based their accounts of the African past partly on oral sources (Delafosse 1912; Palmer 1936; Urvoy 1949) were unsuccessful mainly because of their failure to consider in context the contents, structure, and social meanings of oral accounts (Devisse 1988; Fall 1988; Vansina 1985). But many young African historians considered the oral accounts—or oral traditions, as they were termed—to be relevant historical sources. In using those sources, they faced strong opposition from established academic historians. This opposition led to the development of a school of thought within Africa in which young researchers used oral traditions to write "genuine histories" of the continent. The use of oral traditions was also a way of declaring methodological autonomy as well as a distinctive historical originality for Africa (Devisse 1988:327).

According to Fall (1988), the risk for African history that arose with this development—based as it was on the concept of an irreducible specificity of African societies, exemplified by the importance of "orality"—was and still is that of the emergence of an African fundamentalism (see Blakey, this volume) based on harmonious and romantic reconstructions of the past. Even if such fundamentalism was inescapable in the context of confrontation between colonial systems and African societies, with their incompatible and idealized representations of human cultural achievements, it has now to be critically studied and contextualized. It is now recognized that oral accounts form an interesting and important body of data for the historical and social sciences (Schmidt, this volume), but that their use requires specific methodological tools. For Vansina (1985), oral traditions are not just a source about the past but a "histology" of the past. They are accounts of how people have interpreted their past according to changing social circumstances. It is thus misleading to consider oral accounts simply as raw sources. When considered as hypotheses, similar to the historian's or archaeologist's interpretation of the past, they have to be tested and evaluated according to a problem-oriented research procedure. Oral accounts are therefore a particular kind of historical record. In order to be able to understand their meanings and grasp their complexity, researchers must study the dynamics of at least a part of the social system and the contexts within which the accounts were used and recorded.

Some interesting patterns emerge from the foregoing review of West African archaeology and history in the colonial period. The views of a majority of researchers were congruent with the dominant themes of colonialism. The sociological milieu (Bourdieu 1984; Hull 1988) of archaeologists, historians, social scientists, and other scientists was a very narrow one, a series of interconnected, overlapping, and tightly knit networks of people. They were soldiers, teachers, and civil servants who were obliged in their daily tasks to enforce, directly or indirectly, colonial policies and ideologies. The demic structure that emerged was formalized by the creation of journals and learned societies such as the Société des Africanistes and its journal, *Journal de la Société des Africanistes,* founded in Paris in 1930, and the *Bulletin de l'Institut Français d'Afrique Noire,* founded at Dakar in 1939. These organizations were instrumental in the development of Africanism as a central research interest in the French academies.

There were individual and group differences in both the scope and the explanatory depth of research carried out within the field of Africanist studies. During the climax of the colonial period, at least, a kind of social division of labor seems to have operated. Soldiers, primary school teachers, and clerks often collected data and published descriptive works on features, customs, archaeological sites, and finds they happened to encounter. Following the regulations of French colonial administration, some of them had to send detailed excavation and other reports to their superiors (Waterlot 1909). Soldiers, for instance, were not allowed to publish their discoveries without the formal agreement of their officers. People belonging to the colonial elite—military and medical officers and high-ranking civil servants—used the accumulated data to build grand-scale interpretations in terms of the historical precedence and superiority of white people over black natives, thus reinforcing their *mission civilisatrice*. In this way, to varying degrees, producers of archaeological, historical, and ethnological knowledge participated in the colonial enterprise of political domination, economic exploitation, and cultural alienation. The contrary would have been highly surprising.

Africa to Africans: Pan-Negrism, Pan-Africanism, and Independence

After the colonial military forces crushed African resistance and colonial administrative and economic systems began to be implemented, new encroachments on African land quickly generated serious conflicts (Boahen 1985). Out of these conflicts emerged native political activists and intellectuals who argued in defense of Africans' traditional rights to their ancestral lands and for respect of local customs and social organization. During the colonial period there were no indigenous archaeologists. However, not all of the professional archaeologists working in West Africa agreed consistently with the dominant diffusionist paradigm. Lhote (1952), for instance, disagreed with Mauny (1952, 1953) on the problem of the emergence of iron technology in West Africa, considering it to be the outcome of local developments. Nevertheless, what may be considered a revisionist conception of archaeological, ethnological, and historical knowledge was initiated by scholars who were not archaeologists, historians, and social scientists but intellectuals and political thinkers, novelists and poets. Some of them met as students in universities in France, Great Britain, and the United States in the years following 1920. Most of them were political activists, fighting for the dignity of African peoples, for the freedom of Africa, and against colonial paternalism, cultural alienation, and manipulation of the knowledge that was the main subject of their studies.

The slogan "Africa to Africans" was adopted in 1919 during the first Pan-African Congress, a political conference held in Paris. The major problem facing these pioneers was how to restore African dignity and escape from cultural alienation. The earliest reactions were predominantly cultural and political (Andah 1988; Boahen 1985, 1988; Diagne 1977) and aimed to reappropriate African heritage within the context of struggle for power and legitimacy. Different ways of achieving this goal were explored. Among them were attempts to make an alternative African history: the dominant issue was to study the African past with scientific methods in order to identify the assumptions, biases, and weaknesses of arrogant colonial scholarship and thus to generate a genuine basis for an African revival. The processes are still at work today. H. Sylvestre-Williams, E. W. Blyden, Marcus Garvey, and W. E. B. DuBois were among the most important figures in the earliest stage of this struggle, and their writings and actions were important in Negroes' first attempts at cultural and political revival ("Negro" being the term used in the context of that historical discourse). The importance of intellectuals from the Caribbean in the development of African self-consciousness may have resulted from the exile of so many of them because of political repression, censorship, and bans on historical research, as described by Jalil Sued Badillo during our seminar.

After the abolition of slavery, black peoples from the Americas began a long and difficult struggle for the recognition of their civil rights. The idea of active solidarity with Africans who had to combat economic exploitation and colonialism emerged during the nineteenth century. It was H. Sylvestre-Williams—born in Trinidad, working as a barrister in London, and acting as adviser to African political leaders from British colonies when they came to England for discussions with the Colonial Office—who organized the first African conference in London in 1900. The term *pan-Africanism* was used for the first time during that conference (Mbuyinga 1979; Padmore 1960). Pan-Africanism was a set of political and philosophical ideas that aimed to guide the actions of African peoples in their struggle for liberation, independence, and unity of the continent.

E. W. Blyden was a Liberian from Tobago, a churchman who was the precursor of pan-Africanism. In his books (Blyden 1887, 1890, 1905), he tried to put African history in perspective, to consider it as long-term history—*longue durée*—in which colonialism, instead of being conceptualized as an end, was but a painful episode that would soon be superseded by a grander destiny for Negro Africa. From this perspective, Blyden viewed colonialism as possibly a logical step after the slave trade. His thoughts can be summarized as following two major axes: the importance of Pharaonic Egypt for the history of Africa and its peoples, and the "project" for the unification of West Africa into a unique political entity (Diagne 1977; Fall 1988).

Blyden was fascinated by the history of Pharaonic Egypt and considered it to be the Africans' common heritage because it was a great cultural achievement of Negro peoples. References taken from the Bible, Homer, and Herodotus, along with representations of the great Sphinx, were used as proofs of his arguments of direct historical connections. He believed the peopling of West Africa resulted from migrations from the Nile heartland. Blyden was also fascinated by Islam, especially by West African Moslem communities, and advocated cooperation between

Christians and Moslems in matters of education and culture in a future West African state. He held a quasi-mystical conception of the contribution of Negro Africa to future world civilization:

> Each race is endowed with particular talents, and watchful at the least degree is the Creator over the individuality, the freedom, and independence of each. In the music of the universe each gives a different sound, but all are necessary to the grand symphony. There are several sounds not yet brought on and the feeblest of all is that hither to be produced by the negro, but only he can furnish it. And when he does furnish it, in its fullness and perfection, it will be welcomed with delight by the world. (Blyden 1887, cited in Diagne 1977:303)

Bylden's pan-Negrism was exclusively a cultural and intellectual position, partly because he died in 1912 and did not experience the worst period of colonialism, from 1920 to 1950. Marcus Garvey's pan-Negrism was much more radical and active in political terms. Garvey advocated the return of all African Americans to Africa. His positions were overtly racist and his radical political action did not last long. W. E. B. DuBois played the major role in popularizing the ideas of pan-Africanism in Africa and among African elites and students in western European universities.

The first Pan-African Congress held in Paris, in 1919, was attended exclusively by delegates from Europe and the Americas. The next four meetings were attended by more and more African delegates, and at the fifth congress, in Manchester in 1945, Kwame Nkrumah—delegate from the Gold Coast, present-day Ghana—was appointed secretary of the Pan-African Congress for West Africa.

All these early attempts at African cultural and political revival formed a milieu that nurtured the grand-scale program of Cheikh Anta Diop, which I discuss at length in the next section. After 1945, Anta Diop was studying in France, and in 1952 he became general secretary of the student organization Rassemblement Démocratique Africain (RDA), a confederation of political parties and workers' organizations of the French colonies of West Africa, which had important relations with the Pan-African Congress's permanent secretariat based in London. Because a context of political activism surrounded Anta Diop's research projects, to understand his works it is essential to grasp the dynamics of the demic structure of political factionalism, fusion, scission, and competition between political lines and among charismatic figures in the struggle for independence, as well as changes within French colonial policy-making.

The Program of Cheikh Anta Diop

The Senegalese scholar Cheikh Anta Diop can be considered the most prominent proponent of the use of archaeological and ethnological knowledge, along with linguistics and history, to generate a coherent body of ideas congruent with an African radical nationalism. He never published any information about his formative years and his education in Paris, but it seems that his first book, written between 1948 and 1953—a period he presented as a very difficult time in the struggle against colonialism (Anta Diop 1955:24)—was probably intended as a doctoral thesis. For unknown reasons, it was not accepted by his professors. Although, as Thurstan Shaw (1978:11–12) points out, the Egyptian diffusionism advocated by colonial administrators was also enthusiastically espoused by African writers, if for different reasons (see Dika-Akwa 1980; Obenga 1973), Anta Diop's global research project was more complex than the simple restatement of earlier ideas (see Anta Diop 1955, 1960a, 1960b, 1960c, 1960d, 1962, 1967, 1973a, 1973b, 1973c, 1977, 1980).

Anta Diop believed that African intellectuals should study their past not for intellectual pleasure but as a charter for action in the present. The major purpose of his work was to fight against cultural alienation. He saw the whole body of "scientific" statements on Africa's past in the 1950s to be utilitarian and pragmatic in the sense that it was used to enforce colonial dominance by depriving the natives of any aptitude for cultural achievement. In order to create national self-consciousness, Africans had to study their past critically. Anta Diop saw historical knowledge of past African societies as a strategic tool in the fight against colonialism but also as a crucial instrument in the competition for power and legitimacy among African elites and intellectuals.

At the time of its inception in the 1950s, Anta Diop's research program was rooted in three main ideas: the struggle for the independence of Africa, the creation of a federal and continental African state, and the African and "Negroid" origin of mankind and civilization. This research program was implemented in three major steps. The first was to establish ancient Egypt firmly as the cradle of almost every black African people. The second was to demonstrate the true nature of the links between Pharaonic Egypt and a sample of African peoples and linguistic groups, while ascertaining the Negro identity of the Egyptians. And the third was to consider Pharaonic Egypt as a center of civilization that exerted a tremendous influence upon ancient Greece and consequently upon the whole Western world.

Consequently, the program of Cheikh Anta Diop may be subdivided into a political aspect and a scientific one. In this regard it is similar to Blyden's program, but it is not known whether Anta Diop knew of Blyden's works. The main difference between them was that Anta Diop was, for almost all his life, a radical political activist.

The Political Program

The political part of Anta Diop's activities was wide-ranging. As general secretary of the RDA in Paris, he was situated politically on the left wing and had to keep himself and others to the radical political line of the organization and combat all kinds of factionalism. The preface of his 1955 book is a masterpiece of the political rhetoric of African revolutionaries and radicals. It singles out three kinds of African intellectuals as threats to the African struggle for independence and cultural revival. First were the "cosmopolitans-scientists-modernists," who, victims of cultural alienation, disregarded the study of the African past and considered it useless in the fabric of the modern world. Then came the "intellectual-who-has-forgotten-to-improve-his-Marxist-training," who disconnected his revolutionary knowledge from political practice. Finally, there were the "formalists-antinationalists," who considered national independence of African countries undesirable because of the increasing interdependence of the world's economy. As was common in this political rhetoric, Anta Diop cited no one by name, but political activists and their followers knew exactly which individuals and groups were being stigmatized.

By reading between the lines, it is possible to name some future African statesmen whom Anta Diop must have intended: L. S. Senghor of Senegal in the first category and Houphouet Boigny of Ivory Coast in the third, and many young African Marxists such as Mahmoud Diop and Abdoulaye Wade in the second category. At the beginning, the struggle for independence was not very appealing for many professional African politicians who later jumped on the bandwagon (Mbuyinga 1979). It is well known that some political leaders of West Africa, such as Boigny, were not very enthusiastic about the idea of independence but could do nothing to stop the process. Consequently, after political independence they were obliged to change their discourse and claimed always to have been in the vanguard of the struggle for freedom. Anta Diop, who witnessed all these opportunistic behaviors, sadly wrote the following:

> That was in February 1952, at which time I was acting as the general secretary of the student organization of the RDA, when we

formulated the problems of the political independence of the black continent and the creation of a future federal state. . . . It is certain that at that time, with the exception of Malagasy representatives and the Cameroonian leader Ruben Um Nyobe, not a single franco-phone African politician dared talk of independence, of culture — yes, of culture and African nations. The statements that are pro-claimed today about that subject are close to imposture and are, at the least, flagrant lies. (Anta Diop 1974a:6, my translation)

Also interesting is that all the quotations in the preface to Anta Diop's 1955 book were from Lenin, Stalin, and writers associated with the Chi-nese and Vietnamese experiences — which were at that time exemplary cases of national revolutions that fired the imagination of an important part of the world's intelligentsia, especially that of intellectuals origi-nating in colonies in the present-day Third World. Political struggle was thus geared to face different situations: the changing subtleties of colonial policy-making, which aimed to initiate division and confusion within African nationalist movements, and the variations and diversity of opin-ions and political lines among African intellectuals and politicians.

After debates over the important problem of independence, there were debates about the political nature of independent Africa. For some, such as Anta Diop, Kwame Nkrumah, Sekou Touré, and Modibo Keita, who may be called progressives — that is, revolutionaries and radicals, according to the usual political terminology — future Africa had to be a continental federal state, united against any attempts at neocolonial domination. Anta Diop devoted three books (1960a, 1960b, 1960c) to the study of the cultural unity of Negro Africa, its precolonial history, and the economic and cultural foundations of an African federal state. For the progressives, the African past had to be reappropriated; the Gold Coast was named Ghana, after the famous Ghana empire (ca. A.D. 800–1200), and French Sudan was named Mali, after the Mali empire (ca. A.D. 1200–1500). The project of a federal state was thus considered to be based on a sound and genuine cultural and historical matrix.

For others, such as Boigny, Senghor, and A. Ahidjo, who consid-ered themselves moderate or pragmatic but were called conservative or reactionary by their left-wing political opponents, future Africa would have to be built step-by-step according to the particularities of each country. Together they could move toward greater political and eco-nomic integration at regional levels and then, if successful, at subcon-tinental and continental levels. It was this second position, also termed realistic, that was favored by African heads of states. The Organization for African Unity (OAU), created at Addis-Ababa in 1963, sanctioned the defeat of the radical unitary position. A few years later, in the 1970s, African radicals considered the OAU to be a total failure—a dead end and a mere "syndicate of African heads of states" (Mbuyinga 1979). In Senegal in 1974, with the end of the "one-party system" that had characterized the post-independence political drift of all African states, Anta Diop created a new party, the Rassemblement National Démocratique, to continue the political struggle and popularize his ideas on cultural revival and self-reliance. In 1983, this party split into two parts, and a dissident organization, the Parti de la Libération du Peuple, was created.

Anta Diop's first book (1955), *Nations nègres et culture,* sub-titled *De l'antiquité nègre égyptienne aux problèmes culturels de l'Afrique d'aujourd' hui* (From Negro Egyptian Antiquity to Cultural Problems of Negro Africa Today), captures the essence and scope of his political and scientific program. It is mostly programmatic, with an admixture of political manifesto that is apparent not only in the style of writing but also in explicit statements about the circumstances of the book's production and its aims, together with a *bricolage* of different African systems of values, past and present, and discussions of wide-ranging scientific issues using what were considered sound and rigorous scientific methods. The program is a huge one, and Anta Diop (1979 [1955]: 29–30) confessed that "the whole work is but a sketch in which all the needed details are lacking. It was humanly impossible for a single individual to get a total grasp of all of them. This can be achieved only through the work of many generations of Africans. We are conscious of these weaknesses, and our needs for a rigorous investigation suffer from that situation. However, the main lines are strong enough and the perspectives are right" (my translation).

The Research Program

Anta Diop's research program was already established in his first book, and all his life he labored to elaborate the details of his main arguments on different planes. These planes ranged from dating the past with scientific methods (Anta Diop 1974a) and the anteriority of Negro Egyptian civilization (1967) to historical linguistics (1977), studies of African migrations (1973a), the early emergence of iron technology in Negro Egypt (1973b), and physical and biological anthropology (1967, 1973c, 1980).

Anta Diop considered ancient Egypt the cradle of almost all African Negroes. The idea was not really new (Blyden 1887; Delafosse 1900;

Obenga 1973; Shaw 1978); it was the scope that was different. Ancient Egypt was a part of Africa that had seen a glorious and great civilization; thus, as noted by Shaw (1978:11), it gave added luster to African pride to trace cultural and even physical ancestry to that source. During the colonial period, this argument had been used in a different way — to support the idea of African inability to achieve a high degree of "civilization" without external influence.

Anta Diop used five categories of data to argue that ancient Egypt was the cradle of black Africa. First, he employed ethnological data, integrated within the framework of discussions on totemism, circumcision, kingship, cosmology, matriarchy, and patterns of social organization, to show the existence of general similarities in the structures and the mental templates of Pharaonic societies and most African Negro societies (Anta Diop 1979 [1955]: 204–19). Second, he used historical data gathered from classical Greek authors, travelers, and historians and from the works of later travelers of the eighteenth and nineteenth centuries to demonstrate the close connection between Egypt and Meroitic Sudan, the very early achievement of civilization in the Nilotic Sudan, the rise in power of the Meroitic dynasty of Piankhi, Shabaka, and Sabataka in Upper Egypt, and the color of the skin and the Negro identity of the Egyptians.

Third, Anta Diop used physical and bioanthropological data based on racial typologies of archaeological mortuary populations to show the massive presence of "Negroid" racial traits in those populations, and he attempted to translate the proportions of racial traits into meaningful population figures. He also tested samples of skin from mummies to evaluate their proportions of melanin (1973c). Fourth, he investigated Egyptian hieroglyphic writing to uncover the ancient Egyptians' self-appointed name, *kmt,* meaning black or Negro. He considered artwork, both paintings and sculpture, to display "Negroid" traits, and he presented the Sphinx as a typical Negro. And finally, he employed linguistic data, based on a comparison of samples of vocabulary from Pharaonic Egyptian and some Negro-African languages, to demonstrate the close genetic relationship between the two.

According to Anta Diop, this large body of data was sufficient in itself to ascertain beyond any doubt that Negro ancient Egypt was the cradle of African peoples. He further considered that only lack of integrity, distortion of facts, manipulation of evidence, and even its purposeful destruction had led Egyptologists to different conclusions (Anta Diop 1980:59). He supported his arguments with quotations from Volney, a French scholar and traveler who visited Egypt during the second half of the eighteenth century, about the racial traits of the Sphinx, and from the reply of Champollion-Figeac, one of the founding fathers of Egyptology. Volney described the Egyptians in the following terms:

> They all have puffy faces, swollen eyes, flat noses, thick lips: in short, a real mulatto face. I was tempted to attribute it to the climate, but upon my visit to the Sphinx, its aspect suggested the final words of the story. Seeing this characteristic negro head in all its traits reminded me of a remarkable passage in Herodotus, where he said: "I think that the Colches are an Egyptian colony because they have, like them, black skin and woolly hair." This means that ancient Egyptians were real negroes like all the natives of Africa. (Volney 1787, cited in Anta Diop 1980:57, my translation)

A few years later, Champollion-Figeac (1837:26–27, cited in Anta Diop 1980:59) replied that "black skin and woolly hair, these two physical qualities are not sufficient to characterize the negro race, and Volney's conclusion relative to the negro origin of the ancient peoples of Egypt is obviously extreme and unacceptable." For Anta Diop, this refutation by a major Egyptologist was one of the fundamental tricks of modern colonial history and Egyptology.

The process of the peopling of sub-Saharan Africa was another theme of Anta Diop's research program (1955, 1967, 1973a). As the cradle of almost all African Negroes, ancient Egypt and the Nile Valley witnessed several waves of outward migration that radiated all over the continent. According to Anta Diop (1979 [1955]: 377–403), the Kara of southern Sudan and upper Oubangui, the Kare-Kare of northeastern Nigeria, the Yoruba of southwestern Nigeria, the Fulani, the Poular (ancient Toucoulleurs), the Serer, the Wolof, the Zulu, and others all originated in the Nile Valley. He used archaeological information to trace the routes of migrations and interpreted the burial mounds of the inland Niger Delta as West African versions of the pyramids of the Nile Valley (Anta Diop 1979 [1955]: 349). He considered the megaliths in Senegal, Gambia, and Mali to be markers of the migrations of the Serer from the Nile Valley to the Atlantic coast of West Africa.

In this regard, the Malian site of Tondi-Daro was the subject of debate. The site is an extensive field of megaliths located at the base of a red sandstone hill. It has been interpreted as the material manifestation of an agrarian ritual (Anta Diop 1955). For Maes (1924:31), these stones had been erected by Carthaginians: "For he who knows the psychology of negroes, one can surely ascertain that this undertaking was not executed by the representatives of the Negro race because it represents such a considerable amount of effort, without any immediate utility and bearing no relation to the regular requirements of feeding and reproduction, the only functions which are really appealing to the negro." For Anta Diop (1979 [1955]: 398–99), however, this field of megaliths was further support for his hypothesis concerning the migration route of the Serer people living today in Senegal, who still worship such erected stones.

Negroes left the Nile Valley because of overpopulation and social crisis and penetrated deeper into the continent. Their adaptation to the different ecological conditions they met on the way brought about changes in technological equipment and scientific knowledge; some features vital along the Nile but of no use elsewhere were abandoned and later forgotten (Anta Diop 1979 [1955]: 351). More recently, Anta Diop (1973b) published, in further detail, an article in which he claimed to have identified the Nilotic cradle of peoples from Senegal. The article contains discussions of vocabulary and grammar, comparing Egyptian, Coptic dialect, and Wolof, on one hand, and Nuer, Dinka, Fulani, Serer, and Wolof, on the other. It also discusses a sociopolitical organization based primarily on the evolution of matriarchy in three main stages: early strict matriarchy in stage I (represented by the Nuba Tullushi in the core area), matrilocal postmarital residence in stage II, and bilateral descent in stage III, with patterns of social division of labor and castelike systems.

> The purpose [of the article] is to demonstrate that at a relatively recent period a migratory movement started from the shores of Lake Albert and the Nuba hills (a region inhabited by the Nuer, the Shilluk, the Dinka, etc.) and reached Senegal through a corridor situated between the tenth and twentieth parallels north of the equator, while another migration starting from the same area of the great lakes may have followed the course of the Zaire River to its watershed and from there expanded along the coast, but not farther than Cameroon and the Niger Delta. Peoples from the gulf of Benin, from southern Nigeria to southern Ivory Coast (Ibo, Yoruba, Oyo, Ewe, Akan, Agni, Baoule, etc.), may belong to an earlier migratory wave, coming similarly from the east. (Anta Diop 1973c:769–70, my translation)

The Nilotic cradle of the Senegalian peoples—their *Urheimat*—is therefore located between the Bahr el Ghazzal and the Nile, inhabited today by the Nuba, Nuer, Dinka, and Shilluk.

Anta Diop (1967) also considered ancient Egypt to have been the earliest great civilization of the world. Once civilization had developed there, it radiated all over the ancient world. This great achievement was realized by African Negroes who invented complex social systems, iron metallurgy (1973a), kingship, monotheism, mathematics, science, writing, monumental art and architecture, and sophisticated techniques of mummification (1979 [1955]: 411). Many of the great philosophers and scientists of ancient Greece were trained partly by Egyptians: Pythagoras, Thales, Solon, Archimedes, Eratosthenes, and many others made the trip to Egypt, where science was esoteric and secret. In Greece, science lay in the public domain, where it was progressively integrated into the material world. Eventually, according to what we may refer to as Anta Diop's syllogism, ancient Egypt brought civilization to the entire world. And because ancient Egypt was inhabited by Negroes, it was the Negroes who brought civilization to humankind. Anta Diop thus asserted that black people must assume this glorious past, impose it as an unmistakable fact, and, in continuity with ancient Egypt, revive their national pride in order to reconquer their rightful place in the modern world.

In summary, Anta Diop's thesis is the most radically revisionist and complete system of thought ever proposed by an Africanist concerning the past of Negro Africa. It emerged within the context of the struggle against colonialism and the fight for independence and liberation of the African continent in the 1950s. In this context, he succeeded in demonstrating the weaknesses of colonial rhetoric and the utilitarian nature of an important part of the colonial historical accounts of the African past. Paradoxically, instead of destroying the methodological and theoretical foundations of colonial historical views, Anta Diop helped strengthen the then-current typological and diffusionist paradigms, only reversing some of the waves and streams of the "hydraulic" conception of cultural dynamics. Instead of being considered a mere recipient of ideas, techniques, art, modes of social organization, and cultural traits invented elsewhere, in Anta Diop's work Negro Africa was shown to have played, via Egypt, an important—if not the most important—role in the development of civilization and the dissemination of several cultural traits to Europe.

A new kind of dogmatism, resulting from uncritical and oversimplified presentations of Anta Diop's research, has now become fashionable in many West African francophone universities. According to this dogmatism, "almost everything attests that in the beginning, in remote prehistory, during the Upper Palaeolithic, negroes were dominant. They kept this predominance in civilization and in technological and military superiority all through the millennia of history" (Anta Diop 1967:11).

Alternative Histories as an Unending Process of Selection

The need for alternative histories seems to emerge at particular junctures of social systems; it is based on an assessment of relations of power and conflicts over "true" legitimacy (Chatterjee, this volume; Schmidt, this volume), and it aims to redress a situation of imbalance. Consequently, attempts to generate alternative histories are part of an unending process of selection of the most relevant ideas, theories, and principles that may guide the actions of the members of a society in situations of socioeconomic and cultural confrontation. Alternative histories are therefore geared to reinterpret the dynamics of past societies at different levels of abstraction: metatheoretical or general worldviews, theoretical, methodological, and instrumental. When all these levels are mixed without due attention to their internal consistencies and contradictions, they often result in the production of mythical and dogmatic histories at best, or mystification at worst.

Anta Diop's attempt to make an alternative history of Negro Africa has obliged many Egyptologists and European Africanists to reconsider several ideas they had taken for granted concerning, for instance, the population of Egypt. On biological grounds, if it is considered that humans' bodies are always in a process of adaptation, dark or brown skin was probably less maladaptive than white skin along the Nile Valley. But Anta Diop's program was handicapped by the methods of scientific investigation of his time and by difficulties he met in obtaining samples of the materials needed to carry out his scientific research program. In strict historical terms, his research was framed within a particular paradigm with multiple facets. The typological paradigm was dominant, and dynamic processes were not seriously investigated. Because of its impressive scope in terms of both time and space, Anta Diop's project, as he himself acknowledged, was well beyond the capacities of one individual, and he noted that the work of many generations of African researchers would be necessary to achieve a more accurate picture of the pasts of African societies (Anta Diop 1979 [1955]: 29–30). He also acknowledged the political context of his early writings, up to 1960. For all these reasons, it is not difficult for students of different disciplines to find important flaws in his works (Froment 1988), but such an attitude, based mostly on hindsight, is historically inaccurate and anachronistic. I will present a few examples to clarify my assertion.

Anta Diop's discussions of the physical or bioanthropological material are extremely weak, but such weaknesses are shared by the majority of researchers who have worked in physical anthropology in Africa since the nineteenth century. According to Van Gerven, Carlson, and Armelagos (1973), in order to stimulate archaeologists' interest in saving skeletal materials, physical anthropologists incorrectly proposed that the analysis and classification of those materials could provide information toward the historical reconstruction of cultural traditions. Van Gerven, Carlson, and Armelagos add that such analyses have consistently utilized similarities in skeletal morphology and hypothetical racial affinities to establish biological relationships between skeletal series. Such relationships, once established, have then been assumed to reflect the degree to which populations were culturally related. The three most central features of this approach are (1) a basic orientation toward typological definition and description, (2) a dependence upon admixture (gene flow) as an explanatory model, and (3) a commitment to the objective reality of the racial type and the utility of such concepts as *hybrid* and *atavism* in the reconstruction of racial history (Van Gerven, Carlson, and Armelagos 1973:556).

As MacGaffey (1966) observes, the reason the racial approach was maintained in the physical anthropology of northeastern Africa, in spite of important biological inconsistencies, rests in a deeply rooted structure and philosophy of Western civilization, which calls for an ideology that sanctions as natural and necessary a polarization between rulers and the ruled, the bearers and receivers of culture. Anta Diop was trapped within these biological inconsistencies, which led him to attempt to naturalize social constructs; faced with counterarguments, his main tactics consisted of accusations of mystification. He succeeded, however, in turning the system in the inverse direction. Modern evolutionary biology is the study of population biology with models of natural selection and variations of genotypes and phenotypes. When considered from this point of view, all biological traits—hair, skin color, blood group, size, shape of nose, and so forth—show different complexes of overlapping distribution patterns among the earth's populations (Langaney 1988), resulting from different aspects of natural and cultural processes of selection. Social constructs such as the hierarchy of "races," racism, ethnocentrism, and imperialism have to be countered with arguments based on social processes such as mystification, domination, alienation, exploitation, and divide-and-rule. In this regard, the basic questions are, Who needs the concept of race? and What is its meaning? As Nigerians used to say in the 1970s, "the tiger does not proclaim its 'tigerhood,' it catches its prey and eats it" (in Towa 1973; see Blakey, this volume). As another scholar has noted:

> It is rather well known that in the relations between biology and psychology, this latter one tends to prevail. Racial intolerance develops starting from a collective mind of one's own social condition

and appropriates (phenotypical) differences to project them in terms of social discrimination. It is almost disarming to find the vector of "social status" implied in any turn of cultural development. (Santangelo 1992:189)

But one of the major problems is that Anta Diop, in his more recent writings—up to his death in 1986, a few weeks after the International Conference on the Archaeology of Cameroon—behaved as if nothing new had occurred in African archaeology in general, and especially in West African archaeology, history, linguistics, and social anthropology. For example, his argument about a relatively recent migration of the Serer from their Nilotic cradle could have been strongly modified, if not abandoned, if he had paid attention to more recent archaeological, linguistic, and anthropological research. Since at least the 1960s, the matriarchy described by Bachofen has been seriously reconsidered and shown to have resulted from the confusion of matrilineality as a rule of descent with a sociopolitical regime characterized by the dominance of mothers—*Die Mutterrecht* (Testart 1992). There is no need to have all the aspects of African Negro societies come from only one place, even glorious ancient Egypt. Social creativity is present everywhere. In this regard, an alternative to Anta Diop's alternative is necessary in the historical sciences of West Africa, at least for francophone countries.

It is true that Anta Diop had great difficulty getting the material needed to carry out his research program, partly because of the lack of cooperation from authorities of the Egyptian Antiquity Service, who systematically refused to answer his questions:

> Among the funerary furniture of Toutankhamon exhibited at the Cairo museum, I have noticed a few objects which, if they are authenticated, may show that the use of iron was already well integrated in daily life; such is the case with the metal hinges of Toutankhamon's bed. According to Dr. Ryad, the curator of the museum who was acting as our guide during the visit in November 1971, these metal hinges were made with iron. Back at Dakar, I wrote two letters asking him to check in his records whether these iron hinges do not result from recent restoration of the bed. Unfortunately, I did not receive any answer. (Anta Diop 1974a:6, my translation)

The same thing happened when Anta Diop requested samples of mummy skin for analysis; however, when he succeeded in getting some samples from the Department of Egyptology of the Musée de l'Homme in Paris, he misreported the results of his analysis on melanin (Froment 1986), raising much more skepticism than he expected. His attempts to produce an alternative, scientifically relevant Negro African history were countered by strong resistance, and he was obliged to work in a kind of splendid isolation, suspicious of all researchers who did not share his views.

Developing Other Alternative Histories

The simplest way to launch the new alternative (Andah 1988, 1990b) may be to break away from scientific "provinces" with combined research programs that include, at least, archaeology, history, and anthropology, both biological and social. Under this perspective, the emergence of African societies may be studied within the framework of long-term history. Languages, ethnic groups, ethnonyms, material culture, and modes of social organization result from conscious and "unconscious" processes of selection, and the same is true for research programs, social conditions for research, contexts of production of scientific and cultural knowledge, and, finally, researchers' "minds."

Oral tradition is one of the most characteristic aspects of African societies, and so it deserves the attention of almost all researchers in African social and historical sciences. Oral traditions have been instrumental in bringing to light whole segments of the past of large parts of the world, and more importantly, they provide one way of knowing history from the inside. It is worth emphasizing what I consider to be one of the most important aspects of scientific investigation in general: each kind of description implies a choice of the question asked, a choice of relevant ideas, and a choice of measuring device (Prigogine and Stengers 1984). Making alternative histories is necessarily an unending process partly dependent on the arrow of time and its corollary, changing scientific, political, and social conditions. As noted by Prigogine and Stengers (1984: 212–13), it appears obvious that human societies are immensely complex systems that involve a potentially enormous number of bifurcations, exemplified by the variety of cultures. It is known that such systems are highly sensitive to fluctuations. This situation may lead to both hope and threat: hope because a minute fluctuation may grow, expand, and modify the total structure of the system, and threat because the potential security of stable, durable rules is gone forever. In this regard, an alternative history has to be based on a choice of predominant ideas or hypotheses.

Archaeology may play the role of vanguard in the making of alternative histories in Africa; it has, whether we wish it or not, a political and cultural role. It has already played a significant role in discrediting colonial myths about Africans and their past (Schmidt 1983, this volume; Trigger 1990). But it will also have to refute well-intentioned but highly imaginative claims by some African researchers and intellectuals. Archaeological findings, to paraphrase the words of Trigger (1990: 318), have the power to restrain fantasy if sufficient data are collected and analyzed in a scientifically rigorous fashion. Lack of space precludes an extensive discussion of the subject here, but one example will illustrate the importance of archaeology in the process of making alternative histories (Holl 1990).

Until recently, the archaeology of the western Cameroon grassfields was known only from short notes on surface finds of stone tools published in the 1950s (Jeffreys 1951). Even if some researchers suspected the existence of very ancient settlements, the consensus, based partly on literal interpretations of oral accounts, was that this area was settled only quite recently by waves of immigrants coming from the northeast. Archaeological surveys and excavations beginning in 1974 have shown, however, that the area has been inhabited since at least 9000 B.P. and that iron technology was in use from about the third or fourth century A.D. (Asombang 1988; Maret 1980, 1982; Warnier 1984, 1985). Furthermore, it has been suggested that the high-altitude savanna that comprises the Cameroon grassfields is mainly a by-product of long-term human interference with the environment (Warnier 1984, 1985).

Archaeological surveys and tests excavations have shown that the production of iron artifacts in the grassfields took place within the context of a long-distance trade network controlled by regional centers (Warnier and Fowler 1979). In this center-periphery set of relations, iron tools were exchanged for palm oil from the south and cotton and textiles from northern Nigeria (Rowlands 1986). The nature of the iron-working sites, the technologies used, and the scale of production achieved all contradict the colonial stereotype, according to which African peoples lacked any kind of technological skill and initiative—a stereotype that had been given credibility by the fact that at the time of colonial contact, the Germans observed only highly dispersed and very small-scale smelting furnaces.

In fact, three different types of smelting furnaces are now known to have existed: a low cylindrical furnace, which appears to have been the earliest and most widespread form, in use from the third to the seventeenth century; a larger "clump" furnace, in use from the seventeenth to the nineteenth century; and another form of small bowl furnace similar to the first, which survived as the dominant means of indigenous iron production until the 1940s (Warnier and Fowler 1979). The technology of clump furnaces was a response to the intensification of long-distance trade, the emergence of stratified and competing polities, and an energy crisis. This period of intensive production of iron implements resulted in deforestation, which in turn encouraged further technological advances in order to produce more iron with less fuel. This highly labor-intensive system could be maintained only with sustained demand. The introduction of mass-produced European iron implements during the eighteenth and nineteenth centuries, combined with the effects of the slave trade, caused the whole socioeconomic system to collapse. Clump furnaces were replaced by small bowl furnaces in which iron and slag from an earlier period were recycled and smelted. Competing polities turned to extensive warfare as a means of predatory accumulation. The most likely explanation of this radical change is the failure of the local economic system to compete with the increasing flow of imported European ingots and hoe blanks during the late nineteenth century.

The available archaeological evidence from the western Cameroon grassfields suggests that the encroachment and expansion of European trading networks served to break the complexity of existing local exchange networks and social relations of production, and also to move local communities into more autarkic, or self-sufficient, strategies of resource procurement and consumption. And, more importantly, it appears that it was larger regional systems that were thus destabilized, resulting in increased warfare at the end of the nineteenth century, when colonial powers began to take total control of Africa. Therefore, it is not surprising that they found disturbed social and economic systems (Holl 1979). This case is important because it shows how in some situations, what was presented as African "backwardness" may have been an artifact of exploitation and unequal exchanges initiated by the colonial powers.

Let me conclude this chapter with a metatheoretical statement that is, according to Popper (1991), nonscientific because it is not falsifiable. Such statements, however, whether implicit or explicit, are inescapable, and they may help make sense of the straightforward question, Why make alternative histories? I wish to emphasize the humanistic value of the historical and social sciences, which appeal to individuals both as individuals and as members of societies. The research carried out within these fields of knowledge finds complete justification if it enriches people's experience and helps them to live more abundantly as heirs of all ages and as brothers and sisters to one another (Clark 1968).

Archaeological and historical experiences show that cultural achievement is a complex of interacting processes, both within and beyond any spatio-temporal cultural unit. If we want to build a world of true humanity, we must consider all the levels of human interaction, composed as it is of a nested hierarchy of components. At the bottom is the individual, who belongs to a family, a corporate group, an ethnic group, and a culture. All these components are included in various types of social groupings (bands, chiefdoms, states, empires, etc.), only one of which is the modern "nation-state" (Holl 1990). At the top of the hierarchy, I am inclined to place the vague "humankind," which is admittedly meaningless for some. Historical and social sciences, therefore, have to generate a frame of mind, a vivid consciousness of people's belonging to a world society, transcending but also comprehending regional and even national loyalties.

Race, Nationalism, and the Afrocentric Past

MICHAEL L. BLAKEY

> Tell no lies
> Claim no easy victories . . .
> — *Amilcar Cabral*

"**A**frocentrism," as it has recently been defined, is a consciously ethno-centric approach to understanding the cultures and social issues of the African diaspora. Afrocentrism is meant as a guide for both research and pedagogical programs intended to correct the demeaning distortions of Eurocentric science and education.

The framework of theoretical assumptions that underlies one's understanding of social problems reveals and limits the ways in which one goes about trying to solve those problems. Thus Afrocentrism, like any other theoretical approach, is inherently political. There are many ways to understand our universe, each with limited explanatory, scholastic, and political possibilities. Some interpretations of human society have justified oppressive political and economic systems; others have enhanced our understanding of those systems' inhumanity. Historically, however, these implications of theory have often gone unrecognized, even to the extent that those who formulated and applied theory believed the societal significance of their work was the opposite of its historical effects. Careful and critical political analysis of an evolving school of thought, as I attempt to carry out in this chapter, should assist proponents in identifying their goals more fully.

I will explore the political ideological content of Afrocentrism with which the scholars discussed later are popularly associated, particularly as it bears on questions of race and interpretations of the past. The range of studies in this area is broad and cannot be fully encompassed by this critique, which seeks instead to elucidate some fundamental assumptions and points of view characterizing the scholarship of this school. The following appear to be major, yet not exhaustive, aspects of the Afrocentric school: (1) the notion of a singular African epistemology and culture; (2) the notion of cultural purity and the extricability of a primordial African epistemology and ethos from the multicultural influences of the African diaspora; (3) the notion of naturally occurring and qualitatively delineated biological races; (4) the tendency to favor metaphysical and biological determinants in explaining psychological and social patterns; (5) obfuscation of the role of economic systems in the development of ideology and social relations, and the rejection of theories revealing those relations; (6) the tendency toward racial separatist or supremacist arguments accompanying a cultural nationalist program; (7) opposition to the possibility of social change toward greater equality and harmony in ethnically plural societies; (8) romanticism of feudal society; (9) inattentiveness to cross-cultural comparison or modern human biological diversity; (10) deprecation of the perspectives of all non-African peoples; (11) promotion of research and education concerning neglected African diasporic cultures; (12) reevaluation of ancient Nile Valley societies, placing them at the center of a pan-African culture; (13) promotion of racial vindicationism for the psychological uplift of African-descended peoples; (14) a strong challenge to the ideology of white supremacy coupled with accomodation of notions of racial differentiation and hierarchy; and (15) creation of a Black nationalist ideology.

Asante's Epistemology

Molefe Asante, a major proponent of the Afrocentric school, argues that the "critical perspective I have named *Afrocentricity* . . . means, literally, placing African ideals at the center of any analysis that involves African culture and behavior" (Asante 1987:6). Furthermore, "the term *Afrology* coined in *Afrocentricity: The Theory of Social Change* [Asante 1980] denotes the Afrocentric study of African concepts, issues, and behaviors. It includes research on African themes in the Americas and the West Indies, as well as the African continent. Most of the relevant research involves the systematic exploration of relationships, social codes, cultural and commercial customs, and oral traditions and proverbs" (Asante 1987: 16–17).

Therefore, Afrocentrism constitutes a definitively ethnocentric epistemological stance, advocating one ethnocentric view as the corrective to another (Eurocentrism) and as the most appropriate perspective from which to understand African diasporic concepts, issues, and behaviors.

Such a corrective is advocated as necessary for bringing sophistication to scholarship that is otherwise provincial and parochial by virtue of "the inability to 'see' from several angles." Thus, one is able to "see all the possibilities of the world" (Asante 1987:3). Yet theorists might seek to explicate (rather than advance) the ethnocentric biases of scientific theories, and/or they might seek balance through multicentric approaches. To embrace *one* alternative ethnocentric view seems inadequate for comprehending "several angles" and "all possibilities."

Perhaps the first premise of the Afrocentric school is that knowledge is intrinsically subjective and that ethnocentrism is unavoidable. Yet Europeans "have often assumed that their 'objectivity,' a kind of collective subjectivity of European culture, should be the measure by which the world marches" (Asante 1987:3). It is important to note that the evidence for intrinsic scientific subjectivity, a critique of positivism (the idea that objective knowledge accumulates along with data), has emerged not only from African and Afro-American thinkers but also from Asian American (Hsu 1979) and European and Euro-American thinkers (among the critical theorists and dialecticians). Among these critics of scientific "objectivity," there are certainly examples of persistently imbedded positivistic assumptions (see, for example, Kuhn 1970; Leone, Potter, and Shackel 1987), but there are also those (e.g., Feyerabend 1978) who assert that knowledge is wholly subjective and that nonscientific methods can be superior ways of knowing. Others, such as Gould (1980) and Lewontin, Kamin, and Rose (1984), are sharp Marxian critics of positivism and Eurocentrism, showing the cultural influences of science but not disregarding the value of a materialistic basis for discovery (or the role of intuition) and the possibility of some forms of objectivity.

Unquestionably, European scholars must deal with their pervasive Eurocentrism. Yet the idea that science is subject to cultural and political influences also exists among prominent schools of European thought. What is more, proponents of Afrocentrism themselves often exhibit pronounced positivistic tendencies (which they ascribe solely to Eurocentrism), asserting the validity of Afrocentric knowledge alone for studies of the cultures of the African diaspora. The Afrocentrists' omission of non-Afrocentric critics of Eurocentrism and positivism is consistent with their arguments that only Afrocentricity is capable of adequate criticism.

The Afrocentric school (as I will describe later) rejects Western science as materialistic and mechanistic. Yet the idea of a materialistic (observed, sensed, empirical, or testable) basis for knowledge is not exclusive to Europe but is also part of the traditions of African medical science (Ndeti 1976). A respected African scientist, Cheikh Anta Diop, used material evidence for his own Afrocentric studies. The use of material evidence is more than just Western science. Marxist dialectics (initially European) do not separate mind and body in the Cartesian-mechanistic sense for which Afrocentrists criticize European theories in toto.

More revealing still, theorists from Freud and Marx to Spencer (founder of social Darwinism) are lumped among practitioners of incorrect and wrong-minded approaches to knowledge because their approaches "emerged from Western consciousness." Yet each of these approaches is very different from the others in its conceptualization and political direction. For example, it has been argued (beyond the facts, in my view) that Marxist theory is undifferentiated from social Darwinism, an argument that muddies important epistemological and political waters. A (Marxist) critique of capitalism and class "is not helpful in developing Afrocentric concepts and methods, because it too is a product of a Eurocentric consciousness that excludes the historical and cultural perspectives of Africa" (Asante 1987:8). What, then, are the contributions of W. E. B. DuBois, Paul Robeson, and C. L. R. James, or of Jaques Roumain, Amilcar Cabral, Walter Rodney, Cornell West, and Samir Amin, among Marxian-influenced black thinkers? What of the psychoanalytical influences of Franz Fanon (or even of Francis Cress-Welsing, whom I discuss later)? Are they not Afrocentric? Are their ideas less useful for having been partly borrowed from European scholarship? Does their scholarship exist apart from what it embodies?

Proponents of Afrocentrism argue for a dichotomy between the generic "European" and "African" without giving attention to variation beyond or within those traditions or to the value of epistemological variety, cross-fertilization, and dialectics. The Afrocentric school is guided not so much by "an African perspective" as by a narrow definition of Afrocentrism devised by its Afro-American proponents. Unless one compares and contrasts varied ethnocentric views, Afrocentrism itself cannot be properly defined.

As should become more evident in the following discussion, Afrocentrism clearly is not an internationalist perspective (beyond the African diaspora). It does not recognize class analysis or struggle as important. Nor does it involve a civil rights or human rights program. It contains no antiracist thrust beyond an opposition to Europeans as the source of irrepressible racist behavior. The political content of Afrocentrism is distinctly nationalistic.

This perspective stands, in one respect, in opposition to a critical epistemology and pedagogy of change. A critical approach to the transformation of knowledge should allow students or the public to be empowered and given autonomy when examining society, thinking issues through from several theoretical and ethnocentric angles, comparing their own values to those espoused, and coming to their own conclusions about the influences and merits of ideas. Posed as the only correct way of knowing the African world, Afrocentricity can undermine criticism.

At the same time, as a strong alternative to pervasive Eurocentric positivism, an Afrocentric body of ideas demands criticism by presenting a contrast and choice between the two subjective perspectives, which are made more obviously subjective by the contrast itself. It demands dialectical change. But to what future would the Afrocentrists clear a path? The potential for ideological transformation will be limited by all those ways in which Afrocentrism reproduces, and is like, that which it seeks to oppose. Several such contradictions have already been mentioned. In the following discussion of Afrocentric psychology and popularly associated historical studies, the reactionary trends in the Afrocentric fabric are teased out.

Race, Psychic Unity, and Discordance

Afrocentric psychology is an excellent case of the hidden infiltration of Western and reactionary ideas. Joseph Baldwin, when characterizing psychosocial differences among races, asserts that the "European approach exemplifies a 'humanity versus nature,' or antagonistic, style of orientation, while the African approach, on the other hand, exemplifies a 'humanity-nature' unity. . . . Africans seek to achieve a comprehensive understanding of nature to facilitate a more complementary coexistence with it" (Baldwin 1980:95). He represents Europeans as cognitive and materialistic, whereas he describes the African mind as principally affective and spiritual. It seems contradictory that the European social Darwinists—who were far from progressive—argued a "humanity-nature unity." Eugenic and genocidal programs issued from their (European) respect for nature. Surely all cultures have combined a healthy respect for nature with the opportunistic manipulation of nature. Can excesses of industrial societies be laid at the doorstep of European culture?

The problems inherent in the cognitive-affective dichotomy are more obvious. Baldwin seems unaware of the admonitions of Cheikh Anta Diop, whose work *The African Origin of Civilization: Myth or Reality* (1974b) serves as the archaeological cornerstone of Afrocentric inspiration. Anta Diop (1974b:25) recognized the trap:

Frequently Blacks of high intellectual attainments remain so victimized by this alienation [loss of memory of the African world that was] that they seek in all good faith to codify those Nazi ideas in an alleged duality of the sensitive, emotional Negro, creator of art, and the White man, especially endowed with rationality. So it is with good faith that a Black African poet expressed himself in a verse of admirable beauty: "L'emotion est negre et la raison hellene" (emotion is Negro and reason is Greek).

These same dichotomies are expressed in the depictions of white and nonwhite peoples in the historical and anthropological exhibits of the Smithsonian Institution, the national museums of the United States (Blakey 1983, 1990, 1991). In them, Eurocentrism and white supremacist ideas are the dominant influences. In fact, what is being called "Afrocentric psychology" shares an essential common ground with the old social Darwinism and its intuitive eugenic applications. Racial biology is stressed in a way reminiscent of the racial determinism that legitimized the ideology of white supremacy and eugenic programs during the first half of the twentieth century. What Baldwin calls "definitional systems" of African and European descent groups (characterized by the dichotomies just discussed) are attributed to racial differences. His assertion requires quoting at length:

A definitional system [worldview] therefore represents the ideological basis of a culture or social system. Inherent in the definitional system are those beliefs and behaviors which reflect the *survival thrust* of the collection of people it represents, because it evolved from the *cumulative collective experience* or *social reality* of that particular cultural group. The definitional system thus binds the social system's membership together. It gives them their unique (distinguishable) psychosocial reality. However, it is clear that in order for the collection of people to occupy the same space (geographical relatedness) and time (historical relatedness) long enough for their definitions to achieve group relevance and consensus, necessarily requires the existence of some more concrete and fundamental force to bind them together and anchor their collective identity. Given that *race* (i.e., blood relatedness, kinship, or biogenetic commonality) constitutes the most basic and fundamental binding condition underlying human existence, and ultimately transcends all subsequent or secondary bonds of social unity, then it clearly constitutes the initial force binding people to a similar geography and history through which their similar experiences evolve into a distinct definitional system or world view. (Baldwin 1980:98–99)

These assumptions constitute a reductionist, biological/racial deterministic view. Contemporary population genetics tells us that biological races are arbitrarily defined rather than fundamental or real components of the natural world (see Lewontin 1972). While Baldwin's Afrocentric psychology seeks to counter white supremacy, it actually props up the same assumptions about the significance of race biology in human affairs. It is apologetic in that it does not explore the possibility of solutions to the problems of the African diaspora in multiethnic societies and in that it claims racism as a given, unalterable condition of existence:

> It has been utterly impossible, if we subscribe to historical consistency, for different racial groups to truly integrate their respective definitional orientations and coexist harmoniously within the same sociocultural context. This has particularly been the case with European groups relative to non-European (African) groups. . . . The respective definitional systems, then, must be fundamentally different, racially specific, and, beyond that, incompatible. It is therefore apparent that the survival thrusts of the African and European worlds are distinctly different as well as incompatible. (Baldwin 1980:98–99)

Consider the eugenic view of the Imperial Wizard of the Ku Klux Klan, Hiram W. Evans, in "Negro Suffrage—Its False Theory":

> The first essential to the success of any nation, and particularly of any democracy, is a national unity of mind. Its citizens must be One People (*Ein Volk*). They must have common interests and racial and national purpose. . . . No amount of education can ever make a white man out of a man of any other color. It is a law on this earth that races can never exist together in complete peace and friendship and certainly never in a state of equality. (quoted in Patterson 1970 [1951]:18)

The white supremacist scientific basis for these arguments has been described as being opposed, historically, to African American and other liberal scholarship that sought social change and egalitarian reform (see Blakey 1987; Drake 1980; Rankin-Hill and Blakey 1994). Acceptance of racial deterministic assumptions depreciates the historical development of the ideology of white supremacy. Equally dismissed are the political and economic forces which influenced that development; instead, racism is claimed to be based on ahistorical biological causes. The effects of class differences within black and white communities are ignored.

The "Cress theory" of color confrontation and racism (Cress-Welsing 1970)—a biodeterministic Afrocentric theory—gives no insight into means for solving problems of racial conflict and oppression. Rather, it justifies those problems on unsubstantiated biological grounds, claiming that genocidal behavior is inherent in less pigmented populations because of their sense of inadequacy and envy toward highly pigmented people. The Cress theory assumes that the ideology of white supremacy results from a lack of melanin and is not a historical development that can be influenced by social change.

Recently, the Cress theory has been embellished to explain an immunological, intellectual, and "spiritual" superiority in darkly pigmented people. In his chapter "Esoteric Factors of the Cress Theory," Richard King (1990:13–21) argues that the pineal gland, which produces a melanic neurotransmitter called melatonin, functions best in black people (at times he argues that all people are black, and at other times he makes racial comparisons). The assumption of a relationship between neurological melanin and differences in skin pigmentation is based on inadequate scientific grounds. For example, his only quantitative data are differences in the frequency of pineal calcification between blacks (5 percent of whom have calcified pineals) and whites (30–70 percent of whom have calcified pineals) in a study by Daramola and Olowu (1972).

In addition to making broad leaps of inference and disregarding the complex and powerful environmental factors influencing the pineal gland (as well as the pituitary secretions overly attributed to pineal activity), King admits that differences in pigmentation are related to pineal secretions only during tanning (1990:116). All of this is couched in the metaphysical terms of a pseudo-Egyptian mysticism focusing on what he calls the power of the "Black Dot" ("the eye on the mount . . . the all seeing eye"), which is "the hidden doorway to the collective unconscious; primeval waters, universal forces that nourishes [sic] all life forms, and the hidden doorway through which the transforming soul-energy or Uraeus passes" (1990:20–24). In King's writing (1990, 1994), in fact, we can recognize a synthesis of historical romanticism, Baldwin's spiritual and emotional emphasis, and biological determinism. According to the neuroendocrinological literature, pineal melatonin activity is responsive to sunlight as perceived by the human eye. Melatonin helps regulate day-night physiological cycles (prominently including sleep cycles), irrespective of skin pigmentation. Skin pigmentation and neural melatonin activity do not co-vary because they comprise different physiological systems that serve different adaptive functions.

Afrocentric psychology not only promotes notions of inexorable conflict between races but also unwittingly compels us to conclude that conflicts inexorably take place between individuals who are classified as black. One must wonder about the divisive effects of Indian, European, Asian, and other biological admixtures among the peoples of the African diaspora (or of ancient Egypt, for that matter), particularly as these admixtures bear upon "definitional systems." From the Afrocentric premise, does the diaspora's genetic diversity lead many of us toward what Eurocentric eugenicists like Charles Davenport (Steggerda and Davenport 1929) called "wuzzle-headedness"? How small a biological subgroup must one be contained within to avoid psychiatric illness?

Cress-Welsing (1970, 1990) assumes that on a global scale there is a minority population (whites) without pigmentation, qualitatively distinct from people of color. Racism and capitalism (as the means of carrying out genocidal programs) are attributed to white people's melanin envy and genetic competition with the majority, melanic population. Cress-Welsing's failure to understand that pigmentation differences are quantitative (that there is a gradient among all people in the darkness of their skins) seems to result from adherence to the most literal belief in distinct racial types. (This misconception, in all fairness, is also common in "mainstream" biological anthropology and biomedical studies.) Yet the fact that these differences are merely quantitative compels us, should we accept the Cress theory's connection between color and behavior, to conclude that color differences among those defined as black should also produce, by degree, problems similar to those existing between whites and people of color. Less pigmented people would envy and denigrate more pigmented people to the extent of the incremental differences between them. Differences in intellectual and spiritual characteristics associated with melatonin, as expounded by King (1990, 1994) and popularized by Tony Browder (1989) and Leonard Jeffries, would follow the same pattern. This is obviously a highly divisive implication of melanin theory, yet the recognition of it is so dependent upon realizing the arbitrariness of race that the issue of color differences within groups is never raised.

Under the tenets of Afrocentric psychology, one becomes unable to conceive of criticisms of one's own people, except to criticize them for being influenced by "the other." Afrocentric epistemologists (e.g., Asante 1987) and psychologists alike seek a purer Africanity and attribute all errors or problems to the influences of Europeans. What critical abilities can scholarship exercise when it is led down the garden path cleared by fascistic nationalism?

Another relevant illustration of this problem [European control over the definitional process] involves the furor, primarily in the white community, of [sic] the "moral character" of former President Idi

Amin of Uganda. . . . They even have many so-called black leaders in this country [the United States] echoing this blatant distortion of African social reality, while the masses of our people in Africa appear to hold Brother Amin in the highest esteem. Of course, history readily reveals that whenever black leadership has operated firmly within the definitional context of African reality (à la Marcus Garvey, Malcolm X, and the like), Europeans have defined them in similar terms. (Baldwin 1980:103–104)

Although I fully agree that African and African American leaders have often been unfairly accused of inferior morality and honesty in the context of American racism, the Afrocentric simplification of African-as-good and European-as-evil leads to a lack of criticism that does not empower or enable human progress.

Similarly, Afrocentric perspectives on the ancient history of Africa romanticize a feudal order and legitimate recent human rights abuses perpetrated by oppressive African leaders. On the other hand, the progressive effect of Afrocentricity is to relegate those judgments that can be made to African diasporic people themselves, delegitimizing the authority of the colonial and Euro-American scholarship that has given us a Eurocentric definition of world and national history. It enhances the value of people of African descent (albeit uncritically) in opposition to their historical and continuing denigration by a society deeply imbued with white supremacist ideas. The pendulum swings wide, yet remains within the ideological parameters of a racist society.

Afrocentric anthropologist Dona Marimba Richards's work (1980) embodies several of the problems previously discussed: it dehistoricizes the ideology of white supremacy, claims a racial origin for worldviews and for racism itself, and rejects the notion of progress, consistent with romanticism of the past. Richards argues that progress is an a priori concept that is part of the European worldview. "The idea of progress had an irresistible attraction for Europeans; it was, after all, created out of their own sentiment, their ethos. But it was technological efficiency which 'clinched it'—which provided tangible evidence of material gain and accomplishment" (Richards 1980:65). According to this point of view, the notion of progress led Europeans at their origins to conceptualize the universe as linear, from which it followed that everything in nature could be placed within a hierarchy. These concepts, in turn, led to the ideology of white supremacy and an emphasis on the control of nature. According to this Afrocentric approach, the lineal view of the universe proceeded from the conceptualization of progress and has always been tied to it. In order to support the thesis that a progress-oriented, white racial mentality is a root cause of racism, the concept of progressive change is argued to have preceded the social and economic influences of the industrial revolution with which it is often associated. Richards attempts to show that Plato believed in the idea of progress, contrary to other scholars' views of his philosophy.

Plato certainly adhered to the belief in a chain of being, a belief his student, Aristotle, adopted and to which he added the principle of linear gradation (Scala Naturae) that was later adapted to Christian thought as the "Great Chain of Being." But from Plato's "principle of plenitude" to the Christian notion of "fixity," everything in the universe was believed to have been created at once, never transforming. In fact, the Hellenes idealized their classical past as superior to the present, just as did many subsequent European scholars who returned again and again to Socrates, Plato, and Aristotle as ideals.

Surely linearity set the stage for the particular unilinear conceptualization of progress that would emerge in evolutionary theories during the eighteenth and nineteenth centuries. But these theories of *change* constituted a wrenching and difficult break with European traditions of the Enlightenment, despite the emergence of a contested "doctrine of progress" during the late Renaissance (see Kennedy 1976:1–22 for a review). Even Linneus (who devised Western biological classification) stopped short of a belief in evolutionary change (after all, this was heresy). Malthus believed in the unalterable persistence of a cycle of human misery and inequity. But Buffon, Lamarck, and Darwin did believe in the normalcy of change (Lindroth 1983; Lovejoy 1959) (although even the term "evolution" originally meant to roll out a scroll of predetermined and preexisting phenomena [Gould 1979]). Rather than "clinching" a preexisting view of the world as ever-changing, the industrial revolution (and the emergence of the capitalist mode of production) inspired the development of a notion of change and of progress (of secular and materialistic hope) in contention with the previous feudal Christian and pre-Christian views of fixity and humanistic decline.

This Afrocentric interpretation is epistemologically and politically key. We are asked to abandon the concept of progress (as the primary root of linear-hierarchical schema and therefore of white supremacy). The concept of progress has been used in racist ways that should be solidly critiqued. *But the wide acceptance of the idea that our universe undergoes continuous motion or change is a postfeudal phenomenon, not a genetically or metaphysically white phenomenon.* We are asked to return to a cyclical view of nature because it is "African." Dare we embrace a theory devoid of the prospect of change? The alternative is to hark back to an illusory past, or a real past that is gone.

African Diffusionism

The glorification of feudalism, and especially the focus on Egypt by many Afrocentrics, suggests an emulation of European elitist ideals. One gets the impression that those who advocate a return to these purer African (feudal) ways of thinking and behaving must expect that everyone will acquire his or her own pyramid. The slaves, the masses, the inequities are overlooked. Yet the amount of work devoted to placing Egypt in its proper African context (countering Eurocentric approaches) is an impressive corrective. This work is not exclusive to Afrocentrics— Keita (1981) reviews archaeological research on the African origins of Egyptian civilization, and Bernal (1988) examines the Afro-Asiatic roots of Greco-Roman civilization—but African and African American scholars have long been prominent among the vanguard in correcting the Eurocentric expropriation of Egypt to Western civilization (Anta Diop 1967, 1974b; Douglass 1950 [1854]) and the denial of Egypt's influences upon the ancient Greco-Roman world (James 1954). Throughout black scholarship on Egypt, there has been heard a challenge to a dominating white supremacist interpretation of blacks as either culturally or biologically incapable of equality with whites in "civilized" life. If black scholars have gone so far as to make of Africa the origin of all civilized institutions, it is to be understood as a response to dominant white scholarship since the early nineteenth century, which has gone so far as to attribute those institutions solely to Europe. The central purpose of that Eurocentric approach has been to deny equal humanity to blacks (Anta Diop 1974b; Bernal 1988; Douglass 1950 [1854]; and others).

A profusion of classical and historical studies has appeared in the African American (and to a lesser extent in the African) community since about 1975. As I mentioned earlier, Senegalese scientist Anta Diop's work gave impetus to much of the Egyptology that would follow. Anta Diop used classical, archaeological, and linguistic data to show Egyptian influences on West Africa (for example, on his own Wolof language [1974b: 153–55]). According to Anta Diop, Egypt had for millennia been the center of a pan-African culture that finally collapsed under the weight of foreign conquest, producing a massive exodus to the far reaches of the continent (Holl, this volume). Under the conditions of a tropical climate and its resource abundance, African peoples lost interest in technological development and were lulled into the relatively backward state in which Europeans would later find and exploit them. Although Anta Diop at times relies upon antiquated and untenable racial concepts (for example, the Afro-European origins of Asians), *The African Origin of Civilization* (1974b) is an extraordinarily thoughtful book. Anta Diop is explicit in his attempt to counter white supremacist expropriation of Egypt and is equally forthcoming about the use of his analysis as an ideological foundation for pan-African unity (Anta Diop 1959; Holl, this volume).

Anta Diop's scholarship made Egypt's relationship to the rest of Africa (and the world) similar to that which had been made between Greece and the rest of Europe (and the world). James's *Stolen Legacy* (1954) described the mode of transmission of culture from ancient Egypt to Greece as outright theft of oral and written science and philosophy. Ivan van Sertima, in *They Came Before Columbus* (1976), described influences of the Egyptian twenty-fifth dynasty on Olmec society in Mexico in the eighth century B.C. Following this enormously influential book, van Sertima edited the *Journal of African Civilizations,* from which derive two volumes on early African diffusion to Asia and Europe (van Sertima 1985; van Sertima and Rashidi 1985).

These studies, highly influential in African America, have been largely unread, ignored, or summarily dismissed by Euro-Americans. They display problems in their simplistic racial classifications and inattentiveness to biological parallels between unrelated groups, in periodic excesses of diffusionism and possible cultural appropriation, and in neglecting African societies that were peripheral to the most developed states and classical cultures. Yet these same problems have also been the most enduring tendencies of Eurocentric or "mainstream" scholarship — a scholarship to which the authors of these books address themselves repeatedly.

Interestingly, the cultural relativism that many anthropologists consider the essence of their field's liberal, antiracist tradition seems not to have been embraced by the African diffusionists. It has not been enough for them to assign chiefdoms and bands of hunter-gatherers a different-but-equal status comparable to that of any other form of social organization. In addition, Africans can also claim the origins of the state and a powerful diffusion of ideas on a global scale. The result tends to glorify a feudal order generally, and more specifically, those societies Europeans have historically called theirs but which these diffusionist authors reclaim as their own cultural legacy. I hope the pendulum of criticism will swing back toward a more diverse and embracing anthropological scope

225

of cultural appreciation. Nonetheless, the balance in the debate being brought about by these African diffusionist studies is salubrious.

Although the African diffusionists' studies have been claimed by Afrocentrists, the former researchers do not incorporate racial and biological determinism in their otherwise racial analyses. Nor do they describe a single, generic African worldview (though Anta Diop suggests the historical basis for that notion) or way of understanding the world. They analyze but do not advocate a return to ancient science and philosophy. This is a scholarly thrust related to, but qualitatively different from, that of the Afrocentrist epistemologist Asante or the psychologists. Afrocentric scholars and lay organizations, study groups, and educational pressure groups have often lumped these tendencies together. The question of origins and notions of racial supremacy have often been associated in mainstream Eurocentric scholarship too, where claims of being the first to invent all important things tidy up spurious arguments for genetic superiority. The growing amateur tradition of classical African studies, partly represented by the Association for the Study of Classical African Civilizations, Afrocentric shops, bookstores, films, public ceremonies, schools, and educational initiatives in most major cities in the United States, demonstrates the power of these ideas.

Discussion

The concept of a single, generic, "African" ethos (mentality, worldview, definitional system, etc.) not only obscures the rich diversity of African (and other) cultures but also obfuscates many of the real human achievements and failings in the history of these civilizations. Those achievements and failings both distinguish societies from one another and represent their common forms of social organization, indeed, their common humanity. To deny these facts denies us humans a future as a better, more coherent world community. To romanticize is to deny ourselves an adequate understanding of the real problems and prospects of the past and present with which to build a workable future.

The inextricable multidimensionality of our human cultures and our biologies is equally characteristic of our philosophies. Indeed, Plato also believed that "the physical universe is an exhaustive replica of the real world of ideas that had a single creation, although the illusive world of appearances is *cyclical*" (Kennedy 1976:12, my emphasis). Although that view might have been African inspired (an insight afforded as much by the Anglo-Judeocentric work of Martin Bernal as by the work of others), it is no less an origin of European thought. One might also argue that the notion of *an* "African view" (Richards 1980:76–77) represents an "ideal type" (à la Aristotle) that underlies (and belies) the material reality of the diversity and broad international influences of Africa and the diaspora today and in the past. By showing this common ground between Afrocentric and European philosophy, I do not deny that there is much that is unique about cultural traditions but wish only to point out the inefficacy of an analysis based on an attempt to create separate species from neighboring societies.

Furthermore, much of what is being called African (such as breast-feeding children) in contrast to European (bottle feeding) (Richards 1980) represents cultural practices associated with forms of social organization or degrees of capital penetration independent of region and "race." Unfortunately, these Afrocentric approaches suffer from the lack of an anthropological background, at least one incorporating anthropology as practiced since the first half of the twentieth century. Without a comparative, cross-cultural, or anthropological framework, definitions of Africanity seem contrived. Similarly, definitions of Afrocentrism, in the absence of systematic comparisons with Eurocentric and Asiocentric (Hindocentric, Buddhocentric, etc.) approaches, are unsophisticated. To improve such definitions would be a useful academic undertaking. Nonetheless, the variations and transformations of culture and perspective that would be deduced should be expected to reflect the fact that we humans are always changing ourselves.

This is not to say that variation between ethnic and cultural groups does not exist. Eurocentrism is as real as Afrocentrism. Afrocentrism is what I call the ethnocentric perspective of African-descended people, yet it is diverse and incorporates Eurocentrism among other "isms" and schisms that have influenced our history. Given the historical differences between Europeans and Africans, Afrocentrism as broadly defined, in all of its diversity and complexity, must be appreciated as a condition (for better and worse) of knowledge. There is every reason to foster its contributions, by which I mean simply to foster black scholarship. Yet as defined by some, Afrocentrism is strictly limited in its theory and practice.

Diversity is equally true of African cultures and biologies generally, and especially of the African diaspora with all its historical influences. To believe that continental or diasporic Africans today should prize only part of their rich culture and smite the other is to reject who and what Africans are materially. Such complexity has always been involved in the history of Africans, Americans, Asians, and Europeans, among whom diffusion and exchange have long taken place.

What has been examined here, most critically, is the scholarship of a nationalism that, like examples of European nationalism, glorifies the past and connects a people of the present to that past glory (and future potential) on a racial basis. At the same time, the new African diffusionism raises important questions and is likely to correct many of the inaccuracies brought about by the long history of racism in the anthropological and classical literatures. Our present challenge is to disentangle, wherever possible, the salubrious anti–white-supremacist content of this scholarship from its racial nationalism.

Finally, there is deep irony in the heated public debate about melanin theory. The Afrocentric arguments most openly attacked by Euro-American educators as being racist and poor scholarship are based on biological and racial deterministic premises that were actually developed by mainstream Eurocentric scholars. Those notions underlying the ideology of white supremacy persist today and may, indeed, be on the rise. The use of Western biodeterministic assumptions in support of black superiority is a matter of what Malcolm X once referred to as "chickens coming home to roost."

Eurocentric and Afrocentric ideas of racial supremacy are not, however, truly equivalent in motivation. While the former serves the exploitative purposes of institutional discrimination, the latter seeks to heal a people, some of whom are so wounded by white racism that they take heart in learning that there is anything at all good about the color of their skin. Yet African American scholars have principally engaged the war of ideas on a higher, egalitarian plane throughout their history (see Douglass 1950 [1854], at the origin of the nature-nurture debate) and they should be challenged by their own community (that is how I see the role of this chapter) to continue doing so.

NOTE

Some of the ideas in this chapter were first explored in my position paper for a Howard University task force on African and African American studies that deliberated on the relation of Afrocentrism to the university's curricular reforms. I thank the task force members for forcing me to begin to work these ideas out. I am grateful to the editors of this volume, the other participants in the seminar "Making Alternative Histories," and the School of American Research for the opportunity to fully explore and organize these thoughts in print. Thanks also to Dr. Shomarka O. Keita, who has always debated these issues with me in ways that have heightened my own self-criticism.

Alternative Histories, Alternative Nations

Nationalism and Modern Historiography in Bengal

PARTHA CHATTERJEE

> We must have a history!
> — *Bankimchandra Chattopadhyay*

anajit Guha has recently discussed the conditions and limits of the agenda developed in the second half of the nineteenth century for "an Indian historiography of India" (Guha 1988). It was an agenda for self-representation, for setting out to claim for the nation a past that was not distorted by foreign interpreters. Reviewing the development of historiography in Bengal in the nineteenth century, Guha shows how the call sent out by Bankimchandra Chattopadhyay (1838–94), the foremost literary figure of the time — "We have no history! We must have a history!" — was, in effect, an exhortation to launch the struggle for power. In the historical mode of recalling the past, the power to represent oneself is nothing other than political power itself.

Bankim's observation that "Bengalis have no history" was, strictly speaking, incorrect. In 1880, when he began to write his essays on the history of Bengal (Chattopadhyay 1965), a fair amount of historical writing in Bengali already existed. His objection was that these writings did not contain the true history of Bengal. What he meant by true history was also clear: it was the memory of the glorious deeds of one's ancestors. "There are a few godforsaken *jāti* [people] in this world who are unaware of the glorious deeds of their forefathers. The foremost among them is the Bengali" (Chattopadhyay 1965:330).

The reason for his reproach was that no history of Bengal had been written by Bengalis themselves. "In our judgment, there is not a single English book which contains the true history of Bengal" (Chattopadhyay 1965:336). Why? Because English writers had based their histories of

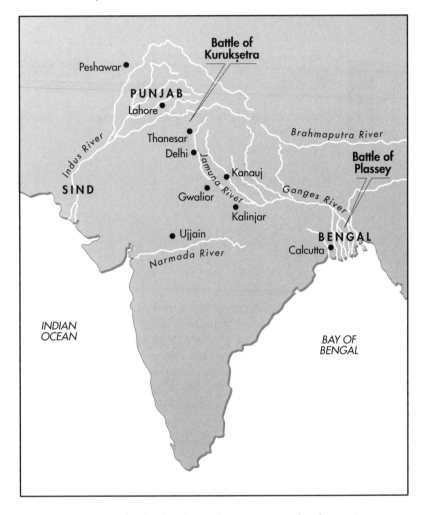

Figure 10.1. Medieval India, showing locations mentioned in chapter 10.

Bengal on the testimonies of foreign Muslim chroniclers; there was no Bengali testimony reflected in them. Consequently, Bengalis could not accept them as their own history. "Anyone who uncritically accepts as history the testimony of these lying, Hindu-hating Musalman zealots is not a Bengali" (Chattopadhyay 1965:336).

It is, of course, a primary sign of the nationalist consciousness that it will not find its own voice in histories written by foreign rulers and that it will set out to write for itself the account of its own past. What is noteworthy in Bankim's nationalist call to history-writing is, first, that whereas he identifies his subject nation sometimes as "Bengali" and at other times as "Indian" (*bhāratavarṣīya*), in both cases the foreign ruler and aggressor is the Muslim; Bankim does not, as is well known, speak of a struggle for power against British rule. Second, the historical conscious-ness he is seeking to invoke is in no way an "indigenous" consciousness, because the preferred discursive form of his historiography is modern European. Third, in 1880, when Bankim was making his exhortation — "Bengal must have a history, or else there is no hope for it. Who will write it? You will write it, I will write it, all of us will write it. Every Bengali will have to write it" — the numerous books being written in Bengali on the history of Bengal and of India, although dismissed by Bankim as "adolescent literature," were actually informed by a historiographic prac-tice that was in no way different from his own (Chattopadhyay 1965: 337). When compared with many other, admittedly less talented Bengali writers of his time, Bankim's views on history were not exceptional.

Elsewhere (Chatterjee 1992), I have examined some of these writ-ings, mainly in school textbooks. None of these books were written by major historians, and none claimed any great originality in histori-cal interpretation. But for that very reason they are good indicators of the main features of a commonly shared discursive form within which Indian nationalist historiography made its appearance. In this chapter I discuss one example selected from this literature.

Before I get to this material from the late nineteenth century, how-ever, let me begin with a text from the very early years of that century. This text will give us an idea of how radical a transformation was effected in the forms of recounting the political events of the past.

A Puranic History

The first three books of narrative prose in Bengali commissioned by the Fort William College in Calcutta for use by young East India Company officials learning the local vernacular were books of history. Of these, *Rājābali* (Śarmanah 1808), by Mrityunjay Vidyalankar, was a history of India — the first history of India in the Bengali language that we have in print. Mrityunjay (ca. 1762–1819) taught Sanskrit at Fort William College and was the author of some of the first printed books in Bengali. When he decided in 1808 to set down in writing the story of "the Rajas and Badshahs and Nawabs who have occupied the throne in Delhi and Bengal," he apparently did not have to undertake any fresh "research" into the subject; he was only writing down an account that was in circulation at the time among the Brahman literati and their land-owning patrons. His book was, we might say, a good example of the historical memory of elite Bengali society at the turn of the century as exemplified in contemporary scholarship.

The book starts with a precise reckoning of the time at which it is being written:

> In course of the circular motion of time, like the hands of a clock, passing through the thirty *kalpa* such as Pitṛkalpa etc., we are now situated in the Śvetavarāha kalpa. Each kalpa consists of fourteen *manu;* accordingly, we are now in the seventh manu of Śvetavarāha kalpa, called Vaivasvata. Each manu consists of 284 *yuga;* we are now passing through the one hundred and twelfth yuga of Vaivasvata manu, called Kaliyuga. This yuga consists of 432,000 years. Of these, up to the present year 1726 of the Śaka era, 4,905 years have passed; 427,095 years are left. (Śarmanah 1808:3–4)

The calendrical system is also precisely noted. For the first 3,044 years of Kaliyuga, the prevailing era (*śaka*) was that of King Yudhiṣṭhira. The next 135 years made up the era of King Vikramāditya. These two eras are now past:

> Now we are passing through the era of the king called Śālivāhana, who lived on the southern banks of the river Narmadā. This *śaka* will last for 18,000 years after the end of the Vikramāditya era. After this there will be a king called Vijayābhinandana who will rule in the region of the Citrakūṭa mountains. His *śaka* will last for 10,000 years after the end of the Śālivāhana era. . . .
>
> After this there will be a king called Parināgārjuna whose era will last until 821 years are left in the Kaliyuga, at which time will be born in the family of Gautabrāhmaṇa in the Sambhala country an *avatāra* of Kalkideva. Accordingly, of the six eras named after six kings, two are past, one is present, and three are in the future. (Śarmanah 1808:8)

Where does the history recorded in *Rājābali* begin?

> In the Satyayuga, the Supreme Lord (*parameśvara*) had planted in the form of an Asvathva tree a king called Ikṣvāku to rule over the earth. The two main branches of this tree became the Sūrya and the Candra *vaṃśa*. The kings born in these two lineages have ruled the earth in the four yuga. Of these, some were able to acquire the greatest powers of dharma and thus ruled over the entire earth con-

sisting of the seven islands. Others had lesser powers and thus ruled over only Jambudvīpa [one of the seven islands] or only Bhāratavarṣa [one of the nine parts of Jambudvīpa] or, in some cases, only the Kumārikākhaṇḍa [one of the nine parts of Bhāratavarṣa]. . . . The accounts of these kings are recorded in the branches of knowledge [śāstra] called the Purāṇa and the Itihāsa. (Śarmanah 1808:6–7)

A few things may be clarified at this point. In Mrityunjay's scheme of history, rulers on earth are appointed by divine will. They enjoy their position to the extent that, and for as long as, they acquire and retain the powers of dharma. By attaining the highest levels of dharma, one could even become ruler of the entire earth. We may wish, in order to distinguish this variety of history-writing from those with which we are more familiar today, to call Mrityunjay's narrative a Puranic or mythical history. Mrityunjay would not have quarreled with this description, not because he was aware of the distinction we are making but because *purāṇetihāsa* was for him the valid form of retelling the political history of Bhāratavarṣa (India).

We cannot accuse the discipline of Puranic history of being sloppy in its counting of dynasties and kings. "In the 4,267 years since the beginning of the Kaliyuga, there have been 119 Hindus of different *jāti* who have become *samrāṭ* (emperor) on the throne of Delhi" (Śarmanah 1808:10). The count begins with King Yudhiṣṭhira of the *Mahābhārata* who heads a list of 28 Kṣatriya kings who ruled for a total of 1,812 years. "After this the actual reign of the Kṣatriya *jāti* ended." Then came fourteen kings of the Nanda dynasty, starting with "one called Mahānanda born of a Kṣatriya father and a Śūdra mother," who ruled for a total of five hundred years. "The Rājput *jāti* started with this Nanda." After this came the Buddhist kings: "Fifteen kings of the Nāstika [atheist] faith, from Vīravāhu to Aditya, all of the Gautama lineage, ruled for four hundred years. At this time the Nāstika views enjoyed such currency that the Vaidika religion was almost eradicated" (Śarmanah 1808:10–12).

Then follows a curious list of dynasties, for the most part unknown in modern historiography, culminating in the rule of the "Chohān Rājput *jāti*," which ends with:

> Pṛthorāy, who ruled for fourteen years and seven months. . . . This is as far as the empire [*sāmrājya*] of the Hindu kings lasted. . . . After this began the *smārājya* of the Musalman. From the beginning of the empire of the Yavanas to the present year 1726 of the Śaka era, fifty-one kings have ruled for 651 years three months and twenty-eight days. (Śarmanah 1808:12–13)

What is interesting about this chronology is the way in which its dynastic sequence passes ever so smoothly from the kings of the *Mahābhārata* to the kings of Magadha and ends with the Mughal emperor Shah Alam II "of the lineage of Amir Taimur" occupying the throne in Delhi at the time of Mrityunjay's writing. Myth, history, and the contemporary—all become part of the same chronological sequence; one is not distinguished from another. The passage from one to another, consequently, is entirely unproblematical. There is not even an inkling in Mrityunjay's prose of any of the knotty questions about the value of Puranic accounts in constructing a "proper" historical chronology of Indian dynasties that would so exercise Indian historians a few decades later. Although Mrityunjay wrote at the behest of his colonial masters, his historiographic allegiances were entirely precolonial.

It would be of some interest to us, therefore, to discover how a Brahman scholar such as Mrityunjay described the end of "the Hindu dynasties" and the accession to the throne at Delhi of "the Yavana emperors." Our curiosity is aroused even further when we discover that the story of the defeat of Prithviraj Chauhan at the hands of Shihabuddin Muhammad Ghuri takes the form of a Puranic tale. The story (Śarmanah 1808) tells how Prithviraj's father had two wives, one of whom was a demoness (*rākṣasī*) who ate human flesh. She had also introduced her husband into this evil practice. One day the *rākṣasī* ate the son of the other queen who, taken by fright, ran away to her brother. There she gave birth to a son who was called Pṛthu. On growing up, Pṛthu met his father. At his request, Pṛthu cut off his father's head and fed the flesh to twenty-one women belonging to his *jāti*. Later, when Pṛthu became king, the sons of those twenty-one women became his feudatories (*sāmanta*). "Because Pṛthu had killed his father, the story of his infamy spread far and wide. Kings who paid tribute to him stopped doing so" (Śarmanah 1808:107). In other words, Prithviraj was not a ruler who enjoyed much respect among his subjects.

It was at this time that Shihabuddin Ghuri threatened to attack Prithviraj:

> When the king heard of the threatening moves of the Yavanas, he called a number of scholars learned in the Vedas and said, "O learned men! Arrange a sacrifice which will dissipate the prowess and the threats of the Yavanas." The learned men said, "O King! There is such a sacrifice and we can perform it. And if the sacrificial block [*yūpa*] can be laid at the prescribed moment, then the Yavanas can never enter this land." The king was greatly reassured by these words and arranged for the sacrifice to be performed with much pomp. When

the learned men declared that the time had come to lay the block, many efforts were made but no one could move the sacrificial block to its assigned place. Then the learned men said, "O King! What Īsvara desires, happens. Men cannot override his wishes, but can only act in accordance with them. So desist in your efforts. It seems this throne will be attacked by the Yavanas." (Śarmanah 1808:109)

Hearing these words, Prithviraj was greatly disheartened and "slackened his efforts at war" (Śarmanah 1808:109). His armies were defeated by Shihabuddin, who arrived triumphantly at Delhi. Then Prithviraj

emerged from his quarters and engaged Śāhābuddīn in a ferocious battle. But by the grace of Īśvara, the Yavana Śāhābuddin made a prisoner of Pṛthurājā. On being reminded that Pṛthurājā was son-in-law of King Jayacandra [Jaichand, ruler of a neighboring kingdom, had already collaborated with Muhammad Ghuri], he did not execute him but sent him as a prisoner to his own country of Ghaznin. (Śarmanah 1808:109–110)

Let us remember that in Mrityunjay's scheme of history, dynasties are founded by the grace of the divine power, and kingdoms are retained only so long as the ruler is true to dharma. The Chauhan dynasty was guilty of such heinous offenses as cannibalism and patricide. That Prithviraj had lost divine favor was already revealed at the sacrificial ceremony. His defeat and the establishment of "Yavana rule" by Muhammad Ghuri were, therefore, acts of divine will. Half a century later, when Puranic history would be abandoned in favor of rational historiography, this account of the battle of Thanesar would undergo a complete transformation. English-educated Brahman scholars would not accept with such equanimity the dictates of a divine will.

Two Mughal emperors are subjects of much controversy in nationalist historiography. Let us note what Mrityunjay has to say about them. On Akbar, Mrityunjay is effusive. "Since Śrī Vikramāditya, there has never been in Hindustan an emperor with merits equal to those of Akbar Shah" (Śarmanah 1808:195). Apart from having a deep sense of righteousness and performing all his duties in protecting his subjects, Akbar also had, according to Mrityunjay, an additional merit:

Because of his knowledge of many śāstra, his spiritual views were skeptical of the doctrines of Muhammad and were closer to those of the Hindus. The kings of Iran and Turan often complained about this. . . . He did not eat beef and forbade the slaughter of cows within his fort. To this day, cow slaughter is prohibited in his fort. (Śarmanah 1808:191, 194)

About Aurangzeb, on the other hand, Mrityunjay has this to say:

> He became very active in spreading the Muhammadī faith. And he destroyed many great temples. Many ceremonies of the Hindus such as the worship of the sun and of Gaṇeśa had been performed in the fort of the Badshah since the time of Akbar; [Aurangzeb] discontinued these practices and issued new rules invented by himself. (Śarmanah 1808:221)

He then adds:

> Although he destroyed many great temples, he was favored by the divine powers at Jvālāmukhī and Lachmanbālā and made sizable grants of land for the maintenance of those temples. He later lived at Aurangabad for twelve years and, on being cursed by a Brahman, died uttering horrible cries of pain. (Śarmanah 1808:221)

Where kings acquire kingdoms and hold power by divine grace, the business of arriving at a verdict on the character of rulers has to be negotiated between kings and gods. The only role the ordinary *prajā* (subject) plays is in bearing the consequences of the actions of these superior entities. Of course, the *prajā* knows the difference between a good king and a bad one, which is why he praises a ruler such as Akbar. And when Aurangzeb dies "uttering horrible cries of pain," perhaps the *prajā* shudders a little at the ferocity of divine retribution, but in the end he is reassured by the victory of dharma. In all this, however, the *prajā* never implicates himself in the business of ruling; he never puts himself in the place of the ruler. In recalling the history of kingdoms, he does not look for a history of himself.

If it was ever suggested to Mrityunjay that in the story of the deeds and fortunes of the kings of Delhi might lie the history of a nation, it is doubtful that he would have understood. His own position in relation to his narrative is fixed—it is the position of the *prajā,* the ordinary subject, who is most often only the sufferer and sometimes the beneficiary of acts of government. It is from that position that he tells the story of Prithviraj's misdeeds or of Akbar's righteousness. The thought would never have occurred to him that because of the associations of "nationality," he, Mrityunjay Vidyalankar, a Brahman scholar in the employment of the East India Company in Calcutta in the early nineteenth century, might in some way become responsible for the acts of Prithviraj or Akbar. *Rājābali* is not a national history because its protagonists are gods and kings, not ordinary people. The bonds of "nation-ness" had not yet been imagined that would lead the historian to identify with a solidarity that is supposed to act itself out in history.

The Construction of a Classical Past

The old historical framework changed radically as the Bengali literati were schooled in the new colonial curricula. Now Indians were taught the principles of European history, statecraft, and social philosophy. They were also taught the history of India as it came to be written from the standpoint of modern European scholarship. The Orientalists had, since the last years of the eighteenth century, begun to "recover" and reconstruct for modern historical consciousness the materials for an understanding of Indian history and society. The English-educated class in Bengal, from its birth in the early decades of the nineteenth century, became deeply interested in this new discipline of Indology.

But curiously enough, the new Indian literati, while they enthusiastically embraced the modern, rational principles of European historiography, did not accept the history of India as it was written by British historians. The political loyalty of the early generation of English-educated Bengalis toward the East India Company was unquestioned, and in 1857, when most of northern India was in revolt, they were especially demonstrative in their protestations of loyalty. Yet by the next decade they were engaged in openly contesting the colonialist interpretation of Indian history. By the 1870s, the principal elements were already in place for the writing of a nationalist history of India.

I have before me the eighteenth edition, published in 1878, of *The History of India* by Tarinicharan Chattopadhyay. Tarinicharan (1833–97) was a product of colonial education, a professor at Sanskrit College, and a social reformer. His textbooks on history and geography were extremely popular and formed the basis for many other, lesser known textbooks. His *History of India* was probably the most influential textbook read in Bengali schools in the second half of the nineteenth century. Its first sentences are striking: "India (*bhāratavarṣa*) has been ruled in turn by Hindus, Muslims and Christians. Accordingly, the history of this country (*deś*) is divided into the periods of Hindu, Muslim and Christian rule (*rājatva*)" (Chattopadhyay 1878:1).

We have passed from the "history of kings" to the "history of this country." Never again will a book like *Rājābali* be written; from now on everything will be the "history of this *deś*." This new history is periodized according to the distinctive character of rule, and this character, in turn, is determined by the religion of the rulers. The identification of country (*deś*) and realm (*rājatva*) is permanent and indivisible. This means that although there may at times be several kingdoms and kings, there is in truth always only one realm, which is coextensive with the country and which is symbolized by the capital or the throne. The *rājatva*, in other words, constitutes the generic sovereignty of the country, whereas the capital or the throne represents the center of sovereign statehood. Since the country is *bhāratavarṣa,* there can be only one true sovereignty that is coextensive with it, represented by a single capital or throne as its center. Otherwise, why should the defeat of Prithviraj and the capture of Delhi by Muhammad Ghuri signal the end of a whole period of Indian history and the beginning of a new one? Or why should the battle of Plassey mark the end of Muslim rule and the beginning of Christian rule? The identification in European historiography between the notions of country or people, sovereignty, and statehood was by now lodged firmly in the mind of the English-educated Bengali.

On the next page of *The History of India,* we have another example of the modernity of this historiographic practice. "All Sanskrit sources that are now available are full of legends and fabulous tales; apart from the *Rājataraṅginī* there is not a single true historical account" (Chattopadhyay 1878:2). The criteria of the "true historical account" had, of course, been set by then by European historical scholarship. That India had no true historical account was a singular discovery of European Indology. The thought had never occurred to Mrityunjay. But to Tarinicharan, it seemed self-evident. We then have a description of the inhabitants of India:

> In very ancient times, there lived in India two very distinct communities [*sampradāy*] of people. Of them, one resembled us in height and other aspects of physical appearance. The descendants of this community are now called Hindu. The people of the other community were short, dark, and extremely uncivilized. Their descendants are now known as Khas, Bhilla, Pulinda, Sāontāl, and other primitive [*jāṅglā,* "of the bush"] *jāti.* (Chattopadhyay 1878:2)

Because there is a lack of authentic sources, the narrative of ancient Indian history is necessarily fragmentary. Gone is the certitude of Mrityunjay's dynastic lists; Tarinicharan states quite clearly the limits to a rational reconstruction of the ancient past:

> European historians have proved by various arguments that the battle of Kurukṣetra took place before the fourteenth century B.C. For a long period after the battle of Kurukṣetra, the historical accounts of India are so uncertain, partial, and contradictory that it is impossible to construct from them a narrative. (Chattopadhyay 1878:16–17)

The narrative he does construct is not particularly remarkable, because he follows without much amendment the history of ancient India as current at the time among British writers on the subject. The only comment that is interesting in these chapters of Tarinicharan's book is the one he makes on Buddhism:

> [The Buddha] became a great enemy of the Hindu religion, which is why Hindus describe him as an atheist and the destroyer of dharma. Nevertheless, the religion founded by him contains much advice of the highest spiritual value. He did not admit anything that was devoid of reason [*yukti*]. No matter how ancient the customs of a *jāti*, if stronger reasons can be presented against the traditional views, then the opinions of at least some people are likely to change. (Chattopadhyay 1878:17)

What is interesting here is that the reasonableness of the religious views of Buddhism is not denied. On the contrary, Buddhism is presented as a rationalist critique from within "the Hindu religion." Otherwise, in accordance with the criterion of periodization, the time of the Buddhist rulers would have had to be classified as a separate period of ancient Indian history. Instead, it is given a place within the "Hindu period."

Although the historical sources for the ancient period are said to be fragmentary and unreliable, on one subject there seems to be no dearth of evidence. That is "the civilization and learning of the ancient Indians." This is the title of chapter 6 of Tarinicharan's book. The main argument is as follows:

> What distinguishes the giant from the dwarf or the mighty from the frail is nothing compared to the difference between the ancient and the modern Hindu. In earlier times, foreign travelers in India marveled at the courage, truthfulness, and modesty of the people of the Arya *vaṃśa;* now they remark mainly on the absence of those qualities. In those days Hindus would set out on conquest and hoist their flags in Tatar, China, and other countries; now a few soldiers from a tiny island far away are lording it over the land of India. In those days Hindus would regard all except their own *jāti* as *mleccha* and treat them with contempt; now those same *mleccha* shower contempt on the descendants of Aryans. Then the Hindus would sail to Sumatra and other islands, evidence of which is still available in plenty in the adjacent island of Bali. Now the thought of a sea voyage strikes terror in the heart of a Hindu, and if anyone manages to go, he is immediately ostracized from society. (Chattopadhyay 1878:32)

Ancient glory, present misery: the subject of this entire story is "us." The mighty heroes of ancient India were "our" ancestors, and the feeble inhabitants of India today are "ourselves." That ancient Indians conquered other countries or traded across the seas or treated other people "with contempt" is a matter of pride for "us." And it is "our" shame that "the descendants of Aryans" are today subordinated to others and are the objects of the latter's contempt. There is a certain scale of power among the different peoples of the world; earlier, the people of India were high on that scale, but today they are near the bottom. Not only physical prowess but also the achievements of ancient Indians in the field of learning were universally recognized:

> In ancient times, when virtually the whole world was shrouded in the darkness of ignorance, the pure light of learning shone brightly in India. The discoveries in philosophy which emanated from the keen intellects of ancient Hindus are arousing the enthusiasm of European scholars even today. (Chattopadhyay 1878:33)

It will be noticed that the opinion of European scholars in this matter is extremely important to Tarinicharan. In fact, all the examples he cites of the excellence of ancient Indian learning—in the fields of astronomy, mathematics, logic, and linguistics—were discoveries of nineteenth-century Orientalists. By bringing forward this evidence, Tarinicharan seems to be suggesting that although Europeans today treat Indians with contempt because of their degraded condition, Indians were not always like this because even European scholars admit that the arts and sciences of ancient India were of the highest standard. This evidence from Orientalist scholarship was extremely important for the construction of the full narrative of nationalist history.

That Tarinicharan's history is nationalist is signified by something else. His story of ancient glory and subsequent decline has a moral at the end: reform society, remove all these superstitions, which are the marks of decadence, and revive the true ideals of the past. These false beliefs and practices, for which Indians are today the objects of contempt, did not exist in the past because even Europeans admit that in ancient times "we" were highly civilized:

> Today we find Hindu women treated like slaves, enclosed like prisoners, and as ignorant as beasts. But if we look a millennium and a quarter earlier, we will find that women were respected, educated, and largely unconstrained. Where was child marriage then? No one married before the age of twenty-four. (Chattopadhyay 1878:33)

Ancient India became the classical age for the nationalist, while the period between the ancient and the contemporary was the dark age of medievalism. Needless to say, this scheme was heartily approved by European historiography. If the nineteenth-century Englishman could claim ancient Greece as his classical heritage, why should not the English-educated Bengali feel proud of the achievements of the so-called Vedic civilization?

Narrative Break

The chapter "Civilization and Learning of the Ancient Indians" closes Tarinicharan's history of ancient India. He then takes the reader outside India, to Arabia in the seventh century. It might seem reasonable to ask why it should be necessary, if one is to talk about a change of historical periods in twelfth-century India, to begin the description from seventh-century Arabia. The answer to this question is obvious, but implicit in that answer is an entire ensemble of assumptions and prejudices of nineteenth-century European historiography:

> Muhammad gave to his followers the name *musalman,* that is, the faithful, and to all other humans the name *kafir* or infidel. . . . Directing his followers to take the sword in order to destroy the *kafir,* he said that God had ordained that those Muslims who die in the war against false religion will go to paradise and live in eternal pleasure in the company of doe-eyed nymphs. But if they run away from battle, they will burn in hell. The Arab *jāti* is by nature fearless and warlike. Now, aroused by the lust for plunder in this world and for eternal pleasure in the next, their swords became irresistible everywhere. All of Arabia came under Muhammad's control, and only a few years after his death the Muslim flag was flying in every country between Kabul and Spain. Never before in history had one kingdom after another, one land after another, fallen to a conqueror with the speed at which they fell to the Muslims. It was impossible that such people, always delirious at the prospect of conquest, would not covet the riches of India. (Chattopadhyay 1878:36–37)

The ground is being prepared here for the next episode, which will result from the clash of this history of the Muslims with the history of Indians. Muslim history originates in, and acquires its identity from, the life of Muhammad. In other words, the dynasty that will be founded in Delhi at the beginning of the thirteenth century and the many political changes that will take place in the subsequent five centuries are not to be described merely as the periods of Turko-Afghan or Mughal rule in India; they are integral parts of the political history of Islam.

The actors in this history are also given certain behavioral characteristics. They are warlike and believe it is their religious duty to kill
infidels. Driven by lust for plunder and visions of cohabiting with the
nymphs of paradise, they are even prepared to die in battle. They are not
merely conquerors but are "delirious at the prospect of conquest" (*digvi-
jayonmatta*), and consequently are, by their innate nature, covetous of the
riches of India.

It is important for us at this point to note the complex relation between the new nationalist historiography and the histories of India produced by British writers in the nineteenth century. Whereas James Mill's
History of British India, completed in 1817, may have been the hegemonic
textbook of Indian history for European Indology, for the first nationalist
historians of India it represented precisely what they had to fight against.
Mill did not share any of the enthusiasm of Orientalists such as William
Jones for the philosophical and literary achievements of ancient India.
His condemnation of the despotism and immorality of Indian civilization was total, and even his recognition of "the comparative superiority
of Islamic civilisation" did not in any significant way affect his judgment
that until the arrival of British rule India had always been "condemned to
semi-barbarism and the miseries of despotic power." Nationalist history
in India could be born only by challenging such an absolute and comprehensive denial of all claims to historical subjectivity (Grewal 1970:
64–97).

Far more directly influential for the nationalist texts we are looking
at was Elphinstone's *History of India* (1841). This was a standard textbook
in Indian universities in the second half of the nineteenth century. The
reason nationalist readers found Elphinstone more palatable than Mill is
not far to seek. As E. B. Cowell, who taught in Calcutta and added notes
to the later editions of Elphinstone's *History,* explained in a preface in
1866, a "charm of the book is the spirit of genuine hearty sympathy with
and appreciation of the native character which runs through the whole,
and the absence of which is one of the main blemishes in Mr. Mill's eloquent work" (Elphinstone 1905:vii). In this spirit of sympathy, Elphinstone wrote entire chapters in his volume *Hindús* titled "Philosophy,"
"Astronomy and Mathematical Science," "Medicine," "Language," "Literature," "Fine Arts," and "Commerce." He also began his volume on "Maho-
metans" with a chapter called "Arab Conquests A.D. 632, A.H. 11–A.D. 753,
A.H. 136," whose first section was "Rise of the Mahometan Religion."

In the second half of the nineteenth century, European Indologi-
cal scholarship seemed to have agreed that the history of Hinduism
was one of a classical age—for some, the Vedic civilization, for others,
the so-called Gupta revival in the fourth to the seventh centuries—

followed by a medieval decline from the eighth to the eighteenth centuries (Inden 1990:117–22). For some, this decline was itself the reason why the country fell so quickly to the Muslim invaders. In any case, the theory of medieval decline fitted in nicely with the overall judgment of nineteenth-century British historians that "Muslim rule in India" was a period of despotism, misrule, and anarchy—this, of course, being the historical justification for colonial intervention.

For Indian nationalists in the late nineteenth century, the pattern of classical glory, medieval decline, and modern renaissance appeared as one not only proclaimed by the modern historiography of Europe but also approved for India by at least some sections of European scholarship. What was needed was to claim for the Indian nation the historical agency for completing the project of modernity. To make that claim, ancient India had to become the classical source of Indian modernity while "the Muslim period" would become the night of medieval darkness. Contributing to that description would be all the prejudices of the European Enlightenment toward Islam. Dominating the chapters in the new nationalist history of India dealing with the twelfth century onward would be a stereotypical figure of "the Muslim" endowed with a "national character": he would be fanatical, bigoted, warlike, dissolute, and cruel.

Muslim Tyranny, Hindu Resistance

The story that begins with the birth of Islam in Arabia does, of course, shift to India, but this happens in stages. Tarinicharan gives long descriptions of the Arab invasions of Sind and the successive raids by Mahmud Ghaznavi into different Indian kingdoms, all of which take place well before the establishment of the so-called Slave dynasty in Delhi in the early thirteenth century. These descriptions have a common pattern that can be clarified by looking at two examples: Tarinicharan's accounts of the invasion of Sind by Muhammad Ibn Kasim and of Mahmud Ghaznavi's attack on Punjab. Muhammad Kasim began his war on Dahir, the king of Sind, in 712:

> Fortune favored him. A ball of fire thrown by his soldiers struck King Dahir's elephant, which panicked and fled from the battlefield. Dahir's troops, thinking that their king had given up the battle, fell into disarray. Later it will be seen that even when Indians had every chance of victory, similar misfortunes often led to their defeat at the hands of the Muslims. (Chattopadhyay 1878:38)

It must be noted that what Tarinicharan calls "fortune" (*daiva*) and "misfortune" (*durddaiva*) are not the same as the *daiva* that was divine intervention in Mrityunjay's narrative. Misfortune here is mere accident, a matter of chance. There is no suggestion at all of any retribution for immoral conduct. It is the misfortune not of kings but of "Indians" that despite deserving to win they have repeatedly lost because of accidents:

> Finally, after displaying much heroism, [King Dahir] was killed at the hands of the enemy. His capital was besieged, but Dahir's wife, displaying a courage similar to her husband's, continued to defend the city. In the end, food supplies ran out. Deciding that it was preferable to die rather than submit to the enemy, she instructed the inhabitants of the city to make necessary arrangements. Everyone agreed; everywhere, pyres were lit. After the immolations [of the women], the men, completing their ablutions, went out sword in hand and were soon killed by the Muslims. (Chattopadhyay 1878:38)

Later in Tarinicharan's *History of India* there are similar stories of defeat in battle. Two features are worth our notice: one, the courage of Hindu women in resisting aggression, and the other, the death in battle of Hindu men as a ritualized form of self-sacrifice. We thus have narrative indices such as "everywhere, pyres were lit" and "completing their ablutions . . . [the men were] killed by the Muslims." The corresponding indices for Muslim soldiers are "driven by the prospect of cohabiting with doe-eyed nymphs" and so forth. The contrast is significant.

Tarinicharan tells another story about Kasim that is part of the same narrative structure. To the courage of Hindu women is added another element: intelligence. And parallel to the story of self-sacrifice is created another story: vengeance on the enemy for the death of one's kin.

> On completing his conquest of Sind, Kasim was preparing to drive further into India when the resourcefulness of a woman became his undoing. Among the women who were captured in war in Sind were two daughters of King Dahir. They were not only of high birth but were also outstandingly beautiful. Kasim thought they would make appropriate presents for the Khalifa and accordingly sent them to his master. The ruler of the Muslims was bewitched by the beauty of the elder daughter and began to look upon her with desire. At this, she burst into tears and said, "It is a pity that I am not worthy of receiving the affections of someone like you, because Kasim has already sullied my dharma." Hearing of this act of his servant, the Khalifa was enraged and ordered that Kasim be sown in hide and brought before him. When this order was carried out, the Khalifa showed Kasim's corpse to the princess. Eyes sparkling with delight, she said, "Kasim was entirely innocent. I had made

the allegation only in order to avenge the deaths of my parents and the humiliation of their subjects." (Chattopadhyay 1878:39)

Let us move to the beginning of the eleventh century and the period of Mahmud of Ghazna. "Of all Muslims, it was his aggressions which first brought devastation and disarray to India, and from that time the freedom of the Hindus has diminished and faded like the phases of the moon" (Chattopadhyay 1878:41). Tarinicharan mentions some of Mahmud's better qualities, such as courage, foresight, strategic skill, and perseverance, but ignores the fact, discussed in Elphinstone, that Mahmud was also a great patron of arts and letters. "Although he was endowed with these qualities, he was also a great adherent, at least in public, of the Musalman religion, a bitter opponent of the worship of idols, and an unyielding pursuer of wealth and fame" (Chattopadhyay 1878:42). This was another trait of the so-called "Muslim character": although faith in Islam was a reason for war, it was not true faith but only an apparent adherence to religion.

When the narrative turns to Mahmud's move against King Anandapal of the Shahiya dynasty, we begin to discern themes that are representations of national unity in the face of adversity:

"The Muslims are determined to destroy the independence of all of India and to eradicate the Hindu religion. If they conquer Lahore, they will attack other parts of the country. It is therefore a grave necessity for all to unite in suppressing the *mleccha* forces." Saying this, the king [Elphinstone writes the name as Anang Pál; Tarinicharan does the same] sent emissaries to all the principal Hindu kings. His appeal did not go unheeded. The kings of Delhi, Kanauj, Ujjain, Gwalior, Kalinjar, and other places joined with Anangapal. Masses of troops arrived in Punjab. Worried by this sudden increase in the strength of the opposition, Mahmud decided, for reasons of safety, to halt near Peshawar. The Hindu forces increased daily. Hindu women from far away sold their diamonds, melted down their gold ornaments, and sent supplies for war. (Chattopadhyay 1878:43–44)

King Anandapal is unlikely to have had the historical foresight to anticipate that the fall of Lahore to Mahmud would lead to "the destruction of the independence of all of India." These are Tarinicharan's words. But by putting them on the lips of the ruler of Punjab, he turns this story into a war of the Hindu *jāti:* "the kings joined with Anangapal," "the Hindu forces increased daily," "Hindu women from far away sent supplies," and so forth. But then came the inevitable stroke of misfortune. "A fire-ball or a sharp arrow flung from the Musalman camp struck the

245

elephant of the Hindu commander Anangapal. The elephant, with the king on its back, fled from the field of battle. At this, the Hindu soldiers fell into disarray" (Chattopadhyay 1878:44).

Coming to the Sultanate and Mughal periods, Tarinicharan's barbs are sharpest when they are directed against Aurangzeb. "Arāñjib was deceitful, murderous, and plundered the wealth of others" (Chattopadhyay 1878:220). "His declaration of faith in the Musalman religion only facilitated the securing of his interests. . . . In truth, Arāñjib would never forsake his interests for reasons of religion or justice" (Chattopadhyay 1878: 173). On the other hand, Tarinicharan has praise for Akbar, although his reasons are informative. It was not Akbar's impartiality in matters of religion but rather his use of the powers of the state to reform both the Hindu and the Muslim religions that made him worthy of praise:

> Akbar attempted to eradicate some irrational practices prescribed in the Musalman religion. He also tried to stop several irrational practices of the Hindus. He prohibited the ordeal by fire, the burning of widows against their wishes, and child marriage. He also allowed the remarriage of widows. . . . Orthodox Muslims were strongly opposed to him because of his liberal views on religion. Many called him an atheist. (Chattopadhyay 1878:191)

Other Claims to a National Past

Not only was Tarinicharan's book reprinted every year, but it also served as a model for many other textbooks. One such was *Questions and Answers on the History of India*. Written by Saiyad Abdul Rahim (1870) of Barisal, it follows Tarinicharan's book very closely. But it makes a few amendments that are significant. First, Abdul Rahim (1870:2) writes the story of the Aryans differently: "The Hindus are not the original inhabitants of India. They came from the west of the river Sindhu and became inhabitants of India by the force of arms." Where Tarinicharan had written "the non-Aryans were included in the Arya *sampradāy*" (Chattopadhyay 1978:4) or "the Aryans established colonies" or "planted the Hindu flag" (Chattopadhyay 1978:27), Rahim changed the description to "became inhabitants of India by the force of arms."

In the remaining part of the historical narrative, Abdul Rahim does not deviate from Tarinicharan. The change comes with the very last question in the book:

> TEACHER. What lesson have you drawn from your reading of the history of Musalman rule?

STUDENT. Arya! This is what I have learnt for certain by reading the history of Musalman rule. To rule a kingdom is to destroy one's life both in this world and in the next. To rule, one must give up for all time the god-given gifts of forgiveness and mercy. How lamentable it is that one must, for the sake of a kingdom, redden the earth with the blood of one's own brother in whose company one has spent so many years of one's childhood. O kingdom! I have learnt well from the history of Musalman rule how you turn the human heart into stone. For your sake, to kill one's parents or one's brothers and sisters, or even to sacrifice the great treasure of religion, seems a matter of little concern. O kingdom, how bewitching are your powers of seduction! (Rahim 1870:40–41)

In spite of having plowed through his book, this student of Tarini-charan has clearly developed little appreciation for the charms of *raison d'état*. Where Saiyad Abdul Rahim writes in his own words, we can still hear the voice of Mrityunjay's *prajā*. But we will not hear it for much longer. If there is no place for Islam in the classical heritage of Indian culture, then in the new mode of historiography it is going to be thought of as constituting an alternative and different classical tradition. Writing a biography of the Prophet in 1886, Sheikh Abdar Rahim cites, as Tarini-charan did, the authority of European scholars to make his claim: "Islam has been far more beneficial to the human *jāti* than the Christian religion. Philosophy and science were first taken to the European continent from the Musalman of Asia and the Moors of Spain. . . . The Musalman of Spain were the founders of philosophy in Europe" (Rahim 1886:173). He also refutes the false accusations made against Islam by Europeans:

All the biographies of the Prophet Muhammad which hitherto have been written in the Bengali language are incomplete. Especially since they have followed English books on the subject, they are in many respects unsuitable for Musalman readers. People of other religions have falsely accused Muhammad of spreading his religion by the sword; a perusal of this book will show how little truth there is in that charge. (Rahim 1886:178)

Further, Abdar Rahim directly refutes the assessment made by Hindu authors of the history of Muslim rule in India: "Although some Musalman rulers have oppressed people on grounds of religion, these were acts contrary to religion and must not lead to a charge against Islam itself" (Rahim 1886:178). In the last decade of the nineteenth century, the journal *Mihir o Sudhākar,* edited by the same Abdar Rahim, would, using almost the same rhetoric as Bankim's *Baṅgadarśan* in the previous decade, call for the writing of "a national history appropriate for the Musalman of Bengal." Responding to that call, Abdul Karim (1863–1943) would write the history of Muslim rule in India (Karim 1898), and Ismail Husain Siraji (1880–1931) the historical ballad *Anal prabāha*. These writers were clearly imbued with the ideas of a modern, English-educated middle class. They were highly conscious of their role as leaders of the people, in this case of the Muslim *prajā* of Bengal. They would not end their books with the lament "O kingdom, how bewitching are your powers of seduction!"

On the contrary, Abdul Karim chose to write his history of Muslim rule in India in the belief that a true account of the glorious achievements of the Muslims in India would produce a better appreciation of their heroism, generosity, and love of learning and create greater amity between Hindus and Muslims. The narrative structure he adopted was, however, exactly the same as that used by the British historians he condemned. His story of Muslim rule in India begins with the birth of Muhammad, the conversion of Arabs to the new monotheistic religion, their "abandonment of false beliefs, false customs, and superstition" and their "acceptance of true religion and morality," and the new feelings among them of fraternity and unity. All this enabled the Arabs to become "a *jāti* of unprecedented power" (Karim 1898:11).

Beginning with the accounts of the early Arab incursions into Sind, however, Abdul Karim takes great care to point out that the Arab military commanders were punctilious in following the codes of honor and justice in warfare:

> [Muhammad Kasim] captured the fort and killed all men bearing arms, but spared all merchants, artisans, and ordinary people. . . . Muhammad then wrote to Hejaz to ask whether the Hindus should be allowed to follow their own religion. Hejaz wrote back to say, "Now that they have accepted our suzerainty and agreed to pay taxes to the Khalifa, they must be protected by us and their life and property secured. They are hereby allowed to worship their own gods." (Karim 1898:40–41)

Abdul Karim is scrupulous in distinguishing between just and honorable conduct of the affairs of state, as approved by Islam, and religious bigotry, to be condemned at all times. His concern clearly was to repudiate the slander that it was a characteristic of Islam as a religion and of Muslims as rulers to be violent, intolerant, and oppressive toward others. This, he suggests, is a calumny spread by European historians; if people would only listen to Muslim historians telling the story of their own past, it would promote the self-esteem of Muslims as a people and elicit the respect of others toward Islamic civilization and tradition. The structure of this historiographic response was, of course, no different from what Bankim had suggested for the Hindu nationalist past.

History as the Source of Nationhood

It is remarkable how pervasive this framework of nationalist history became in the consciousness of the English-educated Hindu middle class in Bengal in the late nineteenth century. In literary and dramatic productions as well as in schools and colleges, this narrative of national history went virtually unchallenged until the early decades of the twentieth century. The idea that "Indian nationalism" is synonymous with "Hindu nationalism" is not the vestige of some premodern religious conception. It is an entirely modern, rationalist, and historicist idea. Like other modern ideologies, it allows for a central role of the state in the modernization of society and strongly defends the state's unity and sovereignty. Its appeal is not religious but political. In this sense, the framework of its reasoning is entirely secular. A little examination will show that compared with Mrityunjay's historiography, which revolved around the forces of the divine and the sacred, Tarinicharan's is a wholly secular historiography.

In fact, the notion of "Hindu-ness" in this historical conception cannot be, and does not need to be, defined by any religious criteria at all. There are no specific beliefs or practices that characterize this "Hindu," and the many doctrinal and sectarian differences among Hindus are irrelevant to its concept. Indeed, even such anti-Vedic and anti-Brahmanical religions as Buddhism and Jainism count as "Hindu" to Tarinicharan. Similarly, people outside the Brahmanical religion and outside caste society are also claimed as part of the Hindu *jāti*. But clearly excluded from this *jāti* are religions like Christianity and Islam.

What, then, is the criterion for inclusion or exclusion? It is one of historical origin. Buddhism and Jainism are "Hindu" because they originated in India out of debates and critiques internal to Hinduism. Islam and Christianity come from outside and are therefore foreign. And "India" is the generic entity, with fixed territorial definitions, that acts as the permanent arena for the history of the *jāti*. What, we may ask, is the place of those inhabitants of India who are excluded from this nation? Several answers are suggested in the historiography we are examining. One answer, which assumes the centrality of the modern state in the life of the nation, is frankly majoritarian. The majority "community" is Hindu; the others are minorities. State policy must therefore reflect this preponderance, and the minorities must accept the leadership and protection of the majority. This view, which today is being propagated with great vehemence in postcolonial India by Hindu-extremist politics, actually has its origin more than a hundred years ago, at the same time that Indian nationalism was born.

The second answer, which also made the distinction between majority and minority "communities," is associated with what is called the politics of "secularism" in India. This view holds that in order to prevent the oppression of minorities by the majority, the state must enact legal measures to protect the rights and the separate identities of the minorities. The difficulty is that the formal institutions of the state, based on an undifferentiated concept of citizenship, cannot allow for the separate representation of minorities. Consequently, the question of who represents minorities necessarily remains problematical and constantly threatens the tenuous identity of nation and state.

There was a third answer as well in the early nationalist historiography. It denied the centrality of the state in the life of the nation and instead pointed to the many institutions and practices in the everyday lives of the people through which they had evolved a way of living with their differences. The writings of Rabindranath Tagore (1861–1941) in his post-Swadeshi phase are particularly significant in this respect. His argument is that the true history of India lay not in the battles of kings and the rise and fall of empires but in the everyday world of popular life, the innate flexibility of which, untouched by conflicts in the domain of the state, allowed for the coexistence of all religious beliefs.

The principal difficulty with this view, which has many affinities with the later politics of Gandhism, is its inherent vulnerability to the overwhelming sway of the modern state. Its only defense against the historicist conception of the nation is to claim for the everyday life of the people an essential and transhistorical truth. Such a defense remains vulnerable even within the grounds laid by its own premises, as is shown rather interestingly in Rabindranath's hesitation in this matter. Reviewing Abdul Karim's history of Muslim rule in India (Thakur 1961:484–87), Rabindranath remarks on the reluctance of Hindus to aspire to an achievement of power and glory that would lead them to intervene in the lives of other people and on their inability to cope with those who do. The political history of Islam and, more recently, the history of European conquests in the rest of the world show, he says, that people who have world-conquering ambitions hide under the edifice of civilized life a secret dungeon of ferocious beastliness and unbridled greed. Compared with this, it often seems preferable to lie in peace in a stagnant pool, free from the restlessness of adventure and ambition.

But, according to Rabindranath, the fortifications put up by the *śāstra* (the scriptural injunctions against close relations with foreigners and travel across the seas)

> have failed to protect India, and conflicts with other peoples have become inevitable. We are now obliged to defend our interests against the greed of others and our lives against the violence of others. It would seem advisable, then, to feed a few pieces of flesh to the beast that lies within us and to have it stand guard outside our doors. At the very least, that would arouse the respect of people who are powerful. (Thakur 1961:484–87)

None of these answers, however, can admit that the Indian nation as a whole might have a claim on the historical legacy of Islam. The idea of the singularity of national history has inevitably led to a single source of Indian tradition, namely, ancient Hindu civilization. Islam is either the history of foreign conquest or a domesticated element of everyday popular life. The classical heritage of Islam remains external to Indian history. The curious fact is, of course, that this historicist conception of Hindu nationalism has had few qualms in claiming for itself the modern heritage of Europe. It is as rightful participants in that globalized domain of the modern state that today's contestants for alternative nations fight each other in the name of history.

Suppressed Histories

There was a fourth answer to the question, What is the place of those inhabitants of India who are excluded from the Hindu nation? It is so unclear and fragmented that it is better to call it only the possibility of an answer. It raises doubts about the singularity of a history of India and also renders uncertain the question of classical origins. This history does not necessarily assume the sovereignty of a single state; it is more confederal in its political assumptions. Surprisingly, there is a hint of this answer in Bankim's writings: "Just because the ruler is of a different *jāti* does not mean that a country is under subjection" (Chattopadhyay 1965:332 [this is volume 2 of Bankimchandra Chattapadhyay's collected works—Eds.]). Indeed, it was Bengal under the independent sultans which Bankim regarded as the birthplace of the renaissance in Bengali culture:

> History tells us that a principal consequence of subjection is that the intellectual creativity of a subject *jāti* is extinguished. Yet the intellect of the Bengali shone more brightly during the reign of the Pathans. . . . Never before and never after has the face of Bengal lit up

more brightly than in these two hundred years. . . . It was Emperor Akbar, upon whom we shower praises, who became Bengal's nemesis. He was the first to make Bengal a truly subject country. . . . The Mughal is our enemy, the Pathan our ally. (Chattopadhyay 1965:332)

There is a great disjuncture in the foregoing passage between the history of India and the history of Bengal. The putative center of a generically sovereign state, coextensive with the nation, also becomes uncertainly located. Bankim notes that the Aryans appeared in Bengal at a much later date; does this weaken the claims of the Bengalis upon the classical heritage of the Aryans?

Many will think that the claims of Bengal and Bengalis have now become less formidable and that we have been slandered as a *jāti* of recent origin. We who flaunt our ancient origins before the modern English have now been reduced to a modern *jāti*. It is hard to see why there should be anything dishonorable in all this. We still remain descendants of the ancient Arya *jāti:* no matter when we may have come to Bengal, our ancestors are still the glorious Aryans. (Chattopadhyay 1965:332)

On the other hand, the question is raised, Who of the Bengalis are Aryans? What is the origin of the Bengali *jāti?* Bankim looked for answers to these questions in a long essay titled "The Origins of the Bengalis" (Chattopadhyay 1965:344–62). The "scientific" evidence he accumulated in support of his arguments will now seem extremely dubious, and this is one of his least remembered essays. But its conclusion was not very comfortable for the writing of a singular history of the Indian nation.

The English are one *jāti,* the Bengalis are many *jāti.* In fact, among those whom we now call Bengali can be found four kinds of Bengalis: one, Aryan; two, non-Aryan Hindu; three, Hindu of mixed Aryan and non-Aryan origin; and four, Bengali Musalman. The four live separately from one another. At the bottom of Bengali society are the Bengali non-Aryans, mixed Aryans, and Bengali Muslims; the top is almost exclusively Aryan. It is for this reason that, looked at from the outside, the Bengali *jāti* seems a pure Aryan *jāti* and the history of Bengal is written as the history of an Aryan *jāti.* (Chattopadhyay 1965:363)

The question is whether these two alternative forms of "national" history—one, a history of the *bhāratavarṣīya* assuming a classical Aryan past centered in northern India, and the other of Bengalis of many *jāti* derived from uncertain origins—contained, in the divergences of their trajectories and rhythms, the possibility of a different imagining of nation-hood. It is difficult now to explore this possibility in positive terms, because the second alternative of the pair has been totally submerged during the last hundred years by the tidal wave of historical memory about Arya-Hindu-Bhāratavarṣa. But the few examples I have considered here show that it would be impossible, according to the line of think-ing introduced by Bankim, to club Pathan and Mughal rule together and call it the Muslim period, or to begin the story of the spread of Islam in Bengal with "Muhammad instructed his followers to take up the sword and destroy the infidels."

It might be speculated that if there were many such alternative his-tories for the different regions of India, then the center of Indian history would not need to remain confined to Aryavarta or, more specifically, to "the throne of Delhi." Indeed, the very centrality of Indian history would then become largely uncertain. The question would no longer be one of "national" and "regional" histories; the very relation between parts and the whole would be open for negotiation. If there is any unity in these alternative histories, it is not national but confederal. We do not yet have the wherewithal to write these other histories. Until we accept that it is the very singularity of the idea of a national history of India that divides Indians from one another, we will not create the conditions for writing these alternative histories.

Alternative Histories

Epistemic Disunity and Political Integrity

ALISON WYLIE

I t has often been said that history is rewritten every generation, the instability of history being an object of nervous derision for those who believe they have science—and objectivity and truth—on their side. In the context of twentieth-century philosophy of science, in the days when the imperialistic ambitions of logical positivists/empiricists were at their height, history was routinely cited as a negative object lesson, a source of examples with which to counter theories that were meant to provide entirely general characterizations of what counts as an explanation, or as confirmation, or as rational judgment in properly scientific research practice (Danto 1985; Dray 1957; Scheffler 1963; Suppe 1977). Insofar as history was assumed to be a respectable (at least quasi-scientific) discipline and the (methodological) unity of science was unquestioned, the difficulties of assimilating history to dominant models of science were attributed to the complexity of the historical subject matter and to the fragmentary and enigmatic nature of historical data; they were treated as puzzles, not as paradigm-challenging anomalies. As confidence in "received view" (logical positivist/empiricist; Suppe 1977) theories of science began to wane, their scope was often restricted; they were intended to capture scientific reasoning only in the heartland of science, usually physics (Salmon 1984). History, much social science, common sense, folk psychology, and other such endeavors were once again set aside as nonsciences in a rearticulation of nineteenth-century divisions of intellectual labor and territory. History has always been something of an intellectual borderland.

In recent years, however, as the unifying ambitions of "received view" philosophy of science have been further undercut, the boundaries separating science from nonscience have eroded from the other direction. That is, developments within philosophy of science, as much as challenges from outside, have made it clear that science—even in the heartland—looks a lot more like history (and other social, human sciences) than had been imagined. It incorporates many features that had been assumed to be distinctive of the humanities and social sciences and to mark their greater ambiguity and instability (see Hesse 1973; Rouse 1987). Internal critiques have made it clear that interesting scientific theories inevitably outstrip all available (and perhaps all imaginable or possible) evidence: no explanatory or generalizing theory of any scope is uniquely determined by the evidence that is subsumed by it or used to support it. Moreover, as in the "interpretive" disciplines, evidence is never autonomous of theory. Data, observational facts, and foundational experience of all kinds inevitably stand as evidence for or against a hypothesis (or theory) only under interpretation; they are constituted as meaningful in light of some specific linguistic and conceptual framework and are mediated (in specific test situations) by an array of auxiliary hypotheses. Together these theses of underdetermination, dependence on auxiliaries, and theory-ladenness—all of them articulated as internal critiques of "received view" philosophy of science by the early 1960s— have decisively undermined any simple empiricist faith in the stabilizing capacity of facts (see, e.g., Hanson 1958; Hempel 1958; Putnam 1962; Quine 1953).

Extending these arguments, a number of post-positivist philosophers of science have since argued that the core sciences must be understood to incorporate an interpretive, hermeneutic dimension (e.g., Follesdal 1979; Harre 1970; Hesse 1960). Kuhn famously drew out the historical implications of these arguments: if the foundations of science are liable to interpretive reconstruction as its theoretical presuppositions change, then science must be subject to disruptive transformations, to a certain generational instability not unlike that which had been presumed distinctive of history. With Kuhn's historical critique, the "received" model of scientific progress through stately accumulation of factual detail and synthesis was decisively undermined (Kuhn 1970). As Newton-Smith (1981:14) observed with sardonic hindsight, there is no escaping the "pessimistic induction" that, judging from the past record of transformations and upheavals in science, even our best, most secure and foundational theories will be decisively disconfirmed within a couple of generations.

The contributions to the seminar "Making Alternative Histories" make it clear that, where history is concerned, models of periodic, generational change are too simple — a thesis that radical critics and sociologists have extended to the natural sciences in recent years. At a purely descriptive level, the patterns of change and dissent evident in "telling the past," archaeologically and historically, are much more complicated than models of orderly (if disruptive) succession suggest. The historiographies developed in this book show that much crucially important history is not "written" at all (although it might be argued that some form of articulate historical consciousness is always immanent) and that when it is written, generational consensus is achieved only with enormous effort, often through direct repression and deliberate canalization, or through various forms of systematic selection, or as a function of artificially and contingently unified reaction against a common enemy.

Sometimes histories proliferate, perhaps most typically at turning points of rupture and disjunction, when selection mechanisms are in disarray. In a discussion of the making of alternative histories in South Africa, Callinicos (1990:285) observes that "as apartheid rapidly loses credibility among even National Party supporters, the gap in history needs to be filled." And it is being filled, not only by the labor and popular/educational movements that generated the people's history projects of the 1980s but also by reactionary forces and by such stalwarts as the *Reader's Digest,* which, Callinicos says (1990:285), recently offered an eager (and paying) public " 'the real story' that can now, at last, be revealed." In this context, historical understanding is as dynamic and fractured as the political situation itself: "To all, from the fascist leader of the AWB [Afrikaner Resistance Movement] to student comrades and worker poets, history is a resource of mobilization, a political weapon activists used to advance current organizational strategies" (Callinicos 1990:285; see also Callinicos 1987).

In these cases, the instability of history reveals not so much an internal dynamic of intellectual extension, elaboration, and transformation — as loyalists to the cause of science might argue — as the operation in and on history of the so-called "external" social and political conditions of its practice. Such cases raise the suspicion that history is always, in different ways and to varying degrees, a political undertaking; whatever commitment practitioners may make to a stance of detached neutrality, their situated interests play a powerful role in shaping the work of history making. The parallel case recently made by sociologists and historians of science is that even unquestionably scientific disciplines are thoroughly cultural (and political) enterprises, like history. Although history may always have been inescapably a creature of its context, this is by no means a distinctive feature setting it decisively apart from the sciences.

This point is by now commonplace. As contentious as it continues to be in some scientific and philosophical circles, I believe it must be accepted as the point of departure for any serious analysis of disciplinary practice (scientific or otherwise), as it has been by all participants in the seminar "Making Alternative Histories." I rehearse it because I am struck by the range of ways in which history is found to work, or to be made to work, in the contemporary political contexts represented in the chapters of this book, and because I want to ask what the implications are of such powerful evidence that history making is situational for the politics of resistance and programs of constructive political action that "alternative histories" are meant to serve. The parallels between these analyses and (much) current thinking about science, especially feminist critiques of science, are striking. In particular, feminist struggles with the disabling implications of (some) deconstructive and postmodern critiques of science may be a useful source of insights in charting a course between an unsustainable objectivism and some of the more extreme constructivist reactions that objectivism's demise has generated.

History at Work

There is, I suggest, a common narrative theme implicit in the historiographic accounts given in this volume of the construction of African, Latin American, Indian, and native North American histories — a theme which, despite its recurrence in widely different contexts, underscores the contingency and plurality of these histories. In all cases, the conditions under which the histories described here have emerged are, immediately or proximately, those of colonial or neocolonial domination marked by a sustained and deliberate delegitimation of the historical consciousness of those whose heritage and identity are in question, sometimes including the systematic erasure of their historical presence. The narrative that unfolds is one of struggle against various forms of dominant history and against the terms of its construction — the structures of opposition, the presuppositions about historical scholarship and authority — where these threaten to infuse and usurp the alternatives.

As Sued Badillo (1992:600) has described the conditions of historical production in the Caribbean, "since the sixteenth century a direct relation has existed between economic exploitation and disinformation." Explicit policies of control and the suppression of historical knowledge have entrenched a conception of the Caribbean as "depopulated, impoverished, or ruined" (Sued Badillo 1992:602) almost from the time of conquest, reinforcing widespread ignorance of the periods in which colonial exploitation was founded and first justified. This conception of Caribbean history turns on a thesis of automatic depopulation or extinction (because of disease) and (voluntary?) abandonment. As such, it serves not only to undermine any sense of indigenous identity but also to absolve colonial powers of responsibility for the alleged disintegration of indigenous society, justifying their subjugation and dispossession of native people.

Once established, this complex of assumptions is perpetuated by historical practices that systematically ignore sources, archaeological and historical, which might counter those assumptions. Sued Badillo (1992: 603) finds that secondary sources are rarely critically scrutinized and that primary sources go largely unexamined even when, by his account, they bear ample testimony to intense and profitable exploitation of Caribbean resources (mineral and agricultural) throughout the sixteenth century, contrary to the presumption of early marginality and the colonial discourse of absence and/or "incapacity and indolence on the part of the region's inhabitants." Even when such sources are considered, the focus is safely on individual personalities and isolated events, not on the political-economic and social processes that established in the Caribbean the systems of colonial rule and capitalism which took possession of America, and certainly not on the emerging histories of surviving indigenous and creole populations. The void, the sense of loss created by this colonial regime of history making, prefigures the politically and economically generated "crisis of identity"—marked by the evocation of a "mythical past" and the "recreation of what is indigenous"—that Sued Badillo describes in chapter 2. Resistance to colonial domination has turned on the recovery of indigenous identity at a popular level, making its "management" crucial to any emergent political power in the contemporary Caribbean.

Handsman and Lamb Richmond describe closely parallel strategies by which the presence of Mahican and Schaghticoke peoples and the integrity and continuity of their communities have been systematically denied by the dominant colonial histories of the northeastern United States. A historical record was created that reinforced assumptions of absence—of abandonment, extinction, and assimilation—which reflect Eurocentric notions of what counts as presence, occupation, and ownership. Because the dominant conventions of history making (and legal adjudication) have enforced exclusive reliance on records created by European observers, it is not surprising that generations of historians would fail to recognize communal ownership or the existence of a population and community that was not manifested in nucleated village settlements. The effect of these historical and legal practices, coupled with an archaeology that has tended to concern itself either with decontextualized artifacts or with ecologistic abstractions, has been to direct attention away from the considerable evidence that survives (in the archaeological record and in collections of material culture) of Mahican and Schaghticoke presence and community life. Euro-American historiography has thus marginalized the historical consciousness that survives, despite all efforts to eliminate it, in contemporary Schaghticoke and Mahican communities.

The assumption underwriting the dominant histories articulated in both the Caribbean and New England contexts is that there is no substantial ("authentic") presence of indigenous peoples who might lay claim to land, resources, or their own (distinctive) cultural identity and thus contest the legitimacy of essentially colonial rights of access and ownership. If this premise is accepted, it can be assumed that there is little or no evidence relating to an indigenous presence in the postcontact/colonial period and that there is, therefore, no point in undertaking systematic investigations of "native" history. This assumption has, in turn, justified successive policies of expropriation and displacement, which, along with the delegitimation of indigenous cultural traditions and wholesale destruction of the archaeological record, ensures that there *will be* no data (or that there will be increasingly little data) that could counter the "vision" of absence central to official history. The theses of extinction, abandonment, and assimilation become self-fulfilling colonial ambitions. The colonial/capitalist systems they serve guarantee their own continuing legitimation by quite literally erasing the records (written, material, cultural, oral) of contingency and historical process that could be used to support the claims of indigenous communities and to counter the encompassing mythology of their inevitable extinction or assimilation. The importance of "making alternative histories" for political movements of resistance and empowerment—the strategies described by Sued Badillo and by Handsman and Lamb Richmond—is unmistakable in these contexts: history must be rewritten if its rationalizing consistency throughout generations of colonial domination is to be challenged.

The mechanisms of erasure and "disinformation" operating in these colonial contexts have direct analogs in all the other cases considered by contributors to this book. The historiographies of continental Latin America, Africa, and India are, in the main, narratives of resistance through the construction of counterhistories. But whereas Sued Badillo, Handsman, and Lamb Richmond detail histories of struggle to articulate and to assert indigenous identity under conditions of what amounts to continued colonial domination, others describe a complex succession of postcolonial (nationalist) histories—alternative histories that have frequently taken on "official" status and have revealed their own capacity to oppress.

In the case described by Chatterjee, this succession includes premodern (if not precolonial) histories of early- to mid-nineteenth-century India as well as nationalist histories incipient since the 1870s and full-blown by the early twentieth century. Patterson's and Vargas Arenas's accounts describe a succession of nationalist histories in Peru, Mexico, and Venezuela since the late nineteenth century, closely paralleled by the succession and diffusion of the African nationalist accounts described by Holl, Andah, Schmidt, and Blakey. In these cases, the colonial histories that the alternatives oppose operate much as they do in the Caribbean and in the northeastern United States. The difference is that, where their agenda cannot be straightforward erasure of an indigenous, colonized "other," it must be one of marginalization by other means.

Typically these histories employ a stock set of strategies for naturalizing conditions of colonial domination, denying an indigenous, colonized population any capacity for historical agency. Colonial interests lie in inculcating standard racist assumptions about the inherent "backwardness" of those who have been subjugated but not annihilated or assimilated. The presumed incapacity of indigenous people for achievement, their failure to manifest "progressive" development, is seized upon in various of the areas prized by Europeans as marks of "civilization": for example, social complexity, agriculture, technology, science, and religious and aesthetic or cultural sophistication. In the process, indigenous cultural identities are at once fragmented and constructed as monolithic (Andah, this volume). Whatever the specific target, colonial "subjects" are denied any identity other than that constructed for them as subjects, and this identity is framed by a series of contrasts with (or reversals of) whatever attributes the dominant colonial population values as distinctive signs of its identity and superiority. It is then entrenched by means of racist assumptions to the effect that these alleged inadequacies are natural and essential to the identity of the subjugated population *as* African, South Asian, American Indian, creole or mestizo, or Latin American indigene, to name those which figure centrally in the chapters assembled here.

The denial of history in these cases follows not from an assertion of the literal absence of an indigenous population but from an assumption of cultural stasis that is established and perpetuated by practices much like those documented by Handsman and Lamb Richmond and by Sued Badillo. These practices include policies of noninvestigation: if there is nothing to be learned but what is manifest in the present (given race-essentialist assumptions), why undertake investigation of local history or prehistory at all? Such practices are evident, as well, in the refusal of colonial and neocolonial history makers to recognize any resources for constructing history but those generated (i.e., written) by the colonial power and its operatives. And where archaeological and ethnographic or oral history resources *are* considered, potentially dislocating evidence that runs counter to entrenched assumptions of stasis and "indolence and incapacity" (to use Sued Badillo's phrase) is deflected by a preoccupation with artifacts and oral traditions as exotica or with large-scale evolutionary and ecological abstractions. Both preoccupations effectively disengage the study of the past from any investigation of the historical processes that have created, and now maintain, conditions of colonial oppression, including the practices of "disinformation" that provide some measure of control of historical consciousness.

The difficulty, however, is that colonial powers with pretensions to modernity do often support programs of "scientific" investigation. At the very least they undertake to catalogue their possessions, and often they seek to glorify their own achievements by documenting those of the cultures they have subjugated. In the process, they frequently turn up material evidence that resists assimilation to assumptions of inherent (racial) incapacity. As Holl (this volume) describes the situation in Africa, the conviction that Africa "has no history," that it was always "backward," and that all vestiges of "cultural evolution and technological change" must be attributed to external influences had to be continuously shored up in the face of archaeological evidence and historical records to the contrary. The diffusionist and migrationist constructions favored by colonial powers were strained to their limits (Schmidt, this volume). This dissonance between evidence and expectation created what Holl described during the seminar discussions as the "dilemma of colonial historical sciences," a dilemma that emerges in one form or another in all the contexts described by participants in the seminar. The rationalizing, modernist impulse to describe completely, to catalogue and document, frequently comes into conflict with the political agendas it was meant to serve. This conflict generates a stock set of responses.

Where the lack of history is explained in terms of environmental and racial determinism, any evidence *of* history—of past achievement (measured, necessarily, in European terms) or of technological, economic, and sociopolitical transformation (including evidence of collapse or devolution)—is attributed to what are, in effect, previous colonial incursions (e.g., Arabs in Africa; Chinese in Peru; Muslims and other groups "from the north" in India). The presumption that indigenous populations are inherently "backward" survives intact, their subjugation is justified (Schmidt, this volume), and it is affirmed that colonialists' burden everywhere has been to enlighten and civilize (Holl, this volume). In present contexts this has required, among other things, the imposition of "rational" standards of historical construction and appeals to racist-evolutionist presuppositions that are distinctively European and/or Western. Drawing on a documentary tradition reaching back beyond the advent of British colonialism, Chatterjee is able to show just how profoundly such assumptions and practices can shape the making of history.

In many of the contexts described in this volume, however, explicitly anticolonial traditions of historical construction have succeeded in displacing such colonial histories, sometimes generating new "official" histories that promote nationalist agendas and the interests of postcolonial elites. Chatterjee traces the emergence of traditions of nationalist history in India from the 1870s; Vargas Arenas and Patterson consider debates over indigenous and national identity dating to the turn of the twentieth century (in Patterson's case, with reference to antecedent debates over the "Indian question" of the 1890s). Sued Badillo likewise describes a struggle to articulate new collective identities that had roots in the seventeenth and eighteenth centuries but became a focus for political struggle in the second half of the nineteenth century. And Holl, Blakey, and Andah describe traditions of pan-African and African nationalist histories that have taken shape since the 1930s, with antecedents, again, in the late nineteenth century. In all cases where these emergent "alternative" histories have come into prominence, the convergence of the historiographic accounts given by the contributors to this volume is especially striking. Each author articulates (or reports) a deep and often militant disaffection with the extent to which the nationalist states or movements that have succeeded colonial governments have taken over—often simply inverted—the essential terms, assumptions, and strategies of the colonial histories they meant to subvert. In this way they are themselves subverted as liberation movements.

As I read these critiques, they suggest that the failure to construct accounts of the past that represent genuine "alternatives" to colonial histories takes at least two general forms. On one hand, old colonial ties frequently persist; former colonies lacking the resources to take full control of the production of their own histories remain dependent, in this respect, on First World centers of power. Schmidt describes the persistence of institutional structures which ensure that First World scholars continue to control access to funding, training, historical sources, and publication and which, in turn, allow those scholars to control the direction and disposition of historical and archaeological research in many Third World contexts (in Schmidt's case, East Africa). There are clear parallels with the situations described by Andah for West Africa, and by Patterson and Vargas Arenas for Latin America.

On the other hand, when nationalist causes do generate rich and vociferous historical traditions of their own, a different kind of colonial influence often persists. Where the historical achievements of indigenous populations were once denied, nationalist histories valorize a glorious indigenous past (e.g., the original *indigenista* activists in Peru and Mexico discussed by Patterson, and the pan-African and Afrocentrist movements discussed by Blakey and Holl). And where these achievements were once attributed to the intercession of external powers, the diverse ethnic groups contained within the domains carved out and ruled by colonial powers are now constituted as a unitary "people"—"true" Indians; the bearers of a pan-African worldview, psychology, and form of life; a romanticized and "homogenized" Andean culture—and cast in the role of historical agent whose manifest destiny is to recapture past glory and complete the project of modernism (Chatterjee, this volume) in and through the emerging nation-state.

Often the processes of cultural diffusion from unitary origins and the arguments for temporal priority typical of colonial accounts reappear in postcolonial histories, now associated with internal, indigenous centers of cultural influence. Holl and Blakey describe how these processes are inverted, in the case of Afrocentric accounts, so that African society becomes the source and progenitor of "civilization." The result is the production of historical constructs which, although they expose "the weaknesses of colonial rhetoric and the utilitarian nature of an important part of the colonial historical accounts of the African past," nonetheless serve to strengthen rather than destroy "the methodological and theoretical foundations of colonial historical views" (Holl, referring to Anta Diop's program). These "foundations" include a range of typological and explanatory conventions that obscure the historical nature of their subjects; Afrocentrism "dehistoricizes" white supremacy (Blakey, Holl) and, just as surely as it valorizes African identity, dehistoricizes it as well. In these cases, romanticized notions—mythologized and nostalgic (Sued Badillo) —of ethnic, racial, and cultural unity obscure significant diversity within modern nation-states (Chatterjee), frequently legitimating brutal policies of assimilation, integration, or subjugation that continue the work of colonial domination, now turned inward or carried out by proxy (Patterson, Vargas Arenas). And when internal difference or historical change *is* recognized, it is circumscribed, as in the construction of sequences of disconnected periods described by Vargas Arenas for Venezuela.

Insofar as historical inquiry operates within the confines of these conceptual frameworks, the mechanisms for perpetuating erasure, strategic ignorance, and repressive essentialism are exactly those associated with the production of colonial history. Whatever the historians' intentions, the effect is to reinforce extant (neocolonial) conditions of intellectual, as well as political and economic, dependence (e.g., Vargas Arenas, Schmidt). The criteria for "achievement" and the conceptions of cultural identity and historical agency that frame historical inquiry continue to be those defined by colonial powers from the nineteenth through the mid-twentieth century (e.g., Andah, Schmidt). Most importantly, they continue to enforce a preoccupation with a "dead" past, a static past, disconnected from the present.

This disconnection takes two forms, at least as described in foregoing chapters. The first is that of ignoring the political-economic dynamics (especially of class struggle) by which the oppressive conditions of contemporary life came into being (Vargas Arenas, Patterson), often characterizing historically constituted conflict as an inevitable outcome of (essential) racial and ethnic difference (Blakey). The second is that of constructing dehumanized histories focused on questions of no relevance to contemporary people or their struggles (Andah, Vargas Arenas, Handsman and Lamb Richmond)—histories which are, in any case, cast in an idiom that is alienating and inaccessible to those whose histories they are (Schmidt). In the making of history, as in many other respects, the oppressive structures of colonial rule are reproduced and internalized by the very movements that had opposed them. At best, such histories offer "no insight into means for solving problems of racial conflict and oppression" (Blakey); indeed, they may be "devoid of the prospect of change" (Blakey). At worst, they may foster and institutionalize conflict along class and racial/ethnic lines in postcolonial contexts (Vargas Arenas, Chatterjee), threatening the very communities they were meant to empower with "dissolution" (Sued Badillo).

The central narrative structure that I discern in these historiographies is, then, explicitly dialectical. Repressive colonial powers have created highly strategic and "selective" histories (to use Holl's term) that legitimate their ambitions and practices, undermining the dignity, will, and capacity for effective collective action of their "subjects." The construction of counterhistories has been, and continues to be, an important locus of resistance to colonial power. But when alternative histories become the "official" histories of nationalist movements, the danger is that they will be defined by the colonial forces they oppose. Often they articulate the same ambitions (pertaining to the same territorial region) and engage the same idiom, units of analysis, and explanatory structures as were typical of colonial histories, now in the interests of promoting the unity, pride, territorial claims, and will of a newly constituted people. In many such contexts, these antitheses to colonial history are in the process of being torn apart by internal (intellectual and political-economic) contradictions. The painful irony, as Chatterjee observes with reference to India, is that the contradictions now erupting into violence frequently arise directly from identity constructs that are thinkable only within the framework of modernist, colonial history, although they were articulated in the interests of liberation from colonial rule.

At this juncture, then, it seems inescapable that "the potential for ideological transformation will be limited by all those ways in which [postcolonial history] reproduces, and is like, that which it seeks to oppose" (Blakey). The challenge is to determine what kind of "dialectical alternative" lies beyond the sharp opposition of thesis and antithesis.

Alternative Histories

A number of recommendations for meeting this challenge have been made by participants in the seminar. These include, first and most centrally, a demand that the questions addressed in historical and archaeological research be redefined (Schmidt). On one hand, attention must be shifted to human lives and agency (Andah), to the lived processes of daily life (Vargas Arenas), and to the concrete conditions, dynamics, and diversity of the lives of "real" or "ordinary" people, "not just the dominant groups or classes" or "abstract formulas" (Andah, Handsman and Lamb Richmond). On the other hand (and these are by no means opposed or exclusive options), the aim of inquiry must be to build a synthetic, explanatory understanding of the political-economic processes by which oppressive power structures were established and are perpetuated in the present (Vargas Arenas, Patterson, Holl).

A second recurrent theme is that the range of resources used to address new questions and to assess the presuppositions that frame the history making enterprise must be substantially broadened. All "relevant" resources must be deployed; in particular, oral traditions and oral history should be credited not only as important sources of interpretive insight but also as historical accounts in their own right. Although the need to critically interrogate these sources (indeed, to "test" them empirically, according to Andah) is affirmed by most who recommend them (Schmidt,

Andah, Handsman and Lamb Richmond, Holl), their importance is recognized to lie not just in their capacity to generate new questions and lines of interpretation but also in their potential to provide a basis for the reciprocal interrogation of documentary and archaeological sources.

Finally, a number of contributors argue that if any significant changes in the orientation or results of history making are to be realized, the political economy of research practice must be changed. At the very least, the sociopolitics and culture of the institutions within which histories are constructed must be reshaped to ensure that they are inclusive of, and responsive to, the needs and interests of those whose history is at issue. Specific recommendations include an insistence that both First and Third World practitioners must focus on questions that are directly "relevant" to those living in the contexts of study; history should be undertaken "for the people" (Schmidt, Vargas Arenas, Andah). By extension, several contributors recommend adopting collaborative practices and creating the institutional structures necessary to sustain them, structures that level power differences, especially when First World researchers take up projects in Third World contexts (Schmidt). And there is strong emphasis on the need to construct and present histories in an idiom that "resonates" with—that is accessible to and engaging of—its popular audience (Schmidt). In many respects, the South African "people's history projects" described by Callinicos (1987, 1990) embody just such a vision of collaborative practice. Certainly Vargas Arenas's educational projects in Venezuela go a long way toward realizing the objective of returning history to those who are normally excluded from it (Vargas and Sanoja 1990), and the research projects described by Schmidt and Andah represent a search for strategies that will build this extraprofessional orientation into the design and conduct of historical research.

As radical as these last recommendations may sound in some archaeological and historical contexts, none is without counterpart in most other fields in the social sciences. Radical sociologists, critics of the colonial entanglements of sociocultural anthropology, and the advocates of "action" research have long insisted that critiques of repressive forms of social science will be met only if the way social scientists do business is substantially altered. The point made time and again is that it will not be enough to take up new questions or to make a commitment to write up "plain language" reports on the results of scholarly research. These measures will be effective only if those whose lives are affected are directly involved in the research enterprise from the outset, as partners, not merely as subjects, as sources of insight, and as progenitors of new lines of evidence. The challenge is to find ways of creating such partnerships effectively where historical and archaeological research is concerned. Although many of the contributors to the seminar and to this book take important steps in this direction, their collective message is that the real work of bringing their critical insights into practice still lies ahead.

Underlying all of these recommendations for doing archaeology and history differently is the concern that it will be crucially important to disembed the presuppositions of inquiry—specifically, presuppositions taken over from colonial historiography—and make them the direct objects of critical scrutiny (Blakey, Schmidt). Several contributors urge, in this connection, that any program for making alternative histories must systematically incorporate reflexive modes of historical practice (Patterson). Because all of their accounts make clear the situated, standpoint-specific nature of history making, the question immediately arises of how practitioners are to build alternative histories—histories that will necessarily reflect a (political) standpoint—and at the same time articulate and challenge the assumptions framing not only the standpoints they challenge but also those they occupy. It is a matter of rebuilding the ship in which you float, continuously, as you travel.

Although this much is acknowledged by all the contributors in principle, there is a sense in which their practice—including both their second-order historiographic practice and the first-order practices of historical construction which they adopt or advocate—remains well within the compass of traditional historical modes of thinking and inquiry, that is, those developed in Europe under the aegis of the Enlightenment. For the most part, the critical arguments presented here condemn colonial and nationalist histories as "bad" history, as histories that fail by their own lights when measured against standard criteria (their own official criteria, as it were) of empirical and conceptual adequacy. In fact, despite frequently voiced suspicions about the efficacy of Western "science" and its attendant preoccupations with objectivity and comprehensive truth, those who make the case against "official" histories rely, almost without exception, on quite standard methods of historical inquiry. They identify internal inconsistencies, gaps, and patent implausibilities in entrenched narratives that flag a repeated failure of the history-making establishment to meet basic requirements of empirical accuracy, rigor, and critical integrity. Moreover, these critics typically call not for an abandonment of such requirements but for a historical practice that conforms more closely (for better or worse) to the regulative ideals of completeness, accuracy, coherence, consistency, and so on, that are constitutive of Western research traditions.

Consistent with this methodological stance, the "alternative" recommended in several cases is to build what Vargas Arenas refers to as histories that oppose the false consciousness inculcated by "official" histories or, alternatively, what Andah described during the seminar as an "authentic cultural history," a historical account of "what actually happened" based on the "real historical facts" that nationalist and "ethnic" interpretations, as much as colonial histories, have tended to ignore or distort. The aim of such alternative histories, according to Andah, is to grasp the "historical reality" of past actors, providing contemporary Africans a "usable past" and making it possible for "real people now long gone to be left some room to speak to us."

The difficulty is, of course, that the challenge these critics bring against colonial and postcolonial nationalist histories calls into question the very notion of "real historical facts," of historical reality, and of a quest for "real" history. These ideals are recognized to be a central part of the legacy of colonial/European history that has "infiltrat[ed]" (Blakey) and compromised the construction of alternative histories and has proved to be the root of renewed oppression in many of the contexts discussed here. Stepping back from the specifics of these critiques, the key reflexive question they raise is that of whether there is a "real" history to be discovered. The methodological corollary seems to be that we must be skeptical, or at least extremely cautious, in engaging programs of research that, to use Lorde's phrase (1984:110), purport to use "the master's tools" to "dismantle the master's house." There is always the danger, to which many of the historiographies presented here give ample testimony, that these tools will define both the task and its outcome.

This worry is an old one: if you build a force that is the counterpart of that which you oppose, you risk reproducing (and internalizing) the oppressive structures you mean to undermine. But what follows from this? A commitment to continuous (historiographic) revolution? Some form of guerrilla historiography made effective precisely because it does not oppose oppressive and hegemonic forces with the *same* force? A decisive break with—a transgression of—modernist, "rational" forms of historiography?

I do not intend these observations as a criticism of the foregoing chapters. Rather, I mean to note what I take to be a dynamic and, I hope, creative tension in all of the projects recommended and represented by the writers assembled here. The juncture at which they stand is strikingly similar to that at which feminist critics of science arrived during the 1980s. The reaction against all things patriarchal and the valorization of all things associated with women—the positions identified with cultural feminism of the 1970s—have been systematically challenged (see, e.g., Echols 1983; hooks 1984). The essentialism of this brand of feminism, its inverted (sometimes biological) determinism, its reification of "femininity," and its failure to recognize the essentially patriarchal and homogenizing nature of such constructs (i.e., the failure to recognize their racist, classist, ablist, often homophobic nature) all parallel closely the features of nationalist movements criticized in these chapters. Although proponents of cultural feminism tended to reject science as a whole as inherently "logocentric" and irredeemably masculinist, those developing closely worked critiques of scientific practice and its products have typically been much less willing to abandon the resources that scientific inquiry has to offer a liberationist movement like feminism. In this connection, Harding (1986) has recommended systematic ambivalence: feminists cannot afford to give up either the emancipatory vision of thoroughly constructivist (postmodern) critiques of science or the insights afforded by "successor science" projects, particularly where the latter are crucial to challenging the historical, social scientific, and biological claims that underwrite patriarchal politics (see Wylie 1987). There is some sense, in this explicitly fractured position, that feminists (and others) should not forsake the "master's tools" altogether—that perhaps these tools can be appropriated, pressed into the service of a political feminist movement, so long as those using them are vigilant in ensuring that they do not delimit the ambitions and political accountability of that movement.

Harding's most recent work (1991) reinforces this suggestion and converges on insights emerging from very different directions in a number of recent feminist analyses of science due, for example, to postanalytic epistemologists such as Code (1991) and Collins (1990), to poststructuralist critics of science such as Haraway (see 1991), and equally to self-avowed feminist empiricists such as Longino (1990). The common thread in these analyses is a concern to articulate an account of knowledge production that recognizes its own contingency and standpoint specificity, that repudiates any quest for a unitary ("master") narrative and any faith in context-transcendent "foundations," and that yet resists the implication that any comparison or judgment of credibility is irreducibly arbitrary, that "anything goes." In this they share the impatience recently expressed by a number of feminists (e.g., di Leonardo 1991) with postmodern and deconstructive trends in the social sciences when these trends move in the direction of a relativism akin to the "ideology of cultural difference" that Handsman and Lamb Richmond question.

The constructive proposals that emerge in this literature—as yet sketches of possibilities just emerging—all turn on the conviction that standpoint specificity should be regarded as a resource, not a liability.

The understanding afforded by divergent standpoints (defined politically, economically, culturally—in any terms which "actors" find salient in contemporary contexts) is a crucial source of critical insight about what a dominant research community may be missing in its investigation of a given subject matter, historical or otherwise. In this spirit, Harding urges that scientific practice be reconstructed so that it incorporates a requirement to assess knowledge claims from a range of standpoints, to discern their silences, limitations, and partialities.

Perhaps this is the sort of reflexivity Patterson has in mind when he calls for continuous critical scrutiny of the presuppositions of practice. What feminist standpoint theorists have added to a general call for such scrutiny is an insistence that it should not be carried out as an abstract exercise in conceptual critique but should depend on a detailed (empirical) understanding of the conditions of knowledge production. This is exactly the project that I understand participants in this seminar to have begun. Far from undermining ideals of objectivity, Harding argues that this project imposes a higher standard of objectivity on the sciences than is embodied in the "neutrality" scientists hope to achieve by ignoring or excluding considerations of difference and context; she refers to it as a requirement for "strong objectivity" (Harding 1991). There are clear parallels in Haraway's discussion of "embodied objectivity" and of the resources afforded by explicit consideration of standpoint in building "situated knowledges" (Haraway 1991), in Code's account of community-based hermeneutic practices (Code 1991, especially chapter 7), and in Longino's arguments for building scientific institutions that enhance the critical integrity of research, bringing value questions into science (Longino 1990, especially chapter 4).

In these emerging standpoint theories, the methods of systematic empirical inquiry developed by Western science (broadly construed, along lines developed by postpositivist philosophers of science in recent years) figure as some of the most effective tools available for building accounts of the world we live in—natural, social, historical—and, crucially, for understanding at a second-order, reflexive level the limits of these accounts. Insofar as those methods can be applied simultaneously to both tasks, I suspect, following Blakey, that they are not necessarily inimical to non-Western cultures and "alternative" worldviews or histories, as heavily implicated as they have been in the articulation of oppressive Enlightenment and colonial traditions.

My own view is that anyone seriously committed to political activism and to the construction of alternative histories as a form of politically self-conscious action will be continuously and acutely aware of just how unforgiving the conditions of action can be and how crucial it is to understand accurately, "realistically," and as completely as possible the forces we oppose if we are to be effective in challenging them (Wylie 1992a). Political self-consciousness enforces a critical awareness of the contingency of knowledge production that does not (necessarily) entail a politically and epistemically paralyzing cynicism about the process of inquiry. What these chapters bring into sharp focus is not a solution but a series of what I have been describing as challenges: those of negotiating the tensions created by a commitment to use the tools of systematic empirical inquiry to rigorously question the authority and presuppositions of scientific inquiry, to turn science and history against themselves when they serve as tools of oppression, and to reclaim their emancipatory potential.

References

Abad y la Sierra, I.
: 1966 *Historia geográfica, civil y natural de la isla de San Juan Bautista de Puerto Rico.* Río Piedras: Editorial Universitaria, Universidad de Puerto Rico.
: 1977 "Viaje a la América." *Boletín de la Academía Puertorriqueña de la Historia* 5(18):19–207.

Acosta Saignes, Miguel
: 1954 *Estudios de etnología antigua de Venezuela.* Instituto de Antropología y Geografía, Facultad de Humanidades y Educación, Universidad Central de Venezuela. Caracas: Tipografía Vargas.
: 1984 *Vida de los esclavos negros en Venezuela.* Caracas: Vadell Hermanos Editores.

Ajayi, Ade J. F., and B. Ikara
: 1985 "Introduction." In *Evolution of political culture in Nigeria,* eds. Ade Ajayi and B. Ikara. Ibadan, Nigeria: Ibadan University Press.

Afigbo, A. E.
: 1986 "Archaeology and the schools." *West African Journal of Archaeology* 16: 155–64.

AGI (Archivo General de Indias, Sevilla)
: Audiencia de Santo Domingo (SD): 10, 15, 49,51, 70, 94, 155, 164, 168, 169, 172, 175, 875, 2280.
: Contratación: 4802.
: Escribanía: 1333.
: Justicia: 70, 98.

Agorsah, E. K.
: 1990 "Ethnoarchaeology: The search for a self-corrective approach to the study of past human behaviour." *African Archaeological Review* 8:189–208.

Aguirre Beltrán, Gonzalo
: 1953 *Formas de gobierno indígena.* Mexico, D.F.: Imprenta Universitaria.
: 1955 *Programas de salud en la situación intercultural.* Mexico, D.F.: Instituto Indigenista Interamericano.
: 1957 *El proceso de aculturación y el cambio socio-cultural en México.* Mexico, D.F.: Universidad Nacional Autónoma de México.

1967 *Regiones de refugio.* Ediciones Especiales, no. 46. Mexico, D.F.: Instituto Indigenista Interamericano.

Akagi, Roy H.

1924 *The town proprietors of the New England colonies: A study of their development, organization, activities and controversies, 1620-1770.* Philadelphia: University of Pennsylvania Press.

Alatas, Syed Hussein

1972 "The captive mind in development studies." *International Social Science Journal* 24(1):9–25.

1977 *Intellectuals in developing societies.* London: Frank Cass.

Albó, Xavier

1987 "From MNRistas to Kataristas to Katari." In *Resistance, rebellion, and consciousness in the Andean peasant world, 18th to 20th centuries,* ed. Steve J. Stern, 379–419. Madison: University of Wisconsin Press.

1990 "Lo andino en Bolivia: Balances y prioridades." *Revista Andina* 8(2): 411–64.

Alimen, Henriette

1955 *Préhistoire de l'Afrique.* Paris: Editions Boubée.

Allen, Charles

1870 *Report on the Stockbridge Indians to the Legislature, Massachusetts: House document no. 13.* Boston: Wright and Potter.

Alvarez Nazario, Manuel

1977 *El influjo indígena en el español de Puerto Rico.* Río Piedras: Editorial Universitaria, Universidad de Puerto Rico.

1990 *El habla campesina del pais: Orígenes y desarrollo del espanol en Puerto Rico.* Río Piedras: Editorial de la Universidad de Puerto Rico.

Anastas, Peter

1973 *Glooskap's children.* Boston: Beacon Press.

Andah, Bassey W.

1973 "Was there a Sangoan industry in West Africa?" *West African Journal of Archaeology* 3:191–96.

1985 "No past! No present! No future! Anthropological education and the African revolution." Inaugural lecture, University of Ibadan, Nigeria.

1987 "Foundations of civilizations in tropical Africa." *West African Journal of Archaeology* 17:vii–x.

1988 *African anthropology.* Ibadan: Shaneson Ltd.

1990a "Prologue." In *Cultural resource management: An African dimension,* ed. B. W. Andah. *West African Journal of Archaeology* 20:2–8.

1990b "The oral versus the written word in the cognitive revolution: Language, culture and literacy." In *Cultural resource management: An African dimension,* ed. B. W. Andah. *West African Journal of Archaeology* 20:18–41.

Anta Diop, Cheikh

1955 *Nations nègres et culture.* 2 vols. Paris: Présence Africaine. (3rd ed. 1979.)

1959 "Afterword." In his *The cultural unity of black Africa,* pp. 209–35. Chicago: Third World Press.

1960a *L'Unité culturelle de l'Afrique noire.* Paris: Présence Africaine.

1960b *L'Afrique noire précoloniale.* Paris: Présence Africaine.

1960c *Les fondements economiques et culturels d'un stat fédéral d'Afrique noire.* Paris: Présence Africaine.

1960d   "Les intellectuels doivent étudier le passé non pour s'y complaire mais pour y puiser des leçons." *La Vie Africaine* 6:10–11.

1962   "Reponse à quelques critiques." *Bulletin de l'Institut Fondamental d'Afrique Noire,* série B, 24:542–74.

1967   *Antériorité des civilisations nègres: Mythe ou vérité historique?* Paris: Présence Africaine.

1973a   "Pigmentation des anciens égyptiens: Test par la mélanine." *Bulletin de l'IFAN,* série B, 35:515–31.

1973b   "La métallurgie du fer sous l'Ancien Empire égyptien." *Bulletin de l'IFAN,* série B, 35:532–47.

1973c   "Introduction à l'étude des migrations en Afrique Centrale et Occidentale: Identification du berceau nilotique du peuple sénégalais." *Bulletin de l'IFAN,* série B, 35:769–92.

1974a   *Physique nucléaire et chronologie absolue.* Dakar: IFAN-NEA.

1974b   *The African origin of civilization: Myth or reality?* Mercer Cook, ed. and trans. Chicago: Lawrence Hill Books.

1977   *Parenté génétique de l'Egyptien pharaonique et des langues negro-africaines.* Dakar: IFAN-NEA.

1980   "Origine des anciens Égyptiens." In *Histoire générale de l'Afrique,* vol. 2, ed. G. Mokhtar, 39–72. Paris: UNESCO.

Apple, Michael W.

1990   *Ideology and curriculum.* London: Routledge.

Apter, D.

1963   *Ghana in transition.* New York: Atheneum.

Arancibia C., Juan

1985   *Honduras: Un estado nacional?* Tegucigalpa: Guyamuras.

Arguedas, José María

1935   *Agua.* Lima: Compañía de Impresiones y Publicidad.

1941   *Yawar fiesta.* Lima: Compañía de Impresiones y Publicidad.

1958   *Los ríos profundos.* Buenos Aires: Losada.

1975   *Formación de una cultura nacional indoamericana.* Mexico, D.F.: Siglo Veintiuno.

1989   *Indios, mestizos y señores.* Lima: Editorial Horizonte.

Arizpe, Lourdes

1978   *El reto del pluralismo cultural.* Investigaciones Sociales, no. 2. Mexico, D.F.: Instituto Nacional Indigenista.

Arrom, José J.

1971   "La vírgen del cobre: Historia, leyenda y símbolo sincrético." In his *Certidumbre de América: Estudios de letras, folklore y cultura,* 184–214. Madrid: Editorial Gredos.

Asad, Talal

1987   "Are there histories of peoples without Europe? A review article." *Comparative Studies in Society and History* 29(3):594–607.

Asante, Molefe K.

1980   *Afrocentricity: The theory of social change.* Buffalo: Amulefi.

1987   *The Afrocentric idea.* Philadelphia: Temple University Press.

Asombang, R. N.

1988   "Bamenda in prehistory: The evidence from Fiwe Nkwi, Mbi crater and Shum Laka rockshelters." Ph.D. dissertation, University of London.

Atherton, J. H.
1983   "Ethnoarchaeology in Africa." *African Archaeological Review* 1:75–104.
Axtell, James
1985   *The invasion within: The contest of cultures in colonial North America.* New York: Oxford University Press.
Babacar, A. O., et al.
1983   *Tegdaust III Recherches sur Aoudaghost.* Institut Mauritanien de la Recherche Scientifique. Paris: Editions Recherche sur le Civilization.
Baldwin, Joseph A.
1980   "The psychology of oppression." In *Contemporary black thought: Alternative analyses in social and behavioral science,* eds. Molefe K. Asante and Abdulai S. Vandi, pp. 95–110. London: Sage Publications.
Balout, Lionel
1955   *Préhistoire de l'Afrique du Nord.* Paris: Arts et Métiers Graphiques.
Baralt, Rafael
1975   *Resumen de la historia de Venezuela.* Caracas: Academía Nacional de Historia.
Bartolomé, Miguel A.
1985   "La desindianización de la Argentina." *Boletín de Antropología Americana* 11:39–50.
Bataillon, Claude
1982   "Notas sobre el indigenismo mexicano." In *Indianidad, etnocido, indigenismo en América Latina,* ed. Francoise Morin, 129–40. Reprinted 1988. Mexico, D.F.: Instituto Indigenista Interamericano.
Bate, Luis
1984   *Cultura, clases y cuestión étnico nacional.* Colección Principios. Mexico, D.F.: Editorial Juan Pablo.
Baud, Michel
1991   "A colonial counter economy: Tobacco production on Española, 1500–1870." *New West Indian Guide* 65(1–2):27–49.
Bauer, Otto
1979   *La cuestión de las nacionalidades y la social democracía.* Mexico, D.F.: Siglo Veintiuno.
Beaudry, Mary, L. J. Cook, and S. Mrozowski
1991   "Artifacts and active voices: Material culture as social discourse." In *The archaeology of inequality,* eds. R. Paynter and R. H. McGuire. Oxford: Basil Blackwell.
Beaver, R. Pierce
1988   "Protestant churches and the Indians." In *Handbook of North American Indians,* vol. 4, ed. W. Washburn, 430–58. Washington, D.C.: Smithsonian Institution Press.
Bee, Robert L.
1990   "Connecticut's Indian policy: From testy arrogance to benign bemusement." In *The Pequots in southern New England: The fall and rise of an American Indian nation,* eds. L. M. Hauptman and J. D. Wherry, 194–214. Norman: University of Oklahoma Press.
Belknap, Jeremy, and Jedidiah Morse
1796   "Report on the Oneida, Stockbridge and Brotherton Indians." Originally published in *Collections of the Massachusetts Historical Society,* first series, 5:

12–32. Reprinted 1955 in *Indian Notes and Monographs,* no. 54. New York: Museum of the American Indian, Heye Foundation.

Bennett, Tony, Colin Mercer, and Janet Woolacott, eds.

1986 *Popular culture and social relations.* Philadelphia: Open University Press.

Bentivenga de Napolitano, C.

1977 *Cedulario indígena venezolano (1501–1812).* Caracas: Instituto de Investigaciones Históricas.

Berkshire Association of Congregational Ministers

1829 *A history of the county of Berkshire, Massachusetts.* Pittsfield, Massachusetts: Samuel W. Bush.

Berman, Edward H.

1983 *The ideology of philanthropy: The influence of the Carnegie, Ford, and Rockefeller foundations on American foreign policy.* Albany: State University of New York Press.

Bernal, Martin

1987 *Black Athena: The Afroasiatic roots of classical civilization, vol. 1: The fabrication of ancient Greece, 1785–1985.* New Brunswick, New Jersey: Rutgers University Press.

Bernstein, Henry, and Jaques Depelchin

1979 "The object of African history: A materialist perspective—II." *History in Africa* 19:17–43.

Berry, L., D. J. Campbell, and I. Emker

1977 "Trends in man/land interaction in the West African Sahel." In *African environment special report,* eds. D. Dalby, R. J. Harrison Church, and F. Bezzar, 83–91. London: International Africa Institute.

Betánces, R. E.

1975 *Las Antillas para los antillanos.* San Juan: Instituto de Cultura Puertorriqueña.

BHPR (*Boletín Histórico de Puerto Rico*).

1921 Vol. 8. Ed. C. Coll y Toste. San Juan, Puerto Rico.

Binford, Lewis R.

1987 "Data, relativism and archaeological science." *Man* 22(3):391–404.

Binsbergen, W. van

1987 "Lykota Lya Bakoya." *Cahiers d'Etudes Africaines* XXVILL 3–4 (107–108): 350–92.

Birdsall, Richard D.

1959 *Berkshire County: A cultural history.* New Haven: Yale University Press.

Blakey, Michael L.

1983 "Sociopolitical bias and ideological production in historical archaeology." In *The socio-politics of archaeology,* eds. J. M. Gero, D. M. Lacy, and M. L. Blakey, pp. 5–16. Research Reports 23, Department of Anthropology, University of Massachusetts, Amherst.

1987 "Skull doctors: Intrinsic social and political bias in the history of American physical anthropology, with special reference to the work of Ales Hrdlicka." *Critique of Anthropology* 7:7–35.

1990 "American nationality and ethnicity in the depicted past." In *The politics of the past,* eds. P. Gathercole and D. Lowenthal, pp. 38–48. London: Allen and Unwin.

1991 "Man and nature, white and other." In *Gelatinizing anthropology,* ed. Faye

Harrison, pp. 8–16. Washington, D.C.: Association of Black Anthropologists and the American Anthropological Association.

Blyden, Edward W.
1887   *Christianity, Islam and the Negro race.* Reprinted 1967. Edinburgh: Edinburgh University Press.
1890   *The African problem and the method for its solution.* Washington, D.C.: Gibson Brothers.
1905   *West Africa before Europe.* London: C. M. Phillips.

Boahen, Adu A.
1988   "Etre historien aujourd'hui: La perspective africaine." In *Etre historien aujourd'hui: L'Histoire et les historiens de l'Afrique contemporaine,* ed. René Rémond, 255–67. Actes du Colloque de Nice. Paris: UNESCO.

Boahen, Adu A., ed.
1985   *Histoire générale de l'Afrique,* vol. 7. Paris: UNESCO.

Bonfil Batalla, Guillermo
1977   *Sobre la liberación del indio.* Nueva Antropología, no. 8. Mexico, D.F.: UNAM.
1987   "Los pueblos indios, sus culturas y las políticas culturales." In *Políticas culturales en América Latina,* eds. Néstor García Canclini et al., 89–126. Mexico, D.F.: Grijalbo.
1989   *México profundo.* Mexico, D.F.: Editorial Grijalbo.

Bonilla, Heraclio
1982   "Etnia, región y la cuestión nacional en el área andina." In *Indianidad, etnocido, indigenismo en América Latina,* ed. Francoise Morin, 87–112. Reprinted 1988. Mexico, D.F.: Instituto Indigenista Interamericano.

Bosch, Juan
1970   *Composición social dominicana: Historia e interpretación.* Santo Domingo, Dominican Republic: Colección de Pensamiento y Cultura.

Boubou-Hama, and J. Ki-Zerbo
1980   "La place de l'histoire dans les sociétés africaines." In *Histoire générale de l'Afrique,* vol. 1, ed. J. Ki-Zerbo, 65–76. Paris: UNESCO.

Bourdieu, Pierre
1984   *Homo academicus.* Paris: Editions de Miniut.

Bourricaud, François
1954   "Algunas características originales de la cultura mestiza en el Perú contemporáneo." *Revista del Museo Nacional* 23:162–73. Lima.

Bower, John
1986   "A survey of surveys: Aspects of surface archaeology in sub-Saharan Africa." *The African Archaeological Review* 4:21–40.

Brain, C. K.
1981   *The hunters or the hunted.* Chicago: University of Chicago Press.

Brasser, Ted J.
1974   *Riding on the frontier's crest: Mahican Indian culture and culture change.* Ethnology Division Paper no. 13. Ottawa: National Museum of Man.
1975   *A basketful of Indian culture change.* Ethnology Division Paper no. 22. Ottawa: National Museum of Man.
1978   "Mahican." In *Handbook of North American Indians, vol. 15: Northeast,* ed. B. Trigger, 198–212. Washington, D.C.: Smithsonian Institution Press.

Brau, Salvador
1972a   *Puerto Rico y su historia.* San Juan, Puerto Rico: Editorial IV Centenario.

1972b   "Las clases jornaleras de Puerto Rico." In *Ensayos: Disquisiciones sociológicas.* Río Piedras, Puerto Rico: Editorial Edil.

Britto García, Luis
1988   *La máscara del poder.* Caracas: Ediciones Alfadil-Trópicos.

Browder, Tony
1989   *From the Browder file.* Washington, D.C.: Browder.

Buitrago Ortíz, C.
1976   *Los orígenes históricos de la sociedad precapitalista en Puerto Rico.* Río Piedras, Puerto Rico: Ediciones Huracán.

Bullen, R., and A. Bullen
1972   *Archaeological investigations on St. Vincent and the Grenadines West Indies.* Report no. 8. Kingston, Jamaica: William L. Bryant Foundation.

Butler, Eva L.
1945   "Sweat-houses in the southern New England area." *Bulletin of the Massachusetts Archaeological Society* 6:11–15.
1946   "The brush or stone memorial heaps of southern New England." *Bulletin of the Archaeological Society of Connecticut* 19:2–11.
1948   "Algonkian culture and the use of maize in southern New England." *Bulletin of the Archaeological Society of Connecticut* 22:3–39.

Callinicos, Luli
1987   "The 'people's past': Towards transforming the present." In *Class, community and conflict,* ed. Belinda Bozzoli, 44–64. Johannesburg: Ravan Press.
1990   "Popular history in the eighties." *Radical History Review* 46(7):285–97.

Canning, E. W. B.
1894   "Indian land grants in Stockbridge." *Collections of the Berkshire Historical and Scientific Society* 5:45–56.

Carlson, Claire, and Russell G. Handsman
1993   "The Fort Hill project. Recovering buried histories: Archaeology at the Weantinock Indian planting fields." *Newsletter of the Conference on New England Archaeology* 12(1):1–2.

Caro Costas, Aida R.
1971   *Antología de lecturas de historia de Puerto Rico.* San Juan, Puerto Rico: Caro Costas (privately printed).

Carr, D.
1986   *Time, narrative, and history.* Bloomington: Indiana University Press.

Carrión, J. M.
1986   "Los orígenes de la nacionalidad puertorriqueña: Comentarios críticos en torno al País de los Cuatro Pisos de José Luis González." *Revista Talleres* 3(3–4).

Caso, Alfonso
1953   *El pueblo del sol.* Mexico, D.F.: Fondo de la Cultura Económica.

Cassa, Roberto
1992   *Los indios de las Antillas.* Madrid: Editorial MAPFRE.

Cassedy, Daniel F., Elise Manning, Bruce Sterling, Christopher Hohman, Tracy Millis, and Mark Rees
1991   *Iroquois gas transmission system: Phase II archaeological evaluations, vol. 4: Connecticut.* Atlanta: Garrow and Associates.

Casson, Lionel
1989   *Periplus Maris Erythraei.* Princeton: Princeton University Press.

Castillo Meléndez, F.
1987 "Población y defensa de la isla de Cuba, 1650–1700." *Anuario de Estudios Americanos* 44:1–87.

Castro Pozo, Hildebrando
1924 *Nuestra comunidad indígena.* Lima: Editorial "El Lucero."
1946 "Social and economic-political evolution of the communities of central Peru." In *Handbook of South American Indians,* ed. Julian H. Steward, 483–500. Bureau of American Ethnology Bulletin 143, vol. 2. Washington, D.C.: U.S. Government Printing Office.

Cero, F., et al.
1980 *Costa Rica: Nuestra comunidad nacional.* San José: Editorial Universidad Estatal a Distancia.

Cha-Jua, Sundiata K., and Robert E. Weems, Jr.
1994 "Coming into focus: The treatment of African Americans in post–Civil War United States history survey texts." *Journal of American History* 80(4): 1408–19.

Chami, Felix
1988a "The coastal Iron Age site in Kisarawe, Tanzania." M.A. thesis, Brown University.
1988b "The excavation of a coastal early Iron Age site in Kisarawe district of Tanzania." *Nyame Akuma* 30:34–35.
1994 *The Tanzanian coast in the first millennium A.D.*: An archaeology of the iron-working, farming communities. Uppsala, Sweden: Societas Archaeologica Upsaliensis.

Champollion-Figeac, J. J.
1839 *Egypte ancienne.* Paris: Firmin Didot.

Chatterjee, Partha
1986 *Nationalist thought and the colonial world: A derivative discourse.* London: Zed Books.
1992 "History and the nationalization of Hinduism." *Social Research* 59:111–49.

Chattopadhyay, Bankimchandra
1965 *Bankim racanabali,* vol. 2. Calcutta: Sahitya Samsad.

Chattopadhyay, Tarinicharan
1878 *Bhāratbarser itihas,* vol. 1. 18th ed. Calcutta.

Chaunu, Pierre
1973 *Conquista y explotación de nuevos mundos.* Barcelona: Nueva, Editorial Labor.

Childs, S. Terry
1995 "Technological history and culture in western Tanzania." In *The culture and technology of African iron production,* ed. Peter Schmidt. Gainesville: University Press of Florida.

Chittick, H. Neville
1968 "The coast before the arrival of the Portuguese." In *Zamani: A survey of African history,* eds. B. A. Ogot and J. A. Kieran, 100–118. Nairobi: East African Publishing House.
1974 *Kilwa: An Islamic trading city on the East African coast.* 2 vols. Memoir 5. Nairobi: British Institute in Eastern Africa.
1984 *Manda: Excavations at an island port on the Kenya coast.* Memoir 9. Nairobi: British Institute in Eastern Africa.

Clark, J. D., ed.
   1982   *The Cambridge history of Africa, vol. 1: From earliest times to c. 500 B.C.*
           Cambridge: Cambridge University Press.
Clark, John G. D.
   1968   *Archaeology and society.* London: Methuen.
Clifford, James
   1988   "Identity in Mashpee." In his *The predicament of culture: Twentieth-century
           ethnography, literature, and art,* 277–346. Cambridge, Massachusetts: Har-
           vard University Press.
Clifton, James A.
   1990   "The Indian story: A cultural fiction." In *The invented Indian: Cultural
           fictions and government policies,* ed. J. A. Clifton, 29–47. New Brunswick,
           New Jersey: Transaction Publishers.
Code, Lorraine
   1991   *What can she know?* Ithaca, New York: Cornell University Press.
Cohen, R., and J. Middleton
   1970   *From tribe to nation in Africa: Studies in incorporation processes.* Scranton,
           Pennsylvania: Chandler.
Cohn, B. S.
   1980   "History and anthropology: The state of play." *Comparative Studies in
           Society and History* 2(2):198–221.
Collins, Patricia Hill
   1990   *Black feminist thought: Knowledge, consciousness, and the politics of empower-
           ment.* New York: Routledge.
Colmenares Goyo, C.
   1989   "Arqueología, herencia cultural y educación." Tesis de grado in anthro-
           pology, School of Anthropology, Universidad Central de Venezuela,
           Caracas.
Connah, G.
   1975   *The archaeology of Benin.* Oxford: Clarendon Press.
Connecticut Archaeological Survey
   1989   *An archaeological survey of Bridge #2425 over the Hollenbeck River in Canaan,
           Connecticut.* Project report 511, prepared for the Connecticut Department
           of Transportation. New Britain: Connecticut Archaeological Survey.
Contreras Alvarez, Gerardo
   1990   *Educación y reforma universitaria.* San José: Ediciones Guayac.
Corchado Juarbe, Carmen
   1985   *El indio: Su presencia en la poesía puertorriqueña.* Río Piedras, Puerto Rico:
           Editorial Universitaria, UPR.
Córdova, P. T.
   1968   "Memorias geográficas, históricas y estadísticas de la isla de Puerto Rico."
           Editorial Coquí, vol. 2. San Juan, Puerto Rico: Edición Facsimilar.
Corretjer, Juan Antonio
   1970   *Yerba bruja: Poemas de Juan Antonia Corretjer.* San Juan: Instituto de Cultura
           Puertorriqueña, Biblioteca Popular.
Cothren, William
   1854   *History of ancient Woodbury, Connecticut,* vol. 1. Waterbury, Connecticut:
           Bronson Brothers.

Cress-Welsing, Francis
  1970   *The Cress theory of color-confrontation and racism (white supremacy): A psycho-genetic theory and world outlook.* Washington, D.C.: Welsing.
  1990   *The Isis (Yssis) papers.* Chicago: Third World Press.
Crew, Spencer R., and James E. Sims
  1991   "Locating authenticity: Fragments of a dialogue." In *Exhibiting cultures: The poetics and politics of museum display,* eds. Ivan Karp and Steven D. Levine, 159–75. Washington, D.C.: Smithsonian Institution Press.
Cruxent, José, and Irving Rouse
  1961   *Arqueología cronológica de Venezuela.* 2 vols. Washington, D.C.: Pan American Union.
Cruz Monclova, Lidio
  1964   *Historia de Puerto Rico siglo XIX,* vol. 3, part 3. Río Piedras, Puerto Rico: Editorial Universitaria.
Cueva, Agustín
  1987   *Tiempos conservadores: América Latina en la derechización de Occidente.* Quito, Ecuador: Editorial El Conejo.
  1989   "Sobre exilios y reinos: Notas críticas sobre la evolución de la sociología sudamericana." *Estudios* 3:10–89.
Cuevas Molina, R.
  1989   "Guatemala: Cultura de oposición, resistencia y liberación." *Estudios* 3: 1–9.
Curtin, Philip D.
  1964   *African history.* Washington, D.C.: Service Center for Teachers of History.
Danto, Arthur C.
  1985   *Narration and knowledge.* Revised edition of *Analytical philosophy of history,* 1968. New York: Columbia University Press.
Daramola, G. F., and Olowu, A. O.
  1972   "Physiological and radiological implications of a low incidence of pineal calcification in Nigeria." *Neuroendocrinology* 9:41–57.
Davenport, C. B., and Morris Steggerda
  1929   *Race crossing in Jamaica.* Washington, D.C.: Carnegie Institution.
De Barros, Philip
  1990   "Changing paradigms, goals and methods in the archaeology of franco-phone West Africa." In *A history of African archaeology,* ed. P. Robertshaw, 155–72. London: James Currey.
Deforest, John W.
  1851   *History of the Indians of Connecticut from the earliest known period to 1851.* Hartford, Connecticut: William James Hammersley.
Deive, C. E.
  1980   *La esclavitud del negro en Santo Domingo.* 2 vols. Santo Domingo, Dominican Republic: Museo del Hombre Dominicano.
Delafosse, Maurice
  1900   "Sur des traces probables de civilisation egyptienne et d'hommes de race blanche à la Côte d'Ivoire." *L'Anthropologie* 11:677–83.
  1912   *Haut-Sénégal-Niger.* Paris: Larose.
  1916   *La question de Ghana et la mission Bonnal e Mézières.* Annuaire et Mémoire du Comité d'Etudes Historiques et Scientifiques de l'AOF, vol. 1.

Departamento de Investigaciones de la Actividad Política
1994   *Las nuevas tendencias políticas del venezolano.* Caracas: Fondo Editorial Venezolano.

Derrida, Jacques
1994   *Specters of Mary.* New York: Routledge.

Devisse, Jean
1988   "L'Histoire et le sociétés: Fonctionnements et problèmes." In *Etre historien
aujourd'hui: L'Histoire et les historiens de l'Afrique contemporaine,* ed. René
Rémond, 325–47. Actes du Colloque de Nice. Paris: UNESCO.

Diagne, Pathé
1977   "Renaissance et problèmes culturels en Afrique." In *Introduction à la culture
Africaine,* eds. O. Balogun, H. Aguessi, and P. Diagne, 213–311. Paris:
UNESCO.

Díaz Polanco, Héctor
1979   "La teoría indigenista y la integración." In *Indigenismo, modernización y
marginalidad,* ed. Héctor Díaz Polanco, 9–40. Mexico, D.F.: Juan Pablo.
1983   *Las teorías antropológicas: El evolucionismo,* vol. 1. Mexico, D.F.: Editorial
Línea.
1985   *La cuestión étnico-nacional en América Latina.* Mexico, D.F.: Editorial Línea.
1987   *Etnia, nación y política.* Mexico, D.F.: Colección Principios, Editorial
Juan Pablo.
1988   "Cultura y política en el pensamiento de Gramsci." *Boletín de Antropología
Americana* 17:63–84.

Dika-Akwa
1980   "Monographie sur la nationalité Bassa." In *Les fils de Hitong: Contribution à
l'étude de l'épopée comme genre,* vol. 2, ed. P. Ngijol Ngijol, 27–56. Yaoundé,
Cameroon: Centre d'Edition et de Production pour l'Enseignement et
la Recherche.

di Leonardo, Micaela
1991   "Gender, culture, and political economy: Feminist anthropology in historical perspective." In *Gender at the crossroads of knowledge: Feminist anthropology in the postmodern era,* ed. M. di Leonardo, 1–50. Berkeley: University
of California Press.

Dincauze, Dena F.
1990   "A capsule prehistory of southern New England." In *The Pequots in
southern New England: The fall and rise of an American Indian nation,* eds.
L. M. Hauptman and J. D. Wherry, 19–32. Norman: University of Oklahoma Press.

Dorfman, Ariel, and Armand Mattelart
1975   *How to read Donald Duck: Imperialist ideology in the Disney comic.* New York:
International General Editions.

Douglass, Frederick
1950 [1854]   "The claims of the Negro ethnologically considered." In *The life
and writings of Frederick Douglass,* ed. Philip S. Foner, 289–309. New York:
International Publishers.

Drake, St. Clair
1980   "Anthropology and the black experience." *The Black Scholar* 11:2–31.

Dray, William
1957   *Laws and explanation in history.* Westport, Connecticut: Greenwood Press.

283

Duany, J.
1985   "Ethnicity in the Spanish Caribbean: Notes on the consolidation of creole identity in Cuba and Puerto Rico, 1762–1868." *Ethnic Groups* 6(2–3): 99–123.

DuBois, W. E. B.
1940   "Dusk of dawn: An essay toward an autobiography of a race concept." In his *Writings*, 549–802. Reprinted 1986 with notes by Nathan Huggins. New York: Library of America.

Dupouy, Walter
1958   "El indio en la historia de Venezuela." *Boletín Indigenista Venezolano* 3–5 (1–4):205–16.

Echols, Alice
1983   "The new feminism of yin and yang." In *Powers of desire,* eds. A. Snitow, C. Stansell, and S. Thompson, 439–59. New York: Monthly Review Press.

Eisenhardt, Evelyn
1987   *On the trail of Connecticut's woodland Indians.* History on the Go! Workbook Series, no. 5. Hartford: Connecticut Historical Society.

Elliot, J. H.
1987   "The Spanish conquest." In *Colonial Spanish America,* ed. L. Bothell, 1–58. Cambridge: Cambridge University Press.

Elphinstone, Mountstuart
1905   *The history of India: The Hindú and Mahometan periods.* 9th ed. London: John Murray.

Ericson, Jody
1991   "The latest of the Mahicans." *Berkshire Magazine* 9(6):18–27.

España Caballero, Arturo
1987   "La práctica social y el populismo nacionalista (1935–1940)." In *La antropología en México: Panorama histórico, tomo 2: Los hechos y los dichos (1880–1986),* ed. Carlos García Mora, 223–88. Mexico, D.F.: Instituto Nacional de Antropología e Historia.

Fage, J. D.
1980   "Evolution de l'historiographie de l'Afrique." In *Histoire générale de l'Afrique: Méthodologie et préhistoire africaine,* ed. J. Ki-Zerbo, 45–64. Paris: UNESCO.

Fahim, Hussein
1982   *Indigenous anthropology in non-Western countries.* Durham, North Carolina: Carolina Academic Press.

Fall, Yoro
1988   "L'Histoire et les historiens dans l'Afrique contemporaine." In *Etre historien aujourd'hui: L'Histoire et les historiens de l'Afrique contemporaine,* ed. René Rémond, 181–218. Actes du Colloque de Nice. Paris: UNESCO.

Favre, Henri
1982   "Capitalismo y etnicidad: La política indigenista de Perú." In *Indianidad, etnocido, indigenismo en América Latina,* ed. Françoise Morin, 113–28. Reprinted 1988. Mexico, D.F.: Instituto Indigenista Interamericano.

Feder, Kenneth L.
1984   "Pots, plants, and people: The late Woodland period of Connecticut." *Bulletin of the Archaeological Society of Connecticut* 47:99–111.
1994   *A village of outcasts: Historical archaeology and documentary research at the Lighthouse site.* Mountain View, California: Mayfield Publishing Company.

Feierman, Steven
   1974   *The Shambaa kingdom: A history.* Madison: University of Wisconsin Press.
   1990   *Peasant intellectuals: Anthropology and history in Tanzania.* Madison: University of Wisconsin Press.
Fernández Méndez, Eugenio
   1976   *Las encomiendas y esclavitud de los indios de Puerto Rico, 1508–1550.* Río Piedras, Puerto Rico: Editorial de la Universidad de Puerto Rico.
Feyerabend, Paul
   1978   *Science in a free society.* London: NLB Press.
Finley, Moses L.
   1987   *Sur l'histoire ancienne: La matière, la forme et la méthode.* Paris: Editions la Découverte.
Fisher, H. J.
   1987   "Sudaness and Sabaan studies: Review article." *Journal of African History* 28:281–93.
Fleury, Eduardo
   1953   *Estudio antropométrico de la colección de cráneos motilones.* Memoria de la Sociedad de Ciencias Naturales La Salle, 13, no. 34. Caracas: Sociedad de Ciencias Naturales La Salle.
Fliegel, Carl John, compiler
   1970   *Index to the records of the Moravian mission among the Indians of North America.* New Haven, Connecticut: Research Publications, Inc.
Florescano, Enrique
   1988   *Memoria Mexicana: Ensayo sobre la reconstrución del pasado, época prehispánica—1821.* México, D.F.: Editorial Joaquín Moritz.
Flores Galindo, Alberto
   1988   *Tiempo de plagas.* Lima: Caballo Rojo.
Follesdal, Dafinn
   1979   "Hermeneutics and the hypothetico-deductive method." *Dialectica* 33: 319–36.
Fonseca, E.
   1989   *Historia: Teoría y métodos.* San José, Costa Rica: Editorial Universitaria Centroamericana.
Fonseca, Oscar, ed.
   1988   *Hacia una arqueología social.* San José: Editorial de la Universidad de Costa Rica.
Forgues, Roland
   1989   *José María Arguedas: Del pensamiento dialéctico al pensamiento trágico: Historia de una utopia.* Lima: Editorial Horizonte.
Frank, Andre Gunder
   1969   *Capitalism and underdevelopment in Latin America: Historical studies of Chile and Brazil.* New York: Monthly Review Press.
Frobenius, Leo
   1987   *La civilisation Africaine.* Paris: Editions Le Rocher.
Froment, Alain
   1988   "Origine et evolution de l'homme dans la pensée de Cheikh Anta Diop: Analyse critique." Lecture read at the University of Yaoundé, Cameroon, 23 February 1988.
Fukuyama, Francis
   1992   *El fin de la historia y el último hombre.* Barcelona: Editorial Planeta.

Gamio, Manuel
    1916   *Forjando patria (pro-nacionalismo)*. Mexico, D.F.: Porrúa Hermanos.
    1922   *La población del valle de Teotihuacán*. 2 vols. Mexico, D.F.: Dirección de Antropología, Secretaría de Agricultura y Fomento.

Gelpi, Elsa
    1993   "Economía y sociedad: Estudio de la economía azucarera en el Puerto Rico del siglo XVI (1540–1612)." Ph.D. dissertation, University of Seville, Spain.

Gifford, D. P.
    1980   "Ethnoarchaeological contributions to the taphonomy of human sites." In *Fossils in the making: Vertebrate taphonomy and palaeoecology,* eds. A. K. Behrensmeyer and P. H. U. Andrew, 93–106. Chicago: University of Chicago Press.

Gil-Bermejo, J.
    1983   *La Española, anotaciones históricas, 1600–1650*. Sevilla: Escuela de Estudios Hispanoamericanos.

Gil Fortoul, José
    1961   "José Gil Fortoul (1862–1942)." In *Pensamiento político venezolano del siglo XIX,* vol. 1, 151–86. Caracas: Ediciones Conmemorativas del Sesquicentenario de la Independencia.

Gladwin, Christina
    1991   *Structural adjustment and African women farmers.* Gainesville: University of Florida Press and Center for African Studies.

Glassberg, David
    1990   *American historical pageantry: The uses of tradition in the early twentieth century.* Chapel Hill: University of North Carolina Press.

Gómez, María
    1947   "Cefalometría en los escolares de Lima." *Boletín del Instituto Psicopedagógico Nacional* (Peru). 6(2):83–129.

González, José Luis
    1980   *El país de los cuatro pisos.* Río Piedras, Puerto Rico: Ediciones Huracán.

González Casanova, Pablo
    1969   *La sociología de la explotación.* Mexico, D.F.: Siglo Veintiuno.

González Casanova, Pablo, ed.
    1984   *Cultura y creación intelectual en América Latina.* Instituto de Investigaciones Sociales de la UNAM. Mexico, D.F.: Siglo Veintiuno.

González Casanova, Pablo, and Guillermo Bonfil Batalla
    1968   *Las ciencias sociales y la antropología: Dos ensayos.* Mexico, D.F.: Centro Nacional de Productividad, Colección Ciencia y Tecnología.

Gordimer, Nadine
    1988   "The essential gesture." In *The essential gesture: Writing, politics and places,* ed. Stephen Clingman, 285–300. New York: Alfred A. Knopf.

Gordon, Linda
    1994   "The treatment of family issues in United States history textbooks: General thoughts and a review of several examples." *Journal of American History* 80(4):1397–1407.

Gould, Stephen J.
    1979   *Ontogeny and phylogeny.* New York: W. W. Norton.
    1980   *The mismeasure of man.* New York: W. W. Norton.

Grant, Charles S.
  1972   *Democracy in the Connecticut frontier town of Kent.* New York: W. W. Norton.
Grewal, J. S.
  1970   *Muslim rule in India: The assessments of British historians.* Calcutta: Oxford University Press.
Gross-Ngate, M.
  1988   "Power and knowledge: The representation of the made world in the work of Park, Charles, Monteil and Delafosse." *Cahiers D'Etudes Africaines* 28:485–511.
Guha, Ranajit
  1988   *An Indian historiography of India: A nineteenth-century agenda and its implications.* Calcutta: K. P. Bagchi.
Hall, Martin
  1984a   "The burden of tribalism: The social context of southern African Iron Age studies." *American Antiquity* 49:455–67.
  1984b   "Pots and politics: Ceramic interpretations in southern Africa." *World Archaeology* 15:262–73.
  1990   "'Hidden history': Iron Age archaeology in southern Africa." In *A history of African archaeology,* ed. P. Robertshaw, 59–77. London: James Currey.
Handsman, Russell G.
  1989   "Algonkian wigwams: An invisible presence, political spaces." *Artifacts* 17(4):19–21. Washington, Connecticut: American Indian Archaeological Institute.
  1990   "The Weantinock Indian homeland was not a 'desert.'" *Artifacts* 18(2): 3–7.
  1991a   "What happened to the heritage of the Weantinock people." *Artifacts* 19(1):3–9.
  1991b   "Illuminating history's silences in the 'Pioneer Valley.'" *Artifacts* 19(2): 14–25.
  1994   "Challenging history's myths in the Berkshires: Mahican Indian people and the Bidwell House acreage." Research report prepared for the Bidwell House Museum, Monterey, Massachusetts.
Handsman, Russell G., and Ann McMullen
  1987   "An introduction to woodsplint basketry and its interpretation." In *A key into the language of woodsplint baskets,* eds. A. McMullen and R. G. Handsman, 16–35. Washington, Connecticut: American Indian Archaeological Institute.
Handsman, Russell G., and Jeffrey H. Maymon
  1987   "The Weantinoge site and an archaeology of ten centuries of native history." *Artifacts* 15(4):4–11.
Handsman, Russell G., and Neil Silberman
  1991   "John DeForest and US: Critical perspectives on the archaeological alienation of Palestinian and Algonkian Indian histories." Paper presented at the annual meeting of the Society for Historical Archaeology, Richmond, Virginia.
Handsman, Russell G., and Lynne Williamson
  1989   "As we tell our stories: Living traditions and the Algonkian peoples of Indian New England." *Artifacts* 17(4):4–34.

Hanson, Norwood Russell
  1958   *Patterns of discovery.* Cambridge: Cambridge University Press.
Haraway, Donna J.
  1991   "Situated knowledges: The science question in feminism and the privilege of partial perspective." In her *Simians, cyborgs, and women: The reinvention of nature,* 183–201. New York: Routledge.
Harding, Sandra
  1986   *The science question in feminism.* Ithaca, New York: Cornell University Press.
  1991   *Whose science? Whose knowledge?* Ithaca, New York: Cornell University Press.
Harre, R.
  1970   *The principles of scientific thinking.* Chicago: University of Chicago Press.
Hart, K.
  1985   "The social anthropology of West Africa." *Annual Review of Anthropology* 14:243–72.
Hasenstab, Robert
  1989   "Workshop on field sampling methods and modeling, held at the CNEA annual meeting, April 9, 1988, Sturbridge, Massachusetts." *Newsletter of the Conference on New England Archaeology* 8(1):3–6.
Hegel, G. W. F.
  1965   *La raison dans l'histoire: Introduction à la philosophie de l'histoire.* Paris: Plon.
Heller, Agnes
  1985   *Historia y vida cotidiana: Aportación a la sociología socialista.* Mexico, D.F.: Grijalbo, Colección Enlace.
Hempel, Carl G.
  1958   "The theoretician's dilemma." In *Concepts, theories, and the mind-body problem,* vol. 2, eds. H. Feigl, M. Scriven, and G. Maxwell, 37–98. Minnesota Studies in the Philosophy of Science. Minneapolis: University of Minnesota Press.
Herrera Fritot, Rene
  1964   *Craneotrigonometría.* Havana: Departamento de Antropología, Comisión Nacional de la Academía de Ciencias de la República de Cuba.
  1965   *Nueva técnica para calcular la capacidad craneana.* Havana: Academía de Ciencias de Cuba, Departamento de Antropología.
Hesse, Mary
  1960   *Models and analogies in science.* Notre Dame, Indiana: University of Notre Dame Press.
  1973   "In defense of objectivity." *Proceedings of the British Academy* 54:275–92.
Hewitt de Alcántara, Cynthia
  1984   *Anthropological perspectives on rural Mexico.* London: Routledge and Kegan Paul.
Heye, George G.
  1921   "A Mahican wooden cup." *Indian Notes and Monographs* 5(2):15–18. New York: Museum of the American Indian, Heye Foundation.
Higham, John
  1989   "Hanging paradigms: The collapse of consensus history." *Journal of American History* 76(2):460–66.
Holl, Augustin F. C.
  1979   *Chefs et notables dans la politique sociale et economique française dans la région*

du Nyong et Sanaga de 1920 à 1940. Masters thesis, Université de Yaoundé, Cameroon.

1990   "West African archaeology: Colonialism and nationalism." In *A history of African archaeology,* ed. P. Robertshaw, 296–309. London: James Currey.

hooks, bell

1984   *Feminist theory: From margin to center.* Boston: South End Press.

Hopkins, Samuel

1753   *Historical memoirs, relating to the Housatunnuck Indians.* Boston: S. Kneeland.

1911   "Historical memoirs relating to the Housatonic Indians." *The Magazine of History with Notes and Queries* vol. 5, extra numbers 17–20. Reprinted 1972. New York: Johnson Reprint Corporation.

Hsu, Francis L. K.

1979   "The cultural problem of the cultural anthropologist." *American Anthropologist* 81:517–32.

Hueck Henríquez, Luis

1993   *El síndrome de Bolívar.* Caracas: Litografía Melvin.

Huffman, T. N.

1970   "The early Iron Age and the spread of the Bantu." *South African Archaeological Bulletin* 25:3–21.

1981   "Snakes and birds: Expressive space at Great Zimbabwe." *African Studies* 40:131–50.

1982   "Archaeology and ethnohistory of the African Iron Age." *Annual Review of Anthropology* 11:133–50.

1986   "Southern Bantu settlement patterns." *Africa* 56(3):280–98.

Hull, David L.

1988   *Science as a process: An evolutionary account of the social and conceptual development of science.* Chicago: University of Chicago Press.

Hunt, Eva

1977   *The transformation of the hummingbird: Cultural roots of a Zinacantecan mythical poem.* Ithaca, New York: Cornell University Press.

Hyden, Goran

1992   "The role of social capital in development: Illustrations from Tanzania." Paper presented at the Center for African Studies, University of Florida, February 6.

Inden, Ronald

1990   *Imagining India.* Oxford: Basil Blackwell.

Irele, Abiola

1991   "The African scholar: Is black Africa entering the Dark Ages of scholarship?" *Transition* 51:56–69.

Isaac, G.

1977   *Olorgesailie: Archaeological studies of a middle Pleistocene lake basin in Kenya.* Chicago: University of Chicago Press.

1984   "The archaeology of human origins: Studies of the lower Pleistocene in East Africa 1971–1981." *Advances in World Archaeology* 3:1–87.

1986   "Foundation stones: Early artifacts as indicators of activities and abilities." In *Stone Age prehistory,* eds. G. N. Bailey and P. Allow, 221–42. Cambridge: Cambridge University Press.

Jaén, María Teresa, Carlos Serrano, and Juan Comas

1976   *Data antropométrica de algunas poblaciones indígenas mexicanas.* México, D.F.: Instituto de Investigaciones Antropológicas, UNAM.

James, George G. M.
    1954   *Stolen legacy.* New York: Philosophical Library.

Jeffreys, M. D. W.
    1951   "Neolithic implements, Bamenda (British Cameroons)." *Bulletin de l'IFAN* 13:1203–17.

Jewsiewicki, G.
    1989   "African historical studies: Academic knowledge as usable past." *African Studies Review* 32–76.

Johnston, H. A. S.
    1967   *The Fulani empire of Sokoto.* Ibadan, Nigeria: Oxford University Press.

Jones, Electa F.
    1854   *Stockbridge, past and present, or records of an old mission station.* Springfield, Massachusetts: Samuel Bowles and Company.

Karim, Abdul
    1898   *Bhāratbarse musalman rājatver itibrtta,* vol. 1. Calcutta: Sanskrit Press Depository.

Karoma, N. J.
    1977   "Towards an organic growth of archaeology in Tanzania." Paper presented in a History Department seminar, University of Dar es Salaam.
    1990   "On the training of archaeologists in East African universities: The Tanzanian experience." Paper presented at the 10th biennial meetings of the Society of Africanist Archaeologists, Gainesville, Florida.

Karp, Ivan, and Steven D. Levine, eds.
    1991   *Exhibiting cultures: The poetics and politics of museum display.* Washington, D.C.: Smithsonian Institution Press.

Kawashima, Yasu
    1969   "Legal origins of the Indian reservation in colonial Massachusetts." *American Journal of Legal History* 13:42–56.

Keen, Benjamin
    1971   *The Aztec image in Western thought.* New Brunswick, New Jersey: Rutgers University Press.

Keita, Shomarka O. Y.
    1981   "Royal incest and diffusion in Africa." *American Ethnologist* 8:392–93.

Kennedy, Kenneth A. R.
    1976   *Human variation in space and time.* Dubuque, Iowa: W. C. Brown.

Kimambo, I. N., and A. J. Temu
    1969   *A history of Tanzania.* Nairobi: East African Publishing House.

King, Richard D.
    1990   *The African origin of biological psychiatry.* Germantown, Tennessee: Seymour-Smith.
    1994   *African origin of biological psychiatry.* Hampton, Virginia: U.B. and U.S. Communications Systems.

Kirkman, James
    1963   *Gedi: The palace.* The Hague: Mouton.

Kirwan, L.
    1986   "Rhapta, metropolis of Azania." *Azania* 21:99–104.

Kittrie, Nicholas N., and Eldon D. Wedlock, eds.
    1986   *The tree of liberty: A documentary history of rebellions and political crime in America.* Baltimore, Maryland: Johns Hopkins University Press.

Klein, R. G.
1983   "Stone Age prehistory of southern Africa." *Annual Review Anthropology* 12:25.

Knight, Alan
1990   "Racism, revolution and indigenismo: Mexico, 1910–1940." In *The idea of race in Latin America, 1870–1940,* ed. Richard Graham, 71–113. Austin: University of Texas Press.

Kohn, Fritzi, and Betty Méndez
1972   *Antropometría de los indios Cariña.* Caracas: Serie Laboratorio de Antropología, Universidad Central de Venezuela.

Kolakowski, Leszek
1969   *The alienation of reason: A history of positivist thought.* Garden City, New York: Anchor Books.
1987   *Histoire du Marxisme.* Paris: Fayard.

Krisólogo, Pedro
1976   *Manual glotológico del idioma Wo'tiheh.* Caracas: Universidad Católica Andrés Bello.

Kuhn, Thomas S.
1970   *The structure of scientific revolutions.* Chicago: University of Chicago Press.
1990   *La tension essentielle: Tradition et changement dans les sciences.* Paris: Gallimard.

Kuper, A.
1980   "Symbolic dimensions of southern Bantu homestead." *Africa* 1:8–23.

Lamb Richmond, Trudie
1987   "Spirituality and survival in Schaghticoke basket-making." In *A key into the language of woodsplint baskets,* eds. A. McMullen and R. G. Handsman, 126–43. Washington, Connecticut: American Indian Archaeological Institute.
1989   "'Put your ear to the ground and listen.' The wigwam festival is the green corn ceremony." *Artifacts* 17(4):24–26. Washington, Connecticut: American Indian Archaeological Institute.
1994   "A native perspective of history: The Schaghticoke nation, resistance and survival." In *Enduring traditions: The native peoples of New England,* ed. Laurie Weinstein, 103–12. Westport, Connecticut: Bergin and Garvey.

Langaney, André
1988   *Les hommes: Passé, présent, conditionnel.* Paris: Armand Colin.

Lange, Dierk
1987   *A Sudanic chronicle: The Borno expeditions of Idris Alauma (1564–1576).* Stuttgart: F. Steiner Verlag.

Langley, P.
1975   "The ethnolinguistic approach to the rural environment: Its usefulness in rural planning in Africa." In *African environment special report,* 4th ed., ed. Paul Richards, 89–101. London: International Africa Institute.

Lantz, Barbara Jo
1985   "Redemption and remembrance: An ethnography of modern Mexican historical narrative." Ph.D. dissertation, Cornell University.

Larco Hoyle, Rafael
1948   *Cronología arqueológica del norte del Perú.* Buenos Aires: Sociedad Geográfica Americana.

Larson, T. B.
1984   "The structure and function of prehistoric social institutions: A social anthropological approach." *Archaeology and Environment* 2:23–30. Umeå, Sweden: University of Umeå.

las Casas, Bartolomé de
1958   *Breve relación de la destrucción de indias.* Madrid: Editorial Atlas, Biblioteca de Autores Españoles, no. 106.

Lavin, Lucianne
1987   "Connecticut's native Americans: Weathering the storm of European contact." *Discovery* 20(2):2–9. New Haven, Connecticut: Yale Peabody Museum.

1988   "Coastal adaptations in southern New England and southern New York." *Archaeology of Eastern North America* 16:101–20.

Leakey, L. S. B.
1936   "Preliminary report on examination of the Engaruka ruins." *Tanganyika Notes and Records* 1:57–60.

Leone, Mark P., and Parker B. Potter, Jr.
1988   *The recovery of meaning: Historical archaeology in the eastern United States.* Washington, D.C.: Smithsonian Institution Press.

Leone, Mark, P. B. Potter, Jr., and P. A. Shackel
1987   "Toward a critical archaeology." *Current Anthropology* 28(3):283–302.

Lewontin, Richard C.
1972   "The apportionment of human diversity." In *Evolutionary biology,* vol. 6, eds. T. Dobzhansky et al., 381–98. New York: Plenum.

Lewontin, Richard C., Steven Rose, and Leon J. Kamin
1984   *Not in our genes.* New York: Pantheon.

Lhote, Henri
1952   "La connaissance du fer en Afrique Occidentale." *Encyclopédie Mensuelle d'Outre-Mer,* 269–72. Paris.

Licha, Isabel, ed.
1991   *Imágenes del futuro social de América Latina.* Caracas: Universidad Central de Venezuela.

Lindroth, Sten
1983   "The two faces of Linnaeus." In *Linnaeus: The man and his work,* ed. Tore Frangsmyr. Berkeley: University of California Press.

Liprandi, Rita, and Ramón Casanova
1991   "El futuro de la educación en America Latina." In *Imágenes del futuro social de América Latina,* ed. Isabel Licha, 141–63. Caracas: Universidad Central de Venezuela.

Lizot, Jacques, and F. Mattei-Muller
1981   "El sistema fonológico Yanomami central." *Boletín Indigenista Venezolano* 20(17):117–43.

Llorens Torres, L.
1967   *América: Estudios históricos y filológicos.* San Juan, Puerto Rico: Editorial Cordillera.

Lockwood, John H., E. N. Bagg, W. S. Carson, H. E. Riley, E. Boltwood, and W. L. Clark, eds.
1926   *Western Massachusetts: A history, 1636–1925,* vol. 1. New York: Lewis Historical Publishing Company.

Longino, Helen E.
1990   *Science as social knowledge: Values and objectivity in scientific inquiry.* Princeton, New Jersey: Princeton University Press.

Lonsdale, J.
1989   "African pasts in Africa's future." *Canadian Journal of African Studies* 23(1): 125–46.

López Cantos, A.
1984   "Emigración Canaria a Puerto Rico en el siglo XVIII." *VI Coloquio de Historia Canario-Americana,* 91–114. Canaria: Cabildo Insular de Gran Canaria.
1985   "La sociedad de Puerto Rico en el siglo XVIII." *Anales* n.s. 1(2):7–29. San Germán, Puerto Rico.

Lorde, Audre
1984   "The master's tools will never dismantle the master's house." In her *Sister outsider,* 110–13. Freedom, California: Crossing Press.

Loring, Stephen
1985   "Boundary maintenance, mortuary ceremonialism and resource control in the early Woodland: Three cemetery sites in Vermont." *Archaeology of Eastern North America* 13:93–127.

Lovejoy, Arthur L.
1959   "Buffon and the problem of species." In *Forerunners of Darwin, 1745–1859,* ed. Bentley Glass, pp. 84–113. Baltimore: Johns Hopkins Press.

Lumbreras, Luis G.
1974   *La arqueología como ciencia social.* Lima: Ediciones Histar.

McBride, Kevin
1989   "Pootatuck Wigwams: Overview of its historic significance and archaeological values." Nomination form for the National Register of Historic Places, prepared for review by the Connecticut Historical Commission, Hartford.

McBride, Kevin, and Nicholas F. Bellantoni
1982   "The utility of ethnohistoric models for understanding late Woodland-contact culture change in southern New England." *Bulletin of the Archaeological Society of Connecticut* 45:51–64.

McDougall, E. A.
1985   "The view from Awdaghust: War, trade and social change in the southwestern Sahara from the 8th to the 15th century." *Journal of African History* 26:1–31.

MacGaffey, Wyatt
1966   "Concepts of race in the historiography of northeast Africa." *Journal of African History* 7:1–17.

McGaw, Judith A.
1987   *Most wonderful machine: Mechanization and social change in Berkshire paper making, 1801–1853.* Princeton, New Jersey: Princeton University Press.

Macías, I.
1978   *Cuba en la primera mitad del siglo XVII.* Seville: Escuela de Estudios Hispanoamericanos.

McIntosh, S. K., and R. J. McIntosh
1980   *Prehistoric investigations in the region of Jenne, Mali: A study in the*

> *development of urbanism in the Sahel. Oxford: British Archaeological* Reports, International Series 89.

1983   "Current directions in West African prehistory." *Annual Review of Anthropology* 12:215–58.

1984   "The early city in West Africa: Towards an understanding." *African Archaeological Review* 2:73–98.

MacLean, George Edwin

1928   *History of Great Barrington, Massachusetts, part II extension: 1882–1922.* Great Barrington: Town of Great Barrington.

Maes, Jean

1924   "Note sur les pierres taillées et garvées, sur les pierres alignées et sur une muraille de pierre en ruine situées près du village de Tundidaro (Soudan)." *Bulletin du Comité d'Études Historiques et Scientifiques de l'A.O.F.* 8:31–38.

Maggs, T.

1976   "Iron Age patterns and Sotho history on the high veld." *World Archaeology* 7:318–32.

Maggs, T., and G. Whitelaw

1991   "A review of recent archaeology research on food producing communities in southern Africa." *Journal of African History* 32:3–24.

Mallon, Florencia E.

1987   "Nationalist and antistate coalitions in the war of the Pacific: Junín and Cajamarca, 1879–1902." In *Resistance, rebellion, and consciousness in the Andean peasant world, 18th to 20th centuries,* ed. Steve J. Stern, 219–31. Madison: University of Wisconsin Press.

Mandell, Daniel R.

1982   "Change and continuity in a Native American community: Eighteenth century Stockbridge." M.A. thesis, Department of History, University of Virginia, Charlottsville.

1992   "Behind the frontier: Indian communities in eighteenth-century Massachusetts." Ph.D. dissertation, Department of History, University of Virginia, Charlottesville.

Mapunda, Bertram

1992   "Main ideas in *Prelude to East African History.*" Paper presented in the Iron Age Archaeology seminar, University of Florida.

Maret, Pierre de

1980   "Preliminary report on 1980 fieldwork in the Grassfield and Yaounde, Cameroon." *Nyame Akuma* 17:10–12.

1982   "New survey of archaeological research and dates for west-central and north-central Africa." *Journal of African History* 23:1–15.

Mariátegui, José Carlos

1928   *Seven interpretative essays on the Peruvian reality.* Reprinted 1971. Austin: University of Texas Press.

1952   *Siete ensayos de interpretación de la realidad Peruana.* Lima: Biblioteca Amauta.

Marquardt, William

1994   "The role of archaeology in raising environmental consciousness." In *Historical ecology: Cultural knowledge and changing landscapes,* ed. Carole Crumley, 203–21. Santa Fe, New Mexico: School of American Research Press.

Marrero, Levi
1972-75   *Cuba, economía y sociedad,* vols. I-V, XIII. Madrid: Editorial Playor.
Martin, P. M.
1988   "Sources and source criticism: A review article." *Journal of African History* 29:537-40.
Mason, R. J.
1986   *Origins of black people of Johannesburg and the southern western central Transvaal A.D. 350-1880.* Occasional Papers of the Archaeological Research Unit. Johannesburg: University of Witswatersrand.
Matos Moctezuma, Eduardo
1979   "Las corrientes arqueológicas en México." *Nueva Antropología* 3(12):7-26. Mexico.
Mauny, Raymond
1952   "Essai sur l'histoire des métaux en Afrique Occidentale." *Bulletin de l'Institut Français d'Afrique Noire* 14:545-95.
1953   "Autour de l'historique de l'introduction du fer en Afrique Occidentale." *Encyclopédie Mensuelle d'Outre-Mer* 109-10. Paris.
1968   "Bibliographie de la préhistoire et de la protohistoire de l'Ouest Africain." *Bulletin de l'Institut Français d'Afrique Noire* 29, série B: 879-917.
Mayer, Enrique
1991   "Peru in deep trouble: Mario Vargas Llosa's 'Inquest in the Andes' re-examined." *Cultural Anthropology* 6(4):466-504.
Mbuyinga, Elenga
1979   *Panafricanisme et neo-colonialisme.* Paris: Publication de l'Union des Population du Cameroun.
Médina, Andrés
1988   "La cuestión étnica y el indigenismo." In *La antropología en México: Panorama histórico, tomo 4, Las cuestiones medulares (etnología y antropología social),* ed. Carlos García Mora, 713-39. Mexico, D.F.: Instituto de Antropología e Historia.
Mejía, Medardo
1970   *Historia de Honduras, tomo 2, El descubrimiento de la mundialización de Honduras.* Tegucigalpa, Honduras: Editorial Andrade.
Meléndez, Carlos
1983   *Historia de Costa Rica.* San José, Costa Rica: Editorial Universidad Estatal a Distancia.
Meléndez Muñoz, Miguel
1961   "El jíbaro en la revolución de Lares." *Revista Instituto de Cultura Puertorriqueña,* no. 10.
1963   *El jíbaro en el siglo XIX.* Barcelona: Editorial Rumbos.
Méndez Lavielle, Guadalupe
1987   "La quiebra política (1965-1976)." In *La antropología en México: Panorama histórico, tomo 2, Los hechos y los dichos (1880-1986),* ed. Carlos García Mora, 339-438. Mexico, D.F.: Instituto Nacional de Antropología e Historia.
Merchant, Carolyn
1989   *Ecological revolutions: Nature, gender, and science in New England.* Chapel Hill: University of North Carolina Press.

Merrell, James H.
  1989   "Some thoughts on colonial historians and American Indians." *William and Mary Quarterly* 46(1):94–119.
Miller, Joseph C., ed.
  1980   *The African past speaks: Essays on oral tradition and history.* Hamden, Connecticut: Archon.
Mochon, Marion Johnson
  1968   "Stockbridge-Munsee cultural adaptations: 'Assimilated Indians.'" *Proceedings of the American Philosophical Society* 112(3):182–219.
Momigliano, Arnaldo
  1992   *Les fondations du savoir historique.* Paris: Les Belles Lettres.
Monge, Carlos
  1976   *Historia de Costa Rica.* 14th ed. San José, Costa Rica: Taller Trejo Hermanos.
Montero, Maritza
  1984   *Ideología, alienación e identidad nacional.* Caracas: Facultad de Humanidades y Educación, Universidad Central de Venezuela.
Morón, Guillermo
  1971   *Historia de Venezuela.* Caracas: Italgráfica.
Moscoso, Francisco
  1984   "Land tenure and social change in Puerto Rico, 1700–1815." Unpublished manuscript, San Juan, Puerto Rico.
Mosonyi, Esteban
  1966   *Morfología del verbo yaruro.* Caracas: Ediciones Universidad Central de Venezuela.
Mudimbe, V. Y.
  1988   *The invention of Africa: Gnosis, philosophy, and the order of knowledge.* Bloomington: Indiana University Press.
Musonda, Francis
  1990   "African archaeology: Looking forward." *African Archaeological Review* 8: 3–22.
Mynter, Ken
  1987   "Leaving New England: The Stockbridge Indians." In *Rooted like the ash trees: New England Indians and the land,* rev. ed., ed. R. Carlson, 30–32. Naugatuck, Connecticut: Eagle Wing Press.
Nadel, S. F.
  1942   *A black Byzantium.* London: Oxford University Press.
Ndeti, Kivuto
  1976   "The relevance of African traditional medicine in modern medical training and practice." In *Medical anthropology,* Francis X. Grollig and Harold Haley, eds., pp. 11–26. Paris: Mouton.
Neale, Caroline
  1985   *Writing independent history: African historiography, 1960–1980.* Westport, Connecticut: Greenwood Press.
Newell, R. R., and A. A. Dekin, Jr.
  1978   "An integrative strategy for the definition of behaviourally meaningful archaeological units." *Palaeohistoria* 20:7–38.
Newton-Smith, W. H.
  1981   *The rationality of science.* London: Routledge and Kegan Paul.

Ngugi Wa Thiongo
  1987   "Foreword." In *Kenya's freedom struggle: The Dedan Kemathi papers,* ed. Maina Wa Kinyatti. London: Zed Books.
Nicholas, George P., and Mitchell T. Mulholland
  1987   *Archaeological locational survey of the Housatunnuk at Skatehook in Sheffield, Massachusetts.* Report from University of Massachusetts Archaeological Services, no. 70. Amherst, Massachusetts.
Nzewunwa, Nwanna
  1990   "Cultural education in West Africa: Archaeological perspectives." In *Politics of the past,* eds. Peter Gathercole and David Lowenthal, 189–202. London: Unwin Hyman.
Obenga, Theophile
  1973   *L'Afrique dans l'antiquité: Egypte pharaonique-Afrique noire.* Paris: Présence Africaine.
Ocampo López, Javier
  1989   *Breve historia de Colombia.* Caracas: Academia Nacional de la Historia de Venezuela, Colección El Libro Menor.
Okpoko, A. I.
  1986   "Archaeology education in Nigeria." *West African Journal of Archaeology* 9: 147–53.
  1991   "Review article: A history of African archaeology." *African Archaeological Review* 9:111–18.
Oliver, Roland, and Brian Fagan
  1978   *Africa in the Iron Age.* Cambridge: Cambridge University Press.
Orcutt, Samuel
  1882   *The Indians of the Housatonic and Naugatuck valleys.* Hartford, Connecticut: Case, Lockwood, and Brainard. Reprinted 1972. Stratford, Connecticut: John E. Edwards.
Otte, E.
  1977   *Las perlas del Caribe: Nueva Cádiz de Cabagua.* Caracas: Fundación John Bulton.
Packard, Randall M.
  1981   *Chiefship and cosmology: An historical study of political competition.* Bloomington: Indiana University Press.
Padilla Escabí, S.
  1985   "El poblamiento de Puerto Rico en el siglo XVIII." *Anales,* n.s. 2:95–132.
Padmore, George
  1960   *Panafricanisme ou communisme.* Paris: Présence Africaine.
Pagden, Anthony
  1982   *The fall of natural man: The American Indian and the origins of comparative ethnology.* Cambridge: Cambridge University Press.
Palmer, H. R.
  1936   *The Borno Sahara and Sudan.* London: John Murray.
Pathy, Jaganath
  1981   "Imperialism, anthropology and the Third World." *Economic and Political Weekly* 6(14):623–27.
Patterson, Thomas C.
  1989   "Political economy and a discourse called 'Peruvian archaeology.'" *Culture and History* 4:35–64. Copenhagen.

1994   "Social archaeology in Latin America: An appreciation." *American Antiquity* 59(3):531–37.

Patterson, William L., ed.

1970 [1951]   *We charge genocide: The historic petition to the United Nations for relief from a crime of the United States government against the Negro people.* New York: International Publishers.

Pedrals, D. P. de

1950   *Archéologie de l'Afrique noire.* Paris: Payot.

Peña Battle, M.

1948   *La rebelión del Bahoruco.* Ciudad de Trujillo, Dominican Republic: Impresora Dominicana.

Picó, Fernando

1979   "Lazos de solidaridad entre los fundadores de Utuado." *Revista Instituto de Cultura Puertorriqueña* 85. San Juan.

1984   *Camuy, bosque y terrón: Del hato ganadero a las estancias de subsistencia.* CEREP Cuadernos, no. 10. Río Piedras, Puerto Rico: Ediciones Huracan.

1985   "Nociones de orden y desorden en la periferia de San Juan, 1765–1830." *Revista de Historia,* no. 2.

1986a   "Esclavos, cimarrones, libertos y negros libres en Río Piedras, 1774–1873." *Anuario de Estudios Americanos* 43:25–33.

1986b   "Los jornaleros de Jayuya a mediados del siglo XIX." *Boletín de la Academia Puertorriqueña de la Historia* 9(36):89–103.

1990   "Caimito: Una comunidad negra y mulata libre al margen de las haciendas azucareras." *Del Caribe* 6(16–17):51–57.

Pike, Frederick B.

1967   *The modern history of Peru.* New York: Frederick A. Praeger.

Pomian, Krzysztof

1984   *L'Ordre du temps.* Paris: Gallimard.

Poole, Deborah, and Gerardo Renique

1991   "The new chroniclers of Peru: U.S. scholars and their 'Shining Path' of peasant rebellion." *Bulletin of Latin American Research* 10(2):133–92.

Popper, Karl

1991   *La connaissance objective.* Paris: Aubier.

Porras, Pedro

1975   *Fase Cosanga.* Quito: Ediciones de la Universidad Católica.

Posnansky, Merrick

1966   *Prelude to East African history.* London: Oxford University Press.

1982   "African archaeology comes of age." *World Archaeology* 13:345–58.

Pouwels, R. L.

1984   "Oral historiography and the Shirazi of the East African coast." *History in Africa* 11:237–67.

Powell, T. G.

1968   "Mexican intellectuals and the Indian question, 1876–1911." *Hispanic American Historical Review* 48(1):19–36.

Pretto, Julio

1947   "Estudios bioantropométricos en los escolares limeños." *Boletín del Instituto Psicopedagógico Nacional* (Peru) 6(2):5–82.

Prigogine, I., and I. Stengers

1984   *Order out of chaos: Man's new dialogue with nature.* Toronto: Bentam Books.

Putnam, Hilary
1962   "The analytic and the synthetic." In *Scientific explanation, space, and time,* eds. H. Feigl and G. Maxwell, 358–97. Minneapolis: University of Minnesota Press.

Quine, W. V. O.
1953   *From a logical point of view.* Cambridge, Massachusetts: Harvard University Press.

Quintero Rivera, Angel
1973   "Background to the emergence of imperialist capitalism in Puerto Rico." *Caribbean Studies* 13(3):31–63.
1979   *Identidad nacional y clases sociales.* Río Piedras, Puerto Rico: Editorial Huracán.
1983   *Historia de unas clases sin historia.* CEREP Cuadernos, no. 9. Río Piedras, Puerto Rico: Ediciones Huracan.
1987   "The rural-urban dichotomy in the formation of Puerto Rico's cultural identity." *New West Indian Guide* 61(3–4):127–44.

Rahim, Saiyad Abdul
1870   *Bhāratbarser itihāser prasnottar.* Dhaka.

Rahim, Sheikh Abdar
1886   *Hajrat mahammader jiban carit o dharmmaniti.* Calcutta.

Rahman, Abdur
1983   *Intellectual colonisation: Science and technology in West-East relations.* New Delhi: Vikas Publishing House.

Rama, Angel
1975   "Introducción." In *Formación de una cultura nacional indoamerica,* by José María Arguedas, ix–xxiii. Mexico, D.F.: Siglo Veintiuno.
1982   *Transculturación narrativa en América Latina.* Mexico, D.F.: Siglo Veintiuno.

Rankin-Hill, Lesley, and Michael L. Blakey
1994   "W. Montague Cobb (1904–1990): Physical anthropologist, anatomist, and activist." *American Anthropologist* 96:74–96.

Real Díaz, J.
1968   *Catálogo de las cartas y peticiones del cabildo de San Juan Bautista de Puerto Rico en el Archivo General de Indias, siglo XVI-XVIII.* San Juan, Puerto Rico: Instituto de Cultura.

Richards, Dona Marimba
1980   "European mythology: The ideology of 'progress'." In *Contemporary black thought: Alternative analyses in social and behavioral science,* eds. M. Asante and A. S. Vandi, pp. 59–79. London: Sage Publications.

Richards, P.
1975   "Alternative strategies for the African environment." In *Africa environment special report,* 1st ed., ed. Paul Richards, 102–17. London: International Africa Institute.

Rivermar Pérez, Leticia
1987   "El marasmo de una rebelión cataclísmica (1911–1920)." In *La antropología en México: Panorama histórico, tomo 2, Los hechos y los dichos (1880–1986),* ed. Carlos García Mora, 89–131. Mexico, D.F.: Instituto Nacional de Antropología e Historia.

Robertshaw, Peter
1990   "The development of archaeology in East Africa." In *A history of African archaeology,* ed. P. Robertshaw, 78–94. London: James Currey.

Rocha, Jaime N.
1987 "La visión integral de la sociedad nacional (1920–1934)." In *La antropología en México; Panorama histórico, tomo 2, Los hechos y los dichos (1880–1986)*, ed. Carlos García Mora, 133–222. Mexico, D.F.: Instituto Nacional de Antropología e Historia.

Rodríguez, Omar
1991 *Etnias, imperios y antropología*. Caracas: Ediciones FACES, Universidad Central de Venezuela.

Rodríguez Demorizi, E.
1945 *Relaciones históricas de Santo Domingo*, vol. 2. Santo Domingo, Dominican Republic: Editora Montalvo.
1970 *Relaciones geográficas de Santo Domingo*. Santo Domingo, Dominican Republic: Sociedad Dominicana de Geografía.

Rosa, W. M.
1989 "La 'confederación de las Antillas' y la novela caribeña del siglo XIX." *Caribbean Studies* 22(3–4):1–11.

Rosenblat, Angel
1954 *La población indígena y el mestizaje en América*. 2 vols. Buenos Aires: Editorial Nova.

Rouse, Irving
1992 *The Tainos: Rise and decline of the people who greeted Columbus*. New Haven, Connecticut: Yale University Press.

Rouse, Joseph
1987 *Knowledge and power: Toward a political philosophy of science*. Ithaca, New York: Cornell University Press.

Rowe, William, and Vivian Schelling
1991 *Memory and modernity: Popular culture in Latin America*. London: Verso.

Rowlands, M.
1986 "Colonialism, archaeology and constituting the African peasantry." In *Comparative studies in the development of complex societies*, vol. 3. Precirculated Papers of the World Archaeological Congress, Southampton. London: Allen and Unwin.

Rubertone, Patricia E.
1989 "Archaeology, colonialism, and 17th-century native America: Towards an alternative interpretation." In *Conflict in the archaeology of living traditions*, ed. R. Layton, 32–45. One World Archaeology Series. London: Unwin Hyman.

Ruiz Zúñiga, Angel
1991 *La tercera república: Ensayo sobre la Costa Rica del futuro*. San José, Costa Rica: Instituto Centroamericano Cultura y Desarrollo.

Sáenz, Moisés
1939 *México íntegro*. Lima: Imprenta Torres Aguire.

Sahlins, Marshall
1985 *Islands of history*. Chicago: University of Chicago Press.

Said, Edward W.
1985 "Opponents, audiences, constituencies, and community." In *Postmodern culture*, ed. H. Foster, 135–59. London: Pluto Press.

Salas, Julio César
1908 *Etnología e historia de tierra firme*. Biblioteca de Ciencias Políticas y Sociales. Madrid: Editorial América.

Salmon, Wesley C.
1984   *Scientific explanation and the causal structure of the world.* Princeton, New Jersey: Princeton University Press.

Sanoja Obediente, Mario
1990   "Ideas sobre el origen de la nación venezolana." In *Discursos de incorporación 1980-1991,* vol. 7, 201-30. Caracas: Academía Nacional de la Historia.

Sanoja Obediente, Mario, and Iraida Vargas Arenas
1989   "Resource management and environmental education." In *Public archaeology and cultural resource management,* ed. Henry Cleere, 64-69. London: Unwin Hyman.

Santana, Roberto
1982   "En la sierra del Ecuador: Reivindicaciones étnicas y agrarias. El caso de un movimiento indígena." In *Indianidad, etnocido, indigenismo en América Latina,* ed. Francoise Morin, 279-96. Reprinted 1988. Mexico, D.F.: Instituto Indigenista Interamericano.

Santangelo, Antonio
1992   *Antropologia e processi di civiltà: La nascita di nuovi valori.* Milan: La Pietra.

Śarmanah [Vidyalankar], Mrityunjay.
1808   *Rājābali.* Serampore: Baptist Mission Press.

Sarmiento, Domingo F.
1947   *Facundo.* Buenos Aires: Circulo Literaria de Buenos Aires.

Scarano, F.
1989   "Congregate and control: The peasantry and labor coercion in Puerto Rico before the age of sugar, 1750-1820." *New West Indian Guide* 63(1-2): 23-40.

Scheffler, Israel
1963   *The anatomy of inquiry.* New York: Bobbs Merrill.

Schiffer, M.
1987   *Formation processes of the archaeological record.* Albuquerque: University of New Mexico Press.

Schmidt, Peter R.
1978   *Historical archaeology: A structural approach in an African culture.* Westport, Connecticut: Greenwood Press.
1983a   "An alternative to a strictly materialist perspective: A review of historical archaeology, ethnoarchaeology, and symbolic approaches in African archaeology." *American Antiquity* 48:62-79.
1983b   "Cultural meaning and history in African myth." *International Journal of Oral History* 4:167-83.
1983c   "More evidence of an advanced prehistoric iron technology in Tanzania." *Journal of Field Archaeology* 10:421-34.
1988   "Eastern expressions of the 'Mwitu' tradition: Early Iron Age industry in the Usambara Mountains of Tanzania." *Nyame Akuma* 30:36-37.
1990   "Oral traditions, archaeology, and history: A short reflective history." In *A history of African archaeology,* ed. P. Robertshaw, 252-70. London: James Currey.
1994   "Historical ecology and landscape transformations in eastern equatorial Africa." In *Historical ecology: Cultural knowledge and changing landscapes,* ed. Carole Crumley, 99-125. Santa Fe, New Mexico: School of American Research Press.
n.d.   *Symbolic and material views of iron technology in East Africa.* Forthcoming.

Schmidt, Peter R., ed.
  1995   *The culture and technology of African iron production.* Gainesville: University Press of Florida.
Schmidt, Peter R., and D. H. Avery
  1978   "Complex iron smelting and prehistoric culture in Tanzania." *Science* 201: 85–99.
Schmidt, Peter R., and Felix Chami
  n.d.   "A new economic history of the East African coast: Recent discoveries in Tanzania." Manuscript.
Schmidt, Peter R., and S. Terry Childs
  1985   "Innovation and industry during the early Iron Age in East Africa." *African Archaeological Review* 3:53–94.
  1995   "Ancient African iron production." *American Scientist* 83:524–33.
Schmidt, Peter R., and N. J. Karoma
  1987   "Preliminary report: Archaeological survey of the western Usambara Mountains, west and southwest of Lushoto, Tanga region, and Kilwa, Kilwa coastal zone, Lindi region." Archaeology Unit, University of Dar es Salaam, Tanzania.
Schmidt, Peter R., N. J. Karoma, A. LaViolette, W. B. Fawcett, A. Z. Mabulla, L. N. Rutabanzibwa, and C. M. Saanane
  1992   *Archaeological investigations in the vicinity of Mkiu, Kisarawe district, coast region, Tanzania.* Occasional Paper no. 1, Archaeological Contributions of the University of Dar es Salaam. Dar es Salaam: University of Dar es Salaam.
Sedgwick, Charles F.
  1898   *General history of the town of Sharon, Litchfield County, Connecticut.* Amenia, New York: Charles Walsh.
Sedgwick, Sarah Cabot, and Christina Sedgwick Marquand
  1939   *Stockbridge, 1739–1939: A chronicle.* Great Barrington, Massachusetts: Barrington Courier.
Sergeant, John
  1743   *Letter to Dr. Colman of Boston (containing a proposal for a more effectual method for the education of Indian children).* Boston: Rogers and Fowle.
Sevilla Soler, M. R.
  1986   *Las Antillas y la independencia de la América Española.* Seville: Escuela de Estudios Hispanoamericanos.
Shaw, Leslie C., Ellen-Rose Savulis, Mitchell T. Mulholland, and George P. Nicholas
  1987   *Archaeological locational survey in the central Berkshires, Pittsfield, Massachusetts.* Report no. 18. Amherst, Massachusetts: University of Massachusetts Archaeological Services.
Shaw, Thurstan
  1978   *Nigeria: Its archaeology and early history.* London: Thames and Hudson.
Shephard, D.
  1982   "The making of the Swahili." *Paideuma* 28:129–48.
Silie, Rubén
  1992   "1492, Descubrimiento, encuentro, invasión: Cómo calificar este hecho?" *Ciencia y Sociedad* 17(3):12–33.
Silvestrini, Blanca, and Luque María Silvestrini
  1987   *Historia de Puerto Rico: Trayectoria de un pueblo.* San Juan: Cultural Puertorriqueña.

Simpson, Lesley Byrd
  1966   *The Encomienda in New Spain: The Beginning of Spanish Mexico.* Berkeley: University of California Press.
Smith, J. E. A.
  1869   *The history of Pittsfield, Massachusetts, from the year 1734 to the year 1800.* Boston: Lee and Shepard.
Sorman, Guy
  1993   *Esperando a los bárbaros.* Bogotá, Columbia: Seix Barral.
Snow, Dean R.
  1980   *The archaeology of New England.* New York: Academic Press.
Spalding, Karen
  1980   "Class structures in the southern Peruvian highlands, 1750–1920." In *Land and power in Latin America: Agrarian economies and social processes in the Andes,* eds. Benjamin S. Orlove and Glynn Custred, 79–98. New York: Holmes and Meier.
Spear, T.
  1989   "The interpretation of evidence in African history." *African Studies Review* 17–24.
Stabb, Martin S.
  1959   "Indigenism and racism in Mexican thought, 1857–1911." *Journal of Inter-American Studies* 1(4):404–23.
Stavenhagen, Rodolfo
  1969   *Las clases sociales en las sociedades agrarias.* Mexico, D.F.: Siglo Veintiuno.
Stavrianos, L. S.
  1981   *Global rift: The Third World comes of age.* New York: William Morrow.
Stepan, Nancy L.
  1991   *The hour of eugenics: Race, gender, and nation in Latin America.* Ithaca, New York: Cornell University Press.
Stern, Steve J.
  1987   "Introduction to part IV." In *Resistance, rebellion, and consciousness in the Andean peasant world, 18th to 20th centuries,* ed. Steve J. Stern, 327–33. Madison: University of Wisconsin Press.
Steward, Julian H.
  1948   "The circum-Caribbean tribes: An introduction." In *Handbook of South American Indians, vol. 4: The circum-Caribbean tribes,* ed. Julian H. Steward, 1–41. Washington, D.C.: Bureau of American Ethnology, Bulletin 143.
  1950   *Area research: Theory and practice.* New York: Social Science Research Council, Bulletin 63.
  1955   *Theory of cultural change.* Urbana: University of Illinois Press.
Steward, Julian H., and Louis Faron
  1959   *Native peoples of South America.* New York: McGraw-Hill.
Steward, Julian H., Robert Manners, Eric R. Wolf, Elena Padilla, Sidney W. Mintz, and L. Scheele
  1956   *The people of Puerto Rico.* Urbana: University of Illinois Press.
Stoller, P.
  1989   "Speaking in the name of the real." *Cahiers d'Etudes Africaines* 113 XXIX 1:113–25.
Suárez Cortés, Blanca E.
  1987   "Las interpretaciones positivistas del pasado y el presente (1880–1910)." In *La antropología en México: Panorama histórico, tomo 2, Los hechos y los dichos*

(1880–1986), ed. Carlos García Mora, 13–88. Mexico, D.F.: Instituto Nacional de Antropología e Historia.

Sued Badillo, Jalil
1978a   *Los Caribes, realidad o fábula.* Río Piedras, Puerto Rico: Editorial Antillana.
1978b   "Introduction: El tema indígena en la historiografía puertorriqueña hasta el 1970." In *Los Caribes, realidad o fábula,* 1–32. Río Piedras, Puerto Rico: Editorial Antillana.
1986   "Primera parte: Siglo XVI." In *Puerto Rico negro,* by Jalil Sued Badillo and Angel López Cantos, 17–195. Río Piedras, Puerto Rico: Editorial Cultural.
1987   "Beatríz: India cubana cimarrona." *Revista Casa de las Américas* 165:11–26. Havana.
1989   *La economía minera en Puerto Rico, 1510–50.* Doctoral thesis, University of Seville.
1992   "Facing up to Caribbean history." *American Antiquity* 57:599–607.

Sued Badillo, Jalil, and Angel López Cantos
1986   *Puerto Rico negro.* Río Piedras, Puerto Rico: Editorial Cultural.

Sullivan, A. P.
1978   "Inference and evidence in archaeology: A discussion of the conceptual problems." *Advances in archaeological method and theory,* vol. 1, ed. M. B. Schiffer, 183–222. New York: Academic Press.

Suppe, Frederick
1977   *The stucture of scientific theories.* 2d ed. Urbana: University of Illinois Press.

Sutton, John
1973a   "Archaeology in Tanzania: Development or under-development?" Paper presented at a meeting of Tanzanian archaeologists, National Museum, Dar es Salaam.
1973b   "Archaeology in the University of Dar es Salaam." Paper presented at a meeting of Tanzanian archaeologists, National Museum, Dar es Salaam.

Sweeney, Kevin M.
1984   "Mansion people: Kinship, class, and architecture in western Massachusetts in the mid eighteenth century." *Winterthur Portfolio* 19(4):231–55.

Tanodi, A.
1971   *Documentos de la real hacienda de Puerto Rico, 1509–19.* Río Piedras: Universidad de Puerto Rico.

Taylor, Charles J.
1882   *History of Great Barrington, Massachusetts.* Great Barrington: Clark W. Bryan.

Téllez Ortega, Javier
1987   " 'La epoca de oro' (1940–1964)." In *La antropología en México: Panorama histórico, tomo 2, Los hechos y los dichos (1880–1986),* ed. Carlos García Mora, 289–338. Mexico, D.F.: Instituto Nacional de Antropología e Historia.

Tello, Julio C.
1923   "Wira Kocha." *Inca* 1(3):583–606. Lima.
1929   *Antiguo Perú: Primera etapa.* Lima: Editado por la Comisión Organizadora del Segundo Congreso Sudamericano de Turismo.
1930   "Andean civilizations: Some problems of Peruvian archaeology." *Proceedings of the 23d International Congress of Americanists,* 259–90. New York: Science Printing Company.

1940 "Origin y desarrollo de las civilizaciones prehistóricas andinas." *Actas y Trabajos Científicos del XXVI° Congreso Internacional de Americanistas (Lima 1939)* 1:589–720. Lima: Librería e Imprenta Gil.

Temu, A., and B. Swai
1981 *Historians and Africanist history: A critique.* London: Zed Press.

Testart, Alain
1992 "La question de l'évolutionnisme dans l'anthropologie sociale." *Revue Française de Sociologie* 33:155–87.

Thakur, Rabindranath
1961 *Rabindra racanabali,* vol. 13. Calcutta: Government of West Bengal.

Third World Network
1993 "Modern science in crisis: A Third World response." In *The "racial economy" of science: Toward a democratic future,* ed. Sandra Harding, 484–518. Bloomington: Indiana University Press.

Thomas, Peter A.
1976 "Contrasting subsistence strategies and land use as factors for understanding Indian-White relations in New England." *Ethnohistory* 23(1): 1–18.

Thorbahn, Peter F.
1988 "Where are the late Woodland villages in southern New England?" *Bulletin of the Massachusetts Archaeological Society* 49(2):46–57.

Tío, Aurelio
1961 *Nuevas fuentes para la historia de Puerto Rico.* San Germán, Puerto Rico: Ediciones Universidad Interamericana.
1966 *Dr. Diego Alvarez Chanca: Estudio biográfico.* San Juan, Puerto Rico: Instituto de Cultura Puertorriqueña y Universidad Interamericana.

Tomlinson, John
1991 *Cultural imperialism: A critical introduction.* Baltimore, Maryland: Johns Hopkins University Press.

Towa, Marcien
1973 *Négritude ou servitude.* Yaoundé, Cameroon: Editions Clé.

Trigger, Bruce G.
1984 "Alternative archaeologies: Nationalist, colonialist, imperialist." *Man* 19: 335–70.
1990 "The history of African archaeology in world perspective." In *A history of African archaeology,* ed. Peter Robertshaw, 309–19. London: James Currey.

Uhle, Max
1910 "Über die Frühkulturen in der Umgebung von Lima." *Verhandlungen des XVI. Internationalen Amerikanisten-Kongresses,* erste Hälfte, 347–70. Vienna: A. Hartleben's Verlag.
1913 "Die Muschelhügel von Ancon, Peru." *Proceedings of the 18th International Congress of Americanists,* part 1, 22–45. London: Harrison and Sons.
1940 "Procedencia y origen de las antiguas civilizaciones americanas." *Actas y Trabajos del XXVII° Congreso Internacional de Americanistas (Lima 1939)* 1: 355–68. Lima: Librería e Imprenta Gil.

UNESCO.
1982 *Final report of the World Conference on Cultural Policies, Mexico City.* Paris: UNESCO.

Urvoy, Yves
1949 *Histoire de l'empire du Bornu.* Paris: Larose.

Utrera, C. de
1973 *Polémica de Enriquillo.* Santo Domingo, Dominican Republic: Academía Dominicana de la Historia.
1979 *Noticias históricas de Santo Domingo,* vol. 3. Santo Domingo, Dominican Republic: Fundación Rodríguez Demorizi.
Valcárcel, Luis E.
1927 *Tempestad en los Andes.* Lima: Biblioteca Amauta, Editorial Minerva.
1943 *Historia de la cultura antigua del Perú,* tomo 1, vol. 1. Lima: Imprenta del Museo Nacional.
1948 *Historia de la cultura antigua del Perú,* tomo 1, vol. 2. Lima: Imprenta del Museo Nacional.
1981 *Memorias.* Lima: Instituto de Estudios Peruanos.
Vallenilla Lanz, Laureano
1961 *Cesarismo democrático.* 4th ed. Caracas: Tipografía Garrido.
Van Gerven, D. P., D. S. Carlson, and G. J. Armelagos
1973 "Racial history and bio-cultural adaptation of Nubian archaeological populations." *Journal of African History* 14:555–64.
van Sertima, Ivan
1976 *They came before Columbus.* New York: Random House.
1985 *African presence in early Europe.* New Brunswick, New Jersey: Transaction Books.
van Sertima, Ivan, and Runoko Rashidi
1985 *African presence in early Asia.* New Brunswick, New Jersey: Transaction Books.
Vansina, J.
1985 *Oral tradition as history.* London: James Currey.
Vargas Arenas, Iraida
1990 *Arqueología, ciencia y sociedad.* Caracas: Editorial Abre Brecha.
Vargas, Iraida, and Mario Sanoja
1990 "Education and the political manipulation of history in Venezuela." In *The excluded past: Archaeology in education,* eds. Peter Stone and Robert Mackenzie, 50–60. London: Unwin Hyman.
Vargas Arenas, Iraida, and Mario Sanoja
1993a "Revisión crítica de la arqueología Suramericana." In *Prehistoria Suramericana: Nuevas perspectivas,* ed. Betty Meggers, 35–43. Washington, D.C., Taraxacum.
1993b *Historia, identidad y poder.* Caracas: Editorial Tropykos.
Vaufrey, R.
1955 *Préhistoire de l'Afrique: Afrique du Nord et Maghreb.* Tunis: Publications de l'Institut des Hautes Etudes de Tunis.
Vázquez León, Luis
1987 "La historiografía antropológica contemporánea en México." In *La antropología en México: Panorama histórico, tomo 1, Los hechos y los dichos (1521–1880),* ed. Carlos García Mora, 139–212. Mexico, D.F.: Instituto Nacional de Antropología e Historia.
Vega, Carlos
1959 *La ciencia del folklore.* Buenos Aires: Editorial Nova.
Veloz Maggiolo, Marcio
1984 "Apuntes sobre autoctonía y etnicidad." *Boletín de Antropología Americana* 10:53–58.

Volney, Constantin François de
  1787   *Voyages en Syrie et en Egypte pendant les années 1783, 1784, 1785.* Paris.
Warnier, J. P.
  1984   "Histoire du peuplement et genèse des paysages dans l'Ouest Camerounais." *Journal of African History* 25:395–410.
  1985   *Échanges, dévelopement et hiérarchies dans le Bamenda précolonial (Cameroun).* Stuttgart: Franz Steiner Verlag.
Warnier, J. P., and I. Fowler
  1979   "A nineteenth-century Ruhr in central Africa." *Africa* 49:329–51.
Washburn, Wilcomb E.
  1987   "Distinguishing history from moral philosophy and public advocacy." In *The American Indian and the problem of history,* ed. Calvin Martin, 91–97. New York: Oxford University Press.
Waterlot, G.
  1909   *Rapport adressé à M. le Gouverneur général de l'A.O.F. sur les recherches faites sur la préhistoire dans la presqu'île du Cap-Vert (Sénégal).* Dakar: Documents IFAN.
Welburn, Ron
  1990   *Council decisions: Selected poems.* Native American Chapbook Series, no. 3. American Native Press Archives. Little Rock: University of Arkansas Press.
Wendorf, F., et al.
  1968   *The prehistory of Nubia.* Dallas, Texas: Southern Methodist University Press.
Wetherbee, Martha, and Nathan Taylor
  1986   *Legend of the bushwacker basket.* Sanbornton, New Hampshire: Martha Wetherbee Basket Shop.
Wilk, R.
  1985   "The ancient Maya and the political present." *Journal of Anthropological Research* 41:307–26.
Wilkie, Richard W., and Jack Tager, eds.
  1991   *Historical atlas of Massachusetts.* Amherst: University of Massachusetts Press.
Willoughby, P. R.
  1991   "Earlier Stone Age archaeology and African studies: A move towards reconciliation." *Canadian Journal of African Studies.*
Wilmsen, E.
  1989   *Land filled with flies: A political economy of the Kalahari.* Chicago: University of Chicago Press.
Wilson, Samuel
  1990   *Hispaniola: Caribbean chiefdoms in the age of Columbus.* Tuscaloosa: University of Alabama Press.
Wojciechowski, Franz L.
  1985   *The Paugussett tribes: An ethnohistorical study of the tribal interrelationships of the Indians in the lower Housatonic River area.* Nijmegen, Netherlands: Department of Cultural and Social Anthropology, Catholic University of Nijmegen.
Wright, Harry Andrew, ed.
  1905   *Indian deeds of Hampden County.* Springfield, Massachusetts: Privately printed.

Wright, H. T.
  1984   "Early seafarers of the Comoro Islands: The Dembeni phase of the
          9th–10th centuries A.D." *Azania* 19:13–59.
Wylie, Alison
  1987   "The philosophy of ambivalence: Sandra Harding on 'the science ques-
          tion in feminism'." *Canadian Journal of Philosophy,* supplementary vol., 13:
          59–73.
  1992a   "Feminist theories of social power: Some implications for a processual
          archaeology." *Norwegian Archaeological Review* 25(1):51–68.
  1992b   "The interplay of evidential constraints and political interests: Recent
          archaeological research on gender." *American Antiquity* 57:15–35.
Zwernemann, J.
  1982   *Culture history and African anthropology.* Stockholm: Uppsala Studies in
          Cultural Anthropology.

Index

Abdul Rahim, Saiyad, 246–47

Africa: dependence upon Western scholastic tradition of, 122–23; historical tradition of, 186, 188–89, 192; historiography of, 150–51, 177–78; map of, 121; technology of, 5, 134–35, 138, 140–42, 209–10. *See also* Africa, archaeology of; East Africa; Egypt; Kenya; Nigeria; Tanzania; West Africa

Africa, archaeology of: changes needed in, 171–72, 175–81; early history of, 190, 191; ethnoarchaeology in, 163–67; European control of, 151; gaps in, 169–71; goal of, 177; an indigenous, 128, 143–47; irrelevance to Africans of, 149–50, 151, 161; methods of, 159–62; need for collaboration between Western and African scholars in, 123; oral tradition and, 131, 170, 171; politics of, 124–36; positive examples of, 162–63; principal subjects studied in, 151–56, 160–62. *See also* Iron working

Afrocentrism, 21–22; assumptions of, 213–14; contributions of, 226–27; defined, 213, 214; diffusionism and, 224–26; epistemology of, 214–17; Marxism and, 216; psychology of, 217–24; racism of, 218–21

Agorsah, E. K., 164, 165

Aguirre Beltrán, Gonzalo, 81–82

Akbar, 246

Allen, Charles, 94

Anandapal, King, 245–46

Andah, Bassey, 11, 144–45, 146, 147

Anta Diop, Cheikh, 196–97, 217–18; flaws in work of, 21, 205–7; political program of, 198–200; research program of, 20–21, 200–204, 224–25

Archaeology: anthropology and, 1–2, 3; challenges written documents, 19; defined, 3; First World vs. Third World, 1–2; politics of, 124–36; social, 62, 63–64; state-sponsored, 8–9. *See also* Africa, archaeology of; Ethnoarchaeology; Mexico; Tanzania

Arguedas, José María, 74–75

Armelagos, G. J., 206

Arusha, 171

Asante, Molefe, 214

Aurangzeb, 246

Bahamón de Lugo, Governor, 37

Baldwin, Joseph, 217, 218–19, 221–22

Bantu, 152, 169

Bantu Studies Project, 130, 131

Bengali history: early colonial, 237–52; Muslims in, 241–42, 243–49, 250, 252; nationalist, 231, 237–53; Puranic, 231–36

SCHOOL OF AMERICAN RESEARCH ADVANCED SEMINAR SERIES

SCHOOL OF AMERICAN RESEARCH ADVANCED SEMINAR SERIES

Published by University of New Mexico Press

Participants in the School of American Research advanced seminar "Making Alternative Histories." Santa Fe, New Mexico, April 1992.

Front row, left to right: Iraida Vargas Arenas, Trudie Lamb Richmond. *Middle row, left to right:* Alison Wylie, Bassey W. Andah, Partha Chatterjee, Jalil Sued Badillo. *Back row, left to right:* Russell G. Handsman, Thomas C. Patterson, Augustin F. C. Holl, Peter R. Schmidt, Michael L. Blakey.